Pledging My Time

Pledging my Time

Conversations with
Bob Dylan Band Members

RAY PADGETT

EWP PRESS

Pledging My Time | Conversations with Bob Dylan Band Members
Copyright 2023 by Ray Padgett, EWP Press

EWP Press
Burlington, Vermont

dylanlive.substack.com

First Edition: June 2023

Hardback ISBN:	979-8-9881781-0-1
Paperback ISBN:	979-8-9881781-1-8
Ebook ISBN:	979-8-9881781-2-5
Front Cover photos:	Bob Dylan and Rob Stoner top left, *photo by Bob Gruen* Dylan and Freddy Koella top right, *photo by Duncan Hume* Dylan and Larry Campbell center, *photo by Alan Cuenca*
Inside Frontispiece photo:	Dylan and Regina McCrary, *photo by Keith W. Criss*
Back Cover photos:	Left to Right: Dylan and Ronee Blakley, *photo by Ken Regan/Camera 5* Dylan and Paul James *photo courtesy of Paul James* Dylan and The Heartbreakers, *photo by Chris Walter* Dylan and Winston Watson, *photo by Manfred Neugebauer*
Typefaces used:	Zooja Pro for book title; Vinyl OT for headlines and photo credits; Adobe Caslon Pro Regular, Italic, and Bold for main text and footnotes

Book design and layout by Noel Mayeske, Mayeske Creative LLC

To Ella,
who at one year old loved "Changing of the Guards"
so much she would get mad if we played anything else

Contents

Introduction

Bob Dylan made it four years into being a professional musician before he made a key decision: He wanted to be in a band. That decision shaped the next fifty-plus years of his career. Ever since he first toured with a band in 1965 — not just *a* band, *The* Band — at just about every show he's played, thousands of them and counting, he's appeared onstage surrounded by fellow musicians.

Like Dylan himself, these musicians seem both accessible and mysterious. Seeing them in person is as easy as buying a ticket, but in general they don't say much about their time with Dylan beyond the occasional interview platitude.

That changes with this book.

Across over 40 interviews, I go deep with a host of Dylan's band members and other musical collaborators, from the '60s all the way into the 21st century. With a few exceptions, these sidemen (and some sidewomen, though Dylan's bands are hardly a model of gender parity) are not famous, but they have in many cases spent years making music with one of the most revered and impenetrable artists in the world. They're the only people alive who can answer questions like, to paraphrase a song:

How does it feel… to stand onstage next to Dylan and realize he's just launched into a song you've never rehearsed?

How does it feel… to spend months on end riding buses and planes with Bob Dylan from town to town?

How does it feel… to be expected to keep these songs fresh every night, with little explicit instruction from the boss?

Alongside band members from every era of Dylan's career, our guest list also includes occasional collaborators, one-off sit-ins, behind-the-scenes touring personnel, and even a notable stage-crasher. I titled the book after his song "Pledging My Time"because that's just what these people did, pledged their time to Dylan and his work. That's what Dylan has done, too; he's pledged his time to us, the fans, across decades of touring and recording. From that perspective, the song's third verse sounds almost like Dylan's invitation to a potential band member: "Won't you come with me, baby? I'll take you where you wanna go." (In some cases, the second half of that verse also comes into play: "And if it don't work out, you'll be the first to know.")

The interviewees here all have one thing in common: They're connected to the live-performance aspect of Dylan's career. These musicians have stood onstage with him, from Newport Folk Festival to Madison Square Garden, playing for audiences from Deadheads to The Pope. The few that aren't musicians — tour managers, sound guys, venue owners — experienced those same things from their vantage point on the other side of the stage curtain.

I'm following Dylan's lead in focusing on concert performances and the people who have played with him onstage (though many also played on records, and we certainly talk about those as well). Over the years, he has consistently made it clear that his heart is first and foremost in live performance, so the musicians with the closest access to Dylan's creative force are those that have logged miles with him on the road. To pick one quote among many that Dylan has given on this subject, in 1999 he told *USA Today*'s Edna Gunderson, "My fixation is in performing, not in making records, although I will make them. Touring is more important to me than getting locked down in a record."

. . . .

Every chapter of this book came from an original interview (or several) I conducted within the last three years. Preserving the flavor of our chats, I present them in Q&A format. Ideally more "A" than "Q" — since this is the first time many of these stories have been told, I edited myself out as much as possible, so you could hear the tales directly from the tellers. My role in these conversations is to coax, nudge, cajole, and ultimately ask the right question that might jog a memory that's lain dormant for decades, then get the hell out of the way.

A few of these conversations have previously run in my email newsletter *Flagging Down the Double E's*. I started that newsletter in early 2020 as a lark, using it as an excuse to write about something I loved: recordings of Bob Dylan concerts throughout history. It was not intended to be a major project, but, for such a seemingly niche topic, it reached a large audience: thousands of subscribers, citations in the *New York Times* and *New Yorker*, and, best of all, putting me in contact with so many Dylan fans across the world. Throughout the newsletter's short lifespan, my most-read entries have been the interviews. *Pledging My Time* collects the best of these newsletter interviews and adds many new ones conducted exclusively for the book. More than half of them are brand-new, in fact, printed here for the first time.

All these interviews have been edited and condensed. Lightly fact-checked too, if it was a clear fix (i.e., someone says the only time they played "Lay Lady Lay" was in Berlin, but it was actually Hamburg). Otherwise, these people were allowed to spin their yarns their own ways. I generally edited out redundancies across interviews, but in some cases I left them in where they showed intriguing patterns. For instance, more than one musician here compares playing with Dylan to jazz — but, in appropriate jazz fashion, they all add different shades to what that means. In a few cases, you'll even notice multiple vantage points on the same story. Two members of Dylan's first Never Ending Tour entourage tell a funny anecdote about pranking Dylan one Halloween, but their memories of the incident differ in interesting ways.

You can read this book in order…but you don't need to. Each conversation stands alone, so if you want to skip right to a particular musician or era you love, go for it. But do circle back. Sometimes the most obscure names have the best stories.

While I've arranged the interviewees more or less in chronological order, even that's fuzzy, because many came in and out of Dylan's orbit over many years. Noel Paul Stookey of Peter, Paul and Mary kicks us off talking about the Greenwich Village scene of the early '60s, but before we're done, we're talking about them together again at Live Aid in 1985. Alan Pasqua's chapter is slotted in the middle due to his time on Dylan's 1978 tour, even though by the end he's talking about rejoining Dylan to record "Murder Most Foul" in 2020. So the chronology jumps around, and you're free to as well.

. . . .

When organist Barry Goldberg was discussing "going electric" with Dylan at Newport, he expressed a sentiment I heard a lot: "I was feeling like I was touched by Bob, by the magic, and that really has never left me to this day. Once you experience something like that with someone like Bob, it doesn't rub off. It stays with you."

If Dylan is, as he famously put it back in 1965, a "song and dance man," these are the people who have sung and danced alongside him. Some have worked with him in the last couple years, some haven't worked with him in decades, but the experience has never left them.

Another keyboard player, Benmont Tench from Tom Petty and the Heartbreakers, put it this way: "You can read about Bob's life, and you can pay attention to what he says, and you can learn from it, but when you play music with somebody of that caliber, you learn something entirely different. It can only be passed on by that person. And those of us who have the opportunity to play with that person can pass on what we took away."

Bob Dylan, Joan Baez and Noel Paul Stookey at the March on Washington, 1963.
Photo by Dan Budnik

Noel Paul Stookey

Noel Stookey is best-known by his middle name: Paul. That's "Paul" as in the hitmaking vocal trio Peter, Paul and Mary. They first found success in the '60s folk music boom and, along the way, helped a certain young songwriter with an acquired-taste voice reach a broader audience. Their "Blowin' in the Wind" was the first time a Dylan-penned song topped a *Billboard* chart (Bob wouldn't top a chart with his own recording until "Murder Most Foul" in 2020).

Six decades on, Stookey's still going strong, pursuing both music and activism. On the music front, he's continued releasing new albums well into his 80s; and on the activism front, he co-founded the nonprofit Music to Life with his daughter to train musicians in social-justice work.

When I called Stookey, we talked about Greenwich Village in the '60s, of course, but also when he spent time with Dylan and The Band up in Woodstock after the motorcycle accident as well as several later run-ins in the '80s.

. . . .

It's an auspicious day for us to be talking, the day after Joni Mitchell's big return to Newport.[1]

That's lovely. I never paid too much attention to Joni's work, but I kept hearing Judy Collins' versions of her work. I was rather closer to Judy than I was to Joni.

There's an obvious parallel there with Dylan versus Peter, Paul and Mary, in terms of one artist helping popularize another.

Yeah, but the Dylan–Peter, Paul and Mary thing was really a natural evolution. When people credit Peter, Paul and Mary with introducing Bob Dylan, I understand

---

1 On July 24, 2022, Joni Mitchell shocked the music world by making her first public performance in many years at the Newport Folk Festival.

it on one hand. On the other hand, I really feel it was inevitable because of the power of the lyrics. The nature of the lyric, and the fact that it was talking about something which was so contemporary, was changing the face of popular music in the '60s, and arguably continued on into the formation of folk-rock in the '70s.

I think inevitably Dylan, regardless of the voice, would have become very popular. Albeit he leaned into it perhaps a bit theatrically, that voice had a certain kind of authenticity to it that people couldn't *deny*. You wouldn't go public with a voice like that unless you really meant it. *[laughs]*

Do you remember your first time encountering him, I assume in one of the Village clubs?

I was the master of ceremonies and a performer at The Gaslight [Café]. I was really not a folkie as much. I had so many hats I wore, honestly. I was not only the master of ceremonies, but I was the maître d' from time to time. The Gaslight was slowly evolving as the premier spot for folk singers to show up. Of course, there was Mike Porco's place, Folk City, but The Gaslight was like the place where Len Chandler, Dave Van Ronk, Tom Paxton hung out.

One night, in through the door comes Bob Dylan. I say, "We have our open mic, we can get you up." The first time he was there, and I don't remember the year, but it was probably 1960, he sang mostly derivatives. Nothing original that I can recall. Honestly, he was in and out.

He came back about a month later, after working a chess club in New Jersey[2], and asked if he could go on. I recognized him and said sure. Knowing ostensibly what kind of music he was going to do, I segued him in between a flamenco guitar player and my own comedy routine.

He got on stage and began to do a folk song called "Buffalo Skinners."[3] It tells the story of a man who's out west. He gets a job working for a group of people skinning buffalo hides. At the end of the season, he wants to move on. He goes to payroll, and they pay him in buffalo skins. He says, "What am I supposed to do with these?" The guy says, "Just take them to the general store and trade them off." So he goes to the general store, and he gets supplies for his trip further west.

Well, Dylan starts singing this song that has those same chords. Only this is the story about a folk singer who works at a chess club in New Jersey. At the end of

---

2   The Cave, a coffeeshop in East Orange where Dylan complained that everyone played chess while he was performing. Playing chess in coffeehouses and clubs was popular in the 1960s; the *New York Times* even had a dedicated "chess editor."

3   Dylan has returned to this song often in his career. Like many old folk numbers it goes by different names. During the Basement Tapes sessions it was "The Hills of Mexico," and in the early Never Ending Tour it was "Trail of the Buffalo."

the gig, the proprietor pays him in chess pieces. "Just take them to the bartender. They're like currency." So Dylan goes, sits at the bar, orders a beer, pays with the king, and gets two rooks in change.

That blew my mind. In retrospect, it is obvious to me that Dylan had a sense of what folk music was. That its reach was much broader than the specific story. That it could communicate concepts borrowing on tried-and-true traditional forms. Shortly after that, I recommended him to Albert Grossman, who was Peter, Paul and Mary's manager. It wasn't too long after that Dylan became part of his stable.

To carry this story further, maybe a year later Albert shows up at The Gate of Horn in Chicago, where Peter, Mary, and I are on the bill with Shel Silverstein, and plays an acetate of two songs that he felt we might enjoy. One of them was "Don't Think Twice, It's All Right" and the other one was "Blowin' in the Wind." Needless to say, both of those songs became hinge points for Bobby.

I think we were just coming off "If I Had a Hammer." It was introducing the concept of music with a message to what had been a popular music format. That's when disc jockeys could still make decisions about the music that they wanted to play, whether it was Buck Herring who would play "Lemon Tree," our first single hit, or whether it was a raft of increasingly socially-minded disc jockeys like Dave Dixon out of Detroit. The music that spoke to a social conscience began to take over the airwaves.

What about those two songs, "Blowin'" and "Don't Think Twice," made them seem like potential Peter, Paul and Mary songs? Obviously they're not being delivered to you in three-part harmony.

We always took a song for its value, not really the performance of the artist who created it or brought it to us. We knew we could do just about anything we wanted to, because we had three very individual voices. The first song we ever did was "Mary Had a Little Lamb," because the three of us had such different versions of all the other folk songs, it was the only one we could agree on.

There was such a natural feel between our voices that no matter who had the lead, the other two would find parts. I think stylistically what Peter, Mary and I were able to do was to accent the meaning of the song. We always made our decisions based on what said the lyric best. If that meant somebody had a solo line, then they had a solo line. If the meaning of the lyric was better advanced by a duet, then we would do it in duet.

How did that express in the lyrics of, say, "Blowin' in the Wind"? Can you think of any

"Blowin' in the Wind" is like an accumulated wisdom, so it was an accumulated vocal. The first line would be delivered as a solo. Second line would be a duet. Third line would be together. The chorus would be in harmony. Then a different person might take a lead on the next verse and be joined a line later by somebody. In a sense, it built. It satisfied our desire to emulate what the song was trying to say, that together we should pay attention to these things.

We would make decisions like that all the time. I have an album out called *Fazz*, a marriage of folk music and jazz. In the release of this album, I looked back at a lot of songs that I'd done in the Peter, Paul and Mary era. I was introducing a lot of alternative jazz chords into the folk milieu. At one point, Peter caught me doing a major seventh chord behind a Woody Guthrie tune. He said, "You don't play major sevenths for Woody!"

Although it struck me at the time as kind of arbitrary, it underlines what I was telling you, that the ultimate decider of whether something should be incorporated in a song, whether it was a vocal or a guitar chord, was what the song was saying. Does this enhance the song or does it detract from the message? Stuck with those stark decisions, life became easier. It might be clever musically, might even sound pretty, but if the song's not supposed to sound pretty for that particular lyric, then don't put it in.

In those early days, are you running into Dylan every couple of weeks in various coffeehouses and clubs?

Pretty intensely for about three months, maybe even as long as six months, I remember we'd hear Bobby at any one of the coffeehouses. Performers, as a rule, went from one coffeehouse to another. Not for employment, but just because they had friends at the other coffeehouse who would call them up on stage to do a guest set.

There was a great interplay between the Figaro, the Bitter End, the Gaslight, the Rienzi, and Gerde's Folk City. A great deal of informational exchange. As a matter of fact, somebody told me that Odetta once played a song on stage with her back to the audience because she didn't want a competitive folk singer that she knew was out in front to steal her chords.

This was just prior to Peter, Paul and Mary beginning to move into clubs like The Blue Angel a little uptown, "bringing the music of the common man to the sophisticated elite" *[said with a touch of sarcasm]*, and then going out on the road. That changed everything. Once you went out on the road, you would stop by The

Gaslight to hear somebody who was happening, but that scene went away pretty quickly. By the time we came back to the Village, everything had gone upscale. That folk explosion was over very quickly.

When you got impressed with him as a songwriter, what was he like as a performer, as an onstage presence?

He was probably nervous, because he was just so introspective. He was very tight-lipped. He was not comfortable. I would say that social graces were not high on his skill list.

What do you mean?

Weak handshakes, mumbled hellos, odd introductions to tunes. I'm not a psychiatrist, but it seems like his natural inclination is to be a loner and quiet. Even though his talent was drawing him to the stage, it was not his most comfortable place to be.

In 1963, you all and Dylan both sang at Dr. King's March on Washington. What was the role of the musicians there that day?

Music was such an important part of the movement. Whether it was The Freedom Singers, whether it was people singing during the marches in Selma, any circumstance that occurred where Civil Rights was being talked about, there was music. Maybe because Pete [Seeger] and "We Shall Overcome" was so much a part of it. Maybe because it's part of folk music's calling to be this connection between human life and the arts. Even the rehearsal that took place in front of the Washington Monument integrated music. Odetta singing, Dylan and Baez singing, us singing, in between the speeches. And then we all marched to the Lincoln Memorial.

Music spoke on a couple of levels, but what it did was focus us on the interconnectivity of all people. When you sing together, you are connected in a way that standing shoulder to shoulder listening to someone speak doesn't do it. That was an important part, and still *is* an important part, of understanding that we're all in this together.

Also in the summer of 1963, Dylan made his first Newport appearance. Elijah Wald's book[4] mentions a private plane that Grossman put his clients on that flew you three and

---

4   *Dylan Goes Electric!: Newport, Seeger, Dylan, and the Night That Split the Sixties* — a fascinating read even if you think you already know the basic story pretty well.

Dylan to Rhode Island. Does that ring a bell?

At that time, Peter, Paul and Mary were doing college campuses. We bought a Lockheed Lodestar. Peter used to call it the Lobster Load-hard. It had three tail fins like the old TWA planes. It really helped a lot because you could fly from campus to campus, small airport to small airport. You didn't have to do transfers, all of that. It was that plane, I think, that you're referring to. It ultimately had one of Dylan's guitars in the back cupboard, as I recall. It may have even been the one that he played electric on in Newport.

Most people denigrated his move from what was viewed as political writing into introspective writing. Phil Ochs, particularly. But as far as I was concerned, that paralleled understanding in my own life. You could talk about politics, but it all got down to being individually responsible. And if you're going to be individually responsible, you got to figure out who you are. I thought Dylan's change was a very natural one, and I think part of an evolution that I mirrored myself when I went spiritual in the late '60s. I don't think he relinquished his concern for the human state; I think he just broadened it, and people weren't ready for that.

Two other songs I wanted to ask you about. The first is "Talkin' Bear Mountain Picnic Massacre Blues." You gave Dylan the article that inspired it?

That was right after his rewrite of "Buffalo Skinners," a day or two days later. Bobby was still in town, still coming to The Gaslight to sing. I was so impressed with what he had done. When I saw the article, I thought, this guy can translate anything into a commonly understood circumstance. I brought him the newspaper. I just handed him the whole clipping. He came back — I swear it was the next night, there might have been a day in between — but he came back very quickly and did "Bear Mountain Picnic Massacre Blues."

So you had given the article to him with the idea that there's a song in this story and he could write it?

Yes. That there was a Bob Dylan song.

What about that newspaper story lent itself to that?

The incongruity. I think Dylan saw incongruity and was able to comment on it handsomely. He could give it a full effect. In the song, don't some people end up washed on shore? I'm not sure that actually happened, but the boat did capsize. His ability to give it bone and structure was pretty amazing. I knew he would, just from the "Buffalo Skinners" tune.

And what is the story behind another talkin' blues, your own "Talkin' Candy Bar Blues." I read Dylan contributed to that, but his verse did not end up on your album. What happened there?

Actually, Dylan I don't think contributed— Oh, yeah, you're right! Wow, your research is great. *[laughs]* Now that you mention it, I had written the "Talkin' Candy Bar Blues," and Albert sent it to Bobby because he liked the concept, but he wasn't sure where the song was going to go.

So it was a work in progress?

It wasn't finished when Bobby saw it. Bobby came back with something that was very stiff. Which surprised me. Or it may not have been stiff; I just may have had my back up.

I'm glad where the tune went, but it didn't use any of Dylan's things. I think he tried two or three verses, and they just didn't sit right with me. Wouldn't I love to find that somewhere in my archives, that original contribution by Dylan?

Did you stay in touch with Dylan after those early Village days?

In terms of actually staying in touch with Dylan later on, our paths crossed a couple of times. We saw him backstage at some television show [a Martin Luther King tribute in 1986] where he butchered lead guitar on "Blowin' in the Wind" with us and Stevie Wonder. It was one of those mishmashes where the producer says, "Oh my gosh, we can get all those names together on the screen, we'll have a sell-out TV show." So they put Dylan and us and Stevie together to do "Blowin' in the Wind" and it was not very good.

Backstage Dylan said, "Are you still with the Lord?" I said, "Oh, yes."

That really came about because of the trip that I made up to Woodstock following his accident. He was going through some changes himself. That was just before he put out *John Wesley Harding*, and, of course, several years before his two born-again albums. He asked me to do a bit part in a film he was doing in Woodstock around the time of the motorcycle accident.

Do you remember what your bit part was in that Woodstock thing?

I was dressed in a white monk's robe. It was outside in some forest someplace, but I'm sure that what I saw mostly was the cutting room floor.

What were you doing in your white monk's robe?

I think I was pontificating. This would've been prior to either of our spiritual experiences.

Did you see any of the shows on the post–Newport tours with The Band?

I think by that time, I was really not paying too much attention to what Bobby was up to, or if it was, it was sporadic.

Peter, Paul and Mary didn't have to contend with a purist criterion. We had already gotten criticized a couple of times as being slick. We just stayed with our acoustic instruments. Though our harmonies were maybe challenging to those who just love Appalachian music, we pretty much did the music we wanted to do. Borrowed from folk artists, changed harmonies sometimes. We wrote a bridge to Phil Ochs' "There But for Fortune." Who's audacious enough to do that? That was all part of our comfort zone. If we felt it needed to be done, then we did it, and hang the fallout.

What I'm saying is, we were caught up in our own world, especially through '69. Then we took six years off for what we fondly refer to as good behavior and didn't get back together again until '78.

If you're doing your own thing after Newport and all, how do you end up in Woodstock doing the film?

Spiritual search. Suspecting that reality is not all it's cracked up to be. Looking for some soul direction. Also, the advent of the Beatles, because that was pretty powerful. That was an arrival on the pop music scene at least as cataclysmic as folk music's arrival was. And really in a direction of self-discovery. A lot of the Beatles tunes were, after you got past "I Want to Hold Your Hand," self-discovery.

That was the big question I put to Bobby, "Have you heard the Beatles? What does that make you want to do as an artist?" That's when Bob said to me, "Well, you got to hear my new album." As if *John Wesley Harding* was his answer to the Beatles. I thought that was curious because, certainly, stylistically it wasn't.

How does "Too Much of Nothing," the Basement Tapes song from around that time, make its way to Peter, Paul and Mary to record?

Probably Albert again, and/or [Bob's] ongoing relationship with Peter. I know we did a very pop version of it.

Years later, you three and Dylan were on the same bill again at Live Aid.

That was not a happy scene, particularly for Mary. The expectation was that we would go on and sing "Blowin' in the Wind" with Bobby to conclude. When he called up Keith Richards and Ron Wood instead, it just…I don't know. I think it permanently drew a line between who Dylan thought he was and what Mary thought the folk community should be.

I remember going over to Dylan's trailer, him sitting on the steps. The assumption was we were going to go on stage later with him, and we never did. We did go for the big finale, but that's all. We never sang at Live Aid ourselves. That was not a good feeling.

Basically, you were only there to sing with Dylan and then he snubbed you?

Uh-huh. Like I said, social skills were not high on Bobby's skill list.

If it's any consolation, many people consider that team-up with Keith Richards and Ron Wood just about the worst performance of his career.

Yes. Even Dylan might agree. I just saw a clip of it recently. Either Ron Wood's guitar went out, or somebody's guitar was not in tune, so they kept shifting off guitars. Nobody else sang really except for Dylan.

To try to draw some value out of that experience, I would have to say, I think what he was trying to do was to reach across predispositions. He was trying to say, "Hey, we're all in this together. Even people that you don't expect are in this together are in this together." I don't think he was doing it for self-glorification. He didn't need that. I don't think he did it because he was buddies with those guys. I think he did it to make a broader statement. I would have to give him the benefit of that.

I haven't heard from Bobby or spoken to him, it's got to be 40 years now. If I was going to encapsulate it, I'd say that we had an affectionate but distant relationship. I think it was really super what he wrote in the Peter, Paul and Mary liner notes about me doing my Charlie Chaplin imitations with flickering lights in The Gaslight. He did have a poetic sense that he could put on paper without music from time to time.

> *Paul then was a guitar player singer comedian–*
> *But not the funny ha ha kind–*
> *His funnyness could only be defined an described by the word "hip" or "hyp"–*
> *A combination a Charlie Chaplin Jonathan Winters and Peter Lorre...*
> *it was one a these nites when Paul said*
> *"Yuh gotta now hear me an Peter an Mary sing"*
> *Mary's hair was down almost t her waist then–*
> *An Peter's beard was only about half grown–*
> *An the Gaslight stage was smaller*
> *An the song they sung was younger–*
> *But the walls shook*
> *An everybody smiled–*
> *An everybody felt good–*

Ethan Signer, Martin Carthy, Richard Fariña, Dylan, and Eric von Schmidt perform a chaotic sing-along at the Troubadour in London, England in January 1963.
Photo by Alison Chapman McLean

Martin Carthy

When Bob Dylan first set foot in London in December 1962, Martin Carthy was waiting.

Not literally, of course. Carthy barely knew who Dylan was. But, already an éminence grise of the insular British folk scene, Carthy was bound to run into a newcomer scouting out the folk clubs sooner or later. Sure enough, the singer encountered Dylan on one of his first nights in town. Carthy even invited him on stage at the King & Queen pub for what many believe is Dylan's first-ever performance on British soil.

Carthy told me about that night, as well as shepherding Dylan around London's burgeoning folk scene on many nights after. Dylan was in town to film a BBC play called *Madhouse on Castle Street*. Carthy was on hand for that. And, when Dylan returned to London sixty years later to perform, Carthy was there again for a warm reunion.

A natural raconteur, Carthy spoke all about his time with Dylan as well as the London folk scene in the '60s more generally. Oh, and about the night the two of them smashed a piano with a samurai sword.

. . . .

How far into your career are you in '62? What gigs are you playing before Dylan shows up in London?

Just little pub gigs. Folk clubs were, more often than not, in the upstairs room of a local pub. That's where it was all born, really.

Who were the key figures on the folk scene there?

There were people like Nigel Denver. He was a drinker, but there were certain songs he could sing very, very well indeed. There were a lot of other guitar players around. Davy Graham, but he was more interested in blues and jazz, and sang the occasional English song.

Was Ramblin' Jack Elliott on the scene yet? I know he spent a number of years in London.

Yes, he was around in the late '50s. I never saw him until a bit later on when he was making a return visit.

I met him through a chap called Rory McEwen. Rory had heard Lead Belly, so being that kind of a person, he went to New York and sought him out. Lead Belly of course was dead, but he got to meet his widow. He's an incredibly polite person, and would never dream of asking to see the guitar until she offered. He stared at the guitar case for a while, and she said, "Open it up." She actually gave him permission to play it. He was ecstatic because he'd studied Lead Belly's guitar playing. He was one of the people who actually was able to do an extremely good Lead Belly on guitar.

[Rory's] brother, Alex, was absolutely crazy about Reverend Gary Davis and went and knocked on his door and took guitar lessons from him. The two of them came back absolutely armed to the teeth with very good guitar playing. Occasionally, Rory would turn up at the Troubadour and would sing a couple of songs and blow everybody away.

Rory lived in a house that was a hangout spot for the folk scene, right? I think I read that Dick Farina and Eric Von Schmidt would stay there.

That's quite likely. The person who actually stayed with him a lot was Carolyn Hester.

One of Dylan's first album credits was playing harmonica on her third record.

That's right. She could really sing. She was encouraged by the amount of attention she got from England to come and do a tour. When she turned up, we were expecting just her. She turned up with her new husband: Dick Farina, as he was known then. He played a dulzaina. It was pretty beaten up, but it had a nice sound. He was full of stories. A lot of it was BS, but that was the nature of the bloke.

Then Dylan shows up in December 1962. How do you first meet?

There used to be a left-wing book and record shop called Collet's. It was a meeting place for folk musicians. I remember going in there one day and picking up the new issue of *Sing Out!*[5]. There's this picture on the front of this bloke, Bob Dylan. I flicked the pages and there was a song of his called "Blowin' in the Wind" and one called "Song to Woody." There was another one, I can't remember what that one was ["Ballad of Donald White"].

Is this the first time you encountered the name Bob Dylan, on the cover of that magazine?

Yes. I was intrigued. I bought the magazine, went home and read it.

Not very long afterwards, I was singing at the King & Queen with a group called Thamesiders. We had a gig on Friday nights. One of the evenings, I looked up and, sitting there in the audience, was the front cover of *Sing Out!*.

We finished a song, and I walked over to him. I said, "Do you want to sing a couple of songs?" He looked at me and said, "Ask me later." "Okay." I just left it.

The interval came and the interval went. He'd got his guitar out in the meantime. The Thamesiders and I sang a couple of songs. I looked at him and he nodded, so he got up and sang three songs. One of them was his talking blues about the John Birch Society. I think he was quite surprised at how much people knew about the John Birch Society, as they were often news over here. He was surprised by the audience reaction. They got the jokes. They laughed at all the right places.

One of the other songs was one of those jazzy ragtime-y things that a lot of the American guys used to do. Then he might well have sung "Blowin' in the Wind." He went down very, very well indeed. He really did.

You'd read his lyrics in Sing Out!, *but was this the first time you had actually heard him sing or perform?*

That was the first time I heard him sing. I thought he was very good. Afterwards, he asked about more clubs. I said, "Well, there's the Troubadour tomorrow night, and I'm one of the residents there. Come and sing." And he did.

Of course, he was with [his manager] Albert Grossman then. One of the things Albert used to do was, any of his charges who he'd accompanied to London, he would take them out to the folk clubs. Because Albert was a folkie. I found out later on that he was rather a good singer. His favorite song, I was told, was a whaling song called "Go to Sea No More." He had operated around Chicago. He was very well known in his area as the person who sang that song.

What happens the next night at the Troubadour?

Well first, he went to what was called the Singers Club.

5   A folk-music magazine in the '60s that published song lyrics.

What became the Singers Club was known as The Ballads and Blues in the '50s. It was basically a left-wing tavern, run for people like Ewan MacColl and Bert Lloyd. There would be various guests in the mid- to late-'50s which included Jack Elliott and Derroll Adams. Derroll and Jack were like a musical item in the West End of London. Derroll had a wonderful line of patter. They were a couple of funny Americans, and they played very well.

The fellow who ran it left the club to become an agent. The club shut down and didn't reopen for a couple of years. When it did, it called itself the Singers Club. They were establishing their identity straight away as a place where you could go and sing songs from your tradition. It wasn't acceptable for an English person to sing American songs.

Really? That was a rule, you could only sing songs from your native country?

I understood it later on. You know, "this is my club. If you want to come and sing at my club, you sing songs that I want to hear." Ewan [MacColl] was very demanding on all his performers. He had a tendency to dismiss people who were not following that line.

So Bob came along. He went to the Singers Club and didn't go down terribly well there. Ewan was a songwriter. His partner then was a young Peggy Seeger. They were both very left-wing, and Bob wasn't political enough for them. He wasn't, as he was being touted at the time by *Sing Out!*, as the inheritor of Woody Guthrie. Ewan and Peggy dismissed him out of hand. Peggy still doesn't like his writing.

Because the songs he performed weren't politically minded enough?

Yeah. "Blowin' in the Wind," as far as they were concerned, was just not interesting. They liked songs that named names. More agitprop stuff was what they liked, and they were good at it. It was hard to argue with.

I think it's a criticism that could be leveled at Ewan that he didn't accept what kids were doing. You could draw kids towards you, but if you just dismissed them out of hand, they'll go somewhere else. That's what people like me did. But there were others who didn't. There were others who just thought that he was the berries.

I know in the Village scene, there was some tension between the staunch traditionalists, "no writing new songs, perform them the way they would be performed back then," and the people wanting to push the songs forward. Was there that tension over there too?

Oh yes, absolutely. It was all really silly. Guitars weren't allowed; that wasn't

I always loved the directness of his delivery.
The thing that I noticed about his present album
[Rough and Rowdy Ways] is that he's actually talking to you.
It's just much more intimate. He's not afraid of change,
even at 81 years old. I'm full of admiration for his nerves.

· ·

"traditional." There was that divide between the traddies and the— I don't know what you would call them. We called them the entertainers.

I was stuck in the middle, because I was serious about the songs, but didn't like being dismissed out of hand. I have my pride.

What happens next? Does Dylan go to the Troubadour later that same night?

He went from the Singers Club down to the Troubadour, which always started about 10:30, 11:00 at night. He sang a couple of songs there.

How did he go over?

He went down very well indeed. He didn't sing the same three songs as he had at King & Queens, I don't think. I know he sang "Don't Think Twice, It's All Right."

I remember one of the Saturday nights he was there, he started to sing this song, "Where have you been, my blue-eyed son." I thought, "Well, I wonder what version of 'Lord Randall' he's going to sing." It very quickly became clear that this wasn't "Lord Randall" at all. This was "A Hard Rain's A-Gonna Fall."

It was spellbinding. When he finished, there was that moment of quiet when the audience just takes in what they've been given. I love it when an audience does that; they wait for just a couple of seconds longer. And then the applause started and it went on for a long time. People had been given something extraordinary, something very new.

He arrived in the middle of December '62, and he was there for a good while because he had been brought over for a play called *Madhouse on Castle Street*, which was a play written by a white Jamaican native who couldn't understand what was going on in England at the time. It was full of Tories, full of Conservatives, and people were just beginning to wake up.

What do you remember about that play? The recording that aired on TV with Dylan in it seems to have been lost.

The BBC deleted it. Stupid bastards. They had a big clear-out at one point, and one of the plays that was cleared out was this.

In the play, the Madhouse on Castle Street was a boarding house full of single rooms, and all these different people lived there. The Madhouse was Britain, and Castle Street was because England was full of castles, and it was still basically run by the upper classes. I only understood that two or three years later.

The man who directed it, Philip Saville, he was a clever bloke. He saw Bob Dylan perform in New York.

And thought of Bob for his play?

Yes, Dylan was given a part. When he went to the first read-through, they gave him the script, and he just said, "I can't do this."[6]

I read you were there for the filming of some of that play.

I was, oh yes. I'd go in regularly. I found the songs that he was singing hilarious. One song he had to sing ["Ballad of the Gliding Swan"], he changed the words: "Lady Margaret's belly is wet with tears / Nobody's been on it for 27 years." I don't believe he sang those words on the recording.

What happened was, they took a break at 9:30 in the evening, then they were going to finish the rest of it off. There was an argument between the technical people and the drama department. They said, "You won't pay us our overtime, so we're not coming back." They all walked off.

They had to redo the whole thing, so Bob got paid twice for this play that he wasn't acting in.

And during the down time when the production is sorting out that dispute, he jets off to Italy for a few days?

That's right. [Before he left], he would always ask me to sing "Scarborough Fair." There was a particular guitar figure I played on it, and he really loved that. When he came back from Italy, he said, "Hey, I got to play you this." He took out his

---

6   They split Dylan's part into two characters to give most of the spoken dialogue to another actor while Dylan mostly just sang.

guitar, and he started to play it. He was playing the figure that I'd worked out, but with a flat pick. He was way too excited, and I don't think he got through the first verse. He looked at me and he said, "I can't do this." He burst out laughing, and that was the end of that.

So, instead of singing "Scarborough Fair," he wrote "Girl from the North Country" with the same music.

The other song he always used to ask for was "Lord Franklin," which is the story of Sir John Franklin and his ill-fated attempt to find the Northwest Passage in the Canadian Arctic. It was a disaster. Everybody died. "Lord Franklin" was a song that Bert Lloyd had put together from bits and pieces. It was always either "Scarborough Fair" or "Lord Franklin" he would ask for.

Asking for these in what context?

At shows. "Sing 'Scarborough Fair!' Sing 'Scarborough Fair!'" And he just loved "Lord Franklin." He wrote a song around that one too ["Bob Dylan's Dream"]. I actually did a recording of it for a tribute album. It's a lovely song. "Ten thousand dollars at the drop of a hat / I'd give it all gladly if our lives could be like that."

You've said he played "Girl from the North Country" for you, to show you the "Scarborough Fair" connection. Did the same thing happen with "Bob Dylan's Dream" that came from "Lord Franklin"?

No, I heard it on the album. With "Bob Dylan's Dream," I remember hearing the song and thinking, that's a nice thing to do, just to write another song about it.

Do you get any money from these rewriting of songs you'd been playing?

It's a traditional song. I didn't write it. It belongs to him, belongs to you, belongs to anybody who wants to claim it. You can't copyright it.

He can copyright "Bob Dylan's Dream." That's fine; he wrote all those words. But it's inspired by "Lord Franklin."

Am I right that the Simon & Garfunkel "Scarborough Fair" was also inspired by your version?

Yes, absolutely. Paul Simon always said he loved [my version]. But he hasn't made any money out of it, and neither have I.

Why is that?

I signed a piece of paper, which I should have taken to a lawyer first to have it explained to me. There had been a court case about it.[7] The publishers over here kept trying to persuade me to say that mine was the original version. I said, "No, it's not my song. I learned it from a recording of Bert Lloyd. Go and talk to him." I don't think they ever did.

After the case was all over, I fell into that trap that people have fallen into a million times. There's a whole pile of contracts and "Oh, you need to sign all these bits of paper. This is this, this is that, this one says you have no further claim on 'Scarborough Fair.'" I said, "Okay, I'll sign it."

What I was doing was handing [my publisher] the ownership of the song that I didn't own. Only now *they* own it. They took all that lovely money that was generated by *The Graduate*. It made millions for them.

Except that, of course, the Simon & Garfunkel song came out as "Scarborough Fair/Canticle." Art Garfunkel wrote the "Canticle," so *he* has made some money, I would imagine.

I think I met Art twice. One of them, he was staring up at the ceiling all the time through. I was talking to Paul, and Art was just ignoring everything that was going on. He was *la-la*-ing something to himself as he was looking up. He was working on the "Canticle." I don't have any complaints about that at all. He wrote that, and he's the only one who made any money.

Getting back to Dylan, there's a photo of you, him, and a whole bunch of people onstage playing at the Troubadour. What's the story there?

Eric Von Schmidt and Dick Farina had just recorded an album. They got fairly stoned doing it, then came down to the Troubadour and took over the stage for some time. I was in the background playing guitar on a couple of things along with Ethan Signer, who was unaffected by the substances because he wasn't interested in that stuff. That's the only time I ever actually played with Bob.

Why do you think you two connected on this initial trip he made?

I don't know. We just hit it off the way you do. I just saw him the other day, and we basically fell into each other's arms. It was lovely, just lovely to see him.

Was this while he was in London performing recently [October 2022]?

Yeah. I happened to be down that way, and I got a message. So I walked into the room and it was arms around, just hugging. "I haven't seen you for ages. How are

---

7   Carthy's music publisher sued Simon on the grounds that Simon had stolen, and copyrighted, Carthy's unique arrangement.

you doing?"

I think the last time we met was when he did a gig tacked onto the end of a tour. He did an open-air gig at Blackbushe Airport, which is this disused airport south of London.

That was decades ago!

Yeah, 1978.

That was the last time you'd seen him before a week ago?

Pretty much. There might have been one other time where you just say hello and wave at each other. This time, it was just the two of us. And it was a total delight. Really was.

Did you attend any of the shows on this latest tour?

I went to the show he did in Hull [a few nights after London]. I was up in the rafters quite a bit, and I couldn't always hear the words, which upset me. But the music was astounding.

Fairly different than what you would've been seeing at the Troubadour in 1962.

Well, he's the same bloke. He's developed astonishingly. It seems to me that he'd actually gone to school in a way, and just worked on his singing, worked on his playing, worked on everything.

When you listen to the new album or his recent material, do you see parallels from the Bob Dylan you knew as a musician way back in the early '60s, even though the sound is totally different?

I always loved the directness of his delivery. The thing that I noticed about his present album *[Rough and Rowdy Ways]* is that he's actually talking to you. It's just much more intimate. He's not afraid of change, even at 81 years old. I'm full of admiration for his nerves.

Going back to that first trip, are there other memories that stand out?

If he came to a gig, he'd always come back to have a cup of tea at Dorothy's and my place. We had a room on Haverstock Hill.

The first time, when he came to three gigs in two days — The King & Queen on Friday, the Singers Club on Saturday for early evening, and the Troubadour from 10:30 on until one o'clock in the morning — afterwards he got a taxi back to where I was living. The first thing Dorothy said was, "I'll put the kettle on. Make a fire, Mart." That's me.

I had a piano, which was a complete wreck. We had used all the easily burned bits [as firewood]. We were now starting on the frame. I had to get a samurai sword out to chop up the piano. Bob stood in front of me and said, "You can't do that! That's a musical instrument." I said, "It's a piece of junk. You couldn't repair that." He looked at me and went, "Well, okay…"

He stood behind me, and I swung at it. After I'd had a couple of swings, I just heard this little voice in my ear: "Can I have a try?"

So I handed him the samurai sword, and he chopped up some piano as well.

You know, I've still got the samurai sword. I didn't think to take the sword with me to our meeting last week.

I don't know what security does if you show up to your meeting with Bob Dylan holding a giant sword.

There you are. That would have come into it, I think.

Did you see Dylan when he returned to London a couple years after that first visit?

Yes, in 1964, I think. We were living in the same house. The telephone went and I picked it up, and it was Bob. He still had the telephone number.
He turned up with a couple other people. He pulled out his guitar and he sang the song that would become a hit for the Byrds, "Mr. Tambourine Man." I was absolutely silenced by it. It was just fabulous. He didn't record it until later.

People who rely on his recordings for when he wrote stuff are misguided. The first time he came over, he sang "Hollis Brown" in '62 or early '63. I think he probably sang it one of the Troubadour nights. He always sang different songs. I remember him singing that song about the kid who went down from Chicago, "The Death of Emmett Till."

He was so prolific, especially with early folk songs. He probably has four times as many he didn't put on the records as those he did.

Oh God, he sang so many songs. I've had people coming up to me and saying, "oh, he always cheated. He had three or four people in the audience recording everything [everyone else played], and then he'd go back and play it and write his songs." No, he didn't. He had a fabulous memory. If he heard something that he liked, he would go back to the hotel and he would try and write down what he could remember. He did it with all sorts of songs. I don't suppose he sang them more than once or twice each. One or two of them turned up on some of those Bootleg Series things, and I recognized them.

One of the famous ones was one of his "Farewell" songs, which he heard Louis Killen sing. It clearly derives from that song that Louis sang ["The Leaving of Liverpool"]. It's just inspired by something that he'd heard that night and he would have gone back to his hotel and just written down what he could remember.

But then we all did. We'd learned how to learn songs on one hearing because it was so hard to get songs. I remember the first couple of times I sang a song I just learned, I'd go back home and I'd sing it to myself, and then sing it out the next night.

It was just wonderful to hear all those anthems he wrote later on. They traced back to England. That period of him being in England had a colossal effect on the way he wrote songs. Especially the melodies.

I have fabulous memories of the warmth of the bloke. One night he sang "Pretty Peggy-O" at the Troubadour. I think I or Dorothy may have asked him to do it. He made up a verse on the spot: "The colonel he is gone, he's long gone. He's fighting with the wild man out in Borneo." He bursts out laughing, and so did the rest of the audience. He had a fabulous sense of fun.

Above: Dylan horsing around on top of a car in Cambridge, Massachusetts, 1964. Left: back of photograph.
Courtesy of Betsy Siggins

9 1964 - Cambridge   2.101BSC
John Cooke
John Sabastian
Bobby Dylan
Vector Mamidis
Paul Rothchild

BY BETSY Siggins

Betsy Siggins

To oversimplify dramatically: What Greenwich Village was to Manhattan, Cambridge was to Boston. Thanks to a preponderance of college students, Cambridge became the nexus of the folk scene a couple hundred miles northeast of New York. And one of the central hubs of that scene was a small folk and jazz club called Club 47.

Betsy Siggins was a founder of Club 47 and oversaw many of its activities. She was college roommates with Joan Baez, who started her career performing on Club 47's stages, and soon knew everyone involved in the East Coast folk scene. That, of course, included Dylan, who popped up a number of times at Club 47 during his folkie days. Siggins got to know him both professionally and personally, and she told me about seeing a young Bob Dylan at Club 47 and Newport Folk Festival and fearing for her life as a passenger in Dylan's car.

. . . .

Before we get to Dylan, could you take me through the early days of Club 47?

It was started as a jazz club by two women who graduated from Brandeis University. They were very keen on jazz. But back in the old days, [the police] thought jazz instruments were more dicey and that the musicians who play jazz may have brought drugs into those places. [The club were soon shut down, and, in order to reopen,] they had to have stringed instruments as part of the deal. That's how it morphed into a folk club, because folk musicians were playing stringed instruments. I guess they thought folk music was more benign. Little did they know.

Joan Baez was a big part of Club 47. Was she there from day one?

She was one of the earliest artists there. She and I met in 1958 when we were freshmen at Boston University. We were both in the theater school. Jim Kweskin and Debbie Green were in the same class. I'm still friends with Joan and Kweskin.

I hear from Kweskin probably every 10 days. Geoff Muldaur too. Geoff was not in our class, but Geoff and I have been friends since, I'm going to say 1960. Tom Rush and I have been friends since 1960 too.

Are all of these folk musicians you're mentioning playing at Club 47 from the earliest days too?

More or less. These people made up the nucleus of artists who were living or going to school in the Cambridge community. It made it easy for them to be performers as well as students.

Did it take time for the club to find its audience?

It didn't happen overnight, but Joan attracted a lot of people. In the very, very early days, it was only her parents who came to see her, but that changed quickly.

At what point does Dylan start showing up at Club 47?

Well, I first met him at Gerde's Folk City in New York. The Charles River Valley Boys [featuring Betsy's then-husband Bob Siggins] were playing at Gerde's from time to time. They were on the same bill with Dylan in those early days.

So we saw a lot of him when we were there. My earliest recollection was Dylan wanting to go out and smoke during the sets at Gerde's. I went along with him and listened to him talk endlessly, interestingly. Hard to fathom where he already was in his head.

How do you mean?

He was very, very complex. He was into French poetry and other things that I was not familiar with, but I loved listening to him. He just went on and on and on. There were just the two of us sitting in Washington Square Park. I was a rapt audience.

Do you remember the first time he took the stage at Club 47?

I want to say it was with Eric Von Schmidt, the performer that evening. They'd all been doing a lot of drinking and carrying on. Dylan got pulled up on stage as a lark. He was very funny, very droll. We still have that recording somewhere.

Would the audience have known who he was at this point?

Yeah. I can't tell you how wide his audience had spread, but I remember going to full concerts of him at Brandeis in New York. He sold out, really rapidly.

Every now and then he'd stay at my house overnight when I was married to Bob [Siggins]. At night, when everyone went to bed, Dylan would stay up all night long typing on my typewriter. He was so prolific. I have a set of unpublished words that he wrote during that time and left in my typewriter after spending the night. They are in the Folk New England archives in Amherst.

Do you remember anything about what they say?

I can tell you the first line: "Well it's early and it's squirrely."

Since he didn't sign them, in the big scheme of things, nobody thought they were worth real money, which is maybe just as well. I suppose I would've sold them to pay the rent, but I couldn't, or I didn't, and now they're part of our history in the archives.

I saw one reference to him sitting in with Carolyn Hester at Club 47.

I don't remember if that happened, but he was playing harp with her in New York at Columbia Records. Was I at that session? I know I was with Dylan when he made one of his early albums. A really nice Black guy [Tom Wilson] was the producer of that album.

Dylan would just invite anybody who was in New York to go along to those rehearsals and performances. Again, we just got to go along with him.

Do you remember anything about the recording session you were at?

I remember it being fabulous. Just the whole process was a surprise to me, because I've never been to a recording before except with the Charles River Valley Boys. When they were in London in 1960, they recorded an album of old-timey music at Dobells Record Shop, which was a very famous place in London back in the late '50s, early '60s. I think Dylan appeared there as well.

You mentioned Eric Von Schmidt. There's that line on Dylan's first album where he talks about learning "Baby, Let Me Follow You Down" at the green pastures of Harvard University. I would imagine that was around one of these scenes, one of these times he was there.

Yes, it was. I don't think he had any idea what he meant when he said that. It was just a throwaway line that became famous.

Dylan wrote in some liner notes for Eric Von Schmidt a few years later a story about going to Club 47 to hear him do his song "Grizzly Bear."[8]

I was there. It was crowded, it was hot. I was standing in the back next to the kitchen when they were carrying on onstage. It was a small space. There was not much distance between the kitchen door and the stage door. That was where I stood for most shows.

Another scene I want to ask you about, you sent me a photo of Bob Dylan on the roof of a car on Mount Auburn Street in Cambridge in 1963. Do you remember anything about that?

I took the photograph. I'm going to say we were headed to the Brandeis concert. Everybody was out getting into cars, and Dylan thought it would be amusing to be on top of the car.

He became so guarded and so private very quickly, it seems. Photos like that from the first few years, that was a moment in his career that it doesn't seem like lasted very long.

I think that's correct. Too many people wanted too much from him too much of the time.

Was that ever an issue at Club 47? I imagine a Bob Dylan drop-in might start causing a scene.

Yes. Oftentimes they were not announced, but the buzz was out in Cambridge. Was he around? Was he in town? Did he have a show nearby? That kind of buzz was constant.

What other memorable Club 47 performers stand out from back then?

Well, I have to give an enormous credit to the early days of the Newport Folk Festivals. Club 47 became a stop-off place for people who had just played at Newport and needed to make a few extra bucks.

It's important that everybody remember that Black musicians were not allowed to stay in hotels. Oftentimes, they stayed with the extended folk family in the Cambridge-Boston community. Reverend Gary Davis stayed on my couch.

---

8   "Of course, we had heard about Eric Von Schmidt for many years. The name itself had become a password. Eventually, after standing in line to meet him, there it was — his doorstep, a rainy day, and he greeted his visitors, inviting them in. He was told how much they liked Grizzly Bear and he then invited the whole bunch to the club, where he was about to perform the thing live. 'C'mon down to the club' he said — "I'm about to perform it live.'" — Dylan's liner notes to Von Schmidt's 1969 album *Who Knocked the Brains Out of The Sky?*

Every now and then he'd stay at my house overnight. Everyone went to bed, and Dylan would stay up all night long typing on my typewriter. I have a set of unpublished words that he left in my typewriter. The first line is "Well it's early and it's squirrely."

He wasn't the only one. We were segregated in Cambridge, as liberal as it was. Elizabeth Cotten could not buy a blouse in a department store in Cambridge. A white friend of mine had to go and buy that blouse for her performance at the club.

Sad.

Yeah. Nonetheless, that's how I met people like The Staple Singers. It was from those early days when they would play the club. They had to play four or five nights because that was the only way we could pay them. Without the early Newport people like Bruce Jackson and Bob Jones, I wouldn't have had that opportunity.

Were you yourself attending Newport every year or did you have to work at the club?

Oh, no, no. I was there.

What was your impression of Dylan in '63, '64 there, when he's still fully acoustic?

He was a magnet. When he performed with Joan in workshops, those were stunning performances. Just the occurrence of them happening and attracting so many people to try to get a read on who he was. People were curious about his ability to write prolifically. He and Joan were a magnificent couple. They really were.

In those days the artists stayed at the Viking Hotel, a very famous hotel in Newport. I was there one night for a performance in the bedroom with Johnny Cash and Bob Dylan. That wasn't planned. They just ended up in a room together. There were maybe 10 or 15 of us in that room. The two of them were so nervous. They both had that leg-shaking syndrome — whether it was from taking uppers or just nervous energy, I don't know.

Speaking of Johnny Cash, there's that early controversy, before the going-electric one, where Dylan started writing more personal songs and Cash defended him to one of the folk magazines[9]. As someone who was deep in that scene yourself, where did you stand on Bob getting a little less political?

We were there for the ride, not to have opinions. I didn't have an opinion.

Did you have the same take on the Newport electric controversy in '65: there for the ride?

Yeah. I thought he could do no wrong. If he wanted to go electric, we all thought that was just fine. You've got thousands of critics who all had different opinions. We weren't among them. We were just his friends.

I read in one of the biographies that right after that Newport '65 performance, he was hanging out with you. It actually said sitting on your lap. I don't know if that's an exaggeration.

That's true. He seemed very dejected at that moment. He plunked himself down on my lap on a rickety chair. I thought, "I don't think this chair is going to hold." It did. I was trying to cheer him up. Why not?

Did you all stay in touch in subsequent years when he wasn't playing folk clubs anymore?

Not so much. He became much more guarded and much more busy. The last time I saw him was, geez, 2009. He and Maria Muldaur are still good friends. It's through Maria that I got a backstage pass to a Boston show in 2009.

He comes off stage and he gives me a hug. He said something to me like, "Well, I guess you're 69 now." I said, "No, I'm 70." He said, "No, you're 69." I said, "No, I'm not. I'm 70!" We bantered back and forth. That was his way of identifying with me and our ages.

Meaning what, "a lot's happened since the early Club 47 days," that sort of thing?

Yes. He was challenging me. "Oh, you're 69, or 70?" Now I'm 83, so a lot more time has gone by.

You sent me another photo of Dylan and your husband in Woodstock on a motorcycle. Do you remember what the story is there?

---

9 "Don't bad-mouth him, till you hear him, Let him start by continuing, He's almost brand new, SHUT UP! ... AND LET HIM SING!" — Cash in a letter to *Broadside* magazine, 1964.

I didn't take that picture, but that was the motorcycle he had the accident on. I can tell you riding in a car with him was sheer fear. He was a terrible driver. When I was in Woodstock staying with Geoff and Maria, many times I would get in a car with Dylan to go to a concert. It would be snowing and he would be otherwise directed in his head, talking a mile a minute. I was living in the fear of my life.

I remember going to Rick Danko's house once and staying there all night long. Everybody was drinking and smoking and carrying on. At some point, somebody said, "The sun's coming up. Let's go outside." We all traipsed outside as the sun was coming up to sing "Amazing Grace" lying in the snow. That was a beautiful, beautiful memory.

Ramblin' Jack Elliott (with T Bone Burnett behind him) performing on the Rolling Thunder Revue, 1975.
Photo by Ken Regan/Camera 5

Ramblin' Jack Elliott

In his book *Chronicles,* Bob Dylan describes the first time he heard an album by Ramblin' Jack Elliott:

The record started to spin and Jack's voice blasted into the room. "San Francisco Bay Blues," "Ol' Riley" and "Bed Bug Blues" go by in a flash. Damn, I'm thinking, this guy is really great. He sounds just like Woody Guthrie, only a leaner, meaner one, not singing the same Guthrie songs, though. I felt like I'd been cast into sudden hell.

Jack was some master of musical tricks. The record cover was mysterious, but not in an ominous way. It showed a character with certain careless ease, rakish looking, a handsome saddle tramp. He's dressed like a cowboy. His tone of voice is sharp, focused and piercing. He drawls and he's so confident it makes me sick. All that and he plays the guitar effortlessly in a fluid flat-picking perfected style. His voice leaps all over the room in a lazy way and he is explosive when he wants to be. You could hear that he had Woody Guthrie's style down pat and more. Another thing — he was a brilliant entertainer, something that most of the folk musicians didn't bother with. Most folk musicians waited for you to come to them. Jack went out and grabbed you.

By the time Dylan was sitting there listening to that album, Jack Elliott had already played all over the world. But his travels are not why he earned the "Ramblin'" moniker. You'll understand where it came from when you read my interview, where my setting-the-scene question led to an unbroken 10-minute monologue from Jack. Even my initial "How are you doing?", a nothing opening that I would cut out of any other interview, got an amusing answer worth including.

He didn't really *ramble*, though. Even pushing 90 years old when we spoke, his storytelling remained sharp, funny, and, even when it got discursive, always came back around to land the point and answer the question. Over the course of an hour and a half, he told me about first meeting Dylan in the Greenwich Village folk scene and then, a decade later, reconnecting with him on the Rolling Thunder Revue in 1975. And, because it's Ramblin' Jack, a whole lot more besides.

. . . .

How are you doing?

I had a little cat experience this morning. He's about eight years old and set in his ways. I had to take him to the vet hospital and get him a hair trim. He's got dreadlocks and about 20 different knots of hair that can't be untied. Very furry cat. In fact, he looks like early Bob Dylan.

You're coming full circle. And speaking of early Bob Dylan, I wondered if you wouldn't mind if we started back in the '60s in the Village.

I met Bob toward the end of 1961. I had been touring Europe for six years singing Woody Guthrie songs and cowboy songs. I was very much in love with Woody's voice and his delivery and his subject matter and his storytelling and his guitar playing.

I started playing guitar myself when I was 16 years old, meeting some really excellent players who played bluegrass music, especially Tom Paley, who taught me a lot. Tom was personally acquainted with Woody Guthrie and used to play with him. I had been listening to some of Woody's records and liking them a lot. Tom gave me Woody's phone number. He said, "Give him a ring. He's a friendly guy." I called him up and he invited me to come over to his house and bring my guitar and play some tunes. I was thrilled.

The next day I called Woody to see about getting over there. He didn't live in Coney Island anymore. They had moved into a new apartment building near the Belk Parkway [in Brooklyn]. It was called Beach Haven Apartments; Woody called it Beach *Heaven*. It was owned by the Trump family. You couldn't be Chinese or any sort of off-color race and have an apartment there. It was stated broadly and plainly in black and white in the paperwork when people would apply to get an apartment.[10]

They got a very nice ground-floor apartment with its own private entrance. It was the type of an apartment that would be suitable for a doctor's office. When I phoned, Woody's wife Marjorie answered. I asked if I might come over, because

10 In 1954, Guthrie wrote lyrics to a song called "Old Man Trump" about Fred Trump's discriminatory housing practices at Beach Haven.

when I spoke to Woody [the day before], he said, "Don't come today, I got a bellyache." Well, it turned out that bellyache was a ruptured appendix. He was now in the hospital.

I waited about three days and decided he must be okay by now and went and visited him [in the hospital]. I brought my big old Gretsch guitar. I could see that he was not feeling well. He was very drugged up with painkillers. When I volunteered to play him a song, he said, "Don't make any noise. The guy in the other bed just got off the operating table."

But he said, "If you go over to the window and look out, you can see my new apartment across the street. My kids are playing in the back. Go over there and introduce yourself to my wife. She'll show you around."

I was there less than an hour; I had been invited to a going away party of some school chums of mine. I hitchhiked up to Westport, Connecticut for the party. My friend Cole Cooper was in the Air Force; he was being transferred out to California. Would I like to help drive out there? Couldn't say no. We had some adventures on the way out and got to Travis Air Force Base. I proceeded to hitchhike the rest of the way to San Francisco. I walked around the city with my guitar, serenading people on the street. I was going to be a troubadour like Woody.

I stayed around the Bay area for about two, three months, then hitchhiked back to New York. I called Woody. He was out of the hospital, all healed up. He was playing at a house party in Greenwich Village. "Got a pencil?" he says. "120 University Place. Bring your guitar."

I showed up. Woody was hanging out in a little closet at this beautiful apartment warming up. There were two or three friends or admirers hanging out with him in the closet, asking for requests. He was charging 10 cents for playing a request. Somebody asked for "The Blue Tail Fly." He says, "That's a Burl Ives tune. I get 15 cents extra for Burl Ives tunes." They paid him the 25 cents and he played "Blue Tail Fly."

I had memorized one or two of the songs off of the records I had heard. My favorite song of all was a song called "Hard Traveling." I played it with Woody at the party, and I was shocked to learn that he couldn't remember the words in a song that he had written. My favorite song.

That evening he offered me a ride back to Brooklyn, where my parents lived. He said, "I'll give you a ride in my Cadillac," which was a 1950 four-door black Plymouth. He called it his Cadillac. I ended up sleeping over at his house and staying there for about two and a half years. 1951, '52, and part of '53.

A lot of stuff happened then. I was gonna be a cowboy. I had gotten a job on a traveling rodeo, grooming horses, $2 a day. Had to eat out of the $2. There was a rodeo clown named Brahmer Rogers, who played guitar and banjo and sang hillbilly songs. He'd entertain us rodeo hands in the stands between the afternoon and evening performance. That was my first inspiration to buy a guitar and try to learn how to play.

I ended up in California in 1954, married a beautiful actress that I met out there, June. June was very much a world traveler. She grew up reading the *National Geographic*, always wanted to see the world, and so did I. I said, "Marry me and we'll travel around the world. I can play the guitar and we can busk on street corners." So we did. We went to Europe. We spent six years over there singing Woody Guthrie songs and cowboy songs. We did so well, we were able to buy a Vespa motor scooter. Went over the Alps with it in a blizzard with my wife and tent and sleeping bags and guitar on the back of that scooter.

Came back to America in 1958, stayed at our same apartment overlooking the Hollywood Bowl. Got invited to do a concert with The Weavers and Brownie McGee and Sonny Terry in the Royal Festival Hall in London in around September of 1958. We went back to Europe, played the concert, ended up staying another three years.

In 1961, ten years after I met Woody, I returned to the US. Went to visit Woody in the hospital, met young Bob Dylan. He'd been visiting Woody for several months by that time. I knew nothing about him. That brings Bob and me together. I'm 10 years older, and I met him 10 years after I met Woody.

I moved into the Earl Hotel on the corner of Washington Square Park. Bob moved in right down the hall from me. I think he was in Room 305 and I was in Room 310. Peter La Farge[11] was right next door.

We had a pretty intense and good friendship for the beginning of 1962. Sometime in, I think it was early '63, Bob [started spending time in] Woodstock and I didn't see much of him after that. He said he was tired of this music business and he was gonna be a painter. I said, "Good luck."

I visited him a couple of times. We rode around Woodstock on our motorcycles. Then he got involved with The Band and started traveling and doing big concerts. I saw him less and less until 1975.

What did you think of Bob Dylan as a performer in those very early days?

It was very unique. He had a style of playing the guitar in the beginning that, at first, was rather rough, but it almost seemed like it was a deliberate, intentional

---

11 Fellow folksinger; Dylan later covered his "Ballad of Ira Hayes."

Dylan came in and handed me a glass of wine. He said, "We were talking about a plan of touring with a station wagon. It'll be you, me and Joan playin' little gigs. Little venues. Could you dig it?" I said, "Count me in, man."

style of playing rough. He strummed it speeding up and slowing down. The way he flat-picked his Gibson guitar— It was a really nice old Gibson, country-western. I often wondered whatever became of that guitar.

It wasn't obvious to me, but everybody else could see that he was imitating me a lot. I didn't know it, because I don't see myself the way others do. They kept poking me and saying, "He's doing you, he's doing you!"

One time, we were behind the curtain waiting to go out on stage. He had his harmonica rack all set up. I had a harmonica rack too, like Woody. If I was doing a song without the harmonica, I would unscrew the little tightening screws on the rack and lower the thing down on my chest so that it would be between me and the back of the guitar. That would scratch the varnish off the guitar.

Bob preferred to leave his setup in place, whether he was using the harmonica or not. He'd just sing and not blow. I said, "I'm tired of scratching the back of my guitar with this thing. We look like the Harmonica Brothers, so have at it. It's all yours." I didn't play much harmonica at all after that.

You two performed together a lot then. There are a few recordings, but not many. What sort of songs would you sing together?

We did blues and Woody Guthrie songs and maybe some old cowboy songs like "Red River Valley." That was my first favorite song in the world, the first song I ever played on the guitar.

Was it hard to sing or play with him given that, as you said, he'd slow down and speed up his rhythm?

He varied the way that he chopped up the strings with the flat pick, but I think he didn't really speed the song up or slow it down. In fact, I've been criticized widely for having that same difficulty. A lot of musicians claim that they can't follow me or play with me.

Maybe that's why you two worked together so well in those days.

If two musicians work together a long time, they get to be able to read each other better. Little changes like that don't throw you.

One specific '60s show where there is a recording is this radio broadcast at the Riverside Church in 1961. You two do the song "Acne,"[12] which is hilarious. Do you remember it?

It was a goofy song. I think it was something he wrote. Bob was singing the words, and I was just doing the "doo-wah, doo-wah" in the background. I'm not a "doo-wah" singer.

You said you weren't at Newport. Did you see any of the shows when he was playing with The Hawks?

No, I don't think. I saw him later with The Band a couple of times. I was at that Last Waltz, in fact, in San Francisco. I remember The Band greeting me backstage when I was waiting for them to go on. They all filed past me and said, "Hello, Uncle Jack." Called me Uncle Jack. It was friendly. I speak Canadian.

[Back in 1966,] I arrived in Woodstock on my motorcycle with Jesse Colin Young and his wife. They were on a Triumph and I was on an AJS 500 single. I called Bob's manager Albert Grossman. Said, "Hi, it's Jack. I just arrived in town. I'd like to come over and see Bob" He said, "Bob's not here. He is in the hospital."

That's all I knew. I stayed in Woodstock a couple of days and saw some other friends and went on down to New York. Never got to see Bob at all at that time.

You would have seen him at the Woody Guthrie tribute concert in 1968. You two shared a bill at that. He played with The Band then too.

I recall in the dressing room, Bob's guitar case was open and I glanced in. There was a photograph of a girl riding a bucking horse. She was a cowgirl from South Dakota, and she had given this photograph to Bob. I thought, *that's cool*.

For a long time, I had a Bob Dylan song that he had typewritten and scratched out and inked over and rewrote some words. It was a song he wanted me to learn and record. And I just— it was a long song and I didn't ever get around to learning it. It lived in my guitar case for about a year. Then one day it just wasn't there anymore. Somebody must have looked in and saw it.

---

12 An extremely silly and slight doo-wop pastiche about getting acne and killing your parents. Some sources say it was written by Eric Von Schmidt.

Oh no!

You can't leave a guitar case open in a dressing room

Wonder whatever happened to that song.

I think it was the one about the miners in Minnesota. It was talking about how there wasn't any more money in mining because they closed the mines and the miners had to get jobs in South America.[13]

Let's talk Rolling Thunder and start at The Bitter End, known as The Other End that summer. It seems like that was the genesis of the whole idea, especially during your show in particular.[14]

That was a very enjoyable evening. I was especially thrilled to see Bob and his buddy Bobby Neuwirth there. Bob's date for the evening was a girl named Patti Smith, who I didn't know at the time. I never paid much attention to what was going on as far as who's Top 40; Bob was much more aware of that than I.

How did it come that Bob got on stage with you at The Other End that night? You played versions of "Pretty Boy Floyd" and "How Long" together, then Bob debuted his new song "Abandoned Love," a very famous recording.

I think I just invited him to come up and sing a song. Then at the end of the evening, after the show was over, Bob and Patti and Bob Neuwirth were having a glass of wine in another room. Bob [Dylan] came in and handed me a glass of wine. He said, "We were talking about a plan of touring with a station wagon. It'll be you, me and Joan [Baez] playin' little gigs. Little venues. Could you dig it?" I said, "Count me in, man."

A few months later I was back in New York again. Neuwirth invited me over to his apartment. He phoned Bob in California and talked to him for quite a while. Then he handed me the phone. Bob said, "Jack, you remember that thing we were discussing about a tour?" I said, "Yes, count me in." He says, "Okay, you're in. See you in November."

That easy, huh?

Less than a minute of discussion. We only said a very few words. All that was

13 The song Elliott is referring to is probably "North Country Blues," off *The Times They Are a-Changin'.*
14 In summer 1975, Dylan was in New York and hanging out at various Manhattan venues while brainstorming the idea for the traveling carnival-esque Rolling Thunder Revue tour.

based on that moment of decision. Pretty heavy.

We ended up with 75 people on the tour, 100 by the end. We played 31 concerts in 35 days. I got to drive the bus. It was actually Frank Zappa's bus that he loaned to Bob for the tour. A bus called Phydeaux. It had a cartoon of a dog running with long floppy ears blowing in the wind.

I wanted to ask you one question about that bus, actually. Joan Baez has talked about a night where you led everyone in a bunch of old yodeling songs on the bus. Was that the sort of thing that would happen often?

We might have been inebriated. I know there was an awful lot of booze.

In one interview, you said that after all those shows, everyone's brains were fried. Was that part of why?

That was very evident. We were all getting a little bit road weary. We would always stay at a hotel 50 miles away from the venue, so that the fans wouldn't be able to come and bother us.

Was Bob Dylan the same person you had known in the early '60s then?

I don't think Bob has ever been the same person from one day to the next.

That's a good way to put it.

He's a Gemini. My father's a Gemini. It's the twins, Gemini. It's difficult to know who you're talking to. I've been around Bob when people were asking him questions, and his most recurrent answer to every question is, "I didn't know that."

Helpful.

Last time I saw Bob was about five years ago. He was playing in Oakland. I called somebody in the band, and they got me a backstage pass. The road manager met me at Will Call and showed me to my seat. I couldn't hear anything out in the audience. After about four songs, I thought I might be able to hear better backstage.

The only place where I could position myself was standing right beside the guy who works the monitors. Now, Bob's looking at him the whole time to tell him, like, "Give me a little more volume on the guitar." He's looking right at him. But Bob is blind without his glasses. He couldn't see me standing right behind the soundman.

I positioned myself so that I could speak to him briefly as he was making his way to the bus at the end of the show. The show ended; he's coming by. I said, "Good show, Bob." He said, "Thanks." I said, "Great to see you, Bob." He says, "It's great to see you, Jack." I said, "You know, Billy Faier[15] is alive and well and owns a house in West Texas." He says, "Whaddya know?" He got on the bus and left.

That was one of my longer conversations with my friend Bob. I'm not sure if I know who he is.

I found recordings of some of your sets from Rolling Thunder. Before Bob came on, what do you remember about playing with that band?

I played the "San Francisco Bay Blues" and some other high-speed, high-energy tunes, with the band backing me up on the last two songs of my set. Then I'd race offstage. Bob would slap me on the shoulder and say, "Good set, Jack," and he'd run out. It was as if I was introducing him, but I didn't say anything verbally. I didn't mention that Bob Dylan was going to be out shortly. I disappeared, and he appeared.

We started off talking about Woody Guthrie. What did it mean to you to have the grand finale of all these Rolling Thunder shows be "This Land Is Your Land"?

I was proud that I was the first person to sing that song in England. The skiffle kids in 1955, they were singing "This Land Is Your Land" along with me. I'm not Pete Seeger and I've never been a leader getting people to sing with me and stuff. They just automatically did it, because they loved that song so much. I couldn't help notice the inexplicable nature of that event, British kids all singing "This land is your land, this land is my land."

Do you remember singing it with everyone to close all of the Rolling Thunder shows?

Oh yeah. I got really tired of that song.

Really?

I had a song that was one of my biggest hits. It was called the "Tennessee Stud." People always demanded it. I got to where I wished I'd never recorded that song. If you do a song every night, week in week out, it gets to be a job. I don't know how Arlo Guthrie could stand to do "Alice's Restaurant."

Are there any moments filming the Renaldo and Clara *movie on that tour that stand out?*

I thought that I was 100% cut out of it, but actually I think I'm in there for about 15 or 16 seconds total.

---

15   A banjo player in the Village folk scene.

There was one shot where we were visiting Plymouth, Massachusetts, where the Pilgrims landed. In 1957, somebody in England built a copy of the Mayflower. I went down to the shipyard the day after she was launched and helped them rig the masts. I love working on ship rigging, so I was honored to be there. I would've liked to have sailed in her, but you couldn't be American. You had to be a British subject to sail in that trip. But they brought along a tape recording of me singing on the ship. The Mayflower sailed over from Plymouth, England to Plymouth, Massachusetts.

Our first [Rolling Thunder] gig was in Plymouth, and they shot some kind of a dramatic scene on board the Mayflower. I wasn't in this particular scene, so I decided to go aloft and check out the rigging and see what condition she was in. I'm up there near the top of the mast. They finished shooting their scene and went ashore to get a sandwich. As they were walking away on the dock, they filmed me up in the rigging.

I yelled, "Ahooooy." Allen Ginsberg said, "What can you see?" I said, "I see a church. I see a hill. I see the Mayflower Restaurant." I thought, "I hope they leave this in." I think it was left in, but it was very brief. Nobody could understand what was going on.

That's true of most of that movie.

I saw that movie when it was five hours long, I went to see it in a movie theater in LA along with my friend Larry Mahan, a rodeo cowboy. Bob's mother was there. I remember introducing Larry to Beatty, Bob's mom. That was quite a movie. It didn't seem to make much sense. All those drama scenes that Bob dreamed up were not related to what we were doing on the tour. We really couldn't call it a documentary. It was more like an Italian opera gone Massachusetts.

Did you enjoy that side of the tour? Not just the concerts, but the filming, the extracurriculars?

I did enjoy the filming, yes. In fact, one of my favorite scenes that I was lucky enough to act in, I think was cut out of the movie in the end.

I'm standing on Plymouth Rock. This is in a museum. It's not a real rock; it's made out of fiberglass. There's this little boat, and it's got about four wax figures dressed as pilgrims in it. I'm standing on the rock, welcoming them to Massachusetts and warning them to be careful when they go ashore.[16]

---

16 Some footage of this did appear in the 2019 movie *Rolling Thunder Revue: A Bob Dylan Story by Martin Scorsese*. In a voiceover, present-day Dylan says, "One thing I can tell you about

It was totally gonzo. I thought it was funny. I don't know if anybody else caught the humor.

What do you remember about the final show at Madison Square Garden? After all these shows of playing in small venues, you're at the biggest, most famous arena in the world.

I had to go through Muhammad Ali's dressing room to get to the bathroom. He preceded me on stage, and he made a remark that his friend, the governor of Tennessee[17], had loaned him an airplane. Muhammad Ali predicted that that man would or should become President. He was booed. Muhammad Ali was booed in Madison Square Garden! Then I came on right after that and they all applauded. I felt bad about that.

The day before that, we went to visit Hurricane Carter in prison. It was all Black people in that prison. They were entertained in a little theater with a stage that they had. They weren't too tickled about our music. I think it was a little bit too strange for them.

Were you around for any of the 1976 shows, the second part of Rolling Thunder?

I was living in Colorado at the time. I went to see that one at Fort Collins.

The famous Hard Rain one.

I was standing right near the front of the stage, and Neuwirth saw me. He reached down and took my hand and pulled me right up on the stage. I sang a song with them. It was a song I didn't know, but Bob Neuwirth yelled the words in my ear. They went right through from my ear to my mouth and out in his microphone. With a slight delay, I'm sure. I was just part of the microphone.

Why didn't you want to go on the tour for the second half, in '76?

I *did* want to go on it. I was a glutton for punishment. I visited Bob at his house and asked if there was any chance of me going along with them on the tour. He was strumming on a guitar, some lick he said he learned from [David] Bromberg. He kept practicing it. He said, "I don't know what the plan is. I heard that Joan Baez is going to be there. And Kinky Friedman."

He was in his own way letting me know that I wasn't going to be on the tour.

Ramblin' Jack: He's more of a sailor than a singer. He can tie a bowline, a clove hitch, and he can tie a rolling hitch, all blindfolded. If you're ever on a boat or sailing ship, you would rather have Ramblin' Jack there as a sailor than a singer."

17 John Jay Hooker, who actually only *ran* for Governor of Tennessee (multiple times), but lost.

Kinky Friedman replaced me.

You might have dodged a bullet. Everyone I've talked to says the feeling wasn't the same the second time out.

The people didn't have that lovely spirit of a family on the road, the camaraderie. It seemed like there was a lot of discomfort and friction between the members of the group.

Did you ever share a stage with him again after Rolling Thunder?

I don't believe so. I think Rolling Thunder was the last time we ever performed together. In fact, Bob and I never did a song together on Rolling Thunder. I was the opening act, and he was the main act.

Technically you sang "This Land Is Your Land" together. With everyone else there too, but you did share a stage.

Yes, the grand finale.

I should let you go. I really appreciate you taking all this time to tell me these stories.

I hope I can help to make it live again, because those were crazy and wonderful times and I do miss it. It was different then than it is now. I don't know if people now can appreciate what we were doing back then, but it's great for someone like you to educate all the young people who weren't there and give them an appreciation for what was happening. It doesn't seem to be happening the same way anymore.

I wish I could bring it back, the magic. I'm with this new cat who looks like early Bob Dylan, but he doesn't appreciate Bob Dylan. He doesn't even know who Bob was. That's okay. *Bob* doesn't even know who Bob was. But I love him.

Dylan and Barry Goldberg warming up at Newport Folk Festival, Newport, Rhode Island, 1965

Barry Goldberg

Blues keyboardist Barry Goldberg didn't go to Newport Folk Festival in 1965 expecting to play with Bob Dylan. He went to accompany guitarist Michael Bloomfield and the Paul Butterfield Blues Band, then got cut from the gig when he arrived. But, in one hell of a consolation prize, he was drafted last-minute to accompany Dylan in his historic, inflammatory going-electric Newport set.

This began a working relationship that would resurface every few years. Goldberg is, as far as I can tell, the only person ever to both produce Bob Dylan and be produced *by* Bob Dylan. He tells me all those stories below, as well as what went wrong when Bob asked him to babysit his kids.

. . . .

We'll start with Newport. The reason you were there in the first place was to play with the Paul Butterfield Blues Band?

Right. Paul had asked me to come with Michael and play. When I got there, their producer said, "No keyboards. I don't hear keyboards with the band." So that was a disappointment.

Had you been playing with them at other shows before?

I would sit in a lot with the band at a club called Big John's in Old Town in Chicago.

How had you originally connected with Bloomfield?

Michael and I were in rival bands in high school, and we would see each other at these teenage sock hop kind of things. His band and my band would play the same gig, so we met each other and we became friends. Later we went to the same high school together.

This must have been when you were pretty young if you're still in high school.

Yeah, 16, 17, when we became aware of each other. He was the MC at a coffeehouse in Chicago, so he asked me if I wanted to appear. I said, "Well, it's primarily folk music and I don't know too much about folk music. I only know one song: 'Michael Row the Boat Ashore.'" He said, "Well, keep playing that over and over. Do different versions of it and no one will know the difference." So that's what I did.

Did it work? Did they not know the difference?

Absolutely.

Then what?

I was mostly playing on Rush Street, which was like the Bourbon Street of Chicago. Mafia running clubs with red velvet and twist music.

Michael got me into actually playing the blues. He said, "You have to come down with me to the South Side and sit in with some of the great masters." First sitting in with Muddy Waters and Howlin' Wolf, then playing with Butterfield. It took me out of that twist element and into more of a relaxed blue jeans and workshirt crowd.

When you're at Newport, talk me through the transition from the disappointment of this producer saying no keyboards in Butterfield to getting involved in Dylan's set.

Bob didn't have a band in mind. He wanted to do this electric thing, and he asked if the Butterfield band would back him up. Bob had said to Michael, "I don't know if my keyboard player, Al Kooper, is going to show up or not." This was at a party in one of the old mansions at Newport with all the folk people like Odetta and Theodore Bikel and Kweskin Jug Band and Joan Baez. Bob said, "Would you like to play with me?" I said yeah. Michael had already brought "Like a Rolling Stone" home with him, the demo, so I was familiar with that.

I went from being so down and bummed out with nothing to do in such a beautiful place to one of the most memorable gigs of my life.

What comes next?

A soundcheck. Peter Yarrow[18] was going crazy. The electric thing was freaking people out. They knew what was coming.

---

18 Of Peter, Paul and Mary, and a Newport organizer.

They were already worried?

Yeah. *Danger zone: Rock and roll.*

There's a video of Bob and you sitting playing organ together. Is the soundcheck where that clip comes from?

That's where that comes from. We were just fooling around. He was playing "This Land Is Your Land." I knew that song, sort of, so we were playing along together.

I know the lineup changed during your three songs. Al Kooper is on organ for "Maggie's Farm" and then he switches to bass for the others and you move over from your piano to his B3. Why?

"Like A Rolling Stone" had different chords. It had a structure which [Butterfield bassist] Jerome Arnold couldn't really pick up on. It wasn't like a blues change or one key. Thank God Al took the bass. He knew the song and the changes, 'cause he played on the record.

Were you nervous before the gig itself?

Excited and nervous at the same time. I've never played for this many people at once. I knew we were doing something really important and different and controversial. Any time you do something controversial, everyone's not going to go along with it and dig it. Some people did, and some people were shocked. I remember it was about 50-50. People remember the boos more than the people who really were into it and dug it.

When I listened to the tapes that were recorded at the time, I felt that "Like A Rolling Stone" came out pretty good. I thought that Bob's vocals were really spirited. That thing came together.

How did you feel about the other two songs, "Maggie's "and "Phantom Engineer"[19]*?*

Emotionally, it really didn't get me off that much. It was a go-for-it kind of thing, like a jam. "Maggie's Farm" was pretty much running wild, although people really liked that. *Some* people. "Like A Rolling Stone" had more passion and emotion to it and feeling.

Because they weren't really used to recording live rock and roll at Newport, whoever was mixing it or miking it wasn't really the best you could hope for. Michael had his amp up to nine or something. All you'd have to tell him was "turn

---

19 The early title of what would eventually be "It Takes a Lot to Laugh, It Takes a Train to Cry."

down" and he would turn up.

How was the sound on stage for you all? Could you hear what was going on?

No. No monitors or anything like that. It was just like, go for it.

Just hope it comes off sort of thing?

Yeah. We played like that before. It was a blues band. I don't think Bob ever did that before, played with a rock and roll blues band like Paul and Michael. But Paul wasn't a part of it. Paul didn't play because Bob was on harmonica.

Was the idea always just to do those three songs with the band?

I imagine it was. Bob was calling it off. I really didn't know. We didn't have a set list or anything like that.

When we left the stage, I felt pretty good about the whole thing. Being there at night at Newport with Bob, his attire all in black, it was really cool for me to be a part of that particular moment. Then there was quite a controversial reaction.

What are you witnessing backstage with all the old guard folk people?

Pretty much chaos.

How so?

They were trying to stop it. Like Alan Lomax[20], I remember he and Albert Grossman got into it physically. I think that carried over from Butterfield and his set. Albert had a lot of moxie, I would say. He just went straight forward like a field general and didn't care. This is what his client, Bob, his number one son, wanted to do, and it was going to happen no matter who was going to be the way. He wasn't afraid of anything.

It was the folkies against the rockers. If this is what Bob wanted to do with his career, so be it. It's a good thing that he made that move because it changed the face of music. What resulted was folk-rock.

You must have been in the minority. You're surrounded by all these folk people who don't like rock, and you're a rock person who doesn't like folk.

I was like a stranger in a strange land.

That famous story about Pete Seeger threatening to cut the cord with an axe, did you have

---

20 Prominent ethnomusicologist and more of a folk purist.

"Oh yeah, sure, Bob Dylan's going to come over to our house.
What, am I gonna make my tuna casserole for him?"
Doorbell rings. She'd been making quiche Lorraine.
I said, "Do you like quiche Lorraine?"
He goes, "Oh yeah, man. Cheese pie!"

. . . .

any awareness of that?

Yeah. He was running around trying to cut the power cord. They didn't know what to do. They were panicking. I'm going like, "Come on, man, it's not that heavy."

Was all this chaos happening before you got on stage or did you walk off stage and you just see everyone losing their minds?

That was during the whole thing. But we just put our heads down and played. Followed our fearless leader into destiny.

Did you get a sense of how Bob was feeling after all that?

He was upset. He didn't feel it was that outrageous. But I guess he knew what he was taking on. He's always been controversial, and this was *really* controversial. Thank God there are people like that that have the balls to do something bold and daring. It threatened a lot of people and a lot of what they do.

You get off stage, there's chaos. What happens next?

We pack up and drive back to Chicago.

What's the conversation like on that car ride back?

I was feeling like I was touched by Bob, by the magic, and that really has never left me to this day. Once you experience something like that with someone like Bob, it doesn't rub off. It stays with you. Whether it was a good gig or not a good gig, it was an important gig.

I was really energized after that. I went back to Chicago and found this great guitar player and singer Steve Miller playing in a storefront in Old Town. We got a band together and called it the Goldberg-Miller Blues Band. I was on my way, man, I was really psyched up. We got the gig at Big John's, which was Butterfield's home ground. He left to go to New York, and Steve and I took over.

We lasted about a year, then we went to New York [in the late '60s]. We should have been booked into the Village, but they had us in this uptown discotheque called the Phone Booth where we opened for the Young Rascals. The Long Island kids really made fun of us. They called us the "fabulous dirties," because we had work shirts, Levi's, and cowboy boots. But all the guys like Butterfield and Dylan came uptown to see us.

When Bob came in, I remember seeing him walking down the street with a trail of people behind him. Not walking *with* him, but walking behind him in single file. Like the Pied Piper.

He came up to me, really friendly. He said, "Man, you don't belong here. You belong with me." He tried to get me to join his band. I said, "Thank you for asking me, but not right now." I was having such a blast playing with Steve. Maybe I should have taken that. It was one of the opportunities that I let pass by. Our band broke up about a year later.

After the Goldberg-Miller Band broke up, I started doing sessions. Michael approached me and said, "I have this concept. It's an all-American music band. We'd play like Motown-influenced, Spector-influenced blues." It wasn't named yet, but it would be called The Electric Flag. The original concept was an all-white band that could play soul music, to show people that white guys have soul.

I was doing a gig at Murray the K's[21] show with Mitch Ryder. On the bill was Wilson Pickett. Michael came down to see the show, and Wilson Pickett's drummer was rocking the whole theater. We couldn't believe it. The theater actually started to move. We looked at each other and thought, "This is our drummer. But how are we going to get him away from Pickett?" Pickett was a gangster, a tough guy. He carried a gun.

We were sharing a room at the Albert Hotel, which was a real fleabag. We took the drummer, whose name was Buddy Miles. On our way, we stopped at a grocery store and got four boxes of Oreo cookies. We laid them down on the bed and started talking to him how we were going to put the band together in San

---

21 Prominent New York City DJ and a big booster of rock and roll in the '60s.

Francisco and he could run the town. He could have all the little hippie girls he wants. He would be the king. King Buddy. After each line, we'd drop an Oreo in his mouth. He eventually agreed to it.

Pickett was so pissed off. We heard rumors that he was after us for a year for stealing his drummer. But Buddy was our drummer now. That whole "white guys can play the blues" thing went out the window.

How does that lead to Dylan producing your album?

We were getting ready to play at Monterey Pop festival, which was even bigger than Newport. There was so much pressure for us to do well in Monterey. Drugs started to take over. We had a jazz trumpet player joining the band who was a junkie. And Michael was an insomniac. He became very irritable and hard to deal with. There was a lot of yelling and shouting. The pressure was too great. Half the band succumbed to the drugs. We had a short run, but a good run.

I was becoming really fucked up on heroin. I moved to LA. I played a session with Gram Parsons. I did a Byrds session.

Is this when you start recording your own albums?

Yeah. I wasn't crazy about my solo records. I was basically just too fucked up.

Does that include the one that Dylan and Jerry Wexler[22] produced [1974's Barry Goldberg]?

No, that was later in the '70s. That was when I got straight.

I was so bad. My uncle was a Supreme Court justice [Arthur Goldberg], and here I am on the streets trading my record collection for heroin. I became an animal. I said, this has got to stop. For two years, I kicked, and I became straight. To this day, I've never used that drug again.

Bob and I renewed our friendship. He would come over to my wife and my apartment on the Upper West Side. We had a piano, and Bob would jam with his guitar. Then when Michael was in town, the three of us would jam together. I remember Bob doing a version of "Tracks of My Tears" that was just unbelievable.

How did you reconnect? You hadn't talked in a while, it sounds like.

I was angry at his relationship with the Grateful Dead. I'm not a Deadhead and I knew he shouldn't be a Deadhead, no matter what. I can't explain it. I know

---

22 Legendary record producer who a few years later would produce Dylan's first two Christian albums, *Slow Train Coming* and *Saved*.

there are a lot of Grateful Dead fans. I had an encounter with Jerry Garcia many years ago at the Fillmore. He thought he was hot shit. I knew he couldn't play his instrument. We had some kind of argument. So I left Bob a message, I said, "Stop being gratefully dead and come over and have dinner and jam." He called me up and said, "I'd love to."

Gail, my wife, was like, "Oh yeah, sure, *Bob Dylan's* going to come over to our house. What, am I gonna make my tuna casserole for him?"

He was supposed to have come over at seven a couple of nights later. 7:30 comes and she was giving me shit. "Yeah, any other fantasies?"

The doorbell rings. It's Bob. He comes in. She'd been making quiche Lorraine. I said, "Do you like quiche Lorraine?" He goes, "Oh yeah, man. Cheese pie!" That was the beginning of our new relationship.

Gail and Sara [Dylan] became really good friends. Bob said, "When Sara and I go to Europe, would you mind coming over to my house in the Village and babysitting our kids?" I said, "Well, all right. How many kids do you have?" He said, "Five."

That's a lot of kids to babysit.

All we had was a dog and two cats! But I said okay.

While he's off in Europe?

Gone for a week. We took them on road trips. We took them to the zoo, to the Met, to FAO Schwarz and bought toys for them. The little one, Jakob, was only two years old, maybe a little older. He could walk, barely. They were like little ducks; they'd walked down Fifth Avenue. Maria, the oldest, would help us with the kids.

Jakob got really sick. The flu. Gail and I took him to the doctor, then nursed him back to health. Bob spoke to the doctor and felt confident that he was okay, so they didn't come back [early]. When they did, he said, "Man, you really did a solid for me. What can I do for you?"

I said, "I'd love to record my own record, and I can't get a deal." No one would take a chance on me. He went and spoke to Jerry Wexler. "Jerry said if I produce it with him, we can do a record at Muscle Shoals." That's how that came about.

What was your experience down at Muscle Shoals?

I loved it down there. I felt really comfortable. We did the record, and the rough mixes were really, really good. But the rough vocals— Jerry Wexler really didn't understand that kind of style. I don't think he even understood how *Bob* did it on vocals. He was used to recording Aretha. I mean, I'm not a singer. Later *Rolling Stone* wrote a review that said I should never be allowed to sing again. They weren't Aretha vocals, but they were funky, down home.

Bob said, "When we leave here, don't let anyone touch it. Just go mix it." They mixed it in Muscle Shoals, and it came out amazing. I really was happy with it. Jerry Wexler calls me up two weeks later. He said, "You have to come and remix the records, get rid of all that reverb, redo all the vocals." He made me articulate each syllable, each vowel. It ruined the record for me. I had to live with that for 25 years.

You fixed it eventually, right? Got the original vocals back on there?

I did. Richard Foos [founder of Rhino Records] said, "I want to put out the only record that Bob ever produced." I said, "You got to let me go in and find the original vocals and put some reverb and echo back on it. Just make it breathe and make it alive and make it rock and roll." So we restored the tape, found the missing vocals, and I got the tracks back to where I thought they should be. I was really happy to have that chance to do that. You *can* go home again, if you really try hard.

What is Bob like as a producer? Is he hands-on?

Not at all. If it sounded right, it was right. He wouldn't say much.

Like when I got to produce him later, you don't produce. You let him do his thing. When an artist *needs* help in the studio, you help. When I produced Percy Sledge years later, I had to go in and edit a lot of the vocals. Each syllable I had to put in, just to get the Percy Sledge vibe. But an artist like Bob, one take, two takes, that's all you're going to get. The first take is usually right, and you don't say anything.

So was it the same when Bob and Wexler were producing you?

Yeah, because Wexler was too afraid to say anything with Bob there. He really didn't say anything until after. Jerry became my really dear friend too, but not in the studio.

Bob sang on your record too, right? Backing vocals on a couple of tracks?

Oh, yeah. We brought his vocals up in the remix. He was just wonderful.
The response to the record wasn't really that good. People were expecting the second coming, and it was far from that.

Maybe having Bob Dylan produce your record is a double-edged sword.

Exactly. Especially because of the way it came out. Jerry dried it all up. The realism, which made it so cool in the beginning, was gone. You could feel the uptightness and the nervousness.

Then a decade later the tables turn and you produce Bob, a cover of Curtis Mayfield's "People Get Ready."

For the movie *Flashback* starring Kiefer Sutherland. I'd done a lot of scoring for TV and movies. Robert Worth, who was Charlie Parker's manager in the old days, was the producer, and he had asked me to do the music. He said, "Do you think you can get Bob Dylan?" I said, "Will Paramount pay for it?" They were the bankroll. They gave Bob $100,000 and let me produce it.

Why "People Get Ready"? Where did that idea come from to do that song?

I don't know. That's what they wanted. I think he recorded it once live with the band.[23] I worked with Howie Epstein on that, the bass player for The Heartbreakers. Howie was a Bob freak. Bob used John Cougar [Mellencamp]'s slide player, Mike Wanchic.

Because it was recorded at Cougar's studio in Indiana?

We actually did it through telephone. I was in LA, and Bob's in Indiana. He would send me the tape, and I would send it back to him. We were on the phone making these changes in the production, but, basically, I had nothing to do musically. It was Bob. I didn't tell him where to sing, any of that.

A good producer doesn't ever interfere if the artist is that great. You don't go messing around with that. You want the greatness to come out, and you know that another ego coming in would fuck that vibe up.

In the '90s, you worked with Gerry Goffin[24] on his own album, and Bob has a couple writing credits on it. The one writing credit you and Bob share is a song called "Tragedy of the Trade." What's the story there?

Gerry was a schizophrenic. He would hear voices. He'd hear Bob's voice more than anyone, giving him a lyric or giving him something. Whenever he got that, he'd put Bob on the credit for the song. That would be Bob's credit on "Tragedy

---

23 A group of backing musicians put together just for this session. The only one Dylan had played extensively with before was Epstein.

24 Brill Building writer with Carole King and others of classics like "Will You Love Me Tomorrow" and "The Loco-Motion."

of the Trade."

Gerry was probably the greatest lyricist of all time, or one of them. Bob was in awe of Gerry. He couldn't believe that someone could sit down and write a whole story in under three minutes. I introduced them in New York. Gerry was living in our building. They would play chess together. I would always ask who won, but it was pretty even.

Above: Harvey Brooks, Dylan, and Robbie
Robertson warm up at Forest Hills, Queens,
New York, 1965.
Right: Brooks, Robertson, Al Kooper
(hidden), Dylan, Levon Helm, and Richard
Manuel (who didn't perform).
Photos by Daniel Kramer/Govinda Gallery

Harvey Brooks

Harvey Brooks first entered Dylan's orbit having never heard a note of his music. Like Barry Goldberg, he wasn't much of a folk person. The bassist was recommended for *Highway 61 Revisited* by Al Kooper and returned to the studio five years later for *New Morning*.

While we talk a bit about both of those albums, our conversation focused on two noteworthy concerts he played with Dylan: In Forest Hills, New York on August 28, 1965, where some of the crowd invaded the stage, and then a calmer show in Hollywood, California on September 3. These were Dylan's first two full concerts with a backing band, following the three-song Newport Folk Festival set in July. They weren't part of a full tour, and the band he played with, a blend of Hawks (Robbie Robertson and Levon Helm) and others (Kooper and Brooks) only backed him for those two shows. They bridged the Newport brouhaha and the full Band tours that followed, where Rick Danko would assume bass duties.

. . . .

Can you tell me how you met Dylan?

I met Bob Dylan through Al Kooper. Al was an old friend of mine; we came out of Queens together. The bass player wasn't working out. Bob asked Al, did he know someone, and Al recommended me. I got a call in between sets at the Sniffen Court Inn, where I was playing, on 36th and 3rd. I reported for duty the next morning. I had never met Bob and didn't know who he was. Never heard his stuff.

You were not a member of the Greenwich Village folk scene, I take it?

Not at that time. I was playing with R&B bands on small little tours. Meeting Dylan, when I walked into the session, he had "Like a Rolling Stone" on, and they were listening to it. That was my first hearing of Dylan. Very impressive, I have to say.

That's quite an entry point. You get there, they've got the song playing. Is there much preamble or do you get down to business immediately?

I go into the studio to tune up. [Michael] Bloomfield comes bursting into the studio, mister energy, and we pretty much got down to business. I knew nobody at all. Luckily, the drummer, a great drummer [Bobby Gregg], was giving me little signals. I had no chance for a rehearsal. It was all spontaneous. Dylan, being the brilliant songwriter that he is, generally knows what he wants to hear. The producer was just there to keep the machines running, and we rolled.

There were a couple other bass players he'd gone through at the Highway 61 *sessions, and Al told you Dylan wasn't thrilled with them. Did you have a sense of what he wanted out of you?*

Basically, he felt comfortable with me. We did a few takes and he liked it. It didn't bother him, let's put it that way. He was looking just to be comfortable with the music. I wasn't forcing anything on him; I was reacting to him. If I was trying to put down an emphatic bass line— I never heard the songs before, and so anything I'm going to do is an impression. That's basically jazz anyway. This was jazz-folk-rock. Impressions.

I have to say, I don't think it's the best playing I've ever done, but I was right there. It was good enough for Grossman to call me up after the session and say, "Bob likes your playing and we have a couple of concerts. Would you like to join?"

I read that there were extensive rehearsals for these two concerts. Do you remember what that looked like?

We had two weeks of rehearsals at Carroll Music Rehearsal Studio. Two weeks solid, just playing. Kooper and I knew the material from playing it, and it was adapting a whole different point of view.

Levon sits right behind the beat. Bobby Gregg, the studio drummer for the album, very on, very solid, pattern orientated. Levon was a reactor. Robbie, on the other hand, was a very tight guitar player. Bloomfield [on the album] was just all over the place. His rhythm was on the beat, off the beat, and playing these great notes. So really different worlds, in that sense, but they gelled.

Not only were we rehearsing, but Levon and I went down to the Village and hung out. So the rhythm section was coming together. We hadn't necessarily thought about it that way, but Levon and I got pretty tight. We had a nice dialogue going on.

Playing-wise, I didn't really know what was brewing at the two concerts. Forest

Hills was pretty amazing. It was a warm day. As the nighttime came on, wind started blowing, it got a little chillier. The audience is far away at a tennis stadium. There was a big green lawn in between us, so we really couldn't see them and weren't really cognizant of them until they attacked the stage, which was pretty funny.

I've seen something about a ruckus onstage. What exactly happened?

There were a couple of guys, we saw them crossing the field. I looked at Bob, Bob looked at me. Bob just said, "Keep playing." We saw the cops tackling this guy. Then Kooper went down behind me. Somebody pulled the stool out from under him.

Levon was a little unsure about why he was there in the first place, because the Hawks were a totally united band. He wasn't sure what was happening anyway. Then when we had this little extra insanity going on. It really was, I think, just some herd intelligence that took over a bunch of people. There was no reason for it. They were not looking to do anybody any harm. Maybe it was a way of heckling, which is not out of the realm of irate folkies.

Before they actually rushed the stage, had you felt any hostility or booing, or was everyone so far away that you didn't even notice?

You could hear it right from the get-go. Murray the K came out, and they weren't ready for Murray the K to be announcing Dylan's show.

What was the issue with Murray the K?

They don't consider him a folk person. Murray the K is a promoter, a businessman. I mean, Murray the K put on great R&B shows and Rock & Roll shows. This audience was not his audience. He really didn't make sense for them — but the whole thing didn't make sense. Bob was stretching, coming into a whole other area, and they wanted to keep it the way was. So there were a lot of boos.

They loved his opening set. They were with him when he was acoustic. The change of demeanor happened when *we* came out. As soon as the instruments came out, that was it. We started to play; they were booing. I think more than anything else, Bob had taken them in, like a symbol of what they wanted to be. He became somebody who was betraying their trust. What he was doing was just extending brilliance, making it more accessible to more people.

Were you in the band prepared for something like that to happen? Newport had happened already. Most of you weren't there, but Kooper was.

We had a little backstage meeting before. Bob said, "It's possible it could get a little rowdy." But we didn't know what kind of rowdy. Then we found out.

How did you feel about everyone's performance musically? Did that throw you off or make you more focused?

I thought we actually played very well. It took the whole set pretty much to get them on our side, but we did. By the end of the set, we had 'em.

What happens after the New York show?

After the set, Bob was gone. I had my car there and Kooper came with me. We drove into Manhattan to Albert's apartment in Gramercy Park. Albert was really happy. Dylan was happy. Everybody was happy. There were lots of laughs about the people running around and the stool getting pulled out from Kooper. In looking back, in rewinding the movie after the show, everybody was feeling good about it. I think Albert, the original Cheshire Cat, had that great understanding of, it doesn't matter if anybody thinks it's good or bad, as long as it happens. And with somebody like Bob, it's always going to be good, even if it's bad.

One thing that struck me listening to the recordings is that in a way you all debuted what would become a big thing: turning his old acoustic songs into electric songs. In your case, it was "I Don't Believe You" and "It Ain't Me Babe." Do you remember how that came about? Did you even know those songs in their earlier incarnations?

No, I wouldn't have. They were folky songs.

I treated all the music the same. I learned it, made my chord charts, and just followed Bob. I was setting down the feel. Both Bobby Gregg and Levon played good bass drum. They're clear with their bass drum figures. I locked in, got together with the keyboard and the guitars. I'm like the middle guy. I got to put those two things together. That was my job and that's what I did.

It was a privilege to have that opportunity. I mean, these are great songs. "Tombstone Blues," "Maggie's Farm." "Ballad of a Thin Man" was killing.

The only two times he ever played "From a Buick 6" were at the two shows you did with him. He never played it again.

That's because we did it so good. How could you follow that up?

What about the LA show at the Hollywood Bowl?

There was a moat of water, but we could see people across the moat in the front

There was a big green lawn in between us, so we really couldn't see them and weren't really cognizant of them until they attacked the stage.

. . . .

row. Movie stars. A very receptive feeling. We had cheers when we came out, as opposed to all these grouchy noises in New York.

I couldn't say if it was better musically. They were two different shows. Bob was right on both times.

Why was LA so different?

For somebody out in the audience, I think they got a more enthusiastic show because we got good feedback from them. It was a little looser; we were in a whole other head space. That first show was tighter. We were trying to be locked, spontaneously locked, in New York. And in LA at the Hollywood Bowl, we were just floating with it.

Dylan's C harp wasn't working, so he said, "Anybody out there got a C harp?" Somebody threw one up. It landed at his feet, and we went on with the show.

Do you have a sense of why the LA crowd was so much more receptive and easygoing than the Forest Hills?

It wasn't Greenwich Village. Which was one, very intellectual; two, very opinionated; three, they always want things to stay the same. It's very ritualized. Change has to be an earthquake or something.

Folk history is amazing, and there's a lot of tradition that was trying to be maintained. Bob came in under the guise of Woody Guthrie, but he was no Woody. I think it was hard for them to handle.

What happened after the LA show?

I had to get back to fly to Detroit. I had a gig that I had taken, and I was committed to it. I was in Detroit for three weeks. My understanding was there wasn't going to be anything for a couple of months.

I called in after the first week to check out what was happening. Mary Martin [Albert Grossman's assistant] had taken Bob to see the rest of the guys in The

Band in Toronto. He loved it. They decided that it made more sense for them to have a whole band that they thought would fit really good with Bob. So they said to me when I called in, "We've made some changes and you're out. Rick Danko is going to come in from The Hawks."

You understand, if you do this thing enough, the gigs come and they go. It's never pleasant to lose a good gig but I understood it. It's showbiz.

Do you have any opinion on Rick Danko as a bass player?

I love Rick. We were good friends. He's a great bass player, great feel, can sing his ass off. I felt Bob did as well with Rick as he did with me, but got his background vocal along with it, which I don't have.

It seems a little odd to just have two shows, not a part of a tour or anything. Do you know what the purpose was?

I think it was to prove a point. He got the East Coast and the West Coast, sold out both places, all kinds of press. Robert Shelton gave a review of it: The band great, Dylan phenomenal, audience bad.[25]

Albert succeeded in what he needed to do. He established Bob coast to coast. All he had to do was fill in the blanks. It established him in the States and opened up that European market, which was as rebellious as the folkies in New York.

Fast-forwarding five years, how'd you get back in the mix for New Morning *in 1970?*

Kooper called me. He said Bob was having a problem. They had gone through a whole lot of musicians in Nashville and here [in New York]. They had about three or four tunes and were looking to get stuff done.

I had seen Bob in Woodstock about two or three weeks before. We played some chess. I guess when they went back to the studio, he said to Kooper, "I saw Harvey, we hung out," and they come back to me. That was good. Very smart of them.

What do you remember about the New Morning sessions compared to Highway 61? Publicly he seems like a different person. Did he seem like that in the studio?

Yeah. First of all, they were pretty burnt out because they'd been having all these problems. Kooper and Dylan were arguing about what should be done. Al had this

---

25 "The electric band and the high-voltage vocalizing raised the level of Mr. Dylan's performance from the intimate introspective vein of the first half to a shouting crackling intensity. The young audience's displeasure was manifested at the end of most of the numbers, by booing and shouts of 'we want the old Dylan.' The young star plowed valiantly on."

whole thing he wanted to do, and Bob wasn't being agreeable. He had his own ideas. We came down, Billy Mundi [drummer] and myself, and I think we turned it around. I'll tell you what, it was fun playing. I think that was really a good album for him because it took him to another place that he needed to be.

Dylan and Richard Alderson consult before a show on the 1966 tour.

Richard Alderson

"Most people identify me with Dylan," Richard Alderson says, despite the sound engineer's work with Dylan only being a blip in a long career.

Two blips, actually: He taped a famous October 1962 show at Greenwich Village's Gaslight Café, one of the first recordings of a Dylan concert. A few years later, he joined Dylan in a more official capacity, touring as his soundman on the famous 1966 run. Put simply: You wouldn't have heard "Judas!" without Alderson's recordings.

. . . .

What was your entry into the Greenwich Village scene in the '60s?

I originally got there in 1955, when I was 18. I came on a Greyhound bus with $75 cash in a little tiny rucksack with my books and a change of clothes in it. I eventually got a job installing hi-fi equipment for Thalia Hi-Fi Audio. I installed hi-fi equipment for all kinds of rich people and well-known musicians.

Right around the corner from the store lived Sherman Fairchild, who was the richest man in America, although I didn't know that. He owned the greater portion of IBM, which was willed him by his father. Sherman was a confirmed bachelor and also a hi-fi enthusiast. He had his own audio company, Fairchild Audio, which never made any money. He hired me to be his personal audio assistant.

Fairchild gave me a mono recorder, a Kudelski Nagra, to use. Through him, I befriended Bob Fine, who recorded all the early Mercury Living Presence26 records. He became my mentor and gave me a bunch of microphones. The first Bob Dylan recording I did was with that Nagra and my microphones. And it was at the Gaslight.

When you showed up at the Gaslight that day, were you involved in the Village scene? Did you know who Bob Dylan was?

---

26 A classical-music label in the '50s renowned for its pristine sound.

I lived at 148 Bleecker Street, and I became friendly with Edward Herbert Beresford Monck, who was known as Chip Monck. He was a famous character in the Village. He convinced everybody from Harry Belafonte to Nina Simone that I was the greatest recording engineer since Tom Edison. He convinced The Village Gate to put in a sound system of mine.

He knew the new owners of the Gaslight, who were the Hoods[27]. They had never had a sound system. So I put in a modest two speakers. It was a tiny little room that held 50 people at most. I mean, that room really didn't need any amplification, but the Hoods wanted to attract more people there.

There were so many folk clubs around there at the time. What was the Gaslight's reputation? Was it just one of many?

One of many, but the Hoods were very nice people. They were more idealists than businessmen. Clarence Hood came from Northern Florida and had a fair amount of money. I think he was a millionaire. But the room never made much money. There was no admission fee when they opened it. People would perform, and they would pass around the basket afterwards. The performers got a percentage of it, and the owners of the club got a percentage. So nobody made a lot.

Were you recording a lot of different artists in those clubs or was Bob Dylan unusual?

I did some recording at the Village Gate surreptitiously. I recorded Thelonious Monk; it was issued a while back as an LP. And Sonny Rollins and John Coltrane. Those were all recorded surreptitiously with one microphone in the ceiling, so they weren't great sound.

Did you put the microphone there when you created the sound system?

I just kind of snuck in and put the microphone in the ceiling. It was only there for about a month. I took it down because I wasn't interested in being a bootlegger or recording things surreptitiously. I wanted to stop it before somebody noticed.

So what was the story behind you recording Dylan at the Gaslight?

Chip came to me and said that Dylan had some new songs and was going to perform them. Dylan hung out at Chip's place. Chip had a room at the Village Gate. Dylan would come in and type away and drink red wine and opine on various subjects. He was a charming young kid who had some talent, but nobody expected him to write the great songs that he was going to write.

---

27 Father and son Clarence and Sam Hood.

It was two nights in a row. I think they were one right after the other, but I can't be sure. The first concert was the old Bob Dylan and the second concert was more or less the new one. It was obvious from the second night on that Dylan was headed for fame.

What was he like as a performer? He had started writing great songs by that time, but did he have stage presence, or was he awkward?

A combination. As he wrote great songs, he grew into his personality. I would rate him originally as kind of mediocre. When he started to write songs, he was the top of the heap. He went from one thing to the other.

I went there and recorded it and played it back for Dylan at my studio in Carnegie Hall.

Do you remember Dylan's reaction?

We smoked a joint. Bob was very happy with the sound, but I felt that he was more focused on his studio recordings for Columbia. Many of the songs are better than they were [on the records]. Certainly "A Hard Rain's a-Gonna Fall" is better on the Gaslight tapes than anywhere else.

Was there talk of releasing your tapes as a live album?

No. I think that Columbia didn't know much about live recording. And he hadn't voiced his originality in public. These concerts at the Gaslight in '62 were afterhours; they were more testing material than anything else.

[When Columbia eventually released *Live at the Gaslight 1962* decades later], they said they searched everywhere for the best possible recordings, but they never came to me. I had the originals all along. They just downloaded a bunch of stuff. It sounds pretty good, but my copies were one-offs directly from the master tapes.

So the official album was your recording, just several generations later, or a totally different recording?

They were my recordings, but they were mishandled. I gave the recordings to Dylan's manager, Albert Grossman, at the time, from which the bootlegs must have originated. I suppose that the copies that were on the internet were copies of copies. But they were really bad versions. Not at all like my tapes.

Did you have any interaction with Dylan or Grossman between the Gaslight era and the '66 tour?

No. When it came time to do the '66 tour, Bob had already gone electric and was looking for somebody that knew amplification. I was one of the few who did.

Harry Belafonte was the first person to use his own sound equipment and have it written into his contract that his sound engineer had to do all the concerts. So I got indoctrinated with Belafonte and I kind of spread it around. I did a bunch of other concerts for Grossman like Peter, Paul and Mary, but I wasn't really interested in doing live sound. I was interested in having a recording studio and being a recording engineer. The live sound was a way to make money. It was a paycheck.

I knew about the Hawks. And I liked [Dylan's] newer songs, certainly. I've remained a fan all along, although I've never seen Dylan's set [since].

What is it like trying to amplify a rock band in those rooms?

None of these places were designed for music. It wasn't really loud enough for the electric band. The acoustic set was fine. Dylan and his guitar were very well amplified, but the band— the drums were loud and the guitars were loud and sometimes the organ. It was difficult to make a good balance because this stage balance wasn't good. People would play loud.

Do the recordings of those '66 shows sound better than it did to the audience at the time?

It's the very same audio. Some of them were good; some weren't. The acoustics of the room had more influence than any of the equipment, because the equipment was always the same. Some concerts were very successful and some concerts were underamplified and some concerts the balance was all wrong.

Do you remember any particular rooms that were challenging?

Royal Albert Hall was a big problem, because it seated about five or six thousand people, and the average place that we performed in was just a couple of thousand at most. We would typically use some speakers that were in the hall, but Royal Albert Hall was designed for acoustic music. It wasn't designed for amplified music.

Dylan had a very good idea what he wanted, but it wasn't available at the time. There was nobody doing amplified sound for rock concerts, period, until a year later. It was started by The Who.

Did that cause tension between you two, on nights when Dylan wanted a sound that your equipment wasn't up to the task of delivering?

Yeah, yeah. But he knew that my limitations were forced on me by circumstance. He just wanted to have it better. And it wasn't. He never took it out on me.

Sometimes it was more hostile than others.

Never any more than 20% of the people were hostile.

There were very few concerts where I felt that it was all negative.

. . . .

From your vantage point from the side of the stage at all these shows, was the audience as hostile as its legend?

I would say that sometimes it was more hostile than others. Never any more than 20% of the people were hostile. Vocally hostile — maybe the others were quiet and hostile. There were very few concerts where I felt that it was all negative. There were those who thought that Dylan should stay acoustic and stay with the folk music team. They were very vocal. And they were encouraged by the press.

Do you remember if you heard the famous "Judas" yell in the moment?

No, I didn't. I didn't pay any attention. It all flowed together and I didn't notice it particularly.

It's interesting that capturing that moment on recording has made that specific show so legendary even compared to the others.

I always felt that Dylan was a rock and roll artist. I never felt that he was a folk artist. Most of that is my particular prejudice. But he became a folk artist because that was the only way that he could express himself. Nobody wrote serious rock and roll songs until Dylan did.

SING OUT!

THE FOLK SONG MAGAZINE
VOLUME 18/NUMBER 4—OCTOBER/NOVEMBER, 1968—$1.00

EXCLUSIVE INTERVIEW WITH BOB DYLAN
INTERVIEW WITH BUKKA WHITE
TEN YEARS WITH THE RAMBLERS
WORDS & MUSIC TO "MR. BOJANGLES,"
"THE WEIGHT" AND OTHERS

Happy Traum interviewed Dylan in Woodstock for this 1968 issue of *Sing Out!* magazine.
Dylan donated an original painting for the cover.

Happy Traum

I first clued into Happy Traum's work when the *Another Self Portrait* Bootleg Series came out in 2013. It included a never-before-heard recording from the 1971 *Bob Dylan's Greatest Hits Vol. II* sessions. The song was "Only a Hobo," an obscure protest-era folk number (some greatest hit!) that you would have thought Dylan left back in his Greenwich Village days. But there it was on the set, performed in a duo arrangement with Happy Traum. The same sessions with Dylan and Traum also yielded several songs that *did* make that second *Greatest Hits* collection: "You Ain't Goin' Nowhere," "Down in the Flood," and "I Shall Be Released." Though the writing of those songs came out of the Basement Tapes work with the Band, the first recorded versions Dylan officially released were done by him and Happy.

By 1971, though, Traum had already known Dylan for a decade. He was a denizen of the Greenwich Village folk scene before Dylan showed up, performing both on his own and with vocal group The New World Singers (and later in a duo with his brother Artie). The Singers had been the first group to record "Blowin' in the Wind" — before Peter, Paul and Mary, before Dylan himself — as well as "Don't Think Twice, It's Alright." He was also on hand when Dylan recorded under the pseudonym Blind Boy Grunt for a compilation to support folk-music magazine *Broadside*. Dylan taught Traum "Let Me Die in My Footsteps" at that session, and Traum was the first to record that song too. So Traum's stories about working with Bob span multiple decades: the '60s, the '70s, and even a few memorable encounters the two had in the '80s.

. . . .

Were you already on the Greenwich Village scene when Dylan first showed up?

Yeah. Not totally professional, but I was doing small things even in the late '50s.

Izzy Young, who owned the Folklore Center[28] and was a godfather to us, put me on a couple of concerts. I teamed up with Dick Weissman, a banjo player later in The Journeymen with John Phillips and Scott McKenzie. We did some midnight concerts at the Provincetown Playhouse. So I was sort of floating around the Village. Until 1960, I was still in college, so all this was between classes.

You were going to college somewhere in New York?

I was at NYU, but their main campus in those days was up in Bronx. I'd take the subway on the weekends, hang out at the coffeehouses, and meet people in Washington Square Park. Then in 1961, I met Gil Turner. Gil Turner was a larger-than-life singer. He was very active in the anti-war marches. In '62, he invited me to join The New World Singers.

Dylan was a big fan of the group, and he'd show up often at the gigs we did. Especially the late-night ones. In those days, you'd play for a week or two at one place. There'd be four or five different sets on the weekend. You might do your last set at one in the morning to five bleary-eyed people scattered around the place. Dylan would often just show up and play. He'd either get onstage with us, or we'd get offstage and he'd do a few songs. One of my strongest, most indelible memories was being at Gerde's Folk City one night, maybe there were a dozen people there, and he sang "A Hard Rain's A-Gonna Fall." I had never heard that song at that point. I almost fell off my chair.

The funny thing was that people would get up and leave in the middle of his set. He wasn't the smooth, cool folk singer that everybody was looking for. He was a little harder-edged. That rough voice. I guess the same thing would've happened if Woody Guthrie was on the stage. They probably would've left for him too.

I imagine it takes at least a little while to get to that "Hard Rain" *moment. Is he making an impression the very first times you see him, or is he one of many singing old folk songs?*

He was never one of many, for some unexplainable reason. He had a charisma that got people buzzing. Even before I saw him or met him, I remember I was at a party and people were saying, "Have you heard this new kid, Dylan, who was hopping freight trains from New Mexico?" He had that mythology about him. He always stood out — and there were some great people playing around the Village back then.

People started to play his songs pretty quickly too. *Broadside* magazine was publishing his songs, and Gil Turner became very close to Bob early on. Gil

---

28 Greenwich Village folk music store that became a nexus of the '50s and '60s folk scene.

immediately started singing his songs. He was the one that Bob taught "Blowin' in the Wind" to, I think before anybody else. Then Gil taught it to us, the New World Singers, one night at Gerde's in the basement. We practiced it there and went up on the stage and sang it. We were immediately struck by what an unusual and amazing song it was.

You were the first to record "Blowin' in the Wind," and I believe subsequently "Don't Think Twice" as well. Is that how those happened?

Yeah. Bob was teaching those songs to Gil, and Gil was teaching them to us. There are other songs. I just put out a new CD, and one of the songs on there is a song of Bob's called "Farewell." That was another song he taught us. We sang it, but never recorded that one. Not too many people did.

It's not an official release, but that's one of the songs you and Bob do together on the so-called Banjo Tape, a bootleg tape recorded in '63 that's been circulating for years.

That was in an apartment, it might have been Gil Turner's. I think it was Gil Turner who was playing banjo and I was playing guitar. It also might have been up at the apartment of Gordon Friesen and Agnes Cunningham, the people who published *Broadside*. They sometimes held gatherings at their apartment. Suze Rotolo[29] was there, I think.

 If you're not paying attention to those things at the time— it wasn't like at that moment I thought, this is a moment I should remember, because it's historically important.

That's a fair point. I'm asking about this specific jam session because there happens to be a recording we can hear today, but were there ten similar things that weren't recorded?

There were several times where Bob came to our apartment in New York and played us his latest songs. I never whipped out a tape recorder. My wife Jane remembers him singing "A Hard Rain's A-Gonna Fall" for us in our living room. Of course, there's no record of that. There were times that he did the same thing here in Woodstock some years later.

When he plays a song like that at a private gathering, is he asking for feedback? Is he just showing off what he's got?

I don't think he was looking for "Oh, that verse should be put somewhere else" kind of feedback. I think he was looking for affirmation. It's hard to imagine, looking at

---

29 Dylan's girlfriend at the time.

his persona now, but he was looking for attention, he was looking for recognition. At that point, it was a small circle of people that recognized his special talents. Maybe a year or two later, he was suddenly on the stage at Carnegie Hall, but back then he was very eager for people to hear and like his stuff. He'd pull out a guitar and just play his latest songs for anybody. It was very charming.

Beyond him busting out "A Hard Rain" for the first time on stage, were there any other performances from those Village days that you remember?

Not specifically. I was a part-timer in the Village even then, even when I was in the New World Singers, because I was living on the Upper West Side. I already had a daughter. In fact, Bob did the liner notes to [the New World Singers'] Atlantic album. He has a paragraph there about my little daughter Merry. To this day, it's very sweet to me that he would have done that.[30]

Did having a family make you an outlier in that scene in those early days?

Pretty much. Most of my contemporaries were more free and easy. Freewheelin', if you want to use a Dylan term. Phil Ochs had a child by '63 or so, but most of my friends were either single or childless. So I missed quite a few of those shows.

You were at the Broadside *sessions too, when Bob was recording a few tracks under the pseudonym Blind Boy Grunt. Was that just a Dylan session or were they recording all the artists for the compilation?*

It was a group grope at Folkways Studio, which was not a big studio. My memory could be wrong, but I think there was just one recording room and one control room and a hallway outside. Pete Seeger, my hero at that point, was there, and Phil Ochs. Mark Spoelstra; the Freedom Singers, who had been making the rounds to raise money for SNCC; Peter La Farge, who was representing American Indian sentiments. Everybody was in a room at the same time, so it was not like we were there by ourselves. When we sang "Blowin' in the Wind," Bob was listening three feet away.

At one point at that session, Bob called me out into the hallway. He had this sheath of typewritten papers in his hand. He said, "Would you sing this song?"

---

30 "I met Happy Traum an' his wife about the same time I guess an' I can remember when their baby girl Merry was born an' now she's over a year old — an' with one laugh out a beautiful Merry you'd know why Happy wants a new an' better world — just look some time at long haired little Merry an' you'd know why anybody'd want a new world — but Happy's got the reason right there in his eyeview ... closer to it than a lot of us are ....."

It's hard to imagine, looking at his persona now, but he was looking for attention, for recognition. Back then he was very eager for people to hear and like his stuff. He'd pull out a guitar and just play his latest songs for anybody. It was very charming.

. . . .

It was "Let Me Die in My Footsteps." I don't know why *he* didn't want to sing it. We rehearsed it for a few minutes in the hallway and put the words on the music stand. It was the first time I ever sang anything in a professional recording studio by myself.

This wasn't a song that you had heard him do in Gerde's or something?

I had not heard this one before that day. He sang it for me. We rehearsed it a couple of times, and then we went in and did it.

The reason it was so meaningful for me to do that song: A little over a year before, I did time in the New York City prison system for refusing to take shelter in a compulsory air raid drill. I was arrested, tried, and sentenced to 30 days in the workhouse. I always thought that this is the reason that Bob wanted me to sing it. That's a song about not taking shelter, not going underground. I sang that, and he backed me up on guitar, and harmony on the chorus.

It's such a poetic song. It reminded me of "Pastures of Plenty" or some of those other Woody Guthrie songs with that imagery that he was so good at conjuring up. There's some lyrics that I thought were pretty startling for, what was he, 21 maybe at that point.

This is another one where yours is the first, and maybe even only version for a while. He didn't release his own until the first Bootleg Series in '91.

Right.

I know there's a whole Woodstock scene in the late-'60s we'll get to, but do you have much interaction in between that and the early Village days?

In those days, he was very good about remembering to give Jane and me comp tickets to his shows. We went to a show at Lincoln Center's Philharmonic Hall in '64. That was the first time I ever heard "Mr. Tambourine Man." Joan Baez was on that show as well.

Then sometime after that, he played Carnegie Hall [October 1965]. That was when he broke The Band out in the second half. It was the first time I ever heard The Band on stage. It took me a while to get used to it. Like everybody else, I just loved the solo Bob Dylan. Hearing the rock-and-roll Bob Dylan was a jolt for me, but I went with it. I just said, "Okay, if that's what he wants to do, that's fine with me."

I think after that I lost touch with him. I didn't see him from probably '64 till '66 or '67 when I came to Woodstock. We came here when he was still recovering from his accident.

What drew you to the Woodstock area?

I had known Woodstock since I was in high school. I went to music and art high school; a lot of the art students would come for the summer. I also knew some of the musicians that were here pre-Albert Grossman, like Billy Faier, a banjo player, and Johnny Herald, who I knew from Washington Square Park and was in The Greenbriar Boys. I played gigs, too, at the Woodstock Playhouse and Cafe Espresso. We always liked Woodstock. Jane was pregnant in 1966, and we decided we needed a place to go for the summer.

Bob reached out to us while we were here. He was in seclusion. Very few people were in touch with him, but he called us. We were renting a little place in Bearsville and he was living up in Byrdcliffe, so we got together. Then the following year, '67, we moved full-time. We actually lived for a while just a stone's throw from Bob's place. We were frequently back and forth. My daughter and his daughter Maria, his oldest[31], spent a lot of time together. Birthday parties, all that stuff. My son Adam and his son Jesse were buddies, but they were very young.

Is there any music-making component to any of these visits, or is it just family get-togethers?

Oh, we used to sit around and play a lot. He was very into that, just trading songs and picking stuff.

He probably hadn't done that as much since the early Village days, when you were there

---

31 Sara's daughter from a previous marriage whom Dylan adopted.

too. Full circle.

I think he related to that a lot, and I think he was trying to regroup after his accident. It wasn't life-threatening, I don't think, but it was serious enough. He didn't have a neck brace when I first met him, but I know he was in one for a while. Yeah, we spent a lot of family time together and a lot of time just hanging out and playing songs. He always liked to play the old folk songs.

Do you remember any examples?

Probably a lot of the ones that he might have done on his *Self Portrait* album. "Copper Kettle" or "Pretty Saro," those kinds of old folk ballads that we all listened to. He liked those old songs.

He played me the *John Wesley Harding* tapes to see what my reaction was. That was a very folky album. Even though he wrote the songs, with a lot of them, he took the melody from old folk songs and English ballads and things. "I Pity the Poor Immigrant" was a melody he learned from probably Ewan McColl ["Come All Ye Tramps and Hawkers"].

Are any of the Band guys around yet at this point?

I met most of them for the first time at a Thanksgiving dinner at Bob's house. They were very accessible, very friendly. Rick, Levon, and Richard particularly. In fact, I have this enduring image of my son Adam, who would've been around two, sitting on the floor in that little entryway to Bob's house. When Levon came in, first thing he did was scoop Adam up in his arms and carry him inside. Levon loved kids. Adam and he were close pretty much 'til the end of his life.

Was it known around town that they were recording what would become the Basement Tapes?

Yeah. I never went to any of those sessions, but I'd been to Big Pink and I knew that they were doing that. The whole idea of those sessions was to make demos of songs that Bob had written so that other people would record them. I remember Bob was very excited when Manfred Mann made a recording of "Quinn the Eskimo." I heard those tapes, and most of them, in my ignorance, I just thought were throwaways. Then suddenly people were making really good versions of them. What did I know?

While you both were in Woodstock, you conducted a lengthy interview with Bob for another folk magazine, Sing Out!, *at a time where he wasn't really doing interviews.*

How did that happen?

I was spending quite a bit of time with Bob in those days. I'd cook at his house, and we'd take walks through the woods. On one of our walks, he just turned to me and he said, "Would you like to do an interview with me for *Sing Out!*?"

Most people don't know *Sing Out!* nowadays, but back in the '50s, '60s, and into the '70s and '80s even, it was the bible of anybody who was interested in folk, acoustic, roots, Americana music. I was editor of *Sing Out!* at the time, which I'd been doing part-time from Woodstock.

So Bob just threw that question at me. I was dumbfounded, but I said, "Of course." I knew that all these major publications like *Life* magazine and the *New York Times* were trying to get interviews with him. He wasn't talking to anybody.

He asked for John Cohen, a really unusual and very insightful person, and a great photographer[32], to do it with me. He had really admired John since his earliest days in New York.

John and I went up to Bob's house for maybe two or three days, a few hours at a time, just sitting and talking to Bob. It was largely John, who was much more free-thinking than I was, who threw the questions at Bob. I think they were questions he thought Bob could run with, because they were more abstract. They weren't about how he brushes his teeth in the morning or whatever.

Even back then, people must have known that he wasn't the easiest interview in the world.

Yeah, all that stuff. So we spent some time, and then we edited it together. Bob gave us this painting for the magazine cover. He'd just been studying painting with a painter who lived right down the road from him. All the proceeds went to *Sing Out!*, which was in dire need of funds.

Do you remember what the impact was? Like you say, much bigger publications than Sing Out! *had been trying to get this scoop.*

The magazine sold tens of thousands of copies and raised a lot of money from it. It's still in anthologies of Dylan interviews and stuff like that. It was a great gift from Bob to the magazine.

Moving to the Greatest Hits Volume II *session, you and Bob recorded duo versions of "You Ain't Goin' Nowhere," "Down in the Flood," and "I Shall Be Released" for that*

---

32 Also a musician and a founding member of the New Lost City Ramblers, a group Dylan has expressed admiration for.

He played Carnegie Hall [October 1965]. That was when he broke The Band out in the second half. It was the first time I ever heard The Band on stage. It took me a while to get used to it. Like everybody else, I just loved the solo Bob Dylan.

. . . .

album, as well as "Only a Hobo" which came out years later. Tell me how that came about.

Some months before, Bob called me and said, "You know, you ought to learn how to play bass." I had no idea why he was saying that, but I figured, if Bob says I should learn bass, there must be a reason. So I borrowed a bass and an amp and messed around with it for a while.

Months after that, he called me and said he was doing a session with Allen Ginsberg in New York. He asked me to come to the studio and bring a bass. I found myself in this room with Ginsberg and Peter Orlovsky and David Amram and Jon Sholle and Gregory Corso and some Buddhist monk. It was this insane scene. Bob was in charge, even though John Hammond was sitting in the control booth, mostly reading a newspaper.

We started playing these totally nutty songs with Allen putting his poetry to music. He was playing his harmonium, and Peter Orlovsky was sitting cross-legged on the floor with finger cymbals. Bob was playing guitar and I was playing bass and Amram was playing French horn, I think, and Jon Sholle was also playing guitar. Gregory Corso was running around making a nuisance of himself, being very obnoxious and disruptive because he wanted some attention. Allen kept having to shut him up.

We started doing these songs like Ginsberg's "Jimmy Berman [Gay Lib Rag]," which was a takeoff on the Carter Family or Flatt & Scruggs' "Jimmy Brown the Newsboy." In 1971, the gay thing wasn't that acknowledged. There were several songs that were all about loving little boys and all that stuff.

So it was a crazy session, but I did become a friend of Allen Ginsberg's and Peter's after that. Every time they came to Woodstock to go to this Buddhist monastery near here, they stayed with us.

I've got a record here that says you, also with Dylan and Allen, played some PBS TV show around the time of the session.

That was an amazing thing I helped organize through a woman who lives in Woodstock. It was a local New York PBS show that was called *Freetime*. She was the producer. I was a musical advisor.

I somehow got Allen and Bob involved in coming to the studio and doing a little interview and playing some songs. The awful thing is that they just didn't keep any tapes. Can you imagine? There's no record kept of that. You would think they would've said, "Okay, this is special."

Not long after that, Bob called me again and said he wanted me to bring a bass again and a guitar and a banjo and come down to the studio in New York. I remember it was a nighttime session, just Bob and me and the engineer. The idea was to do songs of his that other people had had hits of, but that he hadn't recorded before.

The first song we did was "Only A Hobo." The only version of that that had existed was eight or nine years earlier when he was "Blind Boy Grunt" on the *Broadside* record. He sang it on that.

Which is funny, because that makes it about as far from a "greatest hit" as a Dylan song could get.

I know. We did maybe two takes of it and I remember thinking I really didn't play it that well. Bob never said anything. He never said much anyway. Since it never appeared on *Greatest Hits Volume II*, I just figured, okay, that was a big flop. It took 40 years for me to hear it again when it came out on *Another Self Portrait*.

Then we did the three songs that appeared on the *Greatest Hits Volume II*. Basically one or two takes. He wanted to have the feel that we had in his living room. "You Ain't Goin' Nowhere" was the only one where there were overdubs. I just overdubbed the bass, I think.

He's turned you into a real bass player at this point.

My first and only recorded bass! I thought that also came out pretty decent. In fact, [Dylan's son] Jakob told me that was one of his favorite of Bob's tracks. He loved the way that song came out, and I do too. I played banjo, Bob played guitar, and I sang harmony live. With the exception of adding the bass afterwards, it was just like it appears on the record.

Is Dylan giving you any direction on these songs, or if he just starts playing, you know him enough to play along?

I could definitely have used some direction — and I could have used some rehearsal! He was like, "Okay, let's play 'I Shall Be Released.'" I had to come up with a part on the fly. I was feeling my way through it. I sang the harmony part because I knew the song from The Band.

Music from Big Pink *was out already.*

Right. And "You Ain't Goin' Nowhere," The Byrds had done it, but I really wasn't that familiar with that except for the Basement Tapes version, which I thought was a total throwaway. Then he changed the words on the *Greatest Hits* to reference McGuinn because of The Byrds.[33]

Bob, he always liked people who recorded his songs. I think he was always appreciative. Now of course there's too many to be appreciated.

How about "Down in the Flood"? Did you know that one?

I didn't actually. He just threw it out there, and I played whatever bluesy little licks I could come up with to try to get a feel. Again, it might have been just one take.

Were you involved in that Another Self Portrait *box set with some of the outtakes?*

Not at all. In fact, the funny thing is that I was having dinner with Eric Andersen in New York. Eric is very good friends with Steve Addabbo, the engineer that put the box set together. Eric and I having dinner at this Italian restaurant in Midtown and Steve came in and sat down at the table. He said, "You wouldn't believe it, but I've just been listening to you on a tape." I said, "What are you talking about?" He told me he had been mixing "Only A Hobo."

I told him I thought that was gone forever. I thought they just left it on the cutting room floor, that they just trashed it. He said, "No, they wanted it on the record." They must mean Bob, I would assume.

I thought, "Oh my God, they're putting that failure on the record." Then I heard it and I thought, this is actually pretty good.

For decades, you'd remembered it as being this dud.

Well, because Bob never said anything. We just moved on to the next thing. When I heard it back maybe 10 years ago, I just thought, "You know, I did pretty well." I wish I could sing as high now as I did then.

---

33 "Clouds so swift an' rain fallin' in / Gonna see a movie called "Gunga Din" / Pack up your money, pull up your tent, McGuinn / You ain't goin' nowhere."

After the Greatest Hits *thing, what sort of interaction are you having?*

Bob moved to New York in the early '70s from Woodstock. We saw him in his New York house a few times. He told me about the Rolling Thunder thing that he was putting together, but I never pursued it myself because I was on to other things. I was on the road with my brother, recording and having our own careers.

We saw him again in London in '78 when he was doing the *Street-Legal* tour. I managed to talk my way past the guards into Earl's Court. I got backstage, got to hang out with Bob and some of my other friends were on that tour, like [guitarist] Steve Soles who I knew from Woodstock and New York. The very next day my wife and kids were coming to meet me in London, so I got them all tickets. We went two days in a row. That was a great show. Seeing it twice in a row was really fun. Bob invited us back to his hotel after. The whole family went, but he didn't show up. We ended up having lunch with Steve Soles.

I saw him again; he came here to visit us in the '80s. Just a surprise drive-by one day, a whole other story. Then I hadn't seen him until 2001. We went to see him at Madison Square Garden right after 9/11. That was the show where he said, "I'm only doing songs I wrote in New York."[34]

What is that '80s one you mentioned, the drive-by?

We were all sitting at home. I see this strange big black car driving up, and then there was a knock on the window. I look out, and it's Bob. It was a Sunday afternoon, totally unexpected. He was with [backing singer] Clydie King and his son Jesse and somebody else, maybe [manager] Jeff Kramer.

We spent an afternoon listening to records and talking. He said, "What are you listening to?" I said, "Oh, this one you got to hear." I took him into the music room. I played him a record by Paul Brady and I played him "Lakes of Pontchartrain" and "Arthur McBride." He absolutely took note of that.

He covered those not long after.

I know — without crediting Paul Brady! He really listened closely to those records. Then I played him some other stuff that totally did not appeal to him. I was in the middle of Tony Rice infatuation at that point. Tony and I were friends; he was peerless as a guitar player. I thought Bob might like some of his more jazzy compositions, some of his newgrass stuff. There was no reaction to that.

---

34 "You know, most of these songs we're singing tonight were written right here in the city. In New York City. And the ones that weren't written here were recorded here. So nobody has to ask me how I feel about this town."

This must be the same house you had lived in way back when, or how else would he have found you?

Same house. We were building the house when Bob was living in Byrdcliffe. In fact, I have a picture of little Jesse, who was maybe four or five at the time, with my son in front of the construction. Bob knew this house when it was just going up, and he somehow found it again 20 years later.

Jim Keltner drumming for Dylan in Akron, Ohio, 1980. Also pictured is Tim Drummond on bass.
Photo by Eddie Halamay

Jim Keltner

Jim Keltner drums for the sort of artists who can be referred to with one name. Neil. Joni. Mick. Elton. Willie. John…and George…and Ringo.

And, of course, Bob.

In fact, there are few musicians who have worked with Bob Dylan over a longer period of time than Jim Keltner. Their relationship began at a 1971 session where a Leon Russell-led band backed Bob on "Watching the River Flow" and "When I Paint My Masterpiece," recorded for *Bob Dylan's Greatest Hits Vol. II* (a different session than Happy Traum's). It's continued into the 2000s, when Keltner toured as a sudden fill-in when Dylan's main drummer suffered carpal tunnel injuries.

And they worked together quite a bit in between. Keltner played drums on tour during all three of Dylan's "gospel years" from 1979–1981. He played on a wide array of Dylan albums — *Pat Garrett and Billy the Kid, Saved, Shot of Love, Empire Burlesque, Time Out of Mind* — plus other assorted tracks throughout the decades. He even became Bob's go-to drummer for strange one-offs, from the Letterman 10th anniversary special to the who's-who of stars at Dylan's 30th Anniversary Concert Celebration (a.k.a. Bobfest).

Oh, and did I mention Keltner was the sixth Traveling Wilbury? George Harrison even asked him to become an official member, and Jim said no. He still got his own Wilbury moniker: Buster Sidebury.

So there was a lot to cover. We didn't hit it all, but over the course of a long, discursive, and fascinating conversation, I tried to touch on as many of his times playing with Dylan as we could get to.

. . . .

Was the first time you met Dylan the '71 session with Leon Russell?

Yeah. I was over in England with my family and got the call from Leon to meet up in New York with Carl [Radle, bassist] and Jesse [Ed Davis, guitarist]. I didn't realize at the time how important those guys were in my life. We were a rhythm section. I hadn't really done a tremendous amount of stuff yet at that point, but I was doing sessions, and they would be on a lot of them. I always loved the fact that we were all from Oklahoma. There was that little bond.

My memories of that session, they're like a dream, really. Leon was playing and we all joined in. I looked over and saw Bob standing facing the wall. I could see his lips moving. He was writing on a tablet. I thought, "Wow, he's writing the lyrics as we're playing." Adjusting some of the lyrics, rearranging some things to fit the groove. That blew my mind.

His phrasing and stuff is so unique. I just did an interview about Willie Nelson, and we were talking about phrasing being completely original and very much like a jazz player. As I was speaking of Willie, I felt like I was speaking about Bob. There's such a similarity in that they both are completely unique with their vocals, the way their voices sound, and the way they phrase. I put them both in a jazz category. They don't sing like the typical rock singer.

Hearing the playback was just extraordinary. It was like an out-of-body experience for me. That little song was "Watching the River Flow." Even today when I hear it, it just thrills me. It takes me right back. Years later, I always wondered, what would have been if we had been a rhythm section for Bob on many, many things? That's not the way it worked out.

You mentioned him as almost a jazz vocalist. I know you started out doing jazz stuff. Do you think that's one way that you connected working with his music?

That's a strong possibility. It wouldn't have been a conscious thing. For me, playing with Bob has always been one of the most natural things I could do. Maybe you have hit on it. It may be this free feeling that you get when you're playing jazz, like you just need to know the song, know the form, and then go for it. Don't be afraid.

The thing that I love about Bob is his fearlessness. There's a fearlessness from some artists that translates to the musicians playing. When that happens, you get the best from the musicians, because the musicians are not worried about tempo or about whether they're rushing or they're dragging or whether they're not in the pocket. It's not about finding a pocket. It's more about searching for the vibe, searching for the thing that makes the song have life.

I love being able to find a pocket and sit in it, but I also love the exploratory thing where you're letting the song bump you along instead of you bumping the song. It's a great thing that doesn't happen often enough.

For instance, the other day I was talking to my good friend Matt Chamberlain, who's playing drums currently with Bob.[35] He was saying that Bob told him one time before they were recording, "Just play. Don't try to find one thing and settle on it." I may not have gotten that exactly the way he said it, but basically what he was saying was what I've been telling you. Just let the music happen. Don't be trying to find "a part" for the song. That's pretty jazz-like. That's the Bob Dylan that I've always known.

A couple years later you did "Knockin' on Heaven's Door" and the Pat Garrett and Billy the Kid *soundtrack. How does doing a session to soundtrack a movie differ from that first session?*

In those days playing a song in a movie meant watching the film while you're playing. I don't think there's so much of that anymore. The composer usually has everything mapped out.

With Bob, ["Knockin' on Heaven's Door"] was meant to hit your heartstrings hard, because it was a death scene. The shot would go back and forth from this great Mexican actress Katy Jurado to her soulful big brown eyes. She's crying because her husband is dying at the edge of the river. To watch the scene unfold while you're hearing Bob's voice is just— I cried. That was the first time I ever cried [while playing]. I thought, "Jesus, I've got to be careful. I'm going to blow this take."

To be moved to tears while you're playing your instrument is a gift, I think. Now, conversely, I did a session years later with Randy Newman where the lyrics hit me so hard and I couldn't help but laugh. I couldn't laugh out loud, but I was laughing so hard inside that it scared me again in the same way: "Oh, I'm going to blow this take."

Jumping forward a few years again, to the gospel tours, your most extended time with him. I read that you had resisted some invitations to tour with him earlier. Why did you decide to sign on for those?

Bob had asked me to join his touring band a few times, and I was always afraid to for various reasons. Plus I was working so much in those days in the studio that I

---

35 Chamberlain drummed for Dylan in 2019 and 2020 both on tour and on the *Rough and Rowdy Ways* album.

didn't want to miss things. I always figured, if I don't go on the road with him, it would be okay because I'll meet up with him in the studio at some point.

When I'd get a call to go tour with him, it would always be an invitation to come down and play. It was like almost like an audition, except that I knew that I had the gig if I said yes.

I went down this time, and it was a little different. The suggestion was that I come down and sit in the room by myself and listen to his new record *[Slow Train Coming]*. Then, when I'm done hearing it, come upstairs and see Bob. I thought, well, that's interesting.

I got to his studio on Main Street there in Santa Monica and went in the office. The girl turned the music on, and I sat there. One song after the other just started banging me in the head, pulling at my heart. All the corny things you can possibly imagine, they all started happening to me. Here's Dylan again, making me cry — and it was uncontrollable! By the time the whole record was done, I had gone through half a Kleenex box.

I went upstairs and opened the door, and he's sitting there at his typewriter. I said, "Bob, I don't know what you're going to do, but whatever it is, I want to go do it with you." That was it.

We rehearsed a bunch. It felt real natural. He had really great musicians. He had Tim Drummond on bass, and Tim was a great natural player. There was no tidiness about his playing. He was exactly the kind of player that Bob loved, in that he wouldn't figure anything out and then stick with it. He just played according to what was going on at that moment. Then he had Fred Tackett playing guitar. Fred I'd known from Little Feat. We had played on a few sessions together before and he was always really easy and fun to play with. Fred and Tim were incredible. Then he had Spooner [Oldham] on the B3, and Spooner was everybody's hero. The man that played the Farfisa on "When A Man Loves a Woman."

The guy's a legend.

Muscle Shoals legend. But maybe the sweetest person in the entire world. That was the core rhythm section. Oh, and Terry Young the piano player. This guy had chops that were unbelievable.

I just felt surrounded by soul. It was such a soulful band, soulful people. The gospel singing behind him was just absolutely unreal. To me, I was right where I belonged. Because of the nature of the music, I started having kind of a prayer life. And the more you pray, the more confidence you have. Which is part of what prayer is about. It increases your faith.

I love Bob's fearlessness. If you're not fearless, you're afraid. A lot of musicians can smell fear. That comes from being in a studio with artists, making records where everything is on the line. People's careers are being shaped or created. A lot of responsibility. But [fearlessness] makes it fun for the musicians.

We hit the road and got to San Francisco, Bill Graham's place, the Warfield. It's a great place to play. The stage is very close to the audience. The way it's set up is that it goes up in a steep way, so that when you're on the stage, you're almost looking at a wall of people, rather than a sea of people.

I'm sitting there playing behind Bob and looking out at faces. I'll never forget this one guy with a red bandana around his head. I think he was smoking because he had something in his hands, and it probably wasn't a cigarette. He would stand up and say, "Fuck you, Dylan! Rock and roll!" Then right next to him — man this is my memory, clear as a bell — right next to him was a guy sitting with a little sports coat on. He had his wife or his girlfriend and a little baby. He stood up after the "Rock and roll!" guy stood up and said, "We love you, Bob! We love your music!"

It was like that 'til the end of that tour. Like a fight in the audience. Not a literal fight, it was a lot of hollering and carrying on. I just got the impression that Bob loved it because he knew he was hitting a nerve.

Like back when he went electric and caused some of the same reaction.

Exactly. Not that he was trying to. I never get the impression that he was trying to make waves just so that he could get attention. He was doing what he intended to do, and his audience was either going to love it or they were going to hate it.

As we went along, I think people realized that the music is speaking for itself. It's not just that he was talking about Jesus. I think people — nonbelievers, I should say — started realizing it's brilliant music. Because it *was* brilliant music. Those gospel songs are some of the greatest ever written, as far as I'm concerned. You can imagine how much fun it was to be a part of that whole thing. That was the longest I'd ever been with anybody in a band.

We had a night in Seattle that I will never forget. It was a good concert, everything was going well, hitting on all cylinders. We got to the song "Solid Rock," which I loved playing because it was fast and it had a ferociousness to it. Bob was on fire that night, and the words were hitting hard. At the end of the song, there was applause like you'd expect, but it went on for— I think I clocked it at almost five minutes. That can be proven; I have a copy of a board tape. That was an extraordinary event for somebody playing in a band. I can't imagine what it was like for Bob. Five minutes standing ovation for one song that wasn't at the end of the concert. There were moments like that.

That's a long way from some guy in a red bandana yelling "Fuck you."

I guess you'd have to call that a highlight of my playing career. It's just one of those things that you never forget. There were other moments similar during that whole time.

Did you feel the tour changed over the three years? I know a few people came and went, especially among the singers, but did the vibe change?

Yes, it changed. One of the things that changed, that made things easier on the audience, [is that] they were given some of his older songs. The first tour, we played only the songs from *Slow Train*. At each succeeding tour, it seemed like we added more of his classics.[36] The night that we played "Like a Rolling Stone" for the first time, I remember getting chills, because the audience went crazy.

The next thing you did with him after the gospel tours was Empire Burlesque. *At this point, you've done a number of albums and you've done a lot of touring. What's the difference between playing with him in the studio or on a stage?*

With most other artists, playing live with them and playing in the studio is pretty different. When I'm playing on a record, I normally am trying different things. Playing in the studio is a fun adventure kind of thing. Going on the road means rehearsing and learning songs.

Playing with Bob live was not really that different than being in a studio, because the adventurous part was still intact. Like what I told you earlier, he doesn't want to have to hear the same thing over and over, just like I don't want to have to play the same thing over and over.

---

36 The shift was slightly less gradual than that: They did three tours of all-gospel material in 1979 and 1980, then reintroduced a bunch of the older material all at once on Fall 1980's "Musical Retrospective" tour.

There are times when you must play an arrangement exactly the way it's been rehearsed and fleshed out all the time. I did that on the Simon & Garfunkel [reunion] tour, *Old Friends*. If the music is really good, then it's not a job really. It's fun, but it's a disciplined fun.

How did you get involved in the Traveling Wilburys? Was that through Dylan? I know you'd worked with Harrison by then.

That was George completely. George became like a brother. He liked having me around all the time for different things. When he was working on something, I'd be there.

I think it was [Harrison's 1987 album] *Cloud Nine* that preceded the Wilburys. I was at his studio. H.O.T. Studio, we called it — Henley-on-Thames — and we were having a ball. We always had such a ball playing, and especially there at the studio because it was in his home. His home was a massive monastery, Friar Park. Talk about a dream; it was always dreamlike.

Jeff Lynne was working with him on the *Cloud Nine* record. Jeff and George had very similar senses of humor. The crazy English Monty Python humor. The more beers they had, the sillier they would get. We were sitting around one night. I think we had just cut my favorite song on the record, "This Is Love." They're being funny and started making up names for a band. They kept going and going. Finally, they settled on the Traveling Wilburys. They thought that was just hilarious.

Then, after we were done, I heard from George that they had gone to Bob's house and cut this song ["Handle with Care"]. The very next thing I heard was, "Hey, we're going to start a band. We're going to be the Traveling Wilburys. We're going to do a record." So then we started recording.

Speaking of funny names, did one of them give you the nickname Buster Sidebury?

That was George. They expected *me* to be a Wilbury.

At that time, I was thinking you got Roy [Orbison], you got Bob, you got Tom [Petty], you got Jeff, and you got George. That's five guys. One in the middle, two on the sides. If you put another Wilbury in there, then it's unbalanced. Which side would I be on? It is a funny way to think, but I was thinking like that. Plus you've got five icons. I may be considered an icon in the drum world, but that's not what we're talking about here. *[laughs]* It was natural for me to say no.

Then it came to me: I'm a *Sidebury*. George laughed. He loved that. I said, "I'm a Sidebury cousin, your first cousin." I was so close with Tom. He liked that I did that. He always made a big deal out of that in interviews. That's how I became

Buster Sidebury.

The other guys all smoked cigarettes. I had quit. To be in one of those RVs that they have on the studio lot for shooting videos, four guys all smoking cigarettes, it was too much for me. During one of the videos, I jumped off the bus and I went over to Roy. Roy was sitting by himself because he was instructed by his wife, Barbara, "You better not be smelling like smoke when I come to the set!"

We started talking. He said, "This is really fun, isn't it Jim?" I said, "Man, it's incredible. You know, Roy, the guys are all here only because of you, really. They all just want to hear you sing." He said, "Well, I'm the only real *singer* in the band. The other boys are all stylists."

I had to suppress a laugh. It was so true, but it was just so funny the way he said it. Just matter of factly. The first freaking thing I did when I got a chance was tell George. He cracked up and then I told all the guys. "I'm the only real singer in the band. The other boys are all stylists." It's absolutely true.

Was there ever any talk of playing live?

Oh, absolutely. There were plans, big plans to go on the road. We were going to go on a train tour. We were going to take a train across the United States.

What's funny is that everybody assumed that it would be Bob who would nix it. But Bob was on board fully. It turned out to be George. I don't care to speculate on why he didn't want to do it, but he didn't want to.

Too bad.

It certainly is. I think Roy had passed already. That may have figured into it a little bit.

I haven't really spent a lot of time thinking about what a Wilbury tour would have been. I think George's passing has overshadowed that whole thing to me. With George gone, it took a lot of the wind out of it for me. George is younger than me. George should be my little brother that I see all the time. He loved LA [where I live]. He loved Friar Park. We should be going back and forth like we did all those years. It wasn't meant for him to hang around.

Bob is still here, and I'll tell you another thing: George Harrison was Bob Dylan's biggest fan in the world. There wasn't anybody that I've ever known that was a bigger Bob Dylan fan. He knew the lyrics to every Bob Dylan song, old and new.

Moving forward to your next Dylan gig, how did you get involved with the 30th anniversary tribute, known as "BobFest"?

George Harrison was Bob Dylan's biggest fan in the world. There wasn't anybody that I've ever known that was a bigger Bob Dylan fan. He knew the lyrics to every Dylan song, old and new.

. . . .

It might've been Bob that asked me to do it. It was either Bob or George. Or both. Let's see. *[Jim flipping through datebook]* On the 7th [of October], we had a rehearsal with Tom Petty. On the 12th, we had a rehearsal with Sophie B. and the O'Jays, and Johnny Winter. On the 13th, we rehearsed with Clapton and Stevie Wonder, Sinéad, Bob, and the band. Then the 14th we rehearsed with Rosanne Cash, Shawn Colvin, George Harrison, and Lou Reed. Then on the 15th, we rehearsed with Neil Young. Then on the 16th was the gig. On the next day, I started an album with Willie at the Power Station.

Does anyone on that list jump out at you, that you particularly remember?

I remember rehearsing with Neil, then the delight of rehearsing with Stevie. Stevie Wonder was like from another planet. And Clapton. I always loved Eric.

What is it about those three?

Imagine what it would be like: You're at this big deal thing honoring Bob Dylan, and then suddenly there's everybody, the biggest artists of the day. You're playing Bob's music with them. To see them all come together for Bob, that's what knocked me out.

That was the beginning of us playing with Neil Young. Me and [Steve] Cropper and Duck Dunn [both also in the BobFest house band], we went on tour with Neil [the following year]. The band was half of the MGs. Cropper and Duck. It was unbelievable to be playing with those guys live.

Neil is another artist that's very much like Bob. There are just a few of them. Neil is definitely one. Neil, he just wants you to interpret his music. He wants you to listen to him and get with him. That's what we did.

Playing with Duck Dunn on bass was like a dream. Then Cropper's rhythm was unreal. There was a little tension there once in a while. I mean in the music, because Cropper is so strong with his groove and Neil really likes to swim. I was in heaven. I was being able to be as expressive as I wanted to be and float in and out of this incredibly pocketed thing and [then] into the deep part of the water and swim with Neil. It was a great tour. It came together because of BobFest.

One more session to hit on, Time Out of Mind, *one of the great latter-day Dylan albums. Both Bob and Daniel Lanois have talked about the tension between them. Were you one of Bob's people he called in to help?*

Yeah, I was definitely there for Bob. Bob and Lanois were not seeing eye-to-eye on everything. There was a tension there. I've got to say, Bob is not alone in being like this, but I think there are some people who feed off of tension. I'm one of those people. I didn't have any problem with Lanois at all. It was actually more fun for me in a sick kind of way.

What I always loved about that record is the voice was so big. There were a lot of musicians playing all at the same time and, the way it was mixed, so that the music was all in the back, almost blurry in a way, and with the voice really big up in the front, I've always marveled at that.

I remember that Bob asked a question one night when we were all standing around. He said, "Do you like the bits or do you like the overall thing?" What he was referring to was there were so many individual pieces to the music. That's what I think Bob meant about the bits. There were little things musically that were really cool. I said, "I like the bits." Later when the record came out, I knew what had happened. He got the bits that we were referring to. The little musical bits all became like this wall, this background for this huge voice so that the lyrics stood out beautifully.

Eric Clapton, not long ago we were playing together, and he said one of his favorite songs ever is "Tryin' to Get to Heaven."

David Bowie covered that one too.

Oh yeah. That record is very much loved by a lot of artists. The way it was mixed, his voice so big, it's one of my favorite things. When I first heard it, I thought, "Wow, Bob got what he was looking for." Only it didn't happen until later. In the mix, they made it work.

The last tour you did with Bob seemed pretty spontaneous. In 2002, George Receli, Bob's drummer, came down with an injury and you pinch-hit for a few weeks.

He got a serious carpal tunnel problem. Bob wanted me to be in Milan tomorrow.

I said, "Wow, I don't think I can get there that soon." I made it the day after. My first gig was April 21st in Zurich with them. George, a great drummer and really good friend, stayed so that I could— Let's see, what happened? Maybe he played at the sound check.

It looks like for the first show you were at, he played half the show and you played half the show. Then subsequently you just took over.

Right, that's what it was. He played half the show, so that I could get a feel for what they were doing, just the vibe of the whole thing. Then I finished it. That's right.

Even still, it's not like he's playing the same songs you're going to play. You're just thrown on stage to play other stuff.

There again, that's the faith Bob had in me. The trust Bob had in me that I could do the thing that he really loved, which is to just play the music. Just fit in with the music somehow. Don't worry about trying to find a part to play and all that other kind of stuff. Don't worry whether or not you're totally accurate with everything. That doesn't matter. Bob is a real champion of that kind of thinking and so that's why it was easy for me.

Had you ever had to do something like that before with anyone where you had literally no rehearsal?

No way. Like I said, that's Dylan. That was incredible, man, now that I think about it. Those guys all took real good care of me. They would give me signs.

In typical Bob fashion, every night, there's new songs you're being thrown into. It's not like you get through the first show and smooth sailing after that.

That's right. With Bob, you didn't know a lot of times. That's the way it should be, really, if you think about it. There's nothing wrong with having a real good, well-rehearsed show. But I think real artistry is a little more than that. I think that putting the little element of danger or tension or whatever you want to call it into the situation is a good thing in some cases.

Again, that's that fearless thing. If you're not fearless, you're going to be afraid. A lot of the musicians I know, we can smell fear. I know that sounds funny, but that comes from being in a studio with artists, making records where everything is on the line. Time is money, people's careers are being shaped or created. There's a lot of responsibility there. If you sense that somebody is afraid or reticent in some way, then you put that other hat on. The fun ones, the really, really fun ones, like Bob, Willie, Neil, Clapton, they've got that fearless kind of thing. That really makes it fun for the musicians.

The playback is what I'm in the game for. I love hearing the playback to see, "Did we do good? Well, let's try it again" or "That's fantastic, we'll never be able to do it that good again."

Is that how it works at a Dylan session, typically? You'll do a take or two, then everyone goes into the control room?

They're all a little bit different. With Bob, he'll be a little more conventional. The most unconventional is Neil. There's what's called a rundown of the song, and then the first take. Before the rundown, you were just messing about. I have played with Neil Young on records where the messing about *is* the take! You don't even get to the rundown. That can be a little shocking.

Your most recent time playing with Dylan to date comes full circle, because we've talked about Willie Nelson a lot. It's you performing with Dylan and Nelson at the same time, twice. You recorded "Heartland" with them in the '90s and then a decade later, there was this TV special where Bob came out and they do "You Win Again" together, May 2004.

That's a great pairing. In this [Willie] interview, the interviewer had asked me, "Did you play on 'Heartland'?" I said, " I'm not sure. I don't know if there's any drums on that." When I got home I listened and sure enough, there's the drums. I'm going, "I'm a freaking idiot." If you've been playing for 50 years making records, there's certain things just pass through and you just can't remember.

Willie Nelson and Bob Dylan are two of the most distinctive voices in the music business. You know immediately when they're singing and to hear them sing together is beautiful. I love how they sound on "Heartland" together. I don't think they did enough of that. I wish they'd do it again. They're both here, man. They're both on this planet, still commanding all the attention they've ever commanded. Somebody needs to— I'll tell [Dylan manager] Jeff Kramer that. In fact, I'm going to call him as soon as we're done.

You're in a small group of musicians who Bob calls back again and again, over decades. Why do you think he keeps calling you?

I think it's because of our track record together. The very first time meeting him, playing on — it wasn't a gigantic hit, but it certainly was one of his memorable songs — "Watching the River Flow." Then "Knockin' on Heaven's Door" was iconic. Then the gospel years. I think with that kind of track record, he's always going to be thinking of me like that.

One of my favorite times with Bob was during the Wilburys. He was so funny. I wish that people like you and other people who are big fans of his, I wish they could see that side of Bob, but you're never going to have that without special times like that. He used to crack me up like. I told him one time, I said, "Man, you're like a Lenny Bruce throwback." He's just way more personable than what people get to see.

For me, I always feel as long as I'm there for Bob, I'm there for Bob and that's it. I know why I'm there and I know what I'm going to do, which is I'm going to feel Bob out. I can feel it through the playbacks, through whatever he might say, but I'm there because Bob Dylan wants me to be there.

Dylan at Herzl Camp in Webster, Wisconsin in 1957. Larry Kegan is on his left and Louie Kemp is on his right.
Courtesy of Louie Kemp

Louie Kemp

Louie Kemp saw Bob Dylan perform before anyone else in this book. In fact, he was at what might be the first-ever Bob Dylan concert. That is, if you count Talent Night at a Jewish summer camp as a "concert." And, for that matter, if you count a 13-year-old piano-basher named Bobby Zimmerman as "Bob Dylan."

Kemp grew up with Dylan and was there for many of his formative musical experiences. He went his own way in adulthood, founding the Louis Kemp Seafood Company, but found himself back in the fold in the '70s when Bob asked his old friend to accompany him on his return to public life. Kemp tagged along on the 1974 Band reunion tour in an unofficial capacity and then, the following year, became a producer of the 1975–76 Rolling Thunder Revue, where he oversaw just about everything behind the scenes, from organizing the tour route to running the day-to-day activities on the road.

Dylan hired Kemp not in spite of his lack of music-biz experience, but because of it. Bob knew he could trust his childhood friend to always have his back. As Kemp puts it, "I could play as hardball as I wanted because, afterwards, I was going back to the fish business."

. . . .

You were at maybe the first ever Bob Dylan concert, of a sort: Talent Night at Herzl Camp in Minnesota, 1954. What can you tell me about that Bobby Zimmerman performance?

Talent Night is where any of the campers that wanted could exhibit whatever talent they had. Kids would dance, sing Jewish songs, all kinds of stuff. Bobby did a rock and roll exhibition that night. He covered the singers of the day who had an effect on him. Chubby Checker. Little Richard. Jerry Lee Lewis.

You just listed a couple of pianists. Was that his main instrument then?

We had a piano at Herzl Camp in the recreation room and he would go there and pound on it and sing Jerry Lee Lewis, but he also had his guitar. He carried that with him and would play that as well.

One other very early summer camp show is him playing guitar on top of a building for the entire day.

That was about three years later, in '57, our last year there. Traditionally they have a day at the camp where the campers would trade places with counselors to give the campers a chance to exhibit some responsibility. Bobby chose to be the music director of the camp. He spent the whole day on top of the roof of the activity hall. He was up there with his guitar and sang the whole time. Campers and counselors would walk by and listen to him. Our friend Larry Kegan and I spent a lot of time cheering him on and bringing him water. He was the original Fiddler on the Roof.

Then you lost touch for years, until the 1974 tour with The Band. Tell me how you got involved in that.

In '72, his mother had run into me and said, "Bobby would like to see you if you ever get to New York." She gave me his number and I called him; that's how we got back together. I went to Durango, hung out with him when he was shooting the movie [*Pat Garrett & Billy the Kid*] and writing the music, including "Knockin' on Heaven's Door," which he played for me one-on-one before it ever came out.

We were hanging out in the latter part of '73 in LA, and he said, "I'm going to do this tour. If you want to come with me, you're more than welcome." I spent the whole tour with him in '74.

Did you have an official role in '74, or were you just along as a friend?

I was strictly there as Bobby's friend. Once Bill Graham figured that out, he put a rocking chair onstage right next to Levon Helm, where I watched every concert. Best seat in the house.

In fact, the phenomenon of people lighting the lighters after the band went off stage, I might have been one of the closest people who could see it, sitting in my rocking chair prior to the encore. It was on the album cover of that tour [*Before the Flood*].

What was the backstage vibe of the '74 tour? A lot of the subsequent Rolling Thunder story is that, in '74, it was these big generic arenas and playing greatest hits and he was dissatisfied. Did you feel that at the time?

No, it was such an amazing happening. As I recall, they had so many requests for tickets, they had to run a lottery to see who got the tickets. Off the top of my head, 12 million people sent their money to buy tickets for 600,000 seats. Both he and The Band were into the music and the crowds responded amazingly. The whole thing was electrifying.

But it was a lot different than Rolling Thunder. We didn't have contact with the people on a personal basis. It was all limousines and jet airplanes. We fly into a city, go to a nice hotel, eat, go to the concert hall via limousine, come back. The contact was strictly via the music, it wasn't personal. You could tell from the next concert tour, which was Rolling Thunder, Bob wanted to do it differently.

Do you know why Bob asked you to produce Rolling Thunder? You didn't have any concert production experience.

When I was with him out on his farm outside of Minneapolis, after he had come back from cutting *Desire* in New York, he said he had this idea for a different sort of tour. He had mentioned it to one or two concert producers in New York. They all poo-pooed it. They said, "You're too big for that. You got to do a tour like you did last time with big arenas, jets, and limousines." He said, "No, no, I *did* that. I don't want to do that again. I don't want to fly around. I want to drive from city to city so I can get a taste for all these places. I want it to be like an old-fashioned carnival and musical revue. We'll have all kinds of people on the bill. Make it a real happening."

He said all that to me and asked, "What do you think?" I said, "I like it." We went back and forth and brainstormed. We came up with the idea that we won't tell anybody more than a few days ahead of time where the tour's going to be. Bobby yelled, "Yes, not even the people on the tour! They won't even know where it's going to be. It'll surprise everybody."

We were like a couple of kids in a candy store, just bouncing this stuff off each other. "We won't take out any ads! We'll just send our advance person with handbills and break the shows like that." As it turns out, that's what we did. We never spent a penny on advertising. All this is unheard of, of course.

After we went through that whole process, he said, "Okay, Louie, I want you to produce it." I said, "What? I'm a fish guy, not a music guy." He says, "No, no, no. You were on Tour '74 with me, you saw everything from behind the scenes. You can do it." Then he threw a line at me: "If you can sell fish, you can sell tickets." I laughed. He was determined to get me to do it, and I appreciated his confidence in me.

What was your role in the weeks leading up to the first date?

The first thing I did once I left Bobby's farm was I picked up the phone and called Barry Imhoff, Bill Graham's ex-partner. He and Bill were the people who did Tour '74. I got to know both of them very well on that tour. I thought, let me give Barry a call, bounce this idea off him. If he's enthusiastic, maybe I'll hire him. I knew that he had the type of experience I needed for a tour director.

I called Barry and I told him the idea. He was blown away with it. He said, "That's amazing. It's gonna be a huge success." Then he said to me, "What are you going to call this tour?" I said, "That's a good question. I'll get back to you." I called Bobby and said, "Bobby, what do you want to call this?" He paused for a few seconds, *hmm*-ed, and he said, "Let's call it the Rolling Thunder Revue."

I called Barry back and said, "Book everything under the name Rolling Thunder Revue. If they ask you who the principals are, tell them you can't tell and, if they don't like it, you'll go to another venue." He said, "How can you book the venue without telling people who the principals are?" I go, "Just use your power of persuasion."

You're telling a much more experienced concert person what was what. Was that how you saw your role, protecting Bob's vision from the music business?

Absolutely. That's why I was there and that's why I agreed to do it. It was my role to make sure it was actualized the way Bob wanted it, not the way a typical music promoter or industry person would envision it. It was my role to protect his interests, protect his vision, and protect him.

In your book [Dylan & Me], *you mention trouble getting Columbia Records to cough up some money. Where was the money going to come from if they hadn't? Was Bob going to have to fund it himself?*

Well, Bob did fund the startup of the thing until we started selling tickets. He agreed to do that, but I wanted to take some pressure off him financially. I said, "Bobby, you're fronting all the money, but Columbia's going to sell a shitload of your catalog in all these places we're going to. They should be contributing financially." He said, "I don't think they'll do it." I said, "I'm going to go see the president of Columbia."

You know, I'm a fish guy from Duluth. I didn't know who the president of

We were like a couple of kids in a candy store, just bouncing this stuff off each other. "We won't take out any ads! We'll just send our advance person with handbills and break the shows like that." We never spent a penny on advertising.

Columbia Records was. I called the gal who ran [Dylan's] office, Naomi. She laughed at me. She said, "You're not going to get any money from Columbia. I tried before. They said they don't do that sort of thing."

I said, "It's my time, I'm going to waste it. Just give me his name and number and I'll see what I can do." She gave it to me. It was Walter Yetnikoff. So I called the number. His assistant answers. I said, "This is Louie Kemp. I'm a friend of Bob Dylan, producing a new tour that he's going to be doing. I'd like to come up and see Walter about coordinating activity between Columbia and the tour." Half hour later she calls me back. "Mr. Yetnikoff would be very pleased to meet with you." "Tell him I'll be there tomorrow."

Walter was very outgoing and so excited. He'd heard that Bob had a new record that was just fabulous. "Now he's going on this great tour! It's going to be wonderful for his record sales. We're going to get way behind promoting this at every record store, all the disc jockeys, in all the markets. We're going to need the itinerary of the tour and we're going to need to have tickets for every concert that we can give to the record stores and DJs."

Then I say, " Walter, you got to know this isn't an ordinary tour." I explain to him how this tour is different. He was smiling, like, "Wow. You guys are going to really do that?" You could tell it went against the grain of everything he's used to. He wanted to be respectful, but he was amazed that someone of Bob Dylan's stature would be, using a fish phrase, swimming upstream against the current.

After I told him everything, I said, "Walter, because there's no promoters paying like an ordinary tour, everything's coming out of Bob's pocket. We need Columbia to put up some money to help with the tour." Before that, he was smiling and happy. The smile went off his face. He said, "Oh, we can't do that. If we do that for Bob, we have to do that for everybody."

Then I said, "Well, that's too bad, Walter, because if you're not going to be a partner with Bob on this, then I can't cooperate with you. I'm not going to give you an itinerary. I'm not going to give you any tickets. You can just be out there like everybody else on your own."

He just went wild. He said, "You can't do that! You can't do that to us. We're his label. We'll be a laughingstock." I said, "I can and I will. Maybe you can score some tickets on the street."

I turned and I start walking towards the door. He screams out, "Stop, come back!" I turned around, and he said, "Okay, we'll give you a hundred thousand." I said, "Good. I want a check delivered to Bob's office tomorrow morning." He says, "It'll be there." It was.

On the one hand it seems surprising that Bob hired you to do this, but I suppose someone who worked in the music industry would be worried about pissing off the head of Columbia.

That's exactly it. I had no conflicts of interest. I didn't have five or ten other clients that needed the blessings of Walter Yetnikoff and Columbia down the road. Bob knew that and I knew that, and that's why I could play a strong hand. Walter knew that, too.

I used to sell millions of pounds of salmon and herring to Japan. The Japanese were tough to deal with, so I had honed my negotiation skills with the Japanese quite successfully. I used the same skills I had developed there on Walter, and it worked. If you got what they want, they'll pay your price.

Now let's get on the road. In the Scorsese movie, one of the high points was footage of Bob and the band performing at a mahjong tournament for an audience of old ladies. Do you remember how that weird little performance happened?

We were looking for a place outside New York City to do the final rehearsals before we opened in Plymouth, Mass. I said to Barry, "Find a place up in the Cape area where we can get away from the city and not have those distractions." He comes back and says he found us this resort. He said, "They're out of season, so we can rent the whole resort at a good price. There's only one thing, though. They booked a mahjong tournament for that week we're going to be up there, and they said they can't cancel it. We'll have 90% of the resort, but the mahjong ladies will be there." It was really a good deal, so I said, "We can live with that."

In the room next to the rehearsal space, there was a room where all these older Jewish ladies were doing their mahjong. They were very animated, doing their thing. We got the idea that it might be fun if we did something with the mahjong ladies, because we had this camera crew that was always looking for non-concert type footage. We came up with the idea that we would send Allen Ginsberg and Bob in there. We got a hold of the guy who runs the resort. We said, "We wanted to have two of our people go in and entertain the ladies a little bit." "Oh. Okay." He didn't even know what was going on.

He goes in there and he says, "We have a treat for you ladies today. We've arranged for a couple entertainers to entertain." The ladies look up from their mahjong. He says, "We have a poet here who's going to read you some of his poetry. We have a singer. He's going to sing you a song or two." I can't remember what he called him. We didn't use his real name.

It's hard to tell in the footage if they even recognized him.

We didn't identify that it was Bob Dylan, so I don't think they did. Some of them got into it, and others were just polite.

What was a typical show day like for you on the road?

You get up in the morning and, every day, you'd get Chris [O'Dell]'s newsletter[37] under your door. I knew all the information, but the other people didn't. I would tell them where the concert was at, what hall, when to be downstairs, you have meals at such and such a time. That's how the people on the tour knew what was going on. Barry and I had a traveling office with the tour, three or four people.

What were you typically doing during the shows themselves?

I'd go into the crowd and take the temperature of people, get their reactions to see how everything was from the floor. I would pretend to be a random person and talk to people. I never let anybody know who I was.

Bob had a beagle puppy on the tour. What do you remember about Peggy the beagle?

She was a cutie. The problem with Peggy was she wasn't housebroken, so we had the security guys taking care of her. They had their hands full because she was shitting all over the place. They'd bring her, hand her to [Bob] every once in a while, but they pretty well took care of her. It was kind of a joke: where's Peggy going to shit next?

---

37 See my interview with O'Dell for more about the Rolling Thunder tour newsletter, which went well beyond just the basic info.

Rolling Thunder part two, I've always been a big fan of the music, but everyone I talk to says the feeling wasn't the same. Was that your sense as well in '76?

Well, we were in a totally different part of the country. We started off down in Florida and worked our way west; Alabama, Louisiana, Texas, and then north up into Kansas, Oklahoma and Colorado. It was a totally different vibe.

Bob was very serious and he was totally into it. You can see in some of those concerts. The footage from the *Hard Rain* concert in Colorado, I think is amazing footage, just amazing. I think that tour, the performances were in some cases more intense than they were relaxed. It was a different atmosphere, but the shows were great.

Last question, not related to Rolling Thunder but something you mention briefly in your book that I wanted to know more about. What can you tell me about Bob sitting in on your Louis Kemp company fish meeting around that time?

We're in New York, staying at this place on MacDougal Street. I had scheduled a meeting with Aaron Gilman, the president and owner of Vita Foods, which was the largest smoked fish and pickled herring company in the United States. We used to sell them raw material, whitefish from Lake Superior, salmon from Alaska. I said, "Bobby, I'm going over to see a client of mine today." He said, "Can I come with?"

I'd sat in on all his stuff, so he wanted to sit in on my stuff. It didn't make any difference that he was Bob Dylan to the rest of the world. This was Louie Kemp and Bobby Zimmerman, just in each other's lives like you would with any of your friends.

I said, "Sure, if you want to come." [Gilman] had an office in one of the big buildings in Manhattan. We walked in. "Louie Kemp to see Aaron Gilman." "Oh, yes, Mr. Kemp, he's expecting you."

Now, Bobby's just tailing behind me. We get into the office and I said to Aaron, "This is my friend, Bobby." "Oh, fine." We sit down, and were there for about an hour. When the meeting was over, Aaron thanked me for coming. As we left the building and were walking down the street, Bobby said, "That guy is really sharp. It'd be worth it for me to hire him just to make sure everything gets taken care of." Well, this guy you couldn't hire, this guy was a multimillionaire, but that's what Bobby got out of him. He picked up on that right away, that it would be good to have somebody like that on his team looking after his interests.

I went to a fish convention months later, and I run into Aaron. He says to me,

"Louie, why didn't you tell me who your friend was?" I said, "What do you mean?" He said, "After you left, all the young people came rushing into my office and said, 'Do you know who that was you were meeting with?' I said, 'Yeah, sure. That was Louie Kemp.' They said, 'No, the other guy was Bob Dylan!'" Aaron was like, "Bob Dylan? *That* was Bob Dylan?" He knew the name because everybody knows Bob Dylan's name, but he didn't recognize him.

Dylan and Scarlet Rivera rehearsing backstage in Plymouth, Massachusetts, October 31, 1975.
Photo by Ken Regan/Camera 5

Scarlet Rivera

No musician is more closely associated with Rolling Thunder's sound, image, and general vibe than Scarlet Rivera. It's hard to imagine the sound of *Desire* without Rivera's violin, and it's hard to imagine the look of the Rolling Thunder stage without Rivera standing to Dylan's right, wearing elaborate facepaint and some mystical outfit, staring him down.

She also boasts as good an origin story as anyone Dylan's played with: He spotted an intriguing-looking woman walking down the street carrying a violin case, pulled his car over, and voila, Rivera was in his band. We talked about that, of course, as well as life on the road with this ragtag crew.

. . . .

Dylan famously first spotted you on the street from his car. Before then, what was your career looking like?

I flew a one-way ticket to New York City. I had this belief that I was going to break into rock music and do something with the violin that wasn't in music yet. The first paying gig I did was with Ornette Coleman. He introduced me to the Revolutionary String Ensemble, which was very avant-garde jazz-ish music. I took some lessons with Leroy Jenkins, the black jazz violin player. After a couple, he told me I didn't *need* lessons. I also was playing at night with a 13-piece Cuban band to make money.

There's a Blues for Allah *sticker on your violin in the Scorsese movie. Were you in the Deadhead scene?*

No, but I liked that sticker. I related to the skeleton playing the violin, so I put it on my violin and kept it on the whole time. That was my traveling companion.

I gather your first live performance with Bob was at a Muddy Waters show.

That happened the same day that I met Bob. I was walking down 13th street off of 1st Ave. He pulled over and asked, "Can you play that thing?" We ended up in a conversation. Our conversation was short and sweet. Perhaps it knocked him off of his feet, because he said he had to hear me play.

We went to his loft in the Village. He asked me to play along with him. He just didn't give me any information like, "This is what key it's in and here's a chart." After playing for like an hour, he got up abruptly. He said, "I got to go hear a friend play in the Village. You want to come along?"

We jumped back in the car, went a few minutes away to the club The Bottom Line. His friend that was playing was Muddy Waters. I was expecting to watch the whole show from the bar. He went up and did one song with Muddy. At the end of that song, he went to the microphone and said, "Now I want to bring up my violinist."

I was just flabbergasted. I scrambled on stage and yanked the violin out of the case very quickly. It had no amplification; they just put me in front of a microphone. I was listening carefully as the song was going, and Muddy threw me a solo. The whole band turned and watched me while I was soloing, including Muddy and Bob, staring me down. Then they both smiled and that was it.

Was that part of your audition, even if you didn't know it at the time?

Yes. "Let's see how she does live. Let's see how she does throwing her in the middle of something. Let's see how she does under pressure." I pulled it off.

After you finished the Desire *sessions, do you think, that's it? At what point did you find out you were going on tour?*

Before the tour, I got a call from Bob asking me to go to Chicago with him to do a special event. That special event turned out to be the tribute to the man who signed him, John Hammond. Talk about trial by fire! This was live television in front of every major CBS executive and John Hammond. That was a huge amount of belief that I was going to pull that off. It was quite nerve-wracking. As I look closely at my face during [the video of] that tribute, I look a bit petrified.

I still don't know about a tour, but now I'm in touch with [bassist] Rob Stoner and [drummer] Howie Wyeth, because we are the group that continued from being the core band of *Desire* to the John Hammond special. It's possible one of them said something to me. I didn't get a direct call from Bob. I was informed by management, "You were chosen to be part of Rolling Thunder. Here's the tour schedule."

What do you remember from the tour rehearsals?

The band suddenly got huge and included Mick Ronson and Steven [Soles] and T Bone Burnett and Ronnie Blakley. Bette Midler stopped in at least once. It was a big herding of cats. The task went to Rob Stoner to herd the cats and be the musical director.

Was the idea that you would primarily play on the Desire *songs you had just recorded?*

I believe Bob thought I could play on anything that I fit on, including stuff that was not on *Desire*. Although *Desire* was going to be a huge feature, I would end up playing on many other things, like "Just Like a Woman."

*How did your non-*Desire *songs get chosen? Would you just play on things and then at some point someone would say, yes, she sounds good on this song?*

No, I don't think it was that loose. Bob had something to do with whether I was going to be tried out on a song. My participation was going to be very unique and special. It wasn't going to happen just willy-nilly. He was going to pick what he thought I'd sound great on, then we'd try it in rehearsal. There were a lot of band songs that were pretty obvious I probably shouldn't be on; they were too rocking and violin would get drowned out.

I was talking to Rob and his feeling was that your violin functioned in some songs like a lead guitar might. Was that how you thought about it?

It is. I did replace Eric Clapton on *Desire*. The reason that I flew to New York to break into music was not to be the string-section sweet sound that violins have been known for. The way I heard violin, I could replace a lead guitar.

How did you prepare to go on the tour?

Part of my preparation was how it was going to look. I did a lot of shopping to find the incredible outfits that I wore. I found all those hats and I found the raven feather necklace and the long velvet knit thing to the ground. I didn't envision myself face-painting; that just happened when I was on the tour. I connected with a muse that opened a different passageway for me to go into and pull out those symbolic images.

Did you feel like the Desire *songs evolved over the course of the tour?*

Some of them changed, some of them didn't. "Oh, Sister" or "Sara" didn't change. They stayed pretty true to the sound of the album. Things like "Isis" just went through the roof live. It became a fiery, fast, furious, completely different version. "One More Cup of Coffee," I loved the gypsy atmosphere and the mysticism of it, and the interplay between the violin and the harmonica.

I was rereading Sam Shepard's Rolling Thunder Logbook, *and this sentence jumped out at me: "Scarlet is practicing her fiddle scales up and down the hallways in a long black dress, black snakes painted on her cheekbones." Would you often walk around backstage or at the hotel practicing?*

Yes, I would. There was one scene in *Renaldo and Clara* of me running through the hallway because I'm late. I was off practicing my scales and then it was like, "Oh no, I got to get to the stage!"

Speaking of Renaldo and Clara, *there's another scene where it looks like you're reading Dylan's palm. Is that something you actually did or was that staged?*

I'm not a palm reader, but I am a tarot reader. But I only did it for myself. I did not hang out with other people very much on the tour.

Was there anyone that you did connect with?

I really connected with Joni Mitchell. Sometimes I sat with her on the bus. She was a huge inspiration on that tour for me, somebody that I looked up to. I was very withdrawn, but it was nice to be able to step out and connect with her. I'm still friends with her today.

Why do you think you two connected?

I was beyond shy. Even though she is this major persona, she has a shy side of herself as well. We related to each other as artists. That overcame feeling shy. This was going to be the only opportunity we'd probably ever have to be in that close quarters. It was now or never.

What were the biggest differences between the two Rolling Thunders, the fall one, and the spring one?

There was a magic to the first leg of the tour. There was a great sense of harmony amongst all the players. Although the music was as good on the second leg, I think it was a little bit less harmonious. Some element of tension wove itself in that wasn't there in the first one. Perhaps it was because Bob was going through his divorce or maybe there was some more tension with the guitar players and the band, I don't know. There was a little bit less of that magic fairydust glow on the

I replaced Eric Clapton on *Desire*. The reason I flew to New York to break into music was not to be the string-section sweet sound that violins have been known for. The way I heard violin, I could replace a lead guitar.

second one for me.

One word I see thrown around a lot about you is "mysterious." Do you think that is just a function of the fact that you kept to yourself, so people just didn't know you well?

Well, I was a mystical child. Somebody that paints snakes and swords and butterflies and spiders on their face, I would call that reason to consider them a mysterious character.

When the second tour ends, do you have much contact with Bob?

I did for years after. I went to various private things with him, including places in Minnesota, his home state. He introduced me to a childhood friend [Larry Kegan]. When I visited that friend, if Bob was not on tour, he'd come and visit both of us.

What did you think of the Scorsese film?

I was stunned with the live footage, because I had never seen myself perform from a distance on those shows. The interaction between myself and Bob was especially electric. I got a chance to see my facepaint close up as the audience would have seen it.

Did you do that painting yourself? Some of those are pretty impressive.

I did all of these by myself. I did facepaint from the very first show on. In fact, the face-painting was inspired by me originally, and then about a week Bob later started wearing whiteface. Then other people imitated that. He was impressed by the symbolism that I was bringing out. It impressed him enough to want to come up with a theme himself of the whiteface, a symbol as well.

In the semi-fictional movie, they tell a fake story about you taking Bob to a Kiss concert.

The real story is much more interesting, and happens to be true as well. I really was not happy with the insert of Kiss. My face-painting was absolutely not inspired by them.

You don't strike me as a huge Kiss fan.

No. I did not like their music at all.

Did you feel like Rolling Thunder opened doors for your career?

I got a record deal after Rolling Thunder with Warner Brothers. When I got pitched to Warner Brothers, they were highly aware of me being in that show, which is probably the only reason they signed me. I'd assume they would have liked me much better if I had sounded more like a folk singer. I was doing music not like *Desire* at all. It was more like rock fusion.

Was it frustrating that people were pigeonholing you as this Rolling Thunder sound?

They didn't pigeonhole me. I didn't let them. I was doing that music before I left for the tour. If somebody wanted, "Let's just create a whole sound around you that's a copycat of *Desire*," I didn't go that route. My journey was more like, I have to explore all kinds of music and all kinds of genres. Eventually, I came back full circle to roots music, many years later. I would say the music I'm doing now is probably closer to the sound of *Desire*. If I came out with that a year after the tour, it would've been a big deal. I wasn't ready for that then.

Ronee Blakley sings with Dylan during their first meeting at The Other End, New York City, New York, 1975.
Photo by Ken Regan/Camera 5

Ronee Blakley

In the fall of 1975, Ronee Blakley was riding high on her success acting in Robert Altman's movie *Nashville*, which had just been released a few months prior (she'd soon be nominated for an Academy Award). So she posed a double threat on the Rolling Thunder Revue: Not only a singer who'd already released a couple albums, but the only professional actor of the bunch — perfect given that Dylan was attempting to make a movie on the tour.

We talked about filming *Renaldo and Clara* on the road in between shows, duetting with Dylan, and dragging her friend Joni Mitchell along for the ride.

. . . .

How did you first get connected with Dylan?

I went down to The Other End to hear David Blue's show.[38] Paul Colby, the club owner, had shut down the club to the public, and musicians and friends were coming in. I was introduced to Bob by Bobby Neuwirth. Then we started jamming. Bob got up on stage and started playing the piano and singing. I got up on stage with him. We started singing and playing four-handed piano.

After the Other End jam, everybody went back to the Gramercy Park Hotel to party. He asked me to join the tour, and I told him I could not go. They all said, "Nobody says no to Bob Dylan!" But I had a flight to catch the next morning to Muscle Shoals to meet with my band because my second album, *Welcome*, had just come out and I was doing a tour to support the record.

[After the party,] I went back to my hotel by myself and packed up. I think I had the top floor at the Sherry-Netherland, like Elizabeth Taylor or something. Me and my little suitcase. I went out to the airport and called my producer, Jerry Wexler, who told me not to go. He said it's much more important to stay there and

---

38 A singer-songwriter who popped up at some Rolling Thunder shows and was heavily featured (playing pinball) in the *Renaldo and Clara* movie.

work with Dylan. I told him I'd promised the boys, so I got on the plane and went. I rented a car, drove from Huntsville to Muscle Shoals, went to the studio, met with the band and told them. They said, "You got to go with Dylan. That's much more important. We'll do [our tour] afterward."

I went back to my motel and called New York. Amazingly, I called information, and information gave me the number of Bob's hotel. I called the hotel and Dylan got on the phone. I said, "The boys said I can come." He said, "Stay right there. We'll fly you back." Lou Kemp called me and said, "Go back and get on a plane. There will be a ticket there for you. We'll have a limousine pick you up and bring you to the studio."

I went back to Huntsville, got back on the plane, flew back to New York, was picked up, driven to the studio, and recorded "Hurricane" that night.[39]

Tell me about that session.

It's hard to put it into words. I'd never heard it before. I was sharing the mic with Bob, we were face-to-face, nose-to-nose, off one set of lyrics. It was like seven pages of lyrics or something. When we finished one page, I would drop the page to the floor. I still have those papers.

Was it pretty quick, or were you there for hours, doing take after take?

Well, we were there for hours, but it seemed quick. I mean, a few hours *is* quick for an eight-minute song.

I know you knew Joni Mitchell who joined later, but did you know any of the initial group of people before the tour?

I knew Bobby Neuwirth and I knew David Blue. We were all part of the same scene in LA around the Troubadour and the Ash Grove. Bobby was a legendary figure even then. He put the Rolling Thunder Revue together. He's the one who asked the musicians to be in it, the main mover on that. David lived up the road from Joni Mitchell. There was lots of going to each other's shows and just hanging out, being friends, playing music.

I know David Blue wasn't in the band or onstage, but I've read that he was around a lot, and obviously he's in Renaldo and Clara *too.*

---

39 This was Dylan's second go at recording "Hurricane." Record company lawyers ruled that some lyrics in his first pass were potentially libelous, so Dylan re-did the song with new lyrics. Emmylou Harris sang on the discarded original version.

It's hard to know when everybody came and went, because there were so many people to keep track of, and you were trying to do your own portion of the show. I know David was at the motel that we stayed in on the beach because I think that's where he did his pinball stuff [in *Renaldo and Clara*]. He was in and out. I don't think he performed on the tour.

Do you know why he never performed?

The show was long. People were always having their sets cut, because the show was too long with all of us and we all kept inviting people. When I asked Neuwirth if Mitchell could come out, he said no! So I went to Dylan, and he told me yes.

Allen Ginsberg, for example, was originally part of the show, but he was cut completely. He was no longer in the show. He and Peter Orlovsky, his partner, acted as baggage handlers. We'd put our bags outside our hotel door and they would come and pick them up. It was wonderfully strange.

Speaking of how long the shows were, I was rewatching Renaldo and Clara *and you have a featured song, "New Sun Rising." How was it chosen?*

That was complicated. I was hired by Bob as the fourth headliner, billed below Ramblin' Jack Elliott and above Bobby Neuwirth. I was the last headliner signed, while still in rehearsals at SIR, before leaving town. My name was not on the flyers because those were printed before I was hired, but the press took note and published it in *Rolling Stone*.

It started out with me having I think four songs. I was introduced by Neuwirth and came on and did a duet with him. Then I did my song "Dues" and my song "Please" and my song "New Sun," which is the one you're referring to. When Mitchell came out to visit me [in New Haven, Connecticut], she came on and did "Dues" with me.

Then it was decided that Mitchell was going to do some of her own songs. When that happened, the show had to be cut to make room for her songs. They told me that, since I had invited her, that mine would be cut.

Ouch!

Yeah! *[laughs]* My part of the show was shortened to two songs then. I still did the song with Bobby [Neuwirth], "Hank Williams," and I still did "New Sun" but it started to shrink. That's the way the ball bounces.

How did you meet Joni initially?

I met her in Jamaica when I was sailing with David Crosby and Graham Nash on David's boat in 1970. She flew into Kingston to join us. We became close friends after that.

How did you get her to join the tour?

I called her and invited her to come. She did not bring a guitar. She came out just to hang out, and then she decided she wanted to be a part of the show.

I'm sure they mostly blur together, but are there any particular shows on that tour that stand out to you all these years later?

I'm fortunate that the show that "New Sun" is on in *Renaldo and Clara* was a wonderful evening for me. Some nights you sing better than others, and that was a good night for me.

I liked our shows better when they were tighter. Sometimes the audience and the journalists like the shows where more stars appear. It's more exciting for the audience when the guest stars and friends would show up, whether it was Kinky [Friedman], Rick Danko, Roberta Flack. If you ask me, sometimes the show itself was better when it just went straight through with us the way we did it.

Bob never had an off night. He was always great. I never heard him make a mistake. I would often go out and watch from the audience in the dark after the lights went down. Nobody could see me.

We were like a family in a way. Bob did not hang out with us all the time, but, for the rest of us, we would be together every day, every night, riding on the bus. We didn't know where we were going, because it was a secret. We'd only be told on the day of where we were headed.

I wanted to ask about one specific concert, the one at the prison for all the inmates. Do you remember that one?

I do. I can't say I remember everything about it, but I certainly remembered going there, and I remember Hurricane Carter, and I remember the stage. I remember Roberta Flack came out on the bus that day.

Was it a regular Rolling Thunder performance?

Yes, except of course, there's the prison there. They did have a proscenium stage, but of course it was smaller, and we didn't have the sound equipment. All that we had was the hall. It was slightly less majestic. [But] we did a show and they appreciated it and so did we. We were there for a purpose.

Prison is no joke. It's a very serious matter when you go to a prison. I've been to a few. I've performed at La Tuna Federal Prison. I've been to Chino with Joan Baez's sister Mimi Fariña and went on a show there. When you go to a prison, you feel it.

When you're performing a show at a prison, is it tough to get in? Are you having to go through metal detectors?

Not in those days that I recall. What you do have to do is come through a gate that locks. You're behind bars basically. Although at Hurricane's prison, oddly enough, there were not bars. When Hurricane was with us, he was not behind bars. We were all gathering around him.

Speaking of Hurricane, what do you remember about the following night? Did that have a different feel, this big benefit at Madison Square Garden as opposed to small New England towns?

It did. I personally didn't feel that our Madison Square Garden show was our best show, but it was exciting. Muhammad Ali was there. I had done a show with Muhammad, the original Howard Cosell *Saturday Night Live*.[40] Muhammad and I were on that together with Evel Knievel. Johnny Cash was piped in from Nashville via satellite. Muhammad and I stood together and watched Johnny. I was dressed in a long gown, and he was in a blue tuxedo shirt. He said, "That's a pretty dress" and I said, "Well, that's a pretty shirt." In Madison Square Garden, I was the only white person in his dressing room, because we'd already worked together.

Madison Square Garden was incredibly exciting, but there were odd things about it. Everybody was in town meeting with their family and friends and the show changed a little bit. I don't think it should have. Like I said earlier, I think the show was best when it was tight.

Yeah, there were probably more guests at Madison Square Garden than any other show.

Everybody was in town and wanted to get on stage. I don't remember it being that great an evening for me personally. It was big for Hurricane; it earned the money to get him a new trial. It's an historic evening and I'm glad I was part of it.

In terms of the filming side of things, you had just come off of Nashville and now you're thrown into this movie with no script. Was it a big transition to go from Nashville to Renaldo *and* Clara*?*

---

40 A short-lived ABC show with the same name as the much more famous NBC program. In fact, to avoid confusion, the NBC show was titled *NBC's Saturday Night* until after Cosell's show went off the air.

It all seemed natural. It all flowed. It all seemed to be part of one big pageant. That was my life at the time.

One memorable scene in the movie is you at a bar talking with Dylan. Do you remember anything about that?

Yes, of course. I believe that bar was connected to Mama's [Dreamaway Lounge]. She's the woman who sang with Joan Baez and had the bridal dress and all that. A friend of Arlo [Guthrie]'s. Bob and I had that scene in the bar. He was to be a hitchhiking musician. I invited him to join us and come and meet "Bob," because he wasn't supposed to *be* Bob. We shot more scenes related to that, which were great, in which Joan Baez dressed up as Bob. Bob was the musician, and I took him to introduce him to "Bob Dylan," who is Joan Baez. Bob didn't put it in the movie. He said he didn't have the nerve.

You got credited in the film as "Mrs. Dylan." Was that part of the character you were given, or was that just something added later?

It was added later. I really don't know [why], but it's a pretty big compliment.

What did you think of the Scorsese movie, the one that came out last year?

I loved it. There were many different levels to view it on, from the position of being an audience member, from the position of being a cast member, as an experimental film mixing reality and fiction. I made a feature film called *I Played it for You* with my husband at the time, Wim Wenders. I mixed fiction and reality. It's a challenge. Scorsese did a brilliant job to the point where it was confusing even to some of us who were there. That's how convincing it was. We needed somebody to explain it to us. The very first time you see it in an empty room, you're going, "Was that person there? I don't remember them being there."

I know you didn't join for the 1976 Rolling Thunder tour. What did you do instead?

I was opening the movie *Nashville* around the world. I was coming back from Yugoslavia at the airport when I found out I got nominated for an Academy Award. My brother met me at the airport and told me.

Claudia Levy

Like most Dylan fans, I knew Jacques Levy primarily for his role co-writing most of *Desire* with Dylan. I hadn't realized how involved he was with the Rolling Thunder tour until I started talking to the band members. I kept hearing, "Jacques suggested I do this" or "Jacques set it up this way."

Levy was the tour's director, and I was curious what precisely that job entailed. So, when I was running a Rolling Thunder series in my newsletter in 2020, I was thrilled to get an unexpected email from his wife Claudia. Turns out not only was she married to him up until his death in 2004, but they had met just before Rolling Thunder — introduced by their mutual friend Bob Dylan, no less — and she accompanied Jacques on the entire tour. A few months after we spoke, Dylan sold his publishing catalog and Claudia filed a lawsuit over the *Desire* songs Jacques co-wrote, but when we talked she was full of warm memories of her Rolling Thunder experience.

. . . .

Let's start at the beginning. Can you tell me how you met Jacques?

I first met Jacques in the grocery store. He tried to pick me up, and every line he gave me I thought was totally ridiculous. I don't know why I gave him my phone number. He called me a number of times, but I wasn't going to go out with him. It was a non-starter.

Soon after, I met Bob in the Dante Café, where I was working as a waitress, in late May, early June of '75. When he came in, I didn't recognize him. I said, "You look very familiar to me. Are you a dancer?" Because I had studied dance and I had been involved with a lot of dancers. He thought that was very funny. I could see he was writing and it looked to me like he was like writing poetry or something. My graduate degree was poetry, so I said, "Oh, are you a poet"? He said, "Well, I like to write."

So we talked a lot about poetry. He asked me what I did, and I said I was going to go study painting at the Brooklyn Museum school. He said, "Don't go there. You go study with this guy, and he'll change your life." And he sent me to Norman Raeben. He had been Bob's teacher[41], and then he became my teacher.

I spoke to Bob for a couple of days. It was the afternoon; there weren't a lot of people around. I guess it was the third day he was sitting there, the light was coming in in a certain way and you could see the light through his hair. I felt this thing like, "Oh my God. I've just been sitting here casually chatting with Bob Dylan!" I was so flustered. I said to him, "I know who you are." And he said to me, "Does that mean you're not going to talk to me anymore?" Which was the perfect thing to say.

So we became friendly and he invited me to come to the Other End, because he thought he would be playing there. He came in with Jacques and he reintroduced me to Jacques. And that was it.

Did you recognize Jacques from the grocery store?

Yes. He had said to me at the store, "Don't I know you from somewhere?," which I thought was a stupid line. So I said to him at the Other End, "Don't I know *you* from somewhere?" Bob told me that they'd been working together and that they were going to go out to East Hampton. I said to Bob, "You know that Jacques Levy? I really like him. Could you tell him to call me when you get back?"

They were gone for a month and then Jacques called me and said they were going to CBS to record songs and did I want to come? I said yes. When I came in, Emmylou was singing "Oh, Sister." I will never forget that. She was amazing. I went to maybe three of those recording sessions with Jacques. It became clear very quickly that something was afoot between us. So when they decided that they were going to go on tour, Jacques asked Bob if I could come along. Since I was friendly with Bob, Bob said sure.

Can you tell me more about Jacques' work as the director of the show?

Jacques was a man of the theater and they would do these bus and truck tours. He suggested that to Bob. Jacques' idea was that it was going to be a show, not a rock and roll tour. Each musician had a chance to show their stuff. Everyone that was someone had a chance to do that, including Neuwirth, who, as you probably know, is not a great singer, but he gave him a chance. It was very important for Jacques that each musician have their moment. It was them as a band performing. It wasn't just

---

41 Learning painting from Raeben helped inspire how Dylan wrote *Blood on the Tracks*, in particular Raeben's emphasis on dreamlike or nonlinear narratives.

Bob Dylan.

He staged everything. He had Bob come out and not sing right away, but walk through the band as they were performing. People would go "Oh my God, is that Bob? Is that Bob?" Then he had Bob and Joan sitting in chairs across from each other, with the lights down. Then they started to sing and of course everybody went crazy, because you would see that it's Bob and Joan.

There was a curtain too, right? Like dramatically raised to reveal them…

Yes, it was an old-fashioned rolled curtain that Jacques had. It was like theater with the lights on Bob and Joan. They would start to sing together and then that would roll up. Bob had to act those songs and of course Jacques helped him. I know that Patti Smith takes credit for it, but it was Jacques who helped him act the songs where he didn't have a guitar. Jacques coached him 'til early in the morning.

Did you know anyone else on the tour?

The only person that I knew was Jack Elliott. Jack was in love with a woman that I was friends with named Gilma Lee. She had been with Jack in Japan and she had ended their romance. I was hanging out with Gilma a lot. He would call and she would say, "I'm not talking to Jack. You answer the phone." Well, as you probably know, Ramblin' Jack is named Ramblin' Jack not because he moved around a lot. It's because he talks a lot. You talk to Ramblin' Jack and you can be easily on the phone for an hour. So we would talk. He asked me about myself. He would try to get me to persuade Gilma Lee to talk to him.

Jacques knew Allen Ginsberg from Chicago because he was friends with Abbie Hoffman and had been involved at the trial of the Chicago Seven. He and Allen got along quite well, but he didn't love it when Allen would perform with his harmonium during Rolling Thunder. He thought he had to be taken off of the stage. I mean, you couldn't help but love Allen, but it would take the temperature down of the performance. I'm in the end of *Renaldo and Clara* with Allen. I had been studying dance and I told Allen that I was going to teach him how to do the jitterbug. There's a shot me dancing after Ronee Blakley leaves. Bob gave me a credit; it was so sweet he put it in. But Allen wasn't interested in learning the jitterbug.

What was day-to-day life like on the road for you?

For the first few stops, we went around and put signs on lampposts to advertise. People would say to me, "Yeah, right. Bob Dylan isn't going to come here and play the opera house" or whatever. And I'd say, "Well, why don't you go and find out?" In the Scorsese film, you can see how surprised people were that Bob Dylan was coming into town.

The thing is, I was basically quite extraneous. I just watched everybody more than anything. I was having the time of my life. You know, these people became my friends. You're doing a show, you get to be friends like that. I can't tell you how lovely they were. I wanted them to be my family. They were, in a way.

The only person I didn't really get along with, to tell you the truth, was Neuwirth. He gave me kind of a hard time, like I was a groupie or something. I could understand in a way, because there are a lot of things that happen with musicians and girls on tour. But I certainly wasn't one of them. I was coming from a whole different world, and I didn't like the way he cast me as a character.

You said Jacques arranged and choreographed the whole thing in advance, but what work was he doing on the road? Especially after it had been rolling a week or two.

He worked all the time. I hardly saw my future husband during the tour. He would always listen to the show. From the theater, Jacques knew a lot about sound systems, so he would sit at the board with the sound people. It was always a different venue, so you have to make sure that the sound is right, you got to make sure that the lighting is right. It's like any director in the theater. He would watch the show and see how it was going and see if anything needed to be tweaked. He would make the band rehearse if he thought they were not up to snuff. On the second tour, Neuwirth even printed a T-shirt for everyone that said "The I Hate Jacques Levy Fan Club."

He wanted to keep the performances crisp. Jacques hated when you would go to a rock and roll show and you'd have to wait for them to set up. That didn't happen on Rolling Thunder. When the curtain opened on the band, it was like a theatrical opening of the show and they started playing right away.

Only once did that happen, in New Orleans on the second tour, which was really scary. They were playing an old place where they used to do cattle auctions. It was a big round wooden structure with a high ceiling and something happened with the sound system. It wasn't working right. So they were delayed, a lot. People were getting very restless. And, you know, the North is Bob's territory. The South, not as much. They weren't as patient with having to wait. They were stamping and shouting.

Dennis Hopper was there. And Dennis thought the world of himself. He decided that he was going to read a poem and calm everybody down. Jacques was

I met Dylan in the Dante Café. When he came in, I didn't recognize him. "You look familiar to me. Are you a dancer?" He thought that was very funny. I could see he was writing poetry or something. My graduate degree was poetry, so I said, "Oh, are you a poet"? He said, "Well, I like to write."

trying to dissuade him from doing that, but Dennis insisted that it was going to change the whole temperature of the place. And he did it. By the time he was done, we were really scared. The place was shaking. Really literally shaking.

Jacques didn't ruffle. He was not a man who lost his temper or raised his voice. He could figure out how to deal with whatever issues there might be. And he knew that if you had to counter any kind of restiveness, you send out Roger McGuinn. So Jacques said, "Okay, Roger, hit the beaches." And Roger went out and started playing "Eight Miles High." That did the trick.

Roger and Jacques were really great friends, because they had worked together before Jacques knew Bob. Roger came when Jacques was dying and stayed with him 'til the day that he died. It was a wonderful thing. He sang every song they ever wrote to Jacques when he was dying.

Pretty much everyone I've talked to says that the vibe was not as good on the second tour. Was that your and Jacques' experience as well?

Yes, definitely. The first part of the tour was unbelievable. It was idyllic. It was romantic. We were all having a wonderful time, and Bob was very happy. The second part of the tour, he was like a different person. I mean, he was great on stage. There was no point in time that he wasn't really good. But he wasn't a happy camper. You know, everything starts at the top, and it filters through. And that was the case on the second tour.

The first part of the tour, there were no drugs. People weren't doing coke or anything like that. The second part of the tour— I know Mick Ronson was drinking more. There was a different color to things, if you will. There was a kind of tension.

In 2019, your son Julien wrote an article for Vice taking issue with how Scorsese's documentary erased Jacques from the narrative by adding a fictional filmmaker. Can you tell me what you thought?

They invited [my son and I] to this private screening and both of us were sitting there totally freaked out. I was so upset that he didn't give Jacques credit. I was beside myself. I spoke to the woman who was the producer and the editor. I think by that time, it was set and nothing could be changed.

At the opening, I said to Scorsese, "You're a movie director. He was a theatrical director. The two of you had so much in common. And that you would not credit another director's work, I can't understand. I just can't. It really pains me that you didn't do that." And Scorsese got upset. He said, I'm really sorry. He said I should come speak to him again. Then, of course, the pandemic hit.

It just pains me no end that Scorsese took Jacques out of that film and had these people who are just really absurd in there. It totally changes the feeling of what that tour was like.

I'll tell you the real honest truth, I don't care about myself, but I would like Jacques to get proper credit. You see a play, you think of the actors in it, right? You don't think about who directed it. And that was true of Rolling Thunder. Since he was not a guy who was very involved in his ego, it didn't matter to him. But it bothers me.

Bob really liked hanging out with Jacques. They had the most amazing working relationship. You know, people said they have trouble working with Bob or whatever, but they lived together for a month way out in Bob's place on Long Island. Until Jacques died, there was always a feeling of affection between them.

In later years, Bob used to come visit here at my house. We would talk painting because I was somebody he could talk painting to. He loved my kids. I remember Bob giving Julien his harmonica at a concert when he was around five. Now my husband's grandmother played the harmonica, and Jacques had already given Julien his grandmother's harmonica. So when Bob gave Julien the harmonica, Julien turned it down. He said, "Thank you very much, but I already have one."

By that time [around '93 or '94], we had left New York and we were living up in Hamilton. We were both teaching at the university there. Bob wanted to work with Jacques again, but it was really hard. I spoke to him on the phone, and he was trying to figure out a way to get up there so they could work together again. He was very nervous that he would be in a college town and people would see him and not leave him alone. You know, Roger had done it, and Jacques thought he could find a place for Bob where he wouldn't be exposed. But it never worked out. We tried.

Too bad. I would love to hear what they came up with 20 years later.

Jacques would have loved it. He really would have loved it. It had been a very productive relationship. When Bob asked your opinion, he wants to know that you're going to give him your honest opinion. I think that's one of the reasons he liked Jacques so much, because he knew there will be no bullshit. Jacques would tell him the truth.

Chris O'Dell's Rolling Thunder ID.
Courtesy of Chris O'Dell

Chris O'Dell

George Harrison wrote "Miss O'Dell" about Chris O'Dell. Leon Russell's "Pisces Apple Lady" is about her too. She's the "woman down the hall" in Joni Mitchell's "Coyote" and is pictured on the back cover of *Exile on Main St.* But she wasn't just a muse or ingénue. She was, among other things, a tour manager — by some accounts the first woman to ever hold that role.

Among the many tours she managed was Rolling Thunder '75 (and half of '76). She pops up constantly in Larry "Ratso" Sloman's memoir about the tour, *On the Road with Bob Dylan*, as a sort of utility player. One minute she's handing out roast beef sandwiches to the band on the bus, the next she's corralling everyone on a tour of the Vanderbilt houses. In 2009, she wrote her own book too: *Miss O'Dell: My Hard Days and Long Nights with The Beatles, The Stones, Bob Dylan, Eric Clapton, and the Women They Loved.*

. . . .

What does your work look like before the Rolling Thunder tour kicks off?

One of my things was setting up all the logistics, so booking the hotels, booking all the transportation. We were doing it by bus and with motorhomes, so there weren't airline flights to set up. Because the tour was not being advertised publicly, we had to keep it really quiet. Nobody could know the different cities we were going to.

How do you book a hotel without tipping the town off?

We had to use fake names. I'd call up marketing and say, "I have a group I want to book into your hotel." I can't remember what name we used for them, but I don't think it was Rolling Thunder. The hotel didn't know. Nobody knew.

What's a typical day like when you hit the road? What are you doing day to day, city to city?

I usually had to wake up fairly early because whatever was going on that day, we had to start planning for. I didn't worry about what was happening at the gig. That wasn't my responsibility. My responsibility was just dealing with the band members and their families or whoever they decided to bring along.

If we were doing a show, it was really important to get everybody downstairs at the right time, because herding musicians is not an easy job, and then get them to the show. If it was a day we were traveling, it was about collecting luggage and getting everybody ready to get on the bus or the motorhome to leave for the next town.

I just reread the Ratso book and there's a funny scene where you're checking band members off a list to make sure they all made it, like a teacher trying to keep track of unruly children. "Mick Ronson, are you here?" Check.

Pretty much. I'd check them off as they got on the bus. Other tours I'd done, we had flights to catch or chartered planes, so everybody had to be there. This was pretty loose.

During the shows, I didn't have any job. It was a time to relax, to start thinking about the next day. I did try to go out front to watch "One More Cup of Coffee" and "Isis." Those were the two songs I liked the most. [After the show,] there was the herding back on the bus. Then I would go back and write a newsletter after we had our come-down time. The newsletter generally was telling everybody what was going to happen the next day. Although it became like *People* magazine.

You mention the newsletter in your book and it's also in Ratso's book. It had a lot more than just logistics.

It was a little gossipy, I'm afraid to say. I discovered on the very first tour I'd done to do a newsletter so that I didn't have to call everybody up and remind them of everything. I put things in like, where the nearest restaurants were going to be in the next city, just informational stuff.

With that one though, somehow we got into gossip. I signed it by another name [The Zebra Phantom], even though everybody knew I wrote it. It started talking about things that were going on behind the scenes. People would slip me notes under my hotel room with bits of information about other people. It went pretty well for a while and then it didn't work so well anymore.

What changed?

They outed me. The gossip became about me and Sam Shepard. I thought, "Okay,

Joni Mitchell and I were both involved with Sam Shepard at the same time — who by the way was married. She and I actually became friends because of it. After the tour, we kept in touch and talked a lot, discussed how crazy that was.

maybe I better be a little bit more careful."

Did you interact much with Joni Mitchell? I know she started playing "Coyote"[42] on the tour.

Yes, we did. She and I were both involved in a thing with Sam at the same time — who by the way was married. She and I actually became friends because of it. It brought us together. After the tour, we kept in touch and talked a lot, discussed how crazy that was.

Did you ever talk about the line in "Coyote" about you ["he's got another woman down the hall"]?

Oh my God, yes. We had to laugh about it because what can you do? Two women who are doing a thing with the same guy, best thing you can do is get together. When I did the second tour, Joni was on that and Sam wasn't, so we had plenty of time to talk about it.

After Madison Square Garden, did you think that was the end?

No, not at all. That was always the plan to do the East Coast and then fairly quickly the West Coast. I got a call from Barry asking me to come up and start organizing it. I said, "Not unless you give me a raise." I was making, at that time, pretty good money. It was like $500 a week or something. I asked for $700 plus per diem. He said no. I said, "Then I'm not going."

And I didn't until about halfway through the tour, I think they were in San Antonio or something. Barry called me and said, "We need you. Get on a plane and come here right now. I'll give you the money."

---

42 A song reportedly written about the Rolling Thunder love triangle between Mitchell, Shepard, and O'Dell. Mitchell debuted it on this tour.

When I first came on the tour, Bob came up and said, "I'm really glad you're here." Then, after the bus arrived in Fort Worth, he said, "Let's go have coffee." We went up to the restaurant and just sat there talking. That was the day that I learned something about him that I thought was pretty incredible. He was facing the door to the restaurant. My back was turned. We must have been there for an hour talking. At the end of the conversation, when we're getting ready to leave, I turned around and half of the tour was sitting at tables behind us. But his eyes never once left me to indicate that he saw somebody coming in.

Everyone says the vibe in '76 was worse. How did that impact your day-to-day experience on the tour?

A lot more complaints. "This doesn't work, I don't like that." You just look at people getting on the bus, and it would look different. Musically, I think everybody did the best they could, but it was the behind-the-scenes stuff that was like, "Let it be over," which is sad because everyone looked forward to the second one. How do other people describe it?

Similar, just a bad energy. People say Dylan was more distant and less involved, having marital problems, and things flow from the top. If he was grumpy, then the whole energy's not great.

That has a lot to do with it. He was pretty distant. He *is* distant, let's face it *[laughs]*, but I think he was more distant at that time. Personally, I didn't even really put together that he and Sara were having problems during the second tour, even though I knew that. He impacted the whole tour with his moods. He was in a really good space the first tour because it was fun and it was new and it was exciting.

He wasn't ducking [during the first tour]. He ducks stuff. He knows how to keep people away. He fully ignores everybody as though you aren't there, and you feel it. You know there's a barrier around him, so you don't even approach him. That was more on the second tour. The first tour, he was much more interactive. He would call me into the dressing room to find out what the gossip was. People have asked me who did I enjoy touring with the most? Definitely Bob was most fun, on the East Coast tour. People are surprised by that.

David Mansfield onstage on the Rolling Thunder Revue, 1975.
Photo by Ken Regan/Camera 5

David Mansfield

As you've surely noticed by now, I've spoken to a lot of Rolling Thunder personnel. So this chapter will be a bit of a diversion. The only reason I or anyone else cares about Rolling Thunder so much is, first and foremost, the *music*. So let's take a moment to go deep, song by song, through a representative show. I wanted to explore the music, the arrangements, and what it was like to play each song with Dylan and the band. Who better to help me out than the man who played more instruments onstage than anyone else: David Mansfield.

The baby of the tour, Mansfield was all of 19 when he signed on, yet he was, by all accounts, already one of the most talented players in the entire band. He played pedal steel, violin, mandolin, and dobro (he could play guitar too, but figured, with what bandleader Rob Stoner referred to as "an army of guitar players" already, his six-string services weren't needed).

Mansfield gave me a guided tour of every song they played one night of the tour (specifically Hartford, Connecticut on November 24, 1975, though most of these songs were played most nights). Here's David taking us through a Rolling Thunder set, song by song.

. . . .

"When I Paint My Masterpiece"

It had this real carnival atmosphere about it, the sort of raggedy-ass circus arrangement that we played. Also, the fact that Neuwirth and Dylan were singing harmony, and it was anybody's guess what note they might hit at any given point. Neither of them knows how to sing harmony, let's put it that way. Bobby [Neuwirth] is still one of my best friends and I'm saying that with all fondness.[43]

43 This interview was conducted before Neuwirth's passing on May 18, 2022.

I played mandolin on it and had a blast because I did all these chromatic lines in six. I was sort of imitating the way Garth [Hudson] played, which was a lot of fun. Compared to previous versions of that song, Bob revved the amps up on it. It had so much energy. He made this quirky, little mid-tempo song into a really exciting kinetic performance. It was lots of fun every night to be involved.

We had a director, Jacques Levy, so there were all sorts of theatrical elements, a backdrop and curtains going up and stuff. It wasn't just the usual musicians ambling on stage after all the amps had been heated up and guitars tuned. It really felt like a show. This arrangement of "Masterpiece" just made everybody feel like we were in for some special, unpredictable ride.

"It Ain't Me Babe"

I was playing pedal steel guitar and I got to take a big solo that led up to Bob's harmonica solo, which was really thrilling. I came up with this unorthodox, chime-y kind of solo that was a lot of fun to play. I was very young at the time. I probably chose many more notes to play than I would if I was older.

I played pedal steel a lot on the tour, because there was so many damn guitar players. It was like a shootout in the guitar store. It just was one way I could sonically fit into the palette. I certainly wasn't going to try and pick up a guitar. In fact, I think T Bone was playing my guitar.

"The Lonesome Death of Hattie Carroll"

This was the mid-'70s and everybody was using an effects pedal called a phase shifter. We had a lot of them. I mean, Ronson was using one and T Bone was using one. I had an early phase shifter that just had three switches on it. If you pressed all three of them, it would go very fast and it'd sound sort of like an organ. I put that effect on my pedal steel and a lot of times would play way up high, which is sort of a tremolo-y kind of sound.

That was another song where, again, it's like Dylan was like spitting out the words. It was so filled with passion and vitriol that it was very exciting every night to play it. Just to be along for the ride.

"Tonight I'll Be Staying Here with You"

"Tonight I'll Be Staying Here with You" was such a big number for us. I used to love playing on it because it was so intense. I got to do all kinds of dramatic effects on the pedal steel that were really fun.

They did that film, *I'm Not There*, a few years back. We did a concert at [the

Beacon Theatre], and I played that song with My Morning Jacket. They obviously had learned the Rolling Thunder arrangement note for note. Jim James was totally channeling the intense, angry Bob from the '76 tour. It was really fun for one night to recreate that moment from the Rolling Thunder tour. It was a freakish time warp and also reminded me how much I love playing it.

"A Hard Rain's A-Gonna Fall"

We did it as this jaunty, loping shuffle. It was very emblematic of the sound of that tour, the way we played that song. Brimming with energy and really kind of a big party. There were long stretches for Mick Ronson to just strangle his guitar.

With my age, what I knew of Dylan was big radio hits or songs that might have been iconic. I'd never heard songs like "Hattie Carroll" before. I was not a huge Dylan fan. I didn't know that much of his work. It was probably better that way, because I would have been too intimidated if I had really known what a great writer he was. I was much more intimidated about meeting and playing with Roger McGuinn, because I'm a Byrds and Beatles baby.

"Romance in Durango"

Learning to play with him on songs like "Romance in Durango," where he might just hold a note for four seconds sometimes just because he felt like it— it was really all about knowing how to stick like glue to what you're hearing and roll with any changes. After a while, we learned where the fermatas were and what the phrase lengths were and all that kind of stuff. It settled into a groove. I just remember that song being, at least in the beginning, really unpredictable.

That's one thing about not only Dylan, but playing with [Ramblin'] Jack Elliott, is that the phrase length in songs would not always be all that predictable. It was really kind of the old, strange folk music where you might drop a beat or add a beat at the end of a vocal line, depending on how you felt. It really takes some getting used to, just getting the idea out of your head that it was going to be regular four-bar or eight-bar phrases that were always going to repeat the same way every time.

"Isis"

I remember "Isis" more as a spectator than as a participant. Bob was really quite mesmerizing every night doing that song. He dramatically acted out the part as well as sung it. Every night it was electrifying. I just enjoyed being on stage to watch it.

"Dark As a Dungeon"

That was a song that I knew. I learned a lot about country music from the Nitty Gritty Dirt Band's *Will the Circle be Unbroken* record, and things like that. This great folk-country revival by people in the pop world.

"Mama, You Been on My Mind"

[On the tour's much-hyped Bob/Joan reunion:] I was aware that was a big deal. I knew that they had been the king and queen. Joan was so playful with it all. The thing when she started mimicking him, wearing white face makeup and then the same clothes he was wearing. I knew that it was culturally significant in some way.

"Never Let Me Go"

I'd never heard of the song. I knew it wasn't one of his, I could tell that much. That was a fun one to play. I think I pretty much played some straight pedal steel parts on it.

"I Shall Be Released"

Those are the kinds of songs, the more popular ones, that I knew [before the tour]. It was thrilling to play something like that. All of those duo-set songs were just fun, witnessing the playful thing Bob and Joan were doing together and how much goodwill there seemed to be. The audience knew it was a very special moment.

Joan Baez's Set

I think I had a little crush on her. Actually, I *know* I did. I was a little kid at the time. She was quite maternal towards me, and sweet. I remember one time standing at the side of the stage where she was doing her solo set. I was talking to McGuinn, saying, "I think I have a little crush on her." Roger goes, "Don't worry, David, when I was your age, I did too." On the other hand, some of the stuff that she did was so corny that I found myself uneasy around it. Like doing a song like "Please Come to Boston." It was just so white bread.

As I got older, I got to appreciate Joan even more. I had never known Joan in her early career. I had never heard her sing "Bonny Barbara Allen" or "Butcher's Boy." When she first came out, she was this kid. Many years later, I heard her voice on those early records and she was so vulnerable. Nothing like the full-throated folk diva that I met in 1975. I had a great time playing with her, even if some of the stuff rubbed me the wrong way a little bit. For me, the best song of the set with the band was "Diamonds and Rust."

I had a little crush on Joan Baez. I was a kid at the time. She was quite maternal towards me, and sweet. I was talking to Roger McGuinn about it and Roger goes, "Don't worry, David, when I was your age, I did too."

. . . .

Roger McGuinn's Set

It was a thrill. We did "Chestnut Mare" every night, which he'd co-written with Jacques, who had co-written *Desire* and was directing the show. So much of the Byrds' work really was formative for me.

After the tour, a lot of people started to try and put together some projects, continuing the spirit. One of the projects that we tried to put together was a band with Howie, Rob, Ronson, me and Roger. We were going to call it Thunderbyrd. Somehow, it never really gelled. It sounded like three songwriters being backed up by a house band. When we were playing one of Roger's songs, it was just like Roger's band, or one of Mick's songs, like his band, or one of Stoner's, like his.

Roger had to deliver a record to Columbia. We all went out to LA and made a Roger record. I think it's safe to say we all felt really proud of that record, even though it sunk without a trace. It was called *Cardiff Rose*.

"Just Like a Woman"

Those were all the kind of songs that I knew, of course. "Just Like a Woman" has been covered by so many people, besides. I knew the Richie Havens version. Our version of "Just Like a Woman" was reasonably straightforward. No radical surgery, like turning it into a mambo or something.

"Knockin' on Heaven's Door"

"Knockin' on Heaven's Door" was so thrilling. It turned it into this iconic moment. Bob gave McGuinn a verse on it, and then we have this little instrumental breakdown part. I think Roger was picking some pattern on the 12-string, and I would do this chimey thing on the pedal steel guitar. It was very moving every night.

The reason why we had the band configured the way it was, really, it was all about Neuwirth. That band was basically the band that had formed at Neuwirth's club gig that summer in the Village. Whenever Bobby would get hired for a gig, he would flip out, and he would want to be supported by a million people. When he got that gig at the Other End, I think the first advance he got, he bought his friends plane tickets like T Bone, Steven Soles and our friend Cindy Bullens. So his band would be filled with singer-songwriters.

"This Land Is Your Land"

A great, rollicking closer. We were pretty much elbow-to-elbow. It was a real updated hootenanny-style number. The only time that Allen Ginsberg was onstage. Why Bob didn't give him a slot to read a poem, I have no idea. It's also Bob touching all the areas of stuff that he owes a debt of gratitude to. Of course, one of them is Woody Guthrie. How can there be a Bob Dylan without a Woody Guthrie?

It was such a behemoth of a show. At its longest, I think the show was around four hours. It was a big letting-off-steam sing-along at the end, which is just what you need after a night like that.

Above: Luther Rix poses with the boss offstage.
Below: Two of Rix's backstage Polaroids,
of Joan Baez (left) and Dylan and
his wife Sara Dylan (right).
Courtesy of Luther Rix

Luther Rix

Scarlet Rivera always gets called "mysterious," but the most mysterious member of the first Rolling Thunder band is actually percussionist Luther Rix. He was a core member for the entire 1975 tour, but there's relatively little information out there about his role.

That's partly because, by virtue of being a percussionist playing alongside a drummer (Howie Wyeth), it's difficult on the tapes to pinpoint Rix's exact parts — except the unmistakable congas on "Hurricane," of course. It's partly because he doesn't appear in *Renaldo and Clara* except occasionally drumming in the shadowy back of the stage. And it's partly because, by his own admission, he's not much of a self-promoter.

But Rix was nice enough to answer my questions in his first substantial interview ever, both about his role on Rolling Thunder and his career overall.

. . . .

What was your career like before Rolling Thunder?

When I was a teenager, I was a cello student, and a good one. My teacher was in the Washington National Symphony, and *his* teacher was teaching at Indiana University, so I went there as a cello major. After, I think, one semester, I changed my major to percussion. I was in the Midwest for a little while, played a lot of jazz and two seasons with the Indianapolis Symphony.

Then I moved to New York and got into rock and roll. I was with a band which at the time was one of the big psychedelic bands on the East Coast, The Group Image. I played with another band that was quite big in New York for a while called Ten Wheel Drive with Genya Ravan. It's another one of those things that was a real hot prospect that didn't really pan out, but it was fun for a while.

I had some folk-rock background. Before I went on Rolling Thunder, I played with Mary Travers from Peter, Paul and Mary for quite a while. I met Rob Stoner along the way, played with him occasionally with his own thing.

As you probably know, the Rolling Thunder band began gathering momentum like a rolling snowball. Bob would go around to clubs in the Village and hear people play and stuff and ask them if they wanted to do a tour. They all started going around with him, and pretty soon they had a band.

I wasn't in that whole process of getting to go around and have a good time at the clubs. I was hired like a regular musician. They [had] picked a percussionist who didn't work out. Apparently, he was too much of a hardcore Latin percussionist and had a hard time fitting in with the folk-rock thing.

It wasn't hard for me to find things to do with congas and Latin toys because I had a lot of background in that stuff. I also played with Buzzy Linhart, another folk-rock guy who was real hot at the time. When I started with him, it was just the two of us and I played congas and other stuff.

You were first hired to play congas on "Hurricane" on the Desire *album.*

I didn't play on most of the cuts. In fact, I think that "Hurricane" may have been the only one I actually recorded on. I got to play congas on that, and they were [mixed] right up front, which pleased the heck out of me.

What do you remember about that recording session?

It was like a typical Bob Dylan session from what I came to find out, in that Bob picked a take strictly in terms of which vocal rendition he liked the best, and that was the one. It was a common attitude in the folk world. Doesn't matter if there's mistakes or whatever.

When plans for the tour got underway, what do you remember about the rehearsals?

It was pretty loose. The typical thing at rehearsals was, if Bob had a suggestion, he'd whisper something in Rob's ear, and Rob would turn around to the band and say, "Bob said—" *[laughs]* I had a hard time getting used to that. I wanted to say, "Hey man, Bob's right there!" But that was the way it was.

I noticed as time went by that all anybody had to do was walk in the room and go, "Bob says…" and everybody would go, "What? What?" If you said, "Bob says we're all going to go out and take a dump in the snow," people would head to the exits pulling their pants down.

I didn't get to hang with Bob much, but once in a while he'd come over and talk to me for a few minutes. I remember one time, as the tour was winding up, I said,

I remember as the tour was winding up, I said, "I'm really looking forward to getting back and sleeping in my own house." Dylan looked at me like, "What?" Like he was dumbfounded. Such a thing had never occurred to him. His real home was being on the road with the band.

. . . .

"I'm really looking forward to getting back and sleeping in my own house." He looked at me like, *"What?"* Like he was just dumbfounded. Such a thing had never occurred to him. I think that's who he was, and maybe still is. His real home was being on the road with the band.

What was life like on the road?

They were deliberately staying at New England resort hotels in the offseason. We'd go stay at some hotel, and there would never be anybody there. They would just open up some rooms for us and open up the kitchen. Every place we stayed, it was deserted except for the band.

One of the great parts in the Scorsese movie was that mahjong performance where it's you and Dylan right before the tour kicks off playing for a bunch of old ladies. Do you remember that?

That was a real odd event. You have to adjust your playing volume, for sure, when it's just you and a piano, but it sounds pretty good actually. The old ladies looked amused, and maybe slightly puzzled. I thought we were a hit. Ginsberg also read from one of his famous poems. Some of it was really, really obscene; it made *me* uncomfortable. I can only imagine what the old ladies were thinking.

Was that just the sort of thing that would happen on the road, these spontaneous, semi-random happenings?

I'll tell you the truth. My wife Ellen was with me on the tour. We were a little older than a lot of the people on the tour. The hysterical party atmosphere on the band bus was a little too much for us. After a while, we decided to ride on the crew bus where things were much more calm.

We weren't perhaps as social as a lot of people. Like when they went to the Indian Reservation, Ellen and I just took the day off. We talked to Joni Mitchell about it later on, and she said, "Yes, it was pretty weird. When we ate dinner, we were at the long table up at the front of the sanctuary, and the Indians were all sitting there staring at us. We looked like a painting of the Last Supper."

Was that typically your attitude towards all the filming, the extracurricular stuff, that you two would just bag it and do your own thing?

Yes. Honestly, I was glad to have some time away from the tour. So everybody else would be going out filming *Renaldo and Clara*, and I would be laying back. I wasn't in the movie and I'm not sorry about that. I'm not a fan of the movie at all. I think it's just awful.

Did you get along with Howie Wyeth? I would imagine you two had to work together pretty closely on this stuff.

Sure. We didn't discuss the music a lot because, groove-wise, it wasn't all that complicated. I let Howie keep the time. The drummer's the number one guy. I would try to find ways to complement that.

Generally, if there's another drummer, how do you find ways to fit yourself in?

Well, for one thing, Latin music is a little different from American music. You would never hear an American percussionist say, "This is this kind of an instrument, and this is what you play on this instrument." "Wait a minute. I'm going to play that *all the time?*" In Latin music, there's a large degree of truth in that. You can say, "This is the conga, and this is what the congas do." American music is not like that, but when you're playing congas, you have a tendency to go the conga route.

You knew Rob already and we've talked about Howie. Were there any other members of the band or the touring crew that you got along particularly well with?

Allen Ginsberg was a hoot. Quite a character. One time I had a headache and he asked me to tell him where the headache was. I pointed and he said, "I want to massage your eyeballs," and I said okay, because that's the kind of guy he was. You trusted him to know what he was doing and have his heart in the right place. He did it, and he knew just what to do. It really worked.

I'm sure the shows mostly blend together, but do you have any memories of particular shows or particular towns or cities along the way?

The Astrodome thing[44], that was a hoot. Ringo was there, and Dr. John, and Stevie Wonder with his band.

Did you interact with Ringo at all? I would've imagined for a drummer, that one would jump out.

I was not the guy to seek people out and say, "Hey, can I get a selfie?" Not that they had selfies in those days, but I was pretty laid-back. You might've gotten that drift.

Speaking of laid-back, I read in Sam Shepard's book that you meditated before every show.

I was into meditation at the time. When I was with Leonard Cohen, after a while I realized that meditation was making me feel good and feel satisfied, and all that great-sounding stuff, but I had also lost the ambition to do anything new. I wasn't writing, I wasn't practicing, everything seemed okay.

You were too tranquil?

Exactly right. I was all but smug. I just said, "I got to get some of my edge back. I want to be *dis*satisfied." But on the Dylan tour, I was still satisfied.

---

44 A giant Hurricane Carter benefit concert in Houston, Texas in January 1976.

Dylan and Rob Stoner go over the night's setlist in Plymouth, Massachusetts, October 31, 1975.
Photo by Ken Regan/Camera 5

Rob Stoner

Rob Stoner was Dylan's bandleader and bassist for both the 1975 and 1976 legs of the Rolling Thunder Revue, and the first leg of the 1978 World Tour. He played on *Desire* and helped put together Bob's touring bands.

When I spoke with Stoner, we touched on all that, but focused particularly on the transition from 1975 to 1976. Though only a few months separated the two Rolling Thunder tours, the music, and the vibe, couldn't have been more different. Gone was the bonhomie the last few interviews described. Dylan, in the middle of the breakup of his marriage and without the film crew inspiring spontaneous band-bonding outings, turned distant. The music changed too, from joyful gypsy folk-rock to an angry and harder-edged sound closer to punk (which you can hear on the *Hard Rain* live album).

. . . .

You met Dylan several years before Rolling Thunder. Tell me about it.

I was working with John Herald, the lead singer of the Greenbriar Boys. Bob Dylan used to be the Greenbriar Boys' opening act when he first came to New York in the early '60s.[45] The Greenbriar Boys were maybe the most successful and well-regarded of the urban bluegrass groups. I was kind of a well-known bass player and singer in Manhattan. John had hired me as one of his sidemen.

We played a gig in LA in '71 or '72, and Dylan came to the gig to see how the band he had been the opening act for was doing. In the show, John Herald would allow the individual members to each do a little solo segment. Dylan took note of this and saw that I was also a competent lead singer.

After the show, we went back to Kris Kristofferson's hotel room at the Chateau Marmont. Every so often, Dylan and I would pick up guitars, and he would try

---

45 Including at the '61 show Robert Shelton famously reviewed for *The New York Times*.

to stump me regarding obscure bluegrass tunes, since he'd seen me play with this bluegrass group. Bob, being a student of these kind of tunes, would say, "Hey, you know this one?" thinking that he could find one I didn't know. But I knew all these tunes, 'cause I loved them too. Not only did I know the [music], but I knew the words, so I could harmonize with him.

I knew at that time, this guy's auditioning [me] for some future thing. A guy of Bob Dylan's stature would not sit around and jam with an unknown person for hours unless they were checking 'em out to add to their book of potential future hires. I found out subsequently that Bob was in the habit of doing this. He knew the guys in The Band were not going to be working with him forever, and he needed to have a nice group of musicians that he could choose from. So we stayed up 'til dawn jamming on these obscure tunes.

At the conclusion of our initial meeting, Dylan had said, hey man, we're going to do something together some day. At the time, I took that as just one of those platitudes that people always say. But he actually made good on his word.

You were playing a lot around the Village in '75 when he was hanging out there conceiving of Rolling Thunder. Was there a specific moment where he came up to you and asked you the join the band?

His producer Don DeVito telephoned. I knew Don because I was already on Columbia Records as a solo artist. I had country records out. So I get this call from Dylan's producer. "Dylan wants you to come to the studio to see what's wrong with his record *[Desire]*." I was kind of surprised. It had been like four years. I hadn't heard from him.

So of course, I went right uptown to the recording studio. I brought my instrument, but I didn't play. I listened to what was going on. At the conclusion of the session, Dylan takes me aside. He said, "What would you do if this was your session?" I told him, "I would send everybody home. Come back fresh tomorrow night with a much smaller group." And he took my advice. We recorded the whole thing in one session basically. That gave him some confidence in my decision-making ability.

Then I noticed him showing up at my gigs. I had my own band I'd play around the Village in. Dylan would come to my gigs to hear me. About a month after this, he called me to go do a gig with him in Chicago on TV for which we had not rehearsed or anything. For the group that he contracted to do that, he had the same people who played on *Desire*, which was basically the drummer from my band, Howie Wyeth, and a violinist, Scarlet Rivera.

I read an interesting sentence in researching this: "After finishing recording the John Hammond TV special at 2 AM, Dylan walks around Chicago with bassist Rob Stoner before flying directly to Los Angeles."

This was the first time I'd ever gone on the road with Bob Dylan. I mean, the first *day* working with him anywhere other than in the studio. And I'm a guy who likes to stay up late and go for walks at night when there's nobody around and everything is mellow. I used to be in the service, and when I would go to a new port, I'd go walking around all night, just to check out the town.

We had done the TV show and then, later that night, everybody retired to their rooms. But I went out walking. As I'm leaving the hotel, I see Dylan sitting there in the lobby. He says, "Where are you going?" I told him, "I like to go out and take walks late at night and look at stuff." He said, "Oh, I like to do that too!" So we started walking around the town together.

We subsequently ended up doing that on the road on many occasions. It was a great way to wind down after the show, when you still have a lot of energy. We didn't talk much. We were just taking in the sights.

I'd like to fast-forward a little to '76, which I feel is a little undervalued these days. After the '75 leg wrapped, did you know there would be a round two?

No. Every time I ever finished a project with this guy, I had no idea if he'd ever call me again. He didn't put anybody on retainer, he didn't say clear your calendar for this period or that period. Very noncommittal. In fact, for the entire year of 1977, I never heard one word from him.

After the Chicago gig I was talking about a minute ago, I had no idea he was going to call me for Rolling Thunder. Nobody knew there was gonna *be* a Rolling Thunder. Apparently he had been planning it for a while, but he didn't tell anybody. I had no idea if we'd passed the audition, if he'd been satisfied with our work on the TV show or not. It was just like a payday, union-scale gig. I was quite surprised a couple months later when he called and said we're going to do this tour.

And at the end of the '75 tour, it was the same thing! It was a nice handshake, a thank you, they give you your last check, and it's like any tour when it ends. There was some vague talk about, we're going to do it again, but unless you see airline tickets and a check, it's not definite.

It seems like you could have just kept doing the '75 shows in bigger rooms the next year relatively easily — it's mostly the same people, so you'd do mostly the same thing — but the '76 sound is so different. Was that a mandate from him? Did that come through rehearsals?

The rehearsals were kind of nonexistent. We had gone down to Clearwater Florida and taken over this hotel to ostensibly rehearse, but Bob hardly ever showed up. So we didn't know what the hell he wanted! As the bandleader, I would call rehearsals anyway. We'd show up and rehearse without Bob. I'd be singing the songs in his keys as a stand-in.

Even though Bob wasn't there, we tried not to replicate what we'd already done. We knew that was totally redundant. When you hear, say, the *Hard Rain* album or anything from that time, you'll notice that the tunes have been dramatically reworked. That came from basically the rehearsals we did when Bob wasn't present. Then he'd finally show up and he'd say, oh yeah, this is a nice change of pace. Or Bob would have ideas about how to totally rework the tunes. He'd come in and show us one time and then we'd subsequently work on them.

You started singing an unheard Dylan song yourself many nights, "Catfish." How did that happen?

I'd heard Dylan do it at the *Desire* sessions. It was a laid-back folk/blues thing. But I re-envisioned it as a heavy metal song. Because I had Mick Ronson there. I'm trying to emulate Bad Company, the heavy English rock that was popular at that time. That was the only hard rock tune of the whole night.

Did you have to get Bob's sign-off to play his song?

I think I asked him. "Is it cool if I do this tune? You planning to play it?" He said, "Naaah." He didn't regard it as an important tune. It was a throwaway to him.

He knew that he had to do his hits and his recent stuff. When you look at the list of tunes [in '76], it's a few of his hits, but basically he's got a lot of reworkings of tunes from *Blood on the Tracks*. I gotta say, the versions of the *Blood on the Tracks* tunes like "Idiot Wind" and "You're a Big Girl Now," I think they were superior to the original records.

Was that something you all worked out during rehearsals? Did he say, "I want to do more Blood on the Tracks *songs this time."*

He wouldn't say that. Bob is a man of few or no words. He'll just start playing and you better follow him. He'd never tell you, "Oh we're doing a song from *Blood on the Tracks*." He'd just start playing some chords and you start following behind him. After about thirty seconds, you might recognize what song it is, but meanwhile you're just watching his hands, trying to play the right chords.

I mean, some people like to work stuff out meticulously, but Bob was not one

Everybody retired to their rooms. But I went out walking. As I'm leaving the hotel, I see Dylan. He says, "Where are you going?" I told him, "I like to go out and take walks late at night and look at stuff." He said, "Oh, I like to do that too!" So we started walking around the town together.

. . . .

of those guys. He liked to try and surprise people. Not only the band, but the audience. Sometimes he'd start a tune in an actual concert and we'd have no idea what the hell tune he was doing. All we had to do was keep it going. If it worked out, we'd do it on subsequent nights. If not, you never heard the song again.

In an interview you did in 2019, you talked about '76 a little and a quote that struck me was "the bloom was off the rose." What specifically did you mean by that?

The problem is, back then, he was not into repeating himself. The fact that he was going out to do the same thing again didn't sit with well with him. But I think more than that, [there were] marketing mistakes on the '76 tour. They had no idea what Bob's draw would be in those parts of the country. The Southeast for example. They booked him into large places which he could not fill. Many gigs were canceled for lack of ticket sales.

Since then, he's become more realistic, or his people, about his ability to sell tickets. They book him into smaller places. Back then, they were testing the waters, and they thought that his draw in the Northeast was representative of his national draw, but it was not. He was *much* more popular in the Northeast, and always has been, than he was in the hinterlands. So when we went down south, they had a rude awakening. They could not fill these joints. We did great when we played a college. But when they played the Hofheinz Pavilion [in Houston] on May 8, they had to bring Willie Nelson in as the opening act to help the draw. They weren't selling tickets. They had canceled the date before that and they canceled the date after that for lack of ticket sales.

So that's kind of discouraging. You're coming off this heady Rolling Thunder thing and suddenly…people aren't showing up. That takes the wind out of your sails.

How much did that all affect the mood of the band, backstage, the whole feel?

All of that mood stuff in the band is always set by the main guy. The train follows the locomotive. And the locomotive was dragging, discouraged. Like, I'm not selling tickets, this is *embarrassing*. You definitely pick up on that stuff. Of course, everyone's professional. You go out and give it your best shot.

When he played minor league baseball stadiums ten or fifteen years ago, that is Bob Dylan's ideal sized venue. When he comes to New York City, he does not play Madison Square Garden like Billy Joel or Elton.

Yeah, he plays the Beacon these days.

Exactly. Because eventually he wised up to the fact that his draw is more in line with that than the stadium, mega-rock act draw.

Overall, even if it wasn't quite as enjoyable, do you think musically '76 stands up to '75?

Totally! It's got its own vibe. Much more of a punk-rock vibe than the '75 stuff. It just evolved that way. It definitely wasn't just a repeat of the '75 thing. It was more rocking.

What was your feeling about '78? That seemed like a totally different vibe yet again, this big band thing that became the At Budokan *album.*

That was a horse of a different feather. Bob told me he wanted to totally reimagine everything. He wanted to hear himself in a bigger setting with a larger ensemble. We talked about this on the phone. He told me to come out to LA and start auditioning people to put together this large group. He said, I want a horn player, I want girl backup singers.

So we auditioned all these people and ended up with a 12-piece ensemble, which was the largest setting Bob Dylan has ever been heard in. It became just a touring machine that rocked for over a year. Bob finally made some money there.

Did you enjoy it as much as the earlier tours?

You know, it was a different vibe. I can't really compare them. It was a well-oiled machine. Things were a little more predicable than the Rolling Thunder stuff. I was glad to see Bob could go out and do the entire show by himself, which he hadn't been for Rolling Thunder. He had all these other acts to rely on. But he'd get out there night after night, just like Sinatra or Streisand, and do his thing. He was Mr. Entertainment.

Why did you leave after the first leg?

I'm saving that one for my book. Just what the world needs, another old rock and roll guy telling his stories!

Above: Dylan and Kinky Friedman
outside New York City's Lone Star
Cafe, 1983.
Right: Joan Baez, Dylan, Friedman
onstage in Baton Rouge, Louisiana,
1976.
Courtesy of Kinky Friedman

Kinky Friedman

Musician, raconteur, and all-around rabble-rouser Kinky Friedman replaced Ramblin' Jack Elliott on the second leg of the Rolling Thunder tour. This wasn't his first interaction with Dylan, but it might have been the first when they both were sober. Dylan apparently appreciated Kinky's brand of Southern satire, inviting Friedman to regale his audience with songs like "Asshole from El Paso" and "Ride 'Em Jewboy."

In a wonderfully rambling and discursive conversation, Friedman told me all about his (mis)adventures on the road with the Rolling Thunder Revue and beyond, from playing chess in Mexico with Dylan and Dennis Hopper to dueting with Dylan on a shambolic public-access Chabad telethon in the '90s. Plus, a few stories about his good friend (and occasional Rolling Thunder participant) Willie Nelson.

. . . .

Tell me about the first time you met Dylan.

I got instructions to meet at Roger McGuinn's house. When I came in the door, Kris Kristofferson was there. Kris was pretty wired and inspired at the time. There was an obvious groupie type with Kris. Kris said, "Kinky?" The girl and I both said, "Yes."

But the highlight of the party for me was in the next room. I walked in and Bob Dylan was absolutely hammered, on his back on the kitchen floor, singing "Ride 'Em Jewboy." That's the first time I realized he knew my song. He did a pretty serviceable version of it.

You officially joined Rolling Thunder in 1976, but I know you were around for a bit of 1975. How did you join the tour when you were just along for the ride, before you actually started performing?

Bob welcomed me aboard somewhere in New England. Connecticut, I think. That was one of those shows that he did without promotion, which is one of the most remarkable things about that tour. There was absolutely no promotion through radio or any other means. All word of mouth and karma. Almost every show was sold out using that method, which was incredible. For *whoever's* playing. If Jesus Christ was there, he'd have trouble drawing.

Bob opened the evening by saying, "Is anybody here from Texas?" In the audience, there is not a soul wearing any cowboy paraphernalia except me. Ratso leans over and said, "He's talking about you, man! He's sending this out to you." I guess you'd call that some kind of passing in the night.

After that, I would come up and hang out sometimes with the shows. Then Bob asked me if I'd be on the second swing in the South. That tour was terrific. It's like you're wrapped in a cocoon and nothing can hurt you. All you got to do is be on the same stage with somebody that's drawing seven zillion people. It's easy. You're on, and suddenly people are cheering. You tend to forget, "Wait, that's not for me."

Those shows went very well. The crowds particularly liked "Proud to be an Asshole from El Paso," "They Ain't Making Jews Like Jesus Anymore," and "Get Your Biscuits in The Oven and Your Buns in the Bed."

The funny ones cut through, huh?

That's right. That's what they wanted. Sometimes a light hand on the tiller works really well. I thought for a moment that I was going to lose my job because they were laughing so hard. I think Bob had not expected that.

It wasn't long after that that Bob bought me this Jesus coat, with spangles and all kinds of stuff on. During a thoughtless moment, I gave it away to be sold. It's probably worth a small fortune. I heard it was in the Hard Rock Cafe in Israel.

What did the coat look like?

It had a profile of Jesus on each lapel. It had rainbows and palm trees. The guy that made it, Manuel [Cuevas][46], said that the guy who originally ordered it never came back to pick it up.

That's one of my few regrets in life, not hanging onto the Bob Dylan's Jesus coat. Bob was in a little bit of a snit about it, too. He thought selling it was a big mistake. It was worth so much more both spiritually and financially than I let it go for. But then again, it's such an elaborate coat that it kind of steals the show from the artist. Only a few people have the pawn-shop balls to wear it.

---

46 A Mexican fashion designer known for flashy jackets who worked with Nudie Cohn.

Before the full '76 tour kicks off, what do you remember about that big benefit show at the Houston Astrodome?

In the dressing room, there was a rivalry going on. The only two people that seemed to be friendly that would talk to each other were Bobby Neuwirth and me. The others kept to themselves. What happened was that they had to call in Willie as a fireman to bail out Bob with the number of people in the crowd.

The Astrodome is the opposite of the earlier shows like Connecticut with no publicity and sell the place out. Now you're playing a giant stadium. It's hard to fill that thing. You might need Willie.

It would be Bob's preference to play small shows, not to have security men wrapped around him, just to do what he really does best. Bob has argued the point that the shows change terribly. You don't get anything like what you would if 25 people were watching. But the record company would never allow that.

I know that he felt that playing for huge crowds was copping out. It was so easy to do. They were just sheep. They were just following the leader. It was very different from if you got a half a house. He said that that's who the real man is, who can fucking give a great performance when half the seats are empty.

His recent shows are humorous. He plays only the piano. When he finishes the song, he turns around and away from the audience, toddles toward the back of the stage without acknowledging that anybody is in the hall but him. He looks, for all the world, like an old Jewish man on a beach, toddling along at his own pace.

Of course, being in nature a really stubborn Jewish guy, Bob chooses not to do his popular stuff. I'm the kind of guy that loves almost all of his old stuff, and he won't play that to save his soul. That's his response to the audience, all new material. If it's not, it's stuff that very few people know except super Dylan fans. What the hell? I mean, it's his show.

He's also a pretty funny guy off-stage. There's a time Bob and me and Dennis Hopper were going to Yelapa [Mexico] on vacation along with Louie Kemp, Bob's close friend. On the plane, there was no first-class or anything like that. The young girl seated next to Bob could not believe she was sitting next to Bob Dylan. She said, "I can't believe it!" Bob says, "Pinch yourself."

I did win a couple of hundred bucks for Bob at chess. In the marketplace, there was a big chess tournament. Bob put in $200 — I was wearing my Jesus coat, by the way — to back me against the Mexican champ, and I beat him.

That's a high moment in life. Bob put some action in it and was rewarded, and so was Louie. Dennis Hopper, I think, laid back. He was a wiser person in a lot of ways. A very soulful man, Dennis, but then it's hard to get more soulful than Bob. I don't know if being soulful is the point of things. Probably not. Probably a waste of time. It's like Mozart in the gutter.

We've converted our ranch into a camp for kids who have lost their parents in the military. Gold Star families. The first session was two years ago. There was this big guy working on a hot water heater. I told him I just wanted to thank him for all the help volunteering. The guy said, "I'm doing it for Jesus." I told him, "Well, I'm doing it for Moses."

I read a reference to a barbecue that the Rolling Thunder crew did at your parents' house. Was that this same place?

No, that was our home in Northwest Austin. Bob came to that thing. Boy, there were some really odd celebrity types at that, none of which leap to mind. Bob and Joni Mitchell, I'm pretty sure I caught them hosing in my little sister's bedroom. I haven't really confronted Bob about that, but there's no reason not to be doing that. Somebody ought to be hosing somebody.

Really, I'm very high on Dennis Hopper, and on Bob and Willie. These guys have been through a lot. People think it's easy to do this, but it's not. At best, it's reinventing yourself every five minutes. At worst, people get tired of you. They want you to be different than they expected. You've just got to keep going. If you lay out for a period of time that's too long, you'll never get it back.

Willie is coming up on 90 years old.

It's incredible. Willie is an ironman. Very hard to stop him.

Willie had some real sage advice. He called me one night at three o'clock in the morning. He said, "What are you doing, Kink? I said, "I'm watching *Matlock*." Willie said, "Well, turn it off, man. It's bad karma. It's a complete waste of time." He told me I should start writing again. So I followed his advice. I turned it off, and I wrote about 12 songs in a very short period of time.

I called Willie and told him that I had done that. I said, "Willie, how are you doing? I understand there's some rumors about some health issues." Willie said, "You know, it's a little up and a little down." Then he said, "By the way Kinky, what channel is *Matlock* on?"

Willie is a natural comedian. When he'll call, he speaks in a very soft voice. When he says, "Hey, Kinky," I say, "Yeah, who is this?" "It's Willie." "Who?" "It's Willie. You remember me. *[singing]* 'On the road again…'"

Bob is too. Bob is just— he's a shy little booger. Willie is not, but they both contributed incalculably to the music and the memories of lots of people. Bob has always been very kind to me.

One other thing I wanted to ask you about was this video of you two playing this TV telethon for Chabad in 1991. You're singing "Sold American" and Bob's wearing these giant sunglasses, a blue windbreaker, and the traditional tassels [tzitzit], and is accompanying you, sort of, on guitar.

They asked us to do it. Bob had his yarmulke on his head. He was insisting on doing "Proud to be an Asshole from El Paso." Which probably would've had a bigger bang for the buck, I think. But we did "Sold American."

Why didn't you do "Asshole"? Your choice or the TV network's?

It was my worry that it would in some way not be cool for me and Bob to do. It would've worked out; Bob was right on that one: "Go on and do the damn thing." But I didn't. It was just like the Jesus coat. Once you've made a spiritual error, it's very hard to get it back.

Was the plan at one point for Bob to sing? There's a microphone set up in front of him, but he never goes near it. It's mostly random guitar licks.

If you notice, his performance was spotty, but it was funny as hell, actually. Most of the crowd was fervent Orthodox Jews, so they wouldn't have known if Bob were playing the ukulele. I wish we had done "They Ain't Making Jews Like Jesus Anymore" and a few like that, that may have gotten through to the audience a little more.

What do you think of Bob as a guitar player?

He hasn't made the strides that Willie has. Willie has really developed. Both of them, though, have got really fine musicians. Me, not being a fine musician, I know one when I see one. Willie says, "Kinky *thinks* he's a guitar player, but he's not really a guitar player."

At their ages, for both of them to do this is really great. I'm 77 years old, though I read at the 79-year-old level. These guys, I look up to them for wisdom and advice. I got a lot out of being around both of them. I hope to see them soon down the highway.

Dylan and the Rolling Thunder Revue perform in Gainesville, Florida, 1976.
Gary Burke is playing the congas on the right side.
Photo by Frank Beacham

Gary Burke

When Luther Rix left the Rolling Thunder percussionist stool at the end of 1975, Gary Burke took his seat. He played with Dylan and the band dubbed "Guam" for the full '76 tour, including the *Hard Rain* taping.

While many of the musicians who toured during both Rolling Thunder legs complain that the vibe wasn't the same on the second go-round, it was all Burke knew. He was the only full-time bandmember who had not been on the first leg of the tour the previous fall.

He told me about trying to find his way into this established group as the new guy; visiting Bobby Charles' beer fridge; and where the *Hard Rain* headscarves came from.

. . . .

How did you first get involved in Rolling Thunder and the Dylan universe?

In the first half of the tour, the two drummers were Luther and Howie Wyeth. It was a very spontaneous happening, and when it was over, everybody thought it was over. The powers that be decided to start it up again. I have a friend who was an accountant with this tour, and he said they decided to do the second tour to try to make some of the money back that they lost on the first one. The first one, it was really quirky, going to places that were culturally stimulating, but maybe not *box office* stimulating.

Tiny theatres in Lowell, Massachusetts or whatever.

Yeah. It must have been tremendously exciting for the people that were able to experience it in that fashion, but that's a lot of people to haul around.

Anyway, at the start of the '76 tour, Luther's drum chair was open. He went to Europe with Leonard Cohen.

[Before Bob hired me], I had been in New York a year, maybe even less. I was doing a lot of work in the downtown scene with Steve Reich, the real minimalist school. I went to see the Gil Evans Orchestra at the Village Gate, and the percussionist was Sue Evans[47], who played, among other things, timpani. The show blew me away.

About two weeks later, I had my own gig at a club in New York called Trude Heller's. It was after hours, and I was sitting on the steps outside the club. Sue Evans must have been coming back from a gig of her own, and she was walking down the street. As she got near me, I called out to her, "Aren't you Sue? I saw you play with Gil two weeks ago."

She sat down, and we're chatting. She didn't mention anything about the Rolling Thunder tour at that point, but, evidently, she had been asked to do it. She would have been fabulous, but she turned it down. She was a real Manhattan girl; she just basically didn't want to go out on the road, I think.

Not long after, I got a call from Rob Stoner. He said, "I'd like to talk to you about maybe going out with Rolling Thunder, [but first I want to] come and play with you a few minutes." I really wasn't aware of what he was asking me to do, so I was very lackadaisical in my response. I shared a loft with some people down on the Lower East Side. I said, "I got lots of room here, and my kit is set up. Why don't you come over, and we'll do some playing?"

Did you know Rob at this point, or had Sue given him your number?

I do not know him from Adam. He said, "Four or five people recommended you." One of them was Sue Evans. I said, "I know Sue a little bit. I mean, I just met her, but I don't even know who these other people are." He came over; we played for like 10 minutes. He said, "The gig is yours if you want it."

I found it really strange that these people who I did not know recommended me for the gig. I have always looked at it as divine intervention, because I really had nothing to do with it. It was just like somebody picked me off the street to do this, which I guess is in keeping with the Rolling Thunder ethos. I was one more lost soul picked up off the street and brought into the circus.

What's the next step? Rob says you have the gig, he leaves your place. Are there rehearsals?

It stays strange. I was invited to this party of the Rolling Thunder band and crew before going south to Florida. It was sort of like a going-away party. For me, a getting-to-know-you party.

---

47 An accomplished jazz percussionist who played with, in addition to Gil Evans (no relation), Judy Collins, George Benson, and an array of orchestras.

They started passing out contracts for everybody to sign, and I noticed that I wasn't getting one. I went to the promoter, Barry Imhoff, and said, "What's the deal?" He made a call, then he hands the phone to me. I had no idea who I was talking to at first. Again, in keeping with the MO of the whole thing.

It was Bobby Neuwirth. He said, "What's your problem?" I said, "Everybody is getting a contract, and I don't have a contract. If I don't have a contract, I'm not going south. It's that simple." I'm really going Hollywood on him a little bit. I can hear him turn to somebody, and then I recognize the voice. He's talking to Dylan. I didn't know I was on speakerphone, and Dylan was sitting right next to him. That's a real old-school music ploy. Neuwirth could be a real wise ass.

He comes back on with me: "I'll tell you what. We have one question for you to answer." I said, "What is it?" "Do you like music?" I said to him, "No..." and I let it hang there for a second. "...I *love* music." I could hear some muted laughing. He says, "You got the gig, and I promise, you'll have a contract." So I went south for rehearsals.

Did you ever find out why you didn't have a contract in the first place? Easier to fire the new guy if he doesn't work out?

Yeah, that makes a lot of sense. If I were on the other end, I'd keep it that way too. I never really thought about it too much, except for the fact that I knew I was giving up a lot of work to go do this.

Sometimes when you're blindly naive about things, you're much better off. The way I dealt with it at that time has not any semblance of how I would deal with it now. Frankly, I think that's why everything worked out. People recognized a certain bravado. I just didn't know any better.

I flew down to the Belleview hotel in Florida for rehearsals. It looked exactly how it sounds, almost that place in that Peter Sellers movie where he was Chauncey [1979's *Being There*]. A real old school, sprawling wooden hotel with ballrooms and all this kind of stuff.

There was one other issue that I was nervous about. I play left-handed, and I set up my kit left-handed. They were going to use me not just playing percussion alongside Howie on drums, but also to give Howie a breather because the show was coming in at around three to four hours. No one drummer could last that long.

You were worried that his kit would be set up for a right-handed player?

Hell yes. Switching the kit to left-handed would interrupt the flow of the show. So I went into this big elaborate thing of, "Why don't we just get two sets of drums? That way it will take care of any set change on stage." I persuaded them to put another set of drums on stage, which means, of course, renting another set of drums for an entire tour.

I thought I was pulling one over on them. I'm saving my butt here by convincing them to get another set of drums for the betterment of the show. Then I walk into where we're rehearsing. I look, and indeed, there are two sets of drums there. They're both left-handed!

Howie's a lefty too, huh?

Howie was a lefty. I had no idea.

What we ended up doing, which was great, was we did a lot of stuff with double drums. Plus, I had a complete percussion setup, including vibes, congas, orchestra bells, things like this, in addition to the drum set. And, of course, Howie would play piano. He really had an almost Art Tatum stride piano type of thing or Jelly Roll Morton. They even carried an upright piano for him to play, as opposed to a grand. It was a perfect sort of throwback, old school visual.

Do you remember any particular songs that you took over drums for where he was on piano?

There's a pretty funny story about that. Roger McGuinn was of course there. We were doing "Eight Miles High." Roger got sick of doing it, so in a soundcheck he said, "Let's do 'Turn, Turn, Turn.'" Howie wanted to play piano on that, so I went up on drums. We just ran the tune down from the top one time. Of course, everybody played it perfectly; it's in everybody's DNA. At the end of it, Roger turns around and says, "Boy, I forgot how big a hit that was."

The way the show was set up, the revue — not the principals, but the musicians like Mick Ronson, T Bone Burnett, David Mansfield, Steven Soles — we would open the show. Everybody had a tune to do. I would more or less handle the drums on the revue part of the show. Then Kinky would come out, and I would do drums for him and Howie would play piano for all of his tunes. When Dylan would come on, Howie would come over and play drums, and I would move to percussion.

The musicians in the revue became the house band for everybody who came on stage. Allen Ginsberg was there. When we were in Texas, Gary Busey was there. Joni Mitchell was there. People like Dennis Hopper would show up and recite something. Lawrence Ferlinghetti came out at one show and recited the Lord's Prayer.

They were unintroduced, by the way. They just would walk out on the stage. You

**"We have one question for you to answer."
"What is it?" "Do you like music?" I said to him, "No..."
and let it hang there for a second. "...I love music."
I could hear some muted laughing. He says, "You got the gig."**

had to figure it out for yourself. It had the flavor of Mad Dogs and Englishmen[48], this large caravan of people. Because for every person on stage, there had to be ten people off stage. There was tour doctors and tour astrologists.

What is the tour astrologist doing?

They would read the stars and stuff. I mean, I doubt very much they were paid, but they just managed to be part of the whole thing. They would be there all the time.

I just had a feeling that, boy, you're not really going to see this again. This is a last hurrah for this big multi-musical genre happening. Bill Graham would mix up programs, like having The Allman Brothers with Miles Davis on the bill. It would be hard to pull that off these days because there's so much categorizing and labeling. The music business isn't as naive as it was then.

The shows were so long, if you had to go to the bathroom or something, you'd just leave the stage. You'd go backstage and take care of stuff, then come back. No one would miss you.

I remember one time going back there, and I saw one of the guys handling the promotion on the phone. I asked what he was doing, and he said he's booking the next gig. It was that seat of the pants. You can do this with Dylan. You can call up someplace and say, "Would you like to have Bob Dylan tomorrow night in your club?" Who's going to say no?

It led to this barnstorming excitement, because you never knew where you were going to be. The next day you could be playing a rodeo arena.

Is that a real example, a rodeo arena?

There were a number of them. Not your usual college crowds. These were rowdy and aggressive crowds replete with rebel yells and fights. Very loud. Occasionally

48 An iconic '70s Joe Cocker and Leon Russell tour featuring a giant cast of characters.

bloody.

To backtrack, we skipped over what happens in Florida. You hang out for a few days, the rehearsals start. What's your first actual meeting with Dylan?

He didn't show up for a while. He was a real nighthawk. We soon learned, it's not really worth it to come at 3:00 in the afternoon for a rehearsal when Bob isn't going to be there until midnight.

We were in this sort of camp mentality, almost like Parris Island[49]. We would all go to lunch together and would move en masse to different things. The place was not near anything, so you just stayed put.

One day we were told, instead of going to where we're rehearsing, go to this old-school ballroom they had. We were going to shoot a show for Burt Sugarman, the man behind *Midnight Special*. Bob was the MC; he would introduce different segments of the show. He was obviously very uncomfortable doing that. I remember one time he put his glasses on to read the lyrics because there were so many verses he couldn't remember them all. Someone handed him a book of Bob Dylan songs to read the verses from, which I thought was really funny.

Anyway, it wasn't exactly his cup of tea. It felt a little showbiz-y. The word came back the next day that he canned it. I heard he bought it back from Burt Sugarman for a million bucks, never to be shown. At the end of the tour in Fort Collins, we did the *Hard Rain* special. I guess that was to replace that show.

When Bob does finally show up at midnight in the rehearsals, what is the energy?

It was very, very loose. It was more jamming than rehearsing. You got to understand that, except for myself, everybody knew the material. It had this taken-for-granted atmosphere to it that; we already know this stuff and we're just loosening up here playing.

Well, there are a fair number of songs that you all played that he didn't play in the fall. "Maggie's Farm," "I Threw It All Away," "Idiot Wind." Even "Lay Lady Lay," with the new lyrics.

Yeah, the "Lay Lady Lay" thing really upset a lot of people. Instead of a romantic song of let's get together, it was more like a demand.[50]

The whole thing, when everything was hitting on all cylinders, had this edgy punk energy to it. It was a hard rock thing, but it never lost its rootsy feel. "Maggie's

---

49 Marine Corps training facility.
50 Sample lyric: "Forget this dance, let's go upstairs / Let's take a chance, who really cares?"

Farm" was like that too, but I wasn't aware it was new.

Maybe everybody else got a heads up, "We're going to do this coming up. Why don't you listen to it before you get to Florida?" I presumed the other musicians were just going over material that they already knew, because they certainly played that way. I was just trying to get up to speed.

How much interaction as the tour goes on were you having with Dylan himself?

Not a lot. In fact, nobody did to a large degree. He was living a little bit separate from everybody. There was security around him.

For instance, when we would leave a place on the tour, security would go into the room where he was staying and take everything out. Every piece of garbage, everything. They would put it in bags and take it with them so that nobody went in and tried to find the lost verse to "Tangled Up in Blue" or something like that.

That's a tough way to live.

It is. You got the feeling that he was rubbed raw by it all.

He was there with us. Say we were all eating at a restaurant, he would be there, but you just had the feeling that he didn't want to be bothered. People would respect that. Stoner would talk to him a little bit, but I got the feeling that things had changed from the fall. You're trading stories with people, and they would tell you about what they did on the first tour. I'm thinking to myself, that's a lot different than what we're going through.

By that spring, his personal life was not doing so good. His marriage was falling apart.

It's funny you should mention that. When we did play Colorado, where I was set up, I would turn around and there was Sara, his wife, who showed up the night before. She's sitting there in a chair, very regal, with her sons around her. She had on this tiara and just sat there very stone-faced the whole show. I thought, what is going on? So I asked Bob, and he said, "She's just reminding everybody who the matriarch is." I guess even Bob! Yeah, things were a little rough at that point.

Speaking of headgear and Hard Rain, *you all are wearing headscarves or whatever you call them. What's the story there?*

Bob's headgear for the tour had been that white durag he wore. It was like a prison durag with a sort of Arab twist to it.

By the end of the tour, there were a number of wives and girlfriends around. These women cajoled us into wearing them, a goof on Bob and his headgear. Much to our chagrin, at first, but everybody got into it after a while. That concert was [the day before] Bob's birthday. It was a combination of party hats and giving it to the boss a little bit.

And did the boss react when he noticed you all wearing those?

Not an iota. Nothing. It was like, "Nice try, but that's not going to get me."

What else do you remember from that Hard Rain *show? True to the name, I gather it was fairly wet and cold.*

The show is so long, we went through a couple of different climate changes. At one point, it was snowing. I remember when the revue was on stage early on, I looked over and Ronson was playing guitar wearing gloves. He had cut the fingertips off.

I remember looking out, and people were dropping. Usually, it's from heat exhaustion, but in this, it was exposure. I remember one time looking up and they're carrying this guy in a stretcher.

I will tell you one story about "Tangled Up in Blue" from that show. We were staying at the Stanley Hotel, another old historic hotel about a half hour into the woods from Boulder.

Stephen King based The Shining *off of it.*

Yes, exactly. At the last minute we heard, "Bob wants to rehearse. Get down to the ballroom." They were scrambling to get gear set up.

Howie didn't make it. He was under the weather, and they were concerned that I would have to do the whole show on drums, which I hadn't done before. I knew the material, but from the perspective of playing percussion. Most of it, Howie was playing drums.

I remember all we did was we played "Tangled Up in Blue" for about two hours! Because there's a lot of stops in it and things like that; it's an involved arrangement. He wanted us to stop here, start here, stop here. Then he gets on stage the next day and he takes it off in a whole new direction. It was like we didn't even spend any time on it the night before. I'm just hanging on for my life. Eventually, Howie was feeling better, and he showed up about halfway through the Dylan portion of the set.

Dylan lived more in the present than most musicians I know. The most common question I get is, "What's it like to play with Dylan?" I say, "Oh, it was the greatest jazz gig I ever played." People look at me like I am crazy. I don't mean stylistically it was like a jazz gig, but in terms of the mindset. It was very spontaneous. You never know where he's going to go. You weren't given directions ahead of time.

If you look at the footage, you'll see that everybody is just laser-locked on him when they're playing. He would expect you to go there and be with him. We did work off a set list, but they were more suggestions than locked in. Instead of the Ten Commandments, it was the Ten Suggestions.

After the Rolling Thunder tour, I went out on tour with Scarlet Rivera. One day we had a day off in Philly and I said, "Look, they're showing this movie called *The Last Waltz*." We went and saw it. Dylan comes out and stops a song at the end. You can see Levon's eyes get big as saucers. Because he doesn't know where they're going. Nobody knew what the next song was going to be.

When I saw Levon's face, I jumped up. I pointed at the screen and I said, "That's it! Look, he's doing it to them too."

A few years ago, I did a record with Larry Campbell. We got to talking, and he just reaffirmed that nothing really has changed. Larry said that he went through the exact same thing. You got to love that, if you can keep that going for your whole career, that sense of spontaneity and electricity, living out there on the ledge.

Speaking of people who are out there, what was it like working with Kinky Friedman?

I love Kinky. Now we're going to go back to day one. When I went to Florida for the first time and got off the plane, one of the roadies picked me up. I check in to my room, and then nothing. I didn't see the people from that New York party there. I don't know anybody. The place was so big, just a mammoth place you could get lost in.

Finally I get a call from Kinky. I said, "Hi, Kinky, what can I do for you?" He says, "Come on over to my room. I want to meet you." It was like he was being a big brother.

He's a real character, but he's a very loving guy, believe it or not. He took me under his wing and talked about learning the ropes of the tour. Don't let things bug you, just float on top. Stay in the current and you'll be okay. He really made me feel welcome. Oddly enough, the other guy who was like that in his own way was Bobby Neuwirth, too.

Oh, really? He seems like a divisive figure.

Bobby could dress you down in public like nobody, but the one thing about him is he didn't bullshit. He gave it to you straight. If you could handle it, great. If you couldn't handle it, then go back home. He would be that way with me, but you would know that he was telling the truth. So if he told you, "Hoss, you did a good job last night," you knew you did. He wasn't shining you up or blowing smoke.

I got to depend on him a lot, in terms of being a weathervane of what's going on, what to do, what not to do. If we're on a plane going to the next location, I would sit near him, and he would expound to me his philosophies on music. He was maybe a generation ahead of me in terms of the music business. He had a perspective on things that was great to hear.

After the tour was over, we did some gigs together. I remember I did a gig with him at the Bitter End where he decided to stop drinking. He was sweating profusely, he was shaking, really going through the DTs. He wasn't very good that night, but it was very good what he was doing. Two guys walked in from Nashville who were icons and saw him in that condition. He could've let it break him, because he definitely did get more nervous knowing that they were there. But then he gathered himself up and just muscled on. We got through it. I was glad to have been there and shared that with him. He stayed sober from that night on.

Someone else mentioned you all hanging out with Bobby Charles.[51] Does that ring a bell?

Oh yes. One of the sweetest people you would ever want to meet. We played this place called The Warehouse in New Orleans. The word came down that Bobby invited us out to his place. He was living out in the bayou somewhere.

Before we left, we went to Sea-Saint, Allen Toussaint's studio. We were going to record something. We sat down to play, and then it just didn't happen.

The whole Rolling Thunder Revue was going to record something there?

Yeah, just spontaneously do some recording. I remember sitting down at the drums. It was the highest, hardest snare drum I had ever played. I'm thinking, "This is how the drummer for The Meters, Ziggy Modeliste, gets his sound." It was sort of like putting on somebody else's clothes.

Was Toussaint himself there?

I don't remember him being there. We played for a while, and then that was killed. I think we left from the studio to go to Bobby Charles's.

It really, truly was in the bayou. He lived in this little wooden cabin in this swamp. I walk in the screen door, and there are two huge refrigerators side by side. He said, "You want a beer?" He opened up one refrigerator and it's got nothing but beer kegs in it. And he opened up the other refrigerator and it's got nothing but

---

51 Louisiana swamp-rock musician, most widely known for his composition "See You Later, Alligator" but beloved as a cult hero among Southern music aficionados.

mugs chilling.

He played these beautiful songs for us with his acoustic guitar, and piano too. It was stuff he was writing at the time. I remember this one tune in particular he played, I think it was called "Chain of Hearts." It was unfinished at the time. I've looked up his discography since then. I've never seen it come up, but it was just a gorgeous song.

There was a party outside. There were a lot of local characters, and this unusual-looking stew. I said, "Well, what is this?" This guy with a Bowie knife in his belt, somebody you don't want to mess with in a dark alley, says "Oh, it's alligator. I caught this last night." "At night?" "Yeah, that's the time to get them. You bring a flashlight with you, and their eyes glow so you can see where they are. You sneak up to the side of them, reach under and grab one leg, and flip them on the back real quick, and then just slit the throat."

Any other extracurricular adventures with the gang?

It was unusual that we went to Bobby's. I can't remember doing that at all with anybody else.

When we were at the University of Florida, at the Orange Bowl facility, I believe that was the night that Steve Martin joined us. For no other reason than he could. He went up and introduced the whole show. People went nuts when they saw him. I think he actually did the thing with the arrow through his head. He hung out with us for a couple days.

A couple days? He was on the road with you all?

That's the way it was with people, they would show up. It's like you invited them over, you know what I mean? It wasn't just a photo op.

Do you remember anyone else who showed up? You've mentioned Steve Martin, Dennis Hopper, Ferlinghetti.

Joni Mitchell showed up. I mean, she was a performer, but she wasn't scheduled to be there.

What do you remember about her?

I thought, this is going to be interesting, because her music is much more sophisticated. Poetically, she is in a league with Dylan, but terms of harmonically and the chord structure. I got to hand it, the revue pulled it off. It was just like they just turned another switch and did this.

And Willie Nelson was with you all in Texas.

He showed up to do a double bill. It was like two French foreign legions showing up at this venue. We came with our semis and RVs, and he came with his semis and RVs. That show easily hit the six-hour mark.

Before we went on stage, Willie came into our dressing room. Bob was there, and Willie introduced himself. Bob said, "What are you going to do tonight? Why don't you do that thing about the stranger, the guy with the red hair." I'm thinking, "Does he mean 'Red Headed Stranger'?"

There had to be 20-some-odd musicians on stage that night. Two bass players, three drum kits, a fiddler or two, God knows how many guitars. Somebody had a great idea, "Why don't we do 'Will the Circle Be Unbroken'?" As soon as they hit the first chord, it was like complete white noise.

At the end, someone went up to the mic, and said something like, "This has been a real long show, we appreciate you guys hanging out." This one guy who was totally wasted, sprawled over some seats, just yelled, "Play all night long!"

What do you remember about the finale in Salt Lake City?

Not too much about the show, but afterwards there was a meeting. I don't remember Bob being there, but Bobby Neuwirth was like the major domo. He said, "Bob wants to know how you feel. Do you want to keep this thing going, or is this the last night?"

I remember T Bone saying, "I'm going home. I'm going to throw some paint around." I guess he had an art thing going on the side. They got into this whole thing.

It was really a downer meeting. I think people were just tired at that point. It wasn't exactly ending on an uplifting note. You can only keep that energy up for so long. That's what I remember about Salt Lake: It indeed was the finale, but it wasn't necessarily supposed to be.

Were you in that camp of "call it a day"?

I was ready to go for four more years! These guys, they had already been through the wringer once before I got there. They were just burnt out. I remember going back to my room thinking, "This didn't feel good." That's how Rolling Thunder ended: With a whimper, instead of a bang.

Dylan horsing around onstage with Billy Cross in Oakland, California, November 1978.
Photo by Chris Bradford

Billy Cross

1978 was, to that point, the busiest touring year of Bob Dylan's career. By far. *At Budokan* remains the tour's best-known document, but that live album was recorded at some of the year's very first shows. The tour continued for a total of 114 concerts in 10 different countries with one of the biggest bands of Bob's career.

Billy Cross had a busy career before Dylan called on his lead guitar services, playing with Sha Na Na and Jobriath as well as a variety of Broadway musicals, including *Hair,* before moving to Denmark in the '70s, where he was still living when we spoke. He'd also played with Link Wray and Robert Gordon alongside Dylan's Rolling Thunder bassist Rob Stoner, who would lead him to Dylan for that busy 1978 run.

. . . .

How did you get involved in the tour and in Bob Dylan's musical world?

I went to Columbia University with Robbie Stoner. We had this band called Topaz, which was an embarrassment, but nonetheless it existed. When I was back in Copenhagen, Robbie had been playing with Bob on the Rolling Thunder tour, and he had played on the *Desire* record. Then, when Topaz broke up, Bob had contacted Rob again [in late 1977] and said, "Come out to LA, I'm putting a new band together, I'm going to do another tour." They had auditioned about 34 guitar players as far as I know, and Bob simply wasn't satisfied. I don't know why.

Finally, Robbie said, "Well, I got this friend who lives in Copenhagen. It's far away but he's a good player." They called me up, Bob and Rob. They said, "I'm going to give you an airplane ticket and you're going to come over and you're going to audition." And I did.

Arthur Rosato was the main person in the road crew, in charge of putting everything together. I came into the rehearsal place down in Santa Monica and he took me aside and he said, "Look, all the guitar players who have auditioned have been intimidated. What you've got to do is you've got to play loud." I just turned up and played loud.

After the audition Bob walked over to me and said, "What are you doing the next year?" I said, "Well, I hope I'm going to be playing with you." He said, "Yes," and that was that.

Were you surprised at the size and scale of the band? At the time, he wasn't thought of as having these giant bands with backing singers and stuff.

When you're presented with a reality like that, you just accept it for what it is, like kids who accept their parents even if they're weird.

Was it a challenge to make your mark in that environment musically when there's so much else happening?

Well, I wasn't really interested in making my mark. I was interested in doing whatever I could to make the music sound right. I didn't feel that I needed to manifest myself stylistically or personally. I was just so happy to be there.

What's the next thing that happens?

We rehearsed like crazy, just day after day after day after day, in an old gun factory on Ocean Avenue. We would eat really good lunches, great soups, and hang out in this place in Santa Monica.

We still had to audition some people. We had to get a drummer. The keyboards and drums and some of the girls had not been sorted out yet. We went through a bunch of different drummers to play with.

One thing I'm always curious about, and especially with this wild tour, is where the arrangements come from. You got a reggae "Don't Think Twice," that funky "Maggie's Farm," "Love Minus Zero" driven by a flute. Is Bob dictating the arrangements, or were you just jamming until something comes out?

They basically all came from Bob. Bob had a distinct idea on every single song what he wanted to do. Each song had a direction, each song had a genre identity, each song had a presentation that was his.

I came up with some small details, like the intro of "Mr. Tambourine Man." He said to me, "Come up with a guitar intro." I thought, "Oh, Jesus Christ. What am I going to do?" I came up with that. That's about the only thing that I remember that I did that was recognizably significant.

Let's go to Japan. That's probably the most famous part of the tour, because they made a live album out of it. What do you remember from that run?

Musically, we were pretty green. I think we all would've preferred to have recorded shows later in the tour. Bands tend to get better as they play, and we definitely got better.

The shows at the Budokan were interesting because they had guards who stood in the aisles and prevented people from standing up in their seats or getting overly excited. It was a strange feeling. I played in the Soviet Union and there was a similar feeling there. The authorities didn't want the people to emotionally react too strongly, and have that emotion carried into physical behavior. There was a feeling of repression, but it wasn't bad. In America, people will drink as much as they can, and smoke as much as they can, let it all hang out. That was very much not what was happening in Japan.

Is that difficult as a musician? You want a back and forth with the audience, and not really getting it.

Audience communication with the band, it's fun to a certain degree, [but] when I'm on stage playing, I'm really thinking about the music. What's happening, how can I make it sound better, am I doing a good job, is the groove right, is Bob happy, not throwing me any weird looks or anything? Maybe I'll be thinking about a couple of girls in the first row, but mostly, I'll be thinking about the music.

Are you getting feedback from Bob? "This song needs work," etc.

For a person who is as articulate as he has proven to be over his career, on a level with Shakespeare, his communication verbally with people wasn't of the same character as his abilities as a songwriter. He's a very instinctively reactive person. There wasn't a lot of talk about stuff. We kind of did it, and if he felt something wasn't going the right way, we would do something else. He wasn't verbally expressive in terms of negotiating the music.

It's not a thing where you would get notes after: "Hey, the guitar solo sounded wrong."

"On bar 54 of 'Just Like a Woman,' you played an E flat, that's an E natural" — no. It's not like rehearsing for a Broadway show. He was very friendly and very warm. He was lovely, absolutely lovely, considering what he's been subjected to through his life at that point. Everywhere he goes, somebody thinks he's got the answer that's blowin' in the wind. I thought it was unbelievable that he could be as normal and personable and pleasant as he was.

I was looking up some photos of you two and I found a few where he seems to be pulling your hair on stage. He's not someone who's known for goofing around like that. Was that typical?

I don't think he's done it before or after. I must've inspired some sort of ironic distance. Over the years, people have sent me photos of me and Dylan dueling guitars on stage, or him messing up my hair, or pulling up my leather pants, which he did one night. As I said, I found him in relationship to me to be very warm, very loving, very friendly, very understanding, very generous.

I can tell you one specific example, even before he knew me well. I had been away from my wife for quite a while. She's Danish and she had gone back to Copenhagen to start her master's degree. I've been on the road with Topaz with Rob, and I hadn't seen her in quite a while. When I got the [Dylan] gig, I flew her out to be with me in LA while we were rehearsing. I asked management if I could bring her on the road, because it was amounting to an awful long time away. We had been together for four years at that point and those things are tricky with relationships. I was frightened that all the experiences I would have, as opposed to the experiences she didn't have, would bring us further away from one another than was healthy. Management said, "No way, you can't do that."

I had to think, "Do I want to sacrifice my marriage for this gig?" I was very much in doubt. I was tormented by it. I went to Bob and I said, "Bob, I really have a situation here. Lise and I have not been together in about five months, and this would mean another three months that we would be separated. Do you think I could bring her?" He looked at me and said, "Of course you can bring her. I'll make sure that when you pay for a ticket, we take it out of your bulk salary, not after your salary after taxes. We'll get her on the insurance program for the tour. Everything will be set up. Don't worry."

In my book, that's big stuff. It was a warmth and a generosity of spirit that I don't think I've encountered from other people in the business,

Another thing was we both had back difficulties. He had the injuries that he got from the motorcycle accident. I had a gymnastics accident when I was 17 that gave me a disc that would come out every now and then. We used to go swimming together when we were on the road. [Tour manager] Gary would find somebody who had a swimming pool or some public pool and we would be driven over there so we could swim laps to train our backs up. So we spent a good deal more time together than he would have spent with a lot of the other people because of that.

In terms of the concerts themselves, did you have any particular favorite songs to play live?

He wouldn't say anything; he just starts those songs. It'd be 22,000 people out there and you'll hear him play dun-dun-dun-dun-dun and you think, "Okay, here we go." I absolutely adore that. We have a Danish word for it: *befriende*. It means that it frees you up, it allows air under your wings.

. . . .

I think my favorite song is one I didn't play on. *[laughs]* It was the way they did "Tangled Up in Blue," I thought that was unbelievable. I had goosebumps every time he did it. It was just Bob and Steve and Alan[52] and it was remarkable. He always sounds best when there's the least amount of music behind him. He's such an unbelievably great singer that hearing him by himself sometimes is even more powerful than hearing him with a band.

One of the criticisms you see of this tour and album is what you're saying: That there's so many people on stage, that Bob is getting overwhelmed. Did you ever feel, in terms of what you're saying about him being great when it's stripped-down, that sometimes there was almost too much?

Well, I wouldn't say that it was too much, because it managed to function. When you've got that many people on stage, that's not easy on any level. It's not easy in terms of the sound mixing and it's not easy in terms of arranging the instruments. Everybody wants to be a part. Everybody would have a natural inclination to play. I'm a record producer, and the trick is almost always, how can you create the fabric with as few colors as possible and still get the impact?

Every now and then, if I had my druthers, I might have thought that there could have been fewer people involved. The first time I saw Bob play was in 1965, and that was when he did the first show acoustic and then he had the band. It was just enough to cover it, and it was a remarkable concert.

There wasn't one person on [our] stage who wasn't a killer on his instrument. Sometimes I would just lay out and listen to what was going on and then come in occasionally with a musical comment. Bob could have taken just about anybody

---

52 That's Steve Douglas on saxophone and Alan Pasqua on piano.

out of that band except for the bass player and drummer and everything would have been fine, if you know what I mean.

Bob is an exceptionally good guitar player. He's got an unbelievable power in his playing. His rhythm is so strong and his phrasings are so intelligent. His cultural awareness of the musical tradition in which he moves is so complete and so deep, that if you really listen to what he does, it's like going to school.

How does that affect what you're doing as the other guitar player on stage?

It made me shut up a lot. I was much younger then, so I was more of an asshole. I probably played too much.

This is a tour that was relatively consistent night to night. Would a song change much between one show and another, in terms of what Bob was doing on guitar, vocally, or was it laid out the same night to night?

When you got that many people in the band, you can't start taking a left turn where you usually do the right one. They were pretty well worked out. Tempos could change somewhat, but the intensity and the basic feel was more or less the same. Later on, during the American tour, things started to happen where he would just start a song without saying which song it was.

How else did the tour change over the course of the year? This was his longest tour ever at the time.

First of all, we lost Robbie Stoner after the first leg, and he was replaced by Jerry Scheff. That made a difference in the dynamic of the situation.

Robbie takes up a lot of space personally and musically, and Jerry was more laid back. Whereas Robbie's bass playing maybe was more in-your-face, Jerry's was more in the supportive area. They're both great players, it wasn't that one was better than the other, but Robbie's playing is much more upfront, he steps up there. If you look at the Rolling Thunder tour you can really hear that, him and Howie. Howie was the drummer in Topaz. They were an unbelievable unit, Howie and Robbie. They were killer.

Robbie's fire was gone from the band after that, so it was replaced with a more relaxed feel. Robbie was closer to the Sex Pistols and then Jerry was closer to Elvis.[53]

When you start touring to the degree that we toured, there's a certain mental

---

53 Quite close in fact; Scheff played bass for Elvis's Vegas band from 1969 until Elvis's death in 1977.

fatigue that occurs. People change a little bit on the road, things happen, they miss their families, they get tired of hotel rooms. But there were never any conflicts, there was never any time when things were unpleasant. By the time we ended it all, everybody loved each other even more than when we started.

In between tours, you recorded Street-Legal. *What do you remember about those sessions?*

We set up in our rehearsal room, and that was cozy. Don DeVito was a feel-good producer. He makes everybody happy and makes sure that things go as they should and the people make the music they make. He's not like a T Bone Burnett, who goes in and does stuff, or a Roy Thomas Baker, who records everything 14 times, or a Phil Spector, who knows exactly how he wants things. Don was the right producer for Bob in some ways. The sessions were fun and they were very quick and they were very instinctive, the way Bob was.

I wasn't crazy about the sounds that the engineers got. I remember at one point, I was on his case, saying, "Bob, it could sound better, man." He said, "Billy, my records are my music played by me and the people with whom I'm playing in that room on that day. That's what my music is." I thought that was a pretty cool way to look at it.

The sessions were fun; they were not uptight or unrelaxed. But Bob is without a doubt an intense human being. It's not like you're recording with— who's that guy who does "Tequilaland" or whatever?

"Margaritaville"?

Yeah, "Margaritaville." Jimmy Buffett. It's not that. This is a man with an intensity into his articulation as a musician, as a writer, and as singer. This is not for kids. This is very, very elusively powerful stuff.

How were you learning the songs for the album? You hadn't played most of them live.

Essentially Bob would have a song and start playing it, and then the rhythm section would get a pattern together. People will try to figure out where to put their sounds and their colors in.

It's folk music. Music today is much more akin to classical music with a huge arrangement like a Beethoven symphony. You have a pattern, and you put things together around it, and you can take them in and out technically in the studio. The technique of recording is different. This stuff was much more down to earth, worked out like folk music. "Does it sound good? Okay, that's all right then."

I was looking at some of the session logs and I saw there's a bunch of outtakes that haven't ever been released.

I don't really remember the ones we didn't use. David Mansfield did an article in *Rolling Stone*, and they sent it to me. There's this recording from our last gig in Florida, a song that showed up on the first religious record ["Do Right to Me Baby"]. This is the first playing of the song that ever existed, we did it with our band. I had no recollection of it whatsoever. Totally, completely blank.

I want to ask you about one outtake from this era that I bet you do remember, "Legionnaire's Disease." Bob never released it, but you did, with your Delta Cross Band not long after this tour.

We were getting ready to do our third album and were running out of material, but I had all these great tapes from our soundchecks with Bob. Bob would play "Stones in My Passway" and all these old blues things that almost nobody ever heard of.

I'm going through the tapes and all of a sudden, I hear the song and I'm thinking, "Hey, that sounds pretty good." I wrote Bob and said, "Hey, Bob, is it okay if I record this song?" His wonderful lawyer, Jeff Rosen, wrote back and he said, "Yes, Bob says it's great. Here are the proper lyrics." We recorded it and it was a big hit over here.

It's a strange song. A very strange song. Musically, it's pretty close to "Like a Rolling Stone," but it's a strange lyric because it's hard to tell what the attitude is. It's very narrative, you can't tell what the narrator is thinking, which in itself is a strange quality for a song to have. That's what struck me.

You mentioned your blues background. One thing I enjoy about listening to tapes of these shows is you played blues covers sometimes to open. You did "Love Her With a Feeling," "Steady Rolling Man," a bunch. Was that something that evolved out of these soundchecks you're talking about?

If I remember correctly, he would just start them. He wouldn't say anything; he just starts those songs. It'd be 22,000 people out there and we'd be all set up and you'll hear him play *dun-dun-dun-dun-dun* and you think, "Okay, here we go." I love that. I absolutely adore that. We have a word in Danish, it's so perfect for it, *befriende*. It means that it frees you up, it allows air under your wings. When somebody in front of 22,000 people has the confidence and the will to just start a song and the trust in his band to do it.

You probably knew all those songs already, right?

No! Bob would pull these things out, "Hey, have you ever heard of—" He'd give some name I've never heard of in my life and I'd go home to the hotel. There was no internet back then, so I'd call up some people I knew and say, hey man, have you ever heard of Blind Melon Chitlin' or whatever it was.

He was unbelievable. Look, if I knew half of what he's forgotten, I would be one of the most well-educated musicians on the planet. He is really a person who did his homework. His knowledge of American folk history, and that's what the blues is, is unreal. He and Keith Richards, those two people have a passion, a love for that music that is so deep and so totally devoid of commercialism. It's simply affection for the music and tremendous knowledge.

Earlier you mentioned "Slow Train" and "Do Right," where Bob was first dipping his toe into the Christian thing. Did you have any sense that that's what was happening? There's that story of a cross getting thrown on stage while you were with him and that led him down this path.[54] Was there any awareness among you or the band?

No, I saw nothing coming. I was very surprised.

There was a thing in America, being born again. There were certain people in the organization, David Mansfield's girlfriend, for example, and then one of Bob's girlfriends, Alice, she was also into it. Steve Soles was into it and David was into it too for that matter, if I remember correctly. They were all coming out with this Christian shit, and that's not exactly my cup of tea, I'm not religious by any means. I live in Denmark, this is the most irreligious country on the face of the earth, thank God. When those kinds of things came up, I would just back off.

T Bone got born again late in the '70s after Rolling Thunder, because of The Alpha Band. That was David and Steven and T Bone. T Bone was a very charismatic and powerful individual, and I believe he just took everybody along on that. I think he's still pretty religious. I read some stuff he wrote that was unbelievably intelligent, but his imagery was Christian imagery. He's managed to internalize it in a way that works, I think, even though I'm not a great fan of religion on any level. He seems to have the respect for other points of view, and he also sees it as much culturally as he does in terms of actual religious dogma.

You said occasionally it came up backstage or something, what did that look like?

---

54 Bob Dylan recalling a 1978 show in Tucson, Arizona: "Towards the end of the show someone out in the crowd…threw a silver cross on the stage. Now usually I don't pick things up in front of the stage…but I looked down at that cross. I said, 'I gotta pick that up.'…I brought it backstage and I brought it with me to the next town… I said, 'Well…I need something tonight that I didn't have before.' And I looked in my pocket and I had this cross."

Steven. Steven Soles would say something about religious stuff. He was the only one that ever did, really. David never did, Bob never did, Alice, of course, had nothing to do with the tour, and David's girlfriend didn't do it — but she was the one that took Bob to the church, which started the ball rolling.

There was no awareness among the band, for instance, when you're trying out "Slow Train," "Oh, what are these lyrics about?"

There were no religious words in "Slow Train" when he wrote it at the start. I sat next to him when he wrote the song on the bus. He had this notebook he carried around with him and he was writing that song on the bus and we were sitting next to each other. I remember that very distinctly. The original "Slow Train," the only words that were actually recognizable was the chorus. Everything was just sounds and words, you know, he would make up stuff.

Do you have any other memories like the one of "Slow Train," of being around when he was writing or working on something new?

He was always writing. It's just like some people breathe, some people drink beer, some people smoke cigarettes.

Truman Capote was delivering a lecture to some university. He was well into the final phase of his life, when he was irregular, to say the least, and drinking and taking pills and everything else. Somebody in the audience raised his hand. "Mr. Capote, how can I become a writer?" Truman was drunk and he got off on his high horse and said, "You can't. How could you ask that? You don't become a writer; you *are* a writer. You write because you have to write, you write because every day when you wake up, you have to write. It's the first thing you think about in the morning and the last thing you think about before you go to sleep at night. You don't become; you are."

It's a well-known anecdote and, in some ways, it reflects what I perceived as Bob's reality. He writes. That's what he does. He doesn't buy fancy clothing, he doesn't buy snazzy cars, he doesn't need to impress people, he just writes. That's it.

Sometimes, after concerts, we would get together and play. He always had a piano in his room. That was part of a thing on the road. If humanly possible, there will be a piano in his hotel room.

What were those hotel room jams like?

Nothing big. Sometimes, you might end up in Bob's room because he was social and nice and fun to be around. There'd be a piano and sometimes he'd pull out some guitars and play, and sometimes he wouldn't. It was not a big thing. You got to remember that those shows were three and a half hours long. People were bushed.

I bet. I'm surprised it ever happened.

When you're working with somebody who's as dynamically inspirational as Bob was, it's not hard. You never feel tired. He never let us down, even when he was sick. He gave 130% every night, I've never seen anything like that. Not one night in the entire time I played with him did he ever not deliver over 100%.

What do you mean when he was sick?

I think it was a week or so, he had a real bad cold. He's spitting up phlegm all over the place on the stage.

That's like a Michael Jordan–type story where he's got like a fever, he feels like death, goes out and plays a great basketball game, then leaves the court and immediately passes out.

I don't think it's because people feel that they have to. I just think it's because there's no real alternative. I would never try to second-guess why Bob did anything, but my impression was, it wasn't as if he got there and he goes, "Okay, I may be sick but now I'm going to do it." No, I think he just walked down on that stage and that's what he did.

Once I asked him, I think it was in Florida just before the end of the tour, "All this, how can you do it?" He said, "Billy, that's what I do." It was beautiful that way, it was so unpretentious and totally unguarded. Those were his words. "That's what I do."

We started talking about the beginning of the tour and I wanted to ask you about the end of it. Anything you remember in particular about the last show or just how it ended?

There had been a very tragic occurrence, I think in Louisiana. Jimmy Hungerford, one of our riggers, went up to take down the sound system. He did not have a safety belt on, and he fell to his death.

Did that cast a pall or a black cloud over the end of the tour?

Yes. It was shocking. It wasn't what I would have hoped for at the end of the tour. We knew this kid. He was a nice kid. He fell for like 90 feet. He died in [crew member] Roger Danchick's arms. It was just terrible.

By the way, another example of Bob's generosity: Jimmy was from Tennessee or someplace around there. He was a Southern kid and his parents were having a funeral straight off. A lot of us, I think Ian and me and David and Steven, we all went to the funeral. Bob gave us the jet. That must have cost him $15,000, $20,000 to do that, if not more. He just said, "You guys go to that funeral and you take the jet."

We weren't that close with the crew, but the thing is, Bob was in it with everybody. It wasn't like he went first class, and we went coach. Everywhere, it was just a band. That's the way it was set up. He did not remove himself from the other people on the tour. Out for dinner, he would sit next to the bus drivers. That's just the way he was. He was not a snob, he was not fond of himself, he was not in any way acting better than anybody. He was just being a regular guy.

Did you have any other interactions with Dylan after that, or was that closing a chapter?

He came to Copenhagen to play in the '80s, I think it was. I met up with him, and we talked a little bit, then went our separate ways.

He invited me to a show in Odense with my son later. Got us tickets and backstage and everything, but the people who were doing the security whisked him out of there before I got a chance to say hello. I got a message from Jeff that Bob had sent love. I think that after John Lennon was shot, things changed in terms of getting close to anybody, even if they know you.

Alan Pasqua (far left) behind a wall of pianos and keyboards on tour with Dylan in Nuremberg, Germany, 1978.
Photo by Klaudia Kroboth

Alan Pasqua

Alan Pasqua has the most spread-out professional history with Dylan of anyone in this book. In 1978, he played over a hundred concerts with Dylan, Bob's longest tour ever at the time. When the tour ended, they went their separate ways.

Pasqua didn't hear from Dylan again for 39 years.

Then, in 2017, Dylan's office asked Pasqua to record a piece of piano music. For what purpose? They wouldn't tell him. So he recorded something, sent it off, and soon after found himself a new character in the Nobel Prize drama: Dylan recited his long-awaited acceptance speech over Alan's piano recording.

Soon after, Pasqua was actually in the studio with Dylan for the first time in 40 years to record a gender-swapped cover of "She's Funny That Way" for the 2018 compilation EP *Universal Love – Wedding Songs Reimagined*. Then in 2020, they collaborated again on "Murder Most Foul."

. . . .

I've read short versions of how you got involved in the '78 tour, but I wonder if you wouldn't mind telling me the longer version. I gather you were with Eddie Money at the time?

Yes. My first gig after college was with Tony Williams.[55] When that band dissolved, I moved to Los Angeles. The guy that produced the New Tony Williams Lifetime records, his name was Bruce Botnick. When I got to LA, he was the only guy I knew. A couple of weeks after I arrived, he called and said, "I've got this new artist I've been assigned to produce. His name is Eddie Money. We need a piano player to play on his record. Do you want to come over and meet him?"

---

55 Jazz drummer best known for his work with Miles Davis.

I had come from a jazz background, but I had played rock as a kid, so it wasn't something that was foreign to me. I walk in and Eddie says, "Hey, Al, I don't want to hear any jazz shit from you!" Then he sat down at the piano and played me what were going to be his two first big hits, "Baby Hold On" and "Two Tickets to Paradise."

We went out on the road. I think we were in New York doing a rehearsal. We were on a break, and I was standing in the hall, and there's this other guy there. We struck up a conversation. His name was Rob Stoner. I forget what band he was there working with, but he said he was going to be playing with Dylan.

I did this three-month tour with Eddie that ended right before Christmas. I get home and I'm just kind of sitting on the couch, decompressing, and the phone rings. It's Rob. I was living close to Santa Monica, near the Marina, and he said, "I'm in Santa Monica at Bob's rehearsal studio, and I'm putting a band together, auditioning people for next year for a tour. I'd love to get you in on it."

I was so burnt out from the last trip with Eddie. I said to him, "Man, I just got home and I think I'm going to take a break." He said, "Okay, well, good talking to you." I hung up the phone.

Five minutes later, I thought to myself, "Oh my God, what did I just do?" I called him right back. I said, "Hey man… I'm feeling a whole lot better! I'd love to come down and hang out." I went about a mile away from where I was living, down to Bob's rehearsal place. It's a big room with tape recorders, nothing super fancy, just stuff to record music on. Rob was the only one in there.

We started playing some blues and shuffles. He thought he heard something that might be a good fit. He recorded all this stuff, and he put together a tape of me and presented it to Bob. A little bit of time goes by, and Rob calls me and he goes, "Let's do it again." I go back down, we do it again.

After that, I got a call: "We're putting a band together, do you want to come down and play?" The very first day, there were at least, I'm not exaggerating, three drummers, three keyboard players, a bunch of guitarists. Bob showed up and we just started jamming. We weren't really playing any specific songs.

A couple of days later, it's like, "We're going to do it again." That time there were *two* keyboard players and *two* drummers. They started narrowing down the field.

This went on for maybe a week or two. I didn't think I necessarily would get the gig, but the longer I was there, the more I was really into playing with Bob and this band of great musicians. I walked in one day and I was the only keyboard player there.

Nobody said to me, "Congratulations, you've got the gig." With that world, you've got the gig for that day. Depending on how things go, *maybe* you'll have the gig tomorrow. I remember there was one day where it was not a good day, and all of us were dismissed. Then the next day, we all got a call and all of us were brought back in.

So you were fired for 24 hours?

Yes. We were fired for a day. At least I was.

Bob was a great bandleader. I was lucky to play with Tony Williams early on in my life. He learned from Miles Davis. Miles never told him *what* to play, but by *how* Miles played, he showed Tony what he needed to do. I found Bob to be quite a bit similar to Miles.

I never wore my jazz hat in that band, but I let a little bit of that influence leak in, ever so slightly, where I thought it was okay. I didn't know at that time that Bob was a jazz fan.

Were you a big Dylan fan at the time? If he called out something that wasn't a greatest hit during rehearsals, were you likely to know the song?

I was flying blind! He asked me one day if I knew "Positively 4th Street." I freaked, because I didn't know it. I just looked at him and said, "No, man, but I'll learn it." He just looked at me and started laughing. He turned to one of the other guys and said, "He said he'll *learn* it!" I thought, "I'm gone, I'm fired, that's it."

Maybe he appreciated my honesty or my naiveté or whatever it was. I just tried to be myself and enjoy the ride for however long it lasted. It's been interesting that he and I have intersected throughout the years. It's always been a joy for me.

I want to get to those other intersections later, but sticking with that '78 tour, what do you remember about the first shows? They made the live album [At Budokan] so early on, the earliest shows in Japan became the most famous.

It was something that I'd never experienced. That was his first time in Japan, if I'm not mistaken. It was like the Queen. Like royalty. That's how much he mattered to them, coming over there. It was really incredible.

I've got a crazy-ass story. I was playing ping-pong before one of the shows with this guy from China who was just insane, a professional ping-pong player. He hit a shot and I went for it. I ran smack into a steel pole and put a giant gash in my forehead. The tour manager looked at me and went, "Oh, shit. Wrap it up."

They put me in a turban, like a tourniquet on my head, and pumped me full of

Tylenol and said, "Get out there and play." I remember the first bass note, I was like, "Oh my God." But we played the show, and it was a long show. Then after the show, they took me to some— I don't know if it was a hospital, I just remember it was completely dark and this doctor showed up. They put me on a table and they had to stitch me up. I remember him standing on this plastic milk crate. I was thinking, "how sanitary…"

What was a typical day like on the road? I'm assuming you're not getting gashed in the head every day.

Nothing unusual about it. Soundcheck, maybe rehearsal. I don't think he ever, or very rarely did he call a specific rehearsal to go over things during the day. It was very relaxed.

How did you get along with Bob himself?

Look, I've got to be honest, for me to be around somebody like that, I didn't really know how to behave. I mean, I wanted to be his friend and I'm like, "Well, who the hell am I?" The thing that kept us together was that we were all playing music together.

He taught me a lot about how to be a pro. I remember we were in Germany and there were some people in the audience that were planted there, unbeknownst to me. All of a sudden, they started throwing things on the stage. I remember rags soaked in paint were flying by. One of them hit Billy Cross. Bob just stopped, walked off the stage. We followed him. This was not a small gig. It was a big concert, thousands of people.

We're back in our dressing room. We all wore band outfits, and I got back there and I immediately changed into my street clothes. We're sitting there for like a half an hour, and all of a sudden, the door opens. Bob comes in. He sees me and he's like, "Where are you going?" I looked at him and I said, "What do you mean? I'm just waiting for the bus." He said, "We're not going back to the hotel. I'm waiting for these people to leave. There's 15,000 people out there that came to see us, and there's 20 people in the audience that came to ruin the night. We're going to just wait them out."

He said, "Get out of those clothes, man. Put on your gear." So I changed back into the stage clothes and boom, we went out and played a two-and-a-half-hour show. I never forgot that. A lot of people would have just said, "Screw this. I'm out of here," and went back to the hotel.

Wait, why were people throwing rags soaked with paint and whatever else?

I don't know. I think it was some political crap going on.[56]

This was Bob's longest tour ever. How did it change over time? Were people getting burnt out by the end?

It never really changed for me. I was a young guy, 26, so I'm seeing the world for the first time. Every day is just like, "Wow, where are we going today? Far out!" It was incredible. I was so grateful to be there.

Every night for the better part of that year, he and I played two duets ["I Want You" and "Girl from the North Country"]. I looked forward to those two duets every night so much because it was a moment just for me to be alone and play with him and get to do a little bit more than I would normally do as a keyboardist in the structure of the band. It was never a burnout thing for me.

The Street-Legal *sessions were wrapped up in the tour and tour rehearsals. What can you tell me about those sessions?*

It was just a big open room with a linoleum floor. It was not a recording studio by any means. They brought in a mobile truck. We spent a lot of time just trying to get it to sound good.

It didn't take a whole long time to make that record, I remember that. Bob worked on his vocals. We did a number of takes. Don [DeVito, producer] was there, of course, commanding the ship, but it just all went down. The band is new, so we're trying to feel our way in the dark like, "Okay, what do we sound like? Who are we?"

Was that a challenge with such a big band in the studio?

Yes. Ian and myself and Bobbye [Hall, percussionist] and Steve Douglas [sax] and Billy, we were the new guys. Maybe my life in jazz and playing fusion in college— you have to pick your spot. I listened to his earlier records and understood what my role was. It was not about playing wall to wall, necessarily, but making those musical contributions in the space with a band of that size. Everybody had a very specific part to play.

By the time I heard Street-Legal, *it was remastered and sounded great, but I know it was criticized at the time for being muddy. Bob had not wanted anyone to wear headphones or anything, so everything leaked into each other. Do you remember that being an issue*

---

56 A *People* magazine concert review from July 1978 mentions, "Some leftists, apparently angry at the mellowing of the old polemical minstrel, pelted him with eggs at another gig, in Berlin."

I don't recall that record sounding amazing, and I basically attribute that to the room. It's not like you need to be in a chamber with carpet on every surface, but we were in a highly reflective environment with low ceilings. That's not necessarily the greatest place to record. The good part about that was it was a really big space, so there was air. It just wasn't tall. It wasn't high air, so the sound couldn't go up. It went right or left.

So it's bouncing around and bouncing into your mic, other peoples' mics?

Yeah, there was a lot of reflection, and I think people were complaining. I didn't really find it muddy. It sounded more like a live record to me than a studio album, but man, I listen to it now and I think it sounds good.

In terms of the band dynamics you were talking about, did Rob Stoner's departure from the tour early on affect you, since he had been your entry point into that whole world?

It did. I honestly do not know the details of all of that. [I was] surprised by it and saddened by it, because he was the guy that got me in the door.

At that point, I understood what a big machine this was. I knew I was certainly dispensable, so I was like, "Well, this is an amazing gig, and I want to hang on to it for as long as it will go." I went into a little bit of a self-preservation mode. I wasn't going to start going, "Hey, man, why did Rob leave? What happened?" because then I probably would have been out the door, too!

What happens after the tour ends? Is there talk of continuing?

There was no finality. It wasn't like, "Thank you, guys. It's been a great year. I'm going to move on." It was just like, "We're done with the U.S." Amongst us in the band, we just kept tabs on what was going on, and then we heard that there was a new band.

Now to fast-forward, way forward, and get to the Nobel lecture recording. I know from some interviews you did at the time that you didn't even know what it was for.[57] As a pianist, how did you come up with something with so little guidance?

They gave me some direction. I prodded, because I was like, "What am I doing here?" They used the model of early Steve Allen. Piano musings that are slightly

---

57 Pasqua told the *New York Times* in 2017 that Dylan's team asked him to send them 30 minutes of piano music for an undisclosed project.

bluesy, but not really. They're not necessarily connected, but they're not terribly random either. That was just enough for me to go on. I said, "I understand. I think I get what you want."

They needed a certain number of minutes of music, and I say, "Before I give you that, [let me record] three minutes of some stuff and tell me if I'm in the right direction." So I did that, sent it off. I got the call back and they said, "Yeah, that's exactly what we're looking for, so do the rest." I said, "When do you need it by?" They said, "Tomorrow."

What did you think when you heard the end result with Bob's speech overtop?

I was honored to be a part of it, and I was also thankful that they were generous in wanting to give me credit for my work.

There was one other thing that I worked on with him [before "Murder Most Foul"], which was that he did that one track on that record, "He's Funny That Way." We did that at Capitol. I'm trying to recall if the Nobel thing happened before that. It might have, but I didn't see Bob for the Nobel thing. That was all a phone call, and then I went into my studio with my piano and sent them some music.

I believe the Nobel was first. Nobel in 2017 and then "He's Funny" came out a year later.

There was a podium where Vince [Mendoza] was conducting the orchestra, and then to the right of Vince was a mic for Bob, and then to the right of Bob was me on the piano.

It was a really interesting day, because I just read the chart that was written for the piano part and I could see that Bob wanted some things differently. I realized at that moment that I was probably the bridge between him and Vince, because I was the only other person in that room that had history with him. I took it upon myself to try and interpret things for Vince that he could relay to the orchestra.

What do you mean "interpret"? If Bob's saying something that is not clear or is not in like musical-notation form for an orchestra?

There might be like a tempo fluctuation, or he might have wanted to put a pause here or something. That stuff might not have been super-apparent, but I, having had a year of playing music with him, understood what he was trying to get at. I just took it upon myself to go to Bob and say, "Do you want to do this here? What if we try to do this?" There was a comfort factor. He knew me. He didn't know Vince; he didn't know the orchestra people. I was the bridge, and it worked out really nicely. Really cool song, and it was great to see him. I hadn't seen him for a long time. It was just one day, boom, you're driving home like, "Wow, that was a great day of music!"

To bring us up to the present, was your next contact the "Murder Most Foul" session?

Yeah. Jeff [Rosen, Dylan's manager] called and said, "What are you doing?" I said, "When?" He goes, "Tonight."

I said, "I kind of have plans, what's going on?" He goes, "Bob is working and we were thinking maybe of seeing if you had some time." I said, "What other days might be good, Jeff?" and he said, "I don't know. Let me find out and I'll get back to you." I hung up the phone.

I thought about Rob Stoner's initial call to me about going to the first rehearsal when he was putting the [1978] band together. I said, "Oh, man, if this is going to happen, it's going to happen *tonight*." I called Jeff back and I said, "Look, I'll try and clear a path to make it happen tonight. Give me some details." He told me where it was and all that, so I went to the studio.

Blake Mills was there. Benmont [Tench] was there, who is my hero, one of my all-time favorite musicians and people and the greatest B3 player on the planet. I just think the world of him. We were hanging out, and then Bob came out and it was like, "Hey, man." A reunion. Then we went into the studio, and they played [us] the song.

When you say they played you the song, what do you mean?

They were playing a demo. I heard it and I just couldn't believe it. In rock music, things usually have a specific beat and pulse. This was free. The time was free. It was elastic. It wasn't specific to a certain time, feel, or tempo. It just moved and flowed.

When I was done listening to the track, I turned to Bob and I said, "My God, Bob, this sounds to me like *A Love Supreme*." He just stopped and looked at me. I thought, "Oh, I'm going to get fired" again. *[laughs]*

Then we went into the studio. Two or three hours later, we had just a bunch of different takes and it was like, "Okay, fellas. Thanks. We got it." I left going, "What an amazing night. I hope that what I played makes the record." You never know, you know? I was thrilled to find out that it did.

With the Nobel and that, you're kind of his go-to piano guy for these long epics. One's a song and one's not, but as you say, "Murder Most Foul" is almost as loose as playing piano for a Nobel lecture.

I don't know if that's true, but if that's my role, I accept it wholeheartedly. Bottom line is, I think the world of him, and I loved making music with him, and I think that we have some sort of a connection. Musically, spiritually, however it is. Whatever happens in that studio, when people get vulnerable and bare all, it's an amazing experience. It's never work for me. It never, ever feels like work.

I think of him as recording stuff live like you were talking about with Street-Legal, *but "Murder Most Foul" is so long. Was that recorded live or were you piecing bits and pieces together?*

Live.

All 17 minutes?

Yes. Every take that we did, it was the whole— Unless there was a stop because I made a mistake or something, then we'd start over. It was all live.

As a piano accompanist for this long thing with so many words, how do you keep your part interesting? How do you keep yourself engaged?

In our jazz world, we just lost a dear soul, Chick Corea. I was reading some of his advice that he had typed out for somebody, and one of the things that he said was, "Play so that others sound good as well." It's such a beautiful sentiment. Take your ego out of the picture and be there for the song. Be as selfless as you can, and listen and react to what you hear. By reacting, it doesn't mean you have to play *anything*. It might mean you play nothing, and then you come in.

That's the only way it's ever worked for me. In my teaching of other musicians, I stress, don't listen to yourself. Don't worry about the notes that you're playing. You need to be able to *not* play, as well as play, because that's what creates the magic.

In an interview, Fiona Apple said she also played piano on that track. I gather she wasn't at your session, but when you are listening to it, can you pick out who is doing what?

Yes, I can. Benmont's on the left, Alan's on the right, Fiona's in the middle. It's like the early days of stereo. It's a really cool collaboration. She sounded beautiful too.

Bringing it all full circle, in your recent sessions with him, is there any acknowledgment of your history in 1978? Do you talk about it at all?

No, we don't. Perhaps if we were to hang out or go back on the road, that stuff would come up, but I keep things pretty much in the present tense and just let him know how much I appreciate him and how much I love him and how grateful I am.

Regina McCrary and Dylan duet at the Warfield in San Francisco, California, 1979.
Photo by Keith W. Criss

Regina McCrary

In the three years from 1979–1981 when Bob Dylan was performing Christian music, he recorded and toured with a variety of backing singers. But only one singer remained by his side for every single show on every single tour: Regina McCrary. "By his side" sometimes literally, as Dylan and McCrary sang intimate duets at a number of shows, singing into one microphone with him on guitar and her on autoharp (an instrument that Dylan himself taught her).

McCrary has gospel music in her DNA, having grown up singing alongside her father, Reverend Sam McCrary, the leader of gospel pioneers The Fairfield Four. She continues to perform with her family, singing with her siblings in the aptly-named McCrary Sisters. NPR has called them "Nashville gospel royalty."

. . . .

How did you first get involved with that band and with Dylan?

I got a phone call from one of my friends who was singing with him. He was looking for another singer. My friend asked me, was I interested? I said yes. I went to [the hotel where he was staying] in Nashville on Broadway, and I auditioned.

I knew certain songs: "Lay Lady Lay," "Blowin' In The Wind," stuff like that. I did not know who Bob Dylan was if he was standing next to me on the bus stop. Other than a few songs, I never really knew who he was.

I sang three songs. The first song I don't think moved him. The second song made him look, and the third song he jumped up and said, "That's what I want."

Do you remember what the songs were?

The first song was "Everything Must Change," the second song was "Precious Lord Take My Hand," and the third song was "Amazing Grace."

What happened next? Did you leave that day knowing that you had the job?

The young lady who called me about the audition, Carolyn Dennis[58], she started harmonizing with me on "Amazing Grace." After we finished, he jumped up, he said, "Yes, that's the sound I want. That's what I want." We sang it again, and he recorded it on his boom box. Then he said, "You got your job."

He said he wanted me to get my hair braided. I said, "You gonna pay for it?" He laughed and said yes. Then he said, "I want you to see my show."

He wanted me to come to a show on December the 3rd [1978], which happened to be my mother's birthday. I said okay. He said, "Well, how many tickets do you need?" I told him 17. He's like, *"What?"* I said, "I got four brothers, I got three sisters. I have a husband. I have my little boy, myself…" He said, "Don't go no further. You'll have 17 tickets in your name."

My family and I all saw his show. When the show was over, we came backstage, and he met my whole entire family. Then everybody left but my father and I. My dad looked at Bob Dylan and said, "You taking my little girl out on the road?" Bob Dylan said, "Yes." My dad put his hand in Bob's hand and pulled Bob into him ever so gently and said, "Don't make her cry." Bob said, "I promise."

It was about two months later I get a phone call that we're going to record a record [*Slow Train Coming*]. I caught a plane and went to Muscle Shoals, Alabama. When I got there, I'm telling you, we stayed at a big old house. Bob Dylan would go with the band in the studio and record, and then they would come back to the house that we were staying in. They would let [the singers] listen to the music. We would create background parts for the song, and then we would go in the studio and lay down parts.

When did you find out that he had become born again? In December 1978, when you saw that show, it certainly wasn't public knowledge. Did you know when you went to Muscle Shoals that these are going to be gospel-influenced songs?

I knew something, because right before we went into studio to record, there was a big article that came out in Nashville, Tennessee, that said "Bob Dylan confessed to be born again." It didn't matter at the time. Being a professional singer, I was going to do my job. But when I realized what it was I was about to sing, it just made me realize that God always keeps me close to what it is He's called me to do.

I read your son played a role in that record too. Can you tell me that story?

---

58 Then a backup singer on the *Street-Legal* album who would return for *Slow Train Coming* and eventually join the gospel tour the year after McCrary, in 1980. She and Dylan would later marry in 1986. They divorced in 1992.

We were sitting at the house and Bob came back. He and [producers] Jerry Wexler and Barry Beckett had been obviously in a big debate about a particular song. They didn't know if it should go on the record. The debate went on so much between them that he brought the song back to the house for us to listen to it.

As he put it on, the song began to talk about, "I think I'll call it a pig, I think I'll call it a bear." At the time my son was about two, three years old, and when he said, "I think I'll call it a pig," Tony would just bend over and laugh so hard. "Mama! Mama! He said a pig! He said 'I think I'll call it a pig,' Mama." Then they said, "I think I'll call it a bear," and Tony would just fall over and laugh. "Mama, he said, 'I think I'll call it a bear'!" Bob starts looking at Tony. He just started watching him. Every time Bob would call out a name of an animal, Tony would just crack up laughing. Bob said, "That's it. We're going to put the song on the record."[59]

What happens after those sessions? Do you know that there's a tour coming?

When we had finished doing the record, I came home. We were told by his management company that they will get in touch with us. Then we went to Santa Monica. We rehearsed for a few weeks, then we went to New York to do *Saturday Night Live.*

What was that like?

It was amazing. I loved *Saturday Night Live.* I loved watching Gilda Radner and John Belushi and Dan Aykroyd and all of them. To go do *Saturday Night Live* and get to meet all of these guys that I every Saturday sit and watch and laughed at was very exciting.

After that, I went back home for a few weeks, [then back to Santa Monica]. We were in rehearsal for almost three straight months before we went out on the road.

That's a lot of rehearsal.

Well, yeah! He done told the world he's a born-again Christian. He done told the world, "This Jewish man believes in Jesus Christ, and he believes in the Word of God." He is going to go out on the road and do something that, out of all these years, he hadn't done before… but then again, he *had* done. 'Cause if you listen to the lyrics to a lot of his songs, he was speaking positive words of God and love and justice and togetherness and equality. He was speaking all of that in all his other songs. Now he has audaciously told the world that he is a believer in Jesus Christ.

So we're in rehearsals, working up this show, working up this ministry so that

59 The song in question is "Man Gave Names to All the Animals."

when he goes forth, people don't think it's a gimmick. They know that he is real about what it is he's singing about.

Musically, in all those rehearsals, did the band and all the singers gel quickly?

It went well, but see, I'm an old school girl. I go in, I do what I need to do, and then I leave. There was only one person there [Carolyn Dennis] that I had a tight relationship with, and that's because I've been known her since I was seven years old. When rehearsal was over with, I go get me something to eat, go back, listen to the music, rehearse the songs, and then chill out and wake up the next day to go to rehearsal again.

What do you remember about those first shows? You did a whole lot of shows in one place, at the Warfield in San Francisco.

I felt great about it, and the reason why I felt great about it was because I was in my zone. We get to go out there and sing the Word of God and hope that the people that have paid their money to come and hear would receive it. When I get in the zone to walk out on stage, I listen and I look at the people…but I *don't*. I kind of channel spiritually into what it is I'm about to do.

From different articles I read, there were some people pissed off, mad, angry, and booing. Well, guess what? I never heard any of it. I guess God blocked my hearing so that I wouldn't hear that. Because me walking out on that stage by myself, telling the story about an old woman getting on a train, if I had heard some of those people booing, like some of the news articles said they were doing, that would have devastated me. That would have messed my mind and my heart up. I truly have to say that God took all of that away from me. All I know was I went out there focused on what it was I was about to say and what it was I was about to do. That's what I did.

How did it happen that you opened the show each night telling a story?

We were at the theater, we had done soundcheck and everything. I saw Bob scratching his head, and I was like, okay, something ain't right. He's thinking hard. So I walked over to him and I said, "What's wrong?" He said, "Something is missing." I said, "What do you mean?" He said, "This is a great show, but something is missing and I don't know what it is."

I am a jokester, I'm the seventh child out of eight. I come from a family that loves to play games and act silly. I looked at him and I said, "Okay, I know what it is." He said, "What?" I said, "I'm going to walk out on stage, and I'm going to tell

My family came backstage. Everybody left but my father and I. My dad looked at Bob Dylan and said, "You taking my little girl out on the road?" Bob said, "Yes." My dad put his hand in his and pulled Bob into him ever so gently and said, "Don't make her cry." Bob said, "I promise."

this story about this old woman who was crying. She got a letter from her son that had been hurt in Vietnam. They'd been thinking he wasn't going to make it, so he sent a letter to his mom and asked her to come see him one more time. The woman didn't have no money to catch no train, so she got on her knees and prayed to God. An angel appeared and told the old woman to go get on the train, and the woman went and got on the train.

"The conductor came by and asked her, 'Old woman, where is your ticket?' She said, 'Conductor, I don't have a ticket, I don't even have no money. Jesus told me to get on this train. Please don't put me out.' The conductor looked at her and said, 'Old woman, I'm sorry, but I'm going to have to put you off this train.' The woman kneeled down on the side of the railroad tracks and she started singing, 'Father, I stretch my hands to thee… No other help I know…'

"The conductor pulled on the string and waved his hand for the train to start, but the train didn't move. The old woman kept singing, 'Father, I stretch my hands to thee… No other help I know…' The conductor pulled on the string and waved his hand and the train still wouldn't move. She sung one more time, 'Father, I stretch my hands to thee… No other help I know…'

"The conductor got off the train, and he said, 'Old woman, come on, get back on this train.' She said, 'But conductor, you told me if I didn't have no money and no ticket, I couldn't ride this train.' Then the conductor looked at her and said, 'Old woman, *Jesus* got your ticket. Come on and get on board.' The old woman got on the train and the train slowly started to move."

Then I told Bob, "After that, the other girls are going to come out on stage, and the first song we're going to sing is 'If I Got My Ticket, Can I Ride?'"

He looked at me like I had lost my mind. I started laughing. He walked out of the room and came back with Jim Keltner, Tim Drummond, Fred Tackett, and everybody with him. He said, "Tell them what you just told me." I said, "I was playing!" He said, "Well, play again and tell them what you just told me."

I told the whole story over again, except now we're in the dressing room and all the girls, all the background singers, the lighting guy, all of us was in there. I told the story again and, when I told the story, nobody said nothing.

It was about 15, 20 minutes before it was time to go on stage. We, the girls, was putting on our clothes and our makeup and everything. Bob walked in the dressing room and he said, "That's how we're going to open up my show." I said, "No, no, no. I was playing, I was playing!" He said, "Okay, play. Go out there. That's how we're going to open up my show."

I said, "Oh man. You got a quarter?" He said, "A quarter? What do you want a quarter for?" I said, "I need to use a pay phone and call my daddy." "What?" "That story I told you was the story that my dad would tell often in church." My father being a pastor, he would tell stories, and that was one of the stories I remember that he told.

He gave me the money. I called my dad. I said, "Daddy, remember how you used to tell me that my talkin' was going to bless me or was going to curse me?" He said, "Yes." I said, "Well…" and I told him what happened. He started laughing. He told me, "That's a blessing." I said, "Daddy, I can't do this!" He said, "Yes, you can. I'll tell you what to do. When you walk out on that stage, that big bright spotlight that's going to be on you, look into that spotlight." I said, "Why?" He said, "Because God's going to be there, and I'm going to be there. Whenever you get nervous, just look in that light and know we're right there." I said okay.

This is all happening right before you get on stage to do it for the first time?

Right. I went in the room, I prayed, and then it was time for the show to start. I walked out on stage, by myself, and told the story. When I got to the part where it says, "The conductor put the old woman back on the train and, when the old woman got on the train, the train slowly starts to move," at that moment, the piano player starts making sounds to indicate the wheels of the train moving. While the keyboard player was doing that, that was the signal. The other singers came out — because the light at that time was just still on me. I just went from the *[imitates piano sound]* to *[singing]* "If I got my ticket, Lord…" and we went from there.

We did 25 minutes worth of strong gospel. At the end of those songs, the light went down. When the light came back up, Bob Dylan was standing on stage, and we were doing "Gotta Serve Somebody."

A powerful way to open the show every night.

Yes, very powerful.

There's a duet you did with him, the folk song "Mary of the Wild Moor," where you were playing autoharp. Was that the only song you performed an instrument on as well?

Other than tambourine, yes. He taught me the autoharp. He taught me the chords. I didn't know nothing about it.

I enjoyed doing that one. I had heard him do that song by himself and then he decided, "Regina, I want you to learn this song." I was like, "Okay." The challenge was to learn the lyrics and turn around after learning the lyrics to learn the autoharp. "Mary of the Wild Moor" has so many verses to it, it ain't funny.

That's really being thrown in the deep end. Not only learning the song, but then you have to learn a brand-new instrument to play in front of thousands of people.

Oh, yes. An instrument I had never played before.

Was there a lot of that, things getting added as the tour went on that you hadn't rehearsed a bunch? Or things getting changed that you had to learn on the fly?

Bob really never did the same song the same way all the time. There were times that he walked up on stage and you could tell that he was feeling and thinking different. I learned to watch his mouth and watch his feet. That helped me as far as if he changed the phrasing of how he did a song, or he wanted the beat to change, or to slow down or speed up, or put another feel on it. You would watch him, and you could just kick right in.

Did you have particular favorite songs that you liked to sing every night?

I liked "Man Gave Names to All the Animals" because Carolyn Dennis is my son's godmother. When we went in the studio to record it, it was only Carolyn and I singing background on that particular song. Jim Keltner taught me how to play the sticks. When you hear that *donk, de-donk, de-donk*, that's me playing the sticks.

Obviously, it was a very religious show. Was it like that backstage as well?

We prayed before we ever walked out on stage. We all took turns when we circled up before it was time for the show to start. It was awesome to be able to know that everybody was holding hands and everybody was praying. It might have been one or two that wasn't in the circle, but that was okay, too; we prayed for them.

One thing that they didn't include on the Trouble No More *Bootleg Series is the long sermons he gave from the stage. I wonder if those called back to your childhood, even though Dylan is obviously not a traditional preacher.*

This is how I look at it. You can go to school all day long and come out and tell people that you were trained, but are you *called*? I can just say this: I know that from being on the road with Bob Dylan, Bob Dylan has always been called. God called him. Him opening up his mouth and talking about the world and lies and God and quoting scripture was natural for him because he had been told by God to do what he did. For me, it was as perfect as listening to him quote scripture and talk to the people and minister to the people as watching a baby being born. Very natural.

How did you feel later on when he started performing older songs? Did you enjoy performing the greatest hits or had you preferred doing all the new Christian songs?

Let me put it to you like this: I can get up all day long and sing songs about God. I love the Lord, and that's my heart, and that's my passion, and that's who I am. It's my DNA when it comes down to music. I want to always sing songs and introduce people to Jesus Christ. I want to always have a prayer in my heart, on my lips, to help somebody and to be that beacon of light that somebody might need that might be lost. But at the same time, God gave me a job to go on stage and perform with Bob Dylan. I'm glad Bob was singing his gospel music, and when he started adding some of his other music back in, that was okay with me too.

We talked about Slow Train Coming *a lot, but you did* Saved *and* Shot of Love *as well. Does anything jump out at you about the sessions for those two records?*

I love, love, love *Saved*. "Saved" is one of those songs that put that Holy Ghost thing in your feet and you just want to sing and dance. I loved playing the tambourine, and on "Saved," I got to play that tambourine.

Recording the album Saved, *did that feel similar to* Slow Train Coming?

Yes. Going into studio to record *Saved* was truly awesome and powerful too. On *Slow Train Coming*, we didn't know for sure what the songs were until he brought them back to the home where we were all staying, but with *Saved*, we all knew. We were going to go in there and have a Holy Ghost good time.

You wrote a couple songs with him, including "Don't Make Her Cry," inspired by what your father said to him, and "Give Him My All," which you eventually recorded yourself.

How did writing with him happen?

I always reminded Bob of what my dad said. I said, "We're going to eventually have to write this song." He started laughing and he said, "What song?" I said, "The words that my dad said: Don't make her cry." He said okay.

"Give Him My All" was when I was on the road with him. We were on the bus traveling to another city. I had a pen and paper in my hand, and he said, "What are you doing?" I said, "I'm writing a song and I'm stuck. I don't know what to do now." He said, "Can I see it?" I let him see it, and he looked at it. He took the pen, flipped the page and started writing. I said, "What are you writing?" He said, "I'm writing the bridge to the song." He wrote the bridge to "Give Him My All."

How did it come that you decided to record it with your sisters so many years later?

When we recorded our first record, we put "Blowin' in the Wind" on, and I also wanted to put that song on that too, since it was a song that talked about, "got to give God your all." That's what my sisters and I do every time we get up and we sing.

Have you ever recorded "Don't Make Her Cry"?

Not yet. I'm not going to record it. I'm trying to find a male artist that would like to record that. I'm trying to get Buddy Miller to record it. That's my brother from another mother.

You and your sisters sat in with him in concert a couple of times more recently [in 2012 and 2013] for "Blowin' in the Wind." How did those come about?

He came to town and called me. I said, "Do you still end your show with 'Blowin' in the Wind'?" He said, "Yes." I said, "Well, my sisters and I are going to come up there and sing with you." He laughed and said, "Okay, come on."

Did you have to rehearse that with him all these years later or did you guys just go on stage and wing it?

Like I said, when I first met him, that was one of the songs I remembered from way back. My sisters and all of us already knew that. We just showed up on stage and he trusted that we knew what we were doing.

It's nice that you two were still in touch 30 years after you toured with him.

I will always keep up with Bob Dylan. I will always be concerned and will always keep up with him because he's a good man. He's a good man.

Fred Tackett, Spooner Oldham, and Dylan at the *Saved* sessions in Muscle Shoals, Alabama.
Photo by Dick Cooper

Spooner Oldham

"Respect." "When a Man Loves a Woman." "Mustang Sally." Those are but three of the many iconic tracks Spooner Oldham played on as the house keyboard player at FAME Studios in Muscle Shoals, Alabama. He also, with his writing partner Dan Penn, penned songs for The Box Tops, Janis Joplin, and Percy Sledge.

By the time he paired up with Dylan, though, he'd left the swampy South to become an LA session musician, popping up on albums by folks like Linda Ronstadt and Jackson Browne. The studio whiz hadn't actually toured much before Bob brought him on for the first leg of his gospel run. (He would later go on to tour plenty, most notably with his longtime collaborator Neil Young.)

When I called up Oldham to chat, his wife Karen was by his side. And while Spooner is soft-spoken and reticent to toot his own horn, Karen is happy to speak up on his behalf. She was around during Oldham's time with Dylan and has her own stories from the road to share. So an interview with Spooner soon became an interview with Spooner and Karen. I think you'll agree it's for the better.

. . . .

How did you get your start playing with Dylan?

The first two weeks I played with Bob Dylan was at Bill Graham's newly renovated Warfield Theater in San Francisco. It was sold out before we got to the stage, I remember that. That was unusual for me, to experience that kind of thing.

When we drove up in the van — me, Bob, and the band in one car — and approached the building, there was some youngsters out on the sidewalk, maybe 15 or 20. They're standing there with sticks with signs on top. Reminded me of these '60s posters. I thought, "What in the world's going on?" It was protesting his changing from Judaism to Christianity.

I've learned playing with Neil and other people: People will buy tickets to protest. They may leave or they may make a noise, but they'll show up. After about three days of that, it sorta cleared out. People get it out of their system.

It became clear he wasn't simply going to change the entire setlist at that point too, probably.

No. He wasn't going to do anything except just two albums. We were doing the *Slow Train Coming* album, which I had nothing to do with recording-wise. And he had written some new songs that became *Saved*. We recorded that as a touring band. We were doing those two albums and that was it. He wasn't taking requests. "Mr. Tambourine Man" wasn't going to happen.

To back up a little, how did you get involved in the band in the first place?

I never knew exactly. My assumption is, Bob Dylan recorded an album in Muscle Shoals produced by Jerry Wexler and Barry Beckett. Barry Beckett was my personal friend, and I had worked with Jerry Wexler on Aretha Franklin stuff and Wilson Pickett stuff.

When they finished that album, I think Bob needed a keyboard player. The keyboard player on *Slow Train Coming* [Beckett] was a record producer. He worked at Muscle Shoals Sound Studio. That was his studio, he and The Swampers.[60]

So he couldn't tour.

That's my assumption. He had a job. Somebody asked for a reference; either Tim Drummond may have suggested me or Jerry Wexler. Who knows? But it came from that. At the end of that *[Slow Train Coming]* session, he wanted to do a tour and needed a keyboard player. I was recommended.

I lived in Nashville at the time. My wife was pregnant. She was saying, "You need to get a job. Go to McDonald's or something." I said, "It's all right. Something good will happen." Bob called me. He called me himself; he didn't have a manager call me or whatever. I did the tour.

Had you done much touring that extensive before, or were you mostly a studio guy?

I hadn't done much touring. First one I think was Linda Ronstadt and maybe Dickey Betts. I was mostly a studio guy. I didn't want to tour because my thought was, "Why go on the road when I've got a studio job and I can go home every night, sometimes by supper, and go to my own bed?"

---

60 Nickname for Muscle Shoals' legendary crew of backing musicians that earlier included Oldham himself.

Except the more I toured, the more favorable it became to me. I got used to it. Now I've done it so much, I can get into it.

Do you remember much about the rehearsal process? I think it was in Santa Monica at Rundown Studios.

We stayed in a motel on the beach, a little funky place. My wife and daughter Roxanne, a little child three or four years old. Regina McCrary, a background singer from Nashville, she was there on the beach practicing. We were rehearsing two or three weeks.

Karen: They rehearsed for three and a half weeks. Every day for hours and hours and hours. It was nuts. Spooner's never liked rehearsals. He likes the spur of the moment. I stayed a nervous wreck the whole time because I know my husband. He doesn't want to ever play anything the same ever again. Even if it's "When a Man Loves a Woman," that organ that made him world-famous, or if it's Aretha, he's going to change it up. It don't matter. The creativity in Spooner just can't handle it. I think purposely, he tries not to remember exactly like it is.

Spooner: We had Tim Drummond, bass player, who's a longtime friend from Cincinnati. I asked him one time, I said, "Tim, what'd you do before this?" He said, "Well, I played bass with James Brown, and I played bass with Conway Twitty." I thought that was a strange contrast.

Jim Keltner, I had known him a long time. We'd done a lot of session work together in Los Angeles. The black, tall keyboard player I met out there; his name was Terry Young, and his wife Mona Lisa Young was one of the background singers. Fred Tackett, the guitarist, would later be in the Little Feat band.

I remember walking up the stairs to go to rehearse with Bob, and [passing a room with] Terry, Mona Lisa, and the other singers learning these gospel songs which were going to be done as an opening act prior to the band and Bob coming out on stage. I'd hear them every day walking up. They sounded really good.

At the end of the rehearsal, I'm sitting on the steps with Bob outside. Bob says to me, "Are you ready to start rehearsing with the girls?" I said, "Why do that? That guy [Terry] sounds great. I don't see any point." He said, "Well, I never considered that." He hired him. He was already rehearsed.

Oh, so Terry wasn't a part of the band initially? He was married to Mona Lisa and just there helping rehearse.

Well, I don't know Bob's thoughts or Terry's thoughts, but that's the way it sounded to me. I don't think he planned on taking him, but he did. I never told anybody about that because it didn't matter to me. I was just being a little bit lazy, really. I didn't want any more than I already had on my plate.

With two keyboard players now, how did you and Terry divide up the piano and organ parts on the songs you both are playing on?

It developed real easily and quickly. I was playing Wurlitzer electric piano on most of it, Hammond organ on some. I think he was playing an acoustic grand piano on pretty much all of it, except a couple of songs Bob would do solo on the piano.

Did you have any favorite songs to play on stage?

"What Can I Do for You." He'd play harmonica after singing the song and I'd be on the organ. He and I would just improvise the instrumental section. It'd be different every night. It kept getting longer and longer, because we were having fun.[61]

I remember one night on stage, I don't know what song we were doing, but some guy came out of the audience. He got up on stage right in Bob's face, talking the Bible with him or something. Of course, security got him off the stage pretty quick, but Bob said later, "Bring 'em on; I'm ready." He wasn't backing off from the controversy or the questions. He was pretty well prepared for anything.

After the first few shows, when the protesters outside left, do you remember a lot of that? Noise from the crowd or controversy.

The first three nights at Warfield Theatre, I had never experienced this before in my life or since. Okay, first song. Half the audience: clap, clap, clap. Half the audience: boo, boo, boo. I had never been booed before and thought, "How weird is this?" I knew he was singing good, we were playing well, the sound was okay, no faulty technology or anything. I'm trying to figure that out, "What's going on?" As the time went on, I realized people protested his religion. They weren't protesting the songs or his playing ability or singing ability. Religious conflict. *[sighs]*

Karen: I don't believe that.

Spooner: Well, what was it then, Karen? They were half booing, half—

She's saying they were gonna do all this stuff because he wasn't doing what they wanted him to do. No "Mr. Tambourine Man." I felt it was other thing also.

Well, from other people I've spoken to, the whole environment was very religious, with

---

61 Guitarist Fred Tackett also described this Dylan–Oldham interplay as a high point in my interview with him.

When we drove up in the van, there was youngsters out on the sidewalk, maybe 15 or 20. Standing with sticks with signs on top. Reminded me of these '60s posters. Protesting his changing from Judaism to Christianity.

. . . .

Bob praying with you all before every show and giving the long sermons on stage.

Right, right. Well, he was being true to the form of what he perceived as the Christian religious thing. Whatever that was to him. Give up all earthly things. We would stay in pretty modest hotels.

Karen: No, no. Not modest. Cheap.

Spooner: Cheap hotels. *[chuckles]* She's correct.

Karen: We wouldn't even stay in a couple of 'em!

Spooner: Anyway, he was wanting to give an accurate perception to whoever might be looking, I think, as much as anything.

Karen: I think he believed it.

Spooner: Well, he believed it, yeah. He drank the Kool-Aid.

I did notice Bob had a procession, a loyal following. If we'd stay at a motel and the next morning we'd get on a bus and head down the road to the next town, there would be at least two or three cars.

Karen: Hogwash. Twenty!

Spooner: They'd follow us the whole time, the whole tour, in many cities. That's a fact. That's not an exaggeration.

Karen: When we got to Memphis, there was at least 40 cars waiting on us.

Spooner: It was odd. I don't know where they came from. I never tried to figure it out. No way to know why they were doing that. They could have been following me. Who knows? *[Karen: No!]* I'm kidding.

Spooner super fans.

They coulda been following Jim or following Tim, but I will assume they're following Bob Dylan. *[laughs]*

Do you remember playing Saturday Night Live*? Even before the Warfield, that was* *your first public performance. Seems like a high-pressure debut for a new band.*

Well, in a sense, but it was really a boost of confidence to play that first because it's a real test of what you're doing. If it's good, it's going to come off good. If it's bad, it's going to come off bad. I like that kind of pressure and I'm sure he does also. It's good pressure, not bad pressure.

Karen: He got inside my coat.

Spooner: I'll let you tell it. Karen will tell you one of the little episodes after *Saturday Night Live.*

Karen: I don't remember exactly when the guys got to New York to rehearse for *Saturday Night Live*, but I flew in on Wednesday. I was there through the rehearsals until the show Saturday. It was an experience. One of the NBC people came up to us wives, and said, "Donald Trump is signing autographs in the lobby if y'all would like to meet him." I refused. I don't really know if any of the other ladies went, but I just already knew who he was at that time.

It was a good week. Bob seemed to be in a really good place. He looked forward to it.

When we left *Saturday Night Live*, there was so many people trying to follow us that the limousine driver drove in reverse through multiple streets and alleys to get away from the followers. It was just insane.

Then when we got to the hotel, there was maybe 500 people on the sidewalk. It was just hordes trying to get to him. Bob just looked at me. I knew what he meant by the look, and why I knew I'll never know. He literally crawled inside my big coat and disappeared. He was consumed by a tent of my coat; nobody ever saw him.

Wait, you smuggled him into the hotel under your coat?

Karen: I did, I did. We went in through the club that was then part of the hotel. The big fancy disco club that was downstairs. We had to go in through that entrance to get into the hotel. He stayed in my coat until we got into the elevator.

You mean there's people dancing and loud music and you've got Bob Dylan smuggled in your giant coat?

Karen: Exactly. All the way into the elevator. It was absolutely wild. The craziest experience I think I've ever gone through.

Spooner: That night, I learned that he hides from the paparazzi. It scared him, I think. We just kept rolling down the road, though.

Were there any other memorable shows, particular concerts that stand out to you all these years later?

Spooner: Yeah, Toronto. I remember that because there was a lot of cameras. He had three accountants riding on the bus with us. One of them said to me the day before, they're going to have a three-camera shoot of this concert in Toronto. The girls would be wearing black, and the guys need to wear black. I said, "Well, I don't have any black slacks, and *I'm* not going to buy them." So they gave me $60. I went shopping and I bought some slacks.

I saw that film a year ago for the first time. It never came out commercially I don't think, or even underhandedly. I don't know how it got it out to where I could see it even.

Karen: It was in 1980.

Spooner: 1980, yeah. A long time ago for an old man to remember.

What about another unusual gig, the Grammy Awards? Also 1980.

I actually sat in the audience a minute after we played, and it was just boring, boring. It was just another music show to me. I've done a lot of that stuff. I've done it with Neil Young a bunch. It's second nature.

Speaking of clothes, you all are wearing tuxedos. A dress code there, too?

Spooner: It wasn't a code. That's what we choose to do, as smart Southern people. That's me talking now. It's not the management.

Karen: You always had a dress code.

Spooner: Yeah, I always had my own dress code. I know when to dress and how to dress.

Karen: You had your clothes tailor-made in the '60s.

Spooner: Yeah. I don't think they mentioned wearing a tux. They may have.

Karen: They bought 'em! Or rented them. The whole bit. Bob was the only live-playing band that whole Grammys. Everybody else was recorded.

Spooner: The Oscars, I played that recently with Elton John. They make you a suit that's tailor-made. The clothes I had on, I didn't get to carry home. They had my name inside, and they hang it up in the closet there when you leave. It goes to the museum, I guess. That's pretty nice. The Grammys is the same way.

Karen: Same with Neil's movie.

Spooner: Yeah, the *Heart of Gold* thing. There was that guy, Manuel [Cuevas].[62]

---

62 Cuevas is the same person who made the rainbow-Jesus coat Kinky Friedman told me about.

He died, but he's got a partner, a younger man, that makes tailor-made clothes. He made us all clothes for that movie.

What do you remember about recording Saved*? As you said, you weren't on* Slow Train, *but then the whole touring band goes back to Muscle Shoals for the second album.*

Spooner: Yeah, at Muscle Shoals Sound Studio, the second one they had. They left the small one, bought a bigger one down on the river. It had been a naval armory, it was so big. There again, Barry Beckett and Jerry Wexler were producing, the same as *Slow Train Coming.* We were so well rehearsed and had played so many gigs by that, it was just turn on the machine and let's go. Not much to remember about it, really.

Karen: I'll tell the story about Bob in Birmingham. I'll tell a good story before I tell the bad story, or what I consider the bad story.

Bob didn't give any free tickets to any show anywhere. If you had guests, Bob would allow the band to buy them at a cheaper rate, and he'd just take it out of the salaries. When we got to Birmingham, Spooner growing up in Muscle Shoals, of course all of his family and all of our friends wanted tickets. I think we got 33 tickets. Nobody knew we were paying for them. We never told stuff like that.

One or two of the kids — and when I say kids, under 13 — found the roster in our room to the room list of everybody. A couple of them went up to Bob's room and knocked on the door.

Uh-oh.

Karen: Uh-oh is right. So we're already in trouble before the show even occurs. But he was nice to them; he didn't do anything ugly. It was just bizarre trying to keep the kids and everybody corralled so they didn't get in his face. We didn't know they'd gone to his room until probably a week later. Nobody told us.

Anyway, the show went well. After the show, or it may have been during the encores, Barry Beckett came over and sat down next to me. He said, "I really need to go backstage and talk to Bob after the show. Will you please take me backstage with you? They won't let me back there."

I had this immediate "Oh, shit… What do I do? It's his producer. He produced the Grammy-winning album. Surely it's okay." 'Cause I knew you could not carry anybody backstage. I knew that. But it's Barry! His producer!

Now, you have to understand, they started rehearsing in the summer in LA. I don't know exactly when it started, but sometime during that period, Bob started calling me at home. And he'd talk for an hour or two. I had a little one, the house was getting remodeled, my husband's on tour. In other words, I'm crazy as a loon.

You're not getting a lot of sleep.

Karen: No. I'm going, "Why is Bob Dylan calling me?" Spooner's kind of going, "Well, he doesn't talk to me, so it's a good thing he's talking to somebody."

I would tell you what he talked about if I could remember, but it was nothing. He'd talk about…the color of sunshine. I mean, you never knew. You just kinda talked to him. At one point, he did say to me, "You buy most of Spooner's clothes?" I said, "Yeah. When we got married, he had 'em tailor-made, and I didn't feel we could afford to have them tailor-made anymore. I had to buy them off the rack so we could afford to buy me clothes too." And Bob said, "Well, go buy me some."

He liked your eye?

Karen: I guess. But I went and bought him a bunch of stuff, and he didn't like any of it. *[laughs]* I don't know if he told me the wrong sizes, I don't know. All I know is he returned it all to me, and I returned it all to the store. That's the bizarre relationship we had had.

So [at the Birmingham show,] I thought to myself, "Surely to goodness it'll be okay if I take Barry back." You got to understand, I did not feel privileged, I did not stick my nose in, I didn't ever knock on his hotel room door. I never called him, not once. But I just thought, well surely since he talks to me, that it will be okay.

I took Barry backstage. Bob went crazy and threw him out. Bob wouldn't even talk to his own producer. All Barry wanted to know was, do you have a particular microphone you want? Do you have a particular—? It was legit stuff Barry was wanting.

Bob never spoke to me again and hasn't to this day.

You're standing there in the corner witnessing this?

Karen: No, Barry came and told me. Barry was dumbfounded as well. He apologized. He said, "I would have never asked you to do that if I had known."

Like I said, Bob has never spoken to me since. Oh, well! That's a side to Bob that— when he says he doesn't want to be bothered, he doesn't want to be bothered.

I have no clue in the last 40 years if he's changed at all, but my guesses are, no, he hasn't. He is terribly shy. Terribly shy. Spooner was terribly shy. I worked *hard* to get him out of it. It's obvious I'm not shy. Real obvious. I really spent a lifetime trying to get him different. I don't know that anybody could have gotten Bob to change if there'd been somebody working at it. Anyway, that's just something else

I thought of. They talk about him being private, but *Lord.*

Spooner, you did three tours, but not the entire gospel-era run. Why did you leave the band after that?

Spooner: I don't really know how it came to be that I wasn't in the band anymore. It wasn't like "Oh, don't come back" or "You're fired" or anything. I don't remember talking to anybody about it. I just wasn't with him anymore. I wonder. I know he always changed bands, so I didn't expect to stay long. But some of them stayed with him, you're right.

Yeah, Keltner stayed. Regina. All for another year, basically.

Spooner: I don't know what that was about. I don't think I got ugly with him or anything or failed to perform my duty, so I don't know. I'll always wonder, but I don't linger on it because I could care less, really. I've been blessed with opportunities, willing to work, and I don't look back too much too often. Too much to do today and tomorrow, the Lord willing. We moved back to California. Shortly after that, I went out with JJ Cale on the tour and did an album with him. Then I went out with Neil Young.

Karen: We don't know that story, except my brother-in-law unexpectedly died in Florida about the time that they should have gotten back together after being on a break. We were in Florida at my parents' house for well over two weeks. This is the time when there wasn't cell phones and what have you. If they tried to call him and couldn't get him, we have no clue. All I know is he was not brought back for that, and Al Kooper was put in it.[63]

Of course, like I said, Bob was really pissed off at us. If that's why Spooner got fired, it's my fault. Oh well! We ended up going back to California and I became a chiropractor, so I don't care. *[laughs]*

Like he said, we don't know why he was let go. We don't know. After that fiasco, *I* never heard from [Bob] again. He was calling so regular and talking and— I don't know, I can't go there, I never understood it anyway. Why is he calling this crazy woman at home with the baby?

It was just bizarre that the relationship changed after that event in Birmingham. We never knew why Al was brought in and replaced Spooner. The rest of the band, when they came to Nashville to play, just about the whole band came to the house for a chili supper. Spooner went to the show. I stayed home with my child.

---

63 Kooper did join the band not long after, but Willie Smith was Oldham's immediate replacement on keys.

Did you and Dylan have any overlap after you left?

Spooner: I'm trying to think if I ever saw him again after that. I don't remember seeing him anymore. Anyway, I wish him well. I know he's made fortunes many times over, and I got no reason to feel sorry for him. Until he calls me again, I'm here.

Fred Tackett accompanies Dylan at Toronto's Massey Hall, April 1980.
Photo by Lloyd Walton

Fred Tackett

Guitarist Fred Tackett is best known for his work with Little Feat. He worked with the band starting with their iconic third album, *Dixie Chicken*, and continued to collaborate with the band and frontman Lowell George until George's death in 1979. When Little Feat reformed in 1988, Tackett became a full-time member, and he's stayed there ever since. When we spoke on the phone, he was riding the Little Feat tour bus somewhere in the Midwest.

George's sudden passing actually precipitated Tackett's work with Dylan, when the guitarist unexpectedly found himself with free time right as Dylan was putting together his first gospel-era band. Tackett accompanied Dylan for every single show in those three years, from the first year in 1979 when the band was performing exclusively Dylan's new Christian material through the end in 1981 when they were mixing oldies back into the sets. He also joined the touring band to record *Saved* and *Shot of Love*.

In recent decades, Tackett has found time in between his Little Feat duties to appear as a sideman on an absurdly long list of records by everyone from Dolly Parton to Bob Seger. He even recorded with Dylan's son Jakob, on The Wallflowers' quadruple-platinum 1996 album *Bringing Down the Horse*, making him one of the few musicians to collaborate with two generations of Dylans.

. . . .

We'll start with my usual first question. How did you get involved?

Well, I'd been on tour with Lowell George, and he died on that tour [June 29, 1979]. About two weeks after that, I think Jim Keltner and Tim Drummond basically recommended me as somebody to audition.

How did you know those guys?

Well, I'd worked with Timmy Drummond and Jim Keltner on sessions for billions of people over the years. I'd been seeing Drummond, so maybe he had something to do with it. My wife called me up at a session and said, "Hey, we got a call from Bob Dylan's office. They want you to come down and jam with him."

We did that every day for about three weeks. I was driving over every day to Santa Monica, going over mostly his brand-new songs. I remember I was driving down the road and I thought, "Wow, man, three weeks. I wonder when we're going to get to the end of this."

Was it clear that this is an audition? Or that there's a tour?

No. It's just like, "Want to come down and jam?" I kept thinking, "Well, heck, what is the point of all this?" I knew they were going to go out and do a gig or out on tour, 'cause Spooner Oldham and all the band was there, but nobody was really saying much about it.

I mean, I was starting to get a little frustrated. Then I told myself on the way down there, "There's 50,000 guitar players who would love to go spend three weeks jamming with Bob Dylan and Jim Keltner. What are you griping about?"

I think just a couple of days before we were getting ready to leave, Bob called me up on the phone and said, "We're going to go do this *Saturday Night Live* show and then do a tour. Can you play with us?" I went, "Heck yeah, man. Sounds good to me. Have your manager call me and we'll work it out." He goes, "I don't have a manager."

After we did our little rehearsal the next day, he called me into the office he had. He said, "Well, what's the deal?" I started to say, "Well, Bob—" and he held his finger up over his mouth, like, don't talk so loud, and pointed to his ear. He leaned his head over, and I had to lean into his ear. I say, "You know, Bob, I'd normally get session work at double scale." That's like $600 a day or something like that. He leaned back and looked at me like, are you crazy? Then he'd stick his head down again like, talk to me some more. That was just hysterical. He was playing around with me with his great sense of humor. Anyway, it all worked out fine, and that's how I got the job.

The first album Slow Train Coming, *is that out at this point? Do you know those songs?*

Yeah, we were getting ready to go tour behind those songs. Mark Knopfler[64] was doing his own thing. He wasn't going to be on the gig, so they were looking for a guitar player.

---

64 Lead guitarist on the record, from Dire Straits, and later the producer of Dylan's 1984 album *Infidels*.

Knopfler has such a distinctive sound. How do you find your own way into those songs?

Well, first thing I did was stop playing Stratocaster, which is what I normally would play, and start playing a Les Paul so that I would sound different. I knew I wasn't going to compete with what Mark Knopfler was playing. He plays beautiful stuff on that record. I just started playing other stuff that I hoped was *alternatively* as beautiful. Kurt Vonnegut famously said for artists, if you leave home, you're going to run into Mozart on the campus. Do your own thing and don't worry about how many people are so much better than you, because you will run into Mozart.

Bob was playing a Les Paul as well. Finally, at one point, he said, "Hey, you know what, these things are too heavy. Let's go back to the Stratocaster." So we went back to playing Stratocasters again.

Did you have much of a background in gospel music? He's got the backing singers, this big band. It's not what people at the time associated with Dylan's sound, much less lyrical content.

I was a trumpet major in college. So believe me, I played a lot of classic gospel music. I mean, I played trumpet in Jewish churches, Catholic churches, every kind of church. I played in brass choirs at Easter and all kinds of holiday stuff. Over the years, I did a lot of sacred music as opposed to secular music. Tent shows and revivals and masses and everything else. I used to work for J.T. Adams and his Men of Texas. J.T. Adams had a big Methodist Church in Sulphur Springs and he put on these giant tent shows. I played herald trumpet and had 30 pieces of silver in a bag I would shake in front of the mic. Just another gig, man. Just a different employer.

You mentioned Saturday Night Live. *That's a high-pressure first show.*

It was! That was ridiculous. That was when I first saw Lou Marini, who I'd gone to college with in North Texas. He was playing in the *Saturday Night Live* band.

"Blue Lou!" He was in the Blues Brothers movie.

That's right. He was like the best saxophone player in North Texas, him and Billy Harper. I got to reconnect up with him. Gilda Radner loaned us her dressing room so we could hang out there.

We just went out and did our thing, and it came off really good. I remember when we first started playing, I physically couldn't look up. I thought, "I got to raise my head." I couldn't do it because I was so nervous. I was like, stare at your left hand on the guitar and play and don't look up. I just was paralyzed.

I was rewatching those videos, and you're pretty prominent. You're soloing on "Gotta Serve Somebody" and the camera's on you—

That's what it was like playing with Bob. You just jump into deep water and follow along. He wouldn't tell you what he was going to play. I mean, on *Saturday Night Live*, we knew what we were going to do, but in a show, he's liable to start playing anything. It was a great, great, great experience learning to be ready to do anything. Now, when I play with Little Feat, we do whatever. I don't think about it and I don't get nervous about it because of spending those three years playing with Bob.

Speaking of Little Feat, the first time I saw Dylan [in 2004], Richie Hayward was one of the two drummers.

Oh God, I totally had forgotten all about that. Richie was the best, man.[65] Richie was like the Art Blakey of rock n' roll. I mean, he just was one of a kind. Every drummer I've ever met worships Richie. And he was pretty much self-taught. That's why he ended up having such a individual style. It used to drive Lowell *crazy*, because Lowell would go to great extents to get him to play a part, then Richie would immediately forget it. Next time he played the song, he'd play something totally different. Lowell would be, "I just spent two days getting you to play something, man!" Richie would be, "What are you talking about?"

After SNL, *you guys have that long run in San Francisco, a dozen shows in a row.*

I remember we were staying in the Tenderloin area. It was a funky area. Sitting in my room, I could look down and see the hookers on each corner. They had to keep moving, so when the light would change, they would go across. Walk and don't walk, all day long. That's where we were staying.

Was that by choice or was the tour on a tight budget?

I think it was by choice. Just where Bob said he wanted us to stay. I don't even know if he was there. He probably was. He usually stayed the same place we were in.

The shows were great, because every night there was somebody coming to sit in. Carlos Santana was coming down just about every night hanging out. He was very supportive of the spiritualism of Bob's music. He was going, "We're doing the same thing. I have my version of this thing and Bob's got his version."

---

65 Hayward, Little Feat's longtime drummer, passed away in 2010.

Bob would turn the lights on because people were heckling and yelling things. Best comment that I ever saw was a guy in the front row with a poster board: "Jesus loves your old songs."

. . . .

They opened that Dylan Center in Tulsa recently. One of the things they unearthed was footage of Michael Bloomfield with you guys. It was his last time playing with Bob and maybe his last time playing, period.

I think period. I did a bunch of interviews for that about Steve Ripley, who was also playing guitar with us later on. For the first couple of years, it was a smaller band, but then Ripley came in. He was very instrumental in getting that Tulsa museum going, because he lived in Tulsa.

Early on in the run, is there controversy? You hear about people wanting to hear the old hits and Bob's not playing them. Instead he's preaching.

There were occasions where Bob would turn the lights on because people were heckling and yelling things. Mostly like, "Play your old songs." The very best comment that I ever saw was a guy in the front row had a poster board. Written on the poster board was, "Jesus loves your old songs." I thought, "Great point."

That's clever. I'm sure it didn't work.

No, but it was like, yeah, right on.

He had some funny stories. There's some live tapes where he's talking to the audience. He's saying things like, "I went and played at this place and I tried to tell them about Jesus. It was weird, they're making this sound, they're going *boo.*" Like he'd never heard anything like that before. "I don't know what that meant, man. Very weird." That was hysterical.

Speaking of "Jesus loves your old songs," halfway through he does bring back in older stuff. Did you enjoy doing some of the classics?

Oh yeah. I just had shivers that went up down my spine when we started playing "Like A Rolling Stone." When people heard him starting that, the place went nuts. It was this epiphany that happened with the audience and the bands and everybody. I had chills.

Is there a whole other batch of rehearsals? You've got the gospel stuff down and now all of a sudden he's adding 15 or 20 songs.

We went to rehearsal one day and started playing old songs. [He] didn't have an explanation for it, saying, "Okay, we're going to start doing this now." We just started playing old songs again.

We went to San Francisco again a year later and did another residency thing there. Roger McGuinn came down and played, Rick Danko, Maria Muldaur, all kinds of people. I can picture Bloomfield sitting backstage watching television.

Jerry Garcia sat in also at that second run at the Warfield.

That was a funny night. Bob called him out on the second song that we played. Jerry told us later that he was high, man. He was noodling up in the upper register of the guitar, like all the time. When Bob was singing, he's playing *doodle-doodle-ooo*, noodling around and doing all kinds of stuff. Bob's looking over at me like, "What the fuck is going on?"

We got off the set and got in the van. Bob's going, "That's it, I'm not having people sit in with us anymore." I said, "Bob, you gotta bring 'em on the encore. You can't bring someone on out the second song, because they're going to stay there all night."

I think this predates that a little bit, but you guys had that big performance with the Grammys where everyone's dressed to the nines.[66] What do you remember about that?

That was a fun time, man. I had a bowtie. Bob said, "Your bowtie's too big." I had to put on a smaller one. He had one of those clip-on kind of things. I had a more flamboyant and bigger one.

The Doobie Brothers were there. That was the night that they won all kinds of awards. They were friends of ours, so we were hanging with them. Tom Dowd was there in the audience. Rickie Lee Jones — I think she won a Grammy [Best New Artist]. A lot of people that I had worked for, and a lot of albums I played on were being represented. And Bob won!

That always helps. Did you have any favorite songs to play during your time?

---

66 Dylan and the band performed "Gotta Serve Somebody" at the 1980 Grammys. He also won his first Grammy, for the same song.

Some of the ballads were my favorites. The one that Sinéad O'Connor did, "I Believe in You." That's a gorgeous song. Oh God, he had a couple of them that were just beautiful, beautiful, beautiful. I think "Man Gave Names to All the Animals" was probably my least favorite one, but I liked it fine.

What do you remember about going down to Muscle Shoals to record Saved?

[Producer Jerry] Wexler said it was like the old Ray Charles band, because we were just on the road. We drove the bus into Muscle Shoals, checked into our Holiday Inn, went down to the studio, recorded for about five days, then got back on the bus and went to the next gig. Bob said, "Mix it and send it to me." It was old-school.

Were you able to do it so quick because you'd been playing them live?

Yeah. When we were rehearsing for about three weeks before I got the gig, we were rehearsing all the songs off that were going to be on *Saved*. Bob taught us all the new songs.

How does he teach you a song?

He'd just play it on the guitar, start singing and we'd follow along. They're not really complicated musically. You could hear what he was doing. There was never any charts or anything.

Later on, he had a cool way of rehearsing. I would go in early, and he'd say, "Teach the band a song." He would give me a tape that was not one of his songs. We did Bob Seger's "Night Moves." We did The Muppets' "Rainbow Connection."

No kidding.

Yeah. Bob sang the shit out of that. My theory was, he didn't want us to play his songs over and over. I think he didn't want us to get parts, because if you play something four, five, six times, pretty soon you've got yourself this little part and you're going to start to play it all the time. He was trying to keep a little more spontaneity in the band by not having us just beat his songs to death. He'd have us play "Rainbow Connection," or that Neil Diamond song, "Sweet Caroline."

That one they released on the Springtime in New York *Bootleg Series in 2021. It is wild. I don't think that's something that had ever been bootlegged.*

Jim Keltner and I later did a session with Neil Diamond and Burt Bacharach and Carole Bayer Sager, the songwriters. We're standing around sharing a jay. Neil says, "The other day I got this tape from Bob Dylan. He sent me a copy of him singing 'Sweet Caroline'. It's great, but I was really surprised to get it in the mail." Keltner and I both said, "We played on it, man."

We did a good version of "Willin'" [by Little Feat] too.[67] He said, "You got to sing harmony with me." He was a good friend of Lowell's. If you ever saw the back of Lowell's solo album, he's standing there with a rod and a reel and a bunch of seaweed on the end of the hook. Holding it up like it's a specimen fish. That was shot at Bob's house out in Malibu. Bob wanted him to play in the band, but he didn't live that long.

So that's Saved, *and then you record* Shot of Love. *A lot of the same cast of characters, but a different location.*

We did all those sessions at different studios in Los Angeles. One of my best memories is, Bob had a song called "Caribbean Wind." Jimmy Iovine was producing. He called up and said, "Come down early. I want to get a track of this song before Bob shows up to play it to him."

We were all down in the studio. Shelly Yakus was the engineer, Jimmy Iovine's producing, and I'm in a back room with David Mansfield. I'm playing mandolin, and he's playing fiddle. Jim Keltner was baffled off in a corner somewhere. We came in and listened. It was like the A-team studio sound, like all the other sessions that I would've done. A perfect pop-record sound.

We're over at Studio 55, which was Richard Perry's studio. It was an old studio that had been renovated. Richard Perry[68] had made it the top notch. It's where he did the *Nilsson Schmilsson* album and all that kind of stuff. So Bob comes into the studio, and they know that Bob really likes old vintage studios. He's always looking for old mics and the old stuff.

They start telling him that Bing Crosby recorded "White Christmas" here in the studio. Bob's like, "Yeah?" Then they play the track of us doing "Caribbean Wind." Bob turns to one of his gofer guys and says, "Go get me the music for 'White Christmas,' because I can't record any of *my* music here."

Then he goes, "Fred, where are you?" I said, "I'm in the back room here with the mandolin." He goes, "Get your electric guitar and come out here in the room." They got rid of all the baffles around Keltner, and we just all started playing live.

---

67 Though they never performed "Willin'" publicly at the time, Dylan would sing it a few times onstage a decade later.

68 Big hit-making producer for Harry Nilsson, Barbra Streisand, and Carly Simon. *AllMusic* calls him "the most renowned producer in the field of popular music during the 1970s."

We're going through "Groom's Still Waiting at the Altar" and different songs like that.

I look up in the studio, and there's nobody there. Jimmy Iovine and Shelly Yakus just left. The only guy there was the second engineer who was running the tape machine, which was all we really needed, I guess.

Couple specific shows I wanted to ask you about that might be memorable. There's this famous run at Earls Court in London in 1981.

We stayed there several days. Stevie Wonder came to the shows. Eric Clapton was hanging out with us. I had this black beautiful electric 12-string that I would play on "Like a Rolling Stone" and different songs. Clapton came back and said, "Man, George Harrison and I are both out trying to figure out, what's that guitar you've got there, man?" They were all lusting after it.

We went over to Ray Cooper's[69] house. It was right after John Lennon had been assassinated. Julian [Lennon] was hanging out. All the guys were keeping close to Julian during that period.

Then a few weeks later, there's a show in France where there's a blackout and a tragedy.

At stadium shows in France, people would climb up the telephone poles outside. One guy would climb up and then people would start climbing up behind him, trying to see over the edge of the stadium. So people from the bottom were pushing the people on the top up. Finally, some guy hit the live wire on the top. That blew the whole stadium out, and the guy died. They caught one guy trying to cut the power underneath the stadium with a bolt cutter on a different occasion.

Here's a real weird one. Dylan's childhood friend Larry Kegan came out for a few shows to sing. Mostly notable because Dylan played saxophone, which I think is the only time ever. I'm pretty sure he doesn't know how to play the saxophone.

I bet he thought he looked cool. He would walk around backstage with the strap of the sax hanging down. It looked cool, like you're a bebopper. He was just kind of sporting it a little bit, and then he brought it on stage and played a couple notes on it.

You opened almost all the gospel shows with "Gotta Serve Somebody." That's probably still the best-known song of that whole set.

That's a great tune, man. My musical brother Sam Clayton just has discovered

69 British percussionist who's toured with Elton John, Billy Joel, and more.

that, and he plays it every day. It's just so funky, man. Tim Drummond just has the simplest bass part, it's just boom, boom, boom. It's perfect. Great blues.

How about one of the best vocal performances, "When He Returns"?

"When He Returns," that is just a beautiful song, man. Beautiful. He just sang the heck out of it.

What was really amazing about it was he used to play this harmonica thing at the end.[70] This extended version. It was just him and Spooner, and Spooner would feed him these chords and Bob would just keep playing the harmonica. Spooner kept putting what we call substitution chords underneath it. The chords Spooner was playing just made Bob's— even though he was playing the same notes over and over, every time he would play it, it would be sound completely different, because Spooner would put this other chord change underneath him. It was just gorgeous.

When they did the box set of *Trouble in Mind*, I asked the guy, I said, "Man, did you get that cadenza thing that Spooner and Bob would do?" They found the absolute best one man and put it on that box set. That was just absolutely transcendent.

Another song I always liked that never made an album or anything is "Ain't Gonna Go to Hell for Anybody."

That was one of my favorites too. It was funny. "I can manipulate people just like anybody, wine 'em and dine 'em…"

How about "Slow Train," the almost title track of Slow Train Coming?

That's just a classic tune. They're all fun to play. He gave lots of room for improvisation. Sometimes I'd play two or three solos in a song. Then Spooner would play, and the piano player [Terry Young]; everybody had lots of room to jam doing all those tunes.

I guess my last question is, how does it end? You do this last US tour in '81, then is there talk of more?

I had an absolute feeling that this was the end of this particular bunch. He has kept, I guess, this latest band he's had for years and years and years. Back in those days, his bands, you didn't expect them to be lasting that long. The next record would come along and he would hire whoever to work with him.

---

70 I suspect here Tackett means "What Can I Do for You," as his description matches that song more.

Towards the end of the tour, down in Florida, I just had feelings. Every time I'd play a guitar lick or Jim Keltner would play a drum fill, Bob would do this whiplash and look around at you like, "*What* did you just play?"

You mean he was getting grumpy about it?

Yeah, he was like, "What did you just play?" Like he was shocked. Jim Keltner would play a drum fill, and he'd turn around and look like, "What was that? That came out of nowhere." Just a normal drum fill. I started noticing that everybody was standing back as far away as they could get. I thought, "Well, this is pretty much I think the end of this."

In fact, I told him after our last show of that tour in Florida, I said, "Man, it's been a great honor playing with you, man." 'Cause I didn't think we were going to be doing that anymore. And we weren't.

Did the offstage vibe sour a little bit too?

No, no. Just musical. I just think that he was ready to do something else, ready to hear somebody else. It's perfectly normal. Because it isn't a band; it's Bob Dylan. Little Feat is a band. You don't think about changing the instrumentation that much. But with an individual solo artist, you expect the band to be a fluid operation. There's no guarantee that this guy's going to hire you for the rest of your life. You just expect things to come to a natural musical ending, which is what basically happened. We had done it for a long time. Time to go do something else.

Tony Marsico's cheat sheet from his months of rehearsals with Dylan.
Courtesy of Tony Marsico

Tony Marsico

One evening in 1984, Bob Dylan gave one of the most memorable performances of his career. He appeared on David Letterman's fairly new late-night TV show backed by a fairly new band: The Plugz. It would be the only time he'd play with this young Latino punk group — publicly, at least. They had been quietly rehearsing for *months* at Dylan's Malibu house. All for just three songs on this one show: the Sonny Boy Williamson blues tune "Don't Start Me Talkin'" followed by two cuts from his recently released *Infidels* album: "License to Kill" and "Jokerman."

It's about as direct an intersection as Dylan ever had with punk rock. The sound was raw and ragged, in contrast to the far slicker *Infidels*. *Very* ragged, in the case of "Jokerman," which featured an unplanned instrumental interlude while Dylan fumbled around finding the right harmonica for what felt like eons in front of millions on national TV.

To this day, this Letterman appearance is remembered by fans as a classic. One performance from the show, "License to Kill," was included on the 2021 *Springtime in New York* box set. There's also a little Plugz display at the Bob Dylan Center in Tulsa. An impressive legacy for just three songs.

The band technically comprised just two of The Plugz — bassist Tony Marsico and drummer Charlie Quintana — alongside their friend JJ Holiday on guitar. Marsico told me how it all went down.

. . . .

How did you first get connected to Dylan? Do you even know how he discovered or heard you?

Our drummer Charlie's girlfriend, Vanilla, was doing secretarial work for a guy who was working for Dylan. Word was out that Dylan needed some musicians for his "Sweetheart Like You" video. So Vanilla said, "You know, my boyfriend's a drummer." They pieced together the band.

You're not involved yet? They're not asking for a bass player for the video?

No. I was on the outside. I was just hearing the stories from Charlie once in a while.

So how do you get on the inside?

Charlie brought all different musicians up there to jam with Bob.

Where is "there"?

Malibu, at Bob's house. He had a rehearsal studio on his grounds at Point Dume. Charlie would go up there and bring different units. Different bass players, different guitar players. It was kind of odd how I didn't go from the beginning, but whatever, everybody was busy doing their own thing at the time. I was just happy that Charlie was going up there and doing stuff.

Then one day Charlie said, "Hey, you should come up." So we went up there the first time and I guess it clicked.

By the time you were there, was anyone still auditioning or showing up? or were you kind of the last piece of the puzzle?

Once I went up, it was solidified. Not because I'm so great. Maybe Bob just got sick of auditioning people.

You must have been good if he'd been rejecting bassists left and right.

It's not so much that I was good, it's just I was familiar. Charlie and I had played together for a couple years. You get a certain feel with a rhythm section that's used to playing with one another. Me and Charlie had been playing together already for a solid two years, so we were pretty locked in. Bob liked it.

That first day, what happens when you arrive?

The first time I saw him, he came walking up through the weeds on his property with his dog and a walking stick. Like, holy shit, that's Bob Dylan. Just like you see him on the records, you know. It's the same guy.

So the first time you meet him is a little intimidating, but it went away super fast. I mean, we were kinda coming from a whole different place. We were pretty young, early 20s. As fascinated as we were that it was Bob Dylan, it wasn't like we were playing with The Clash or somebody who we really were into at the time.

Things kind of clicked, and we just kept getting invited back. We'd get a call: "Come up Wednesday," "Come up Thursday." Some of them would go all day, like eight hours with lunch and coffee breaks in between.

Did you have a sense early on of what the point of all this was? He's putting together a band to tour, he's thinking of a record…

No. We were told he just wanted to jam with some younger guys. It was never like he's putting together a band for a tour or an album. We didn't think much of it really at the time.

The word we're using is "jamming," but can you talk about what specifically that means? What are you actually doing for eight hours a day?

We wouldn't really talk about what we were doing. We would just we go in the room. Bob would take out the guitar and just start strumming a couple chords. We all just fall in and jam on something.

Is he singing or is this mostly instrumental?

It was mostly instrumental, though he would mumble under stuff. Not really sing words.

Some of these are songs, some are things I think he's working on in his head. We recognize a few of the older songs, but it was a lot of just getting a groove and a vibe.

So we would just play on a song for 15, 20 minutes, looking out over the Pacific. It was a whole different experience than what we were used to. We didn't do that in our punk bands, where the songs were two minutes long.

Is it musically satisfying, or are you looking at your watch by minute 15 of the same song?

Totally satisfying. Are you kidding? There was none of that "we're working" vibe. We're making music and it feels good.

So how long does this go on?

It went on and off for over a year, broken up into different sections. You know, just whenever they'd call. We were still doing Plugz gigs, so a lot of times we'd be kind of burnt out from the night before. We took a break for the holidays [at the end of

1983], and we thought that was it, then we got called back for more.

And you're not getting impatient at some point, like what are we doing here?

You got to realize we're kids with no money. So we're just like, he's paying us to come up there, we're working for Dylan and getting to play music. So yeah, we always loved going up there because it was so different from what we're used to. We're used to playing in the shittiest of rehearsal rooms. To go up there and play in this beautiful rehearsal house overlooking the ocean, it was another world. We were like, how the hell did we go from that to this?

Talk me through this cheat sheet. That's such a fun artifact. What was the context in which you're jotting down all these notes and song titles and stuff?

That's like a second-generation cheat sheet. The first would just be a quick scribble. When we were starting jams, I would stop playing and jot stuff down, because we didn't really talk. I'd make notes what songs were like, just to refresh my memory of the feel of the song. I haven't looked at that in a long time, but I did look when you sent it to me and I see the word "Stones" on there, to remind me it sounded like the Rolling Stones.

And then after a bunch of times, I started putting two and two together and putting some titles to these songs. So I guess that was the master cheat sheet you sent me. Some of the song titles are still really wrong I think. I just tried to piece it all together so I'd have a master list of what we were doing.

And that was just a fraction of it, really. 'Cause a lot of times we would jam on songs that would definitely have no titles. Just some kind of weird jams, you know?

But that's my scribbling. It only makes sense to me, because I don't write music per se. So when you see music notes and stuff, it's all totally wrong and embarrassing. If any musician would look at that, they'd go, "What the hell is this?" It's just chicken scratch, but it was enough to trigger something when we would start a song. I would look at it and go, "okay, it's *that* song."

It's hard for me to imagine Bob Dylan doing "Gimme Some Lovin'."

I know, it's crazy, right? He loved playing that one, too. He was rocking out.

And it's not just the four of you, I gather. Clydie King [Dylan's regular backing singer and duet partner then] is there at least part of the time.

Oh yeah, Clydie showed up a lot. Having her around was mind-blowing. She would just sing along with us. What a sound. They had quite a connection together.

We didn't know what we were going to play. If it sounds raw, that's why. I figured we'd play at least one from *Infidels*, but when we were walking out on stage, he just said, "Sonny Boy in E." It was like, oh, shit, here we go.

You could see the musical history between them.

You look at this cheat sheet, and maybe a third or a quarter of the songs are his, and they're all fairly obscure. "Heart of Mine," "Watered Down Love," "Saved." Do you know any of these songs?

No, I didn't recognize any of them.

Did you ever do like any of the famous ones you might have known?

No, we never did the obvious ones, ever. It was always obscure stuff. Since I wasn't a fan at the time, I didn't know what was a Dylan song and what wasn't, so I would just write titles down. If it appears on those cheat sheets that I didn't know much about Dylan, it's true, I didn't.

Once during rehearsals, the cops showed up, right?

The neighbors used to complain. As far away as the houses were next to Bob — which was quite far, the property was pretty large — sound travels. We played loud. We'd been told before to turn it down.

That one day [when the cops came], Bob just hightailed it into the back room. He just said, "Tell them you're playing with Waylon Jennings."

Did you?

Yeah, we did. Charlie went out and said it, but they know it's Bob Dylan. You could see them all trying to peek in the door. I think they were just there to see Bob, not really scold him so much.

And I gather both you and Dylan to some degree are taping these rehearsals. How is that working?

I always used to bring a boombox with me to every Plugz rehearsals, and later in

The Cruzados when we changed our name. I liked to record stuff and go home and listen, see what works and what doesn't. People said, "Bob let you tape stuff?" I was so young and naive, I didn't think to ask. He probably really didn't want me recording this stuff, but I never thought twice about it.

Bob had this big reel-to-reel tape machine. He liked to record the stuff and listen to it later too, but Bob didn't know how to work the reel-to-reel. Every time he tried to use it, the reels would just go flying and spinning. It was a clusterfuck. So it came to him asking me, "Hey Tony, did you get that song on tape?" It was just me pushing the buttons randomly. I'd push them in the middle of songs.

So would you copy tapes for him?

No, we never really sat around listening to anything, honestly. I would listen back at home to try put a title on something if it was possible, just so I wouldn't come in half-assed. I'd know what songs are what.

There's one of these tapes that circulates. Is that one of yours?

That's one my cassette tapes. They sound terrible. It was a boombox, you know. It wasn't set up for sound. It was set up just so I could learn some songs.

You probably had a lot of cassettes by the end. Did you hang on to the others?

Unfortunately I don't have any of them anymore. The disappeared over the years. I don't really save much stuff anymore. When the Bob Dylan Center in Tulsa opened, they asked me if I had any my cassette tapes for the museum. I said I don't.

How are you spending the downtime at Dylan's place when you're not playing music?

JJ, our guitar player, he would make the coffee all the time. Bob loved JJ's coffee. We'd just sit around and bullshit. Talk about what was going on in the news at the time. We talked about music a little bit. MTV was hot at the time; Bob was asking questions about it. It's like your buddies do when you're sitting around at rehearsal.

So, how does this transition from an amorphous year of on-and-off jamming into knowing that you're going to be playing on Letterman's show?

Bob had mentioned, "Hey, we might go to Hawaii and play something for a record convention." That never happened. And then one day he came in and asked us, "Did you ever hear of David Letterman?" I don't think he knew about him at the time. It was like MTV; Letterman was real new.

So we're like, "Hell yeah, we know that show." I thought he was the funniest comedian. That show was really wacky back when it first came on. So he asked us if we want to go to New York and do the show.

So what happens next?

We got together for a couple hours in New York the day before the show, just to jam a little. Bob stopped in a little bit, but we pretty much went cold to Letterman. We never knew until the minute we walked out on stage which songs we were gonna play.

So if it sounds rough and ready, scattered and crude— I try not to read stuff, but over the years you hear, "Oh those guys sucked." "That was really crude." Well yeah, it was. We didn't really rehearse. We never did like other bands do, go rehearse your set. It's not like that with Bob. We just came out jamming in a room and next thing you know, we're on TV playing these songs, not knowing what key the songs are in, not knowing the songs really, and then Bob not telling us anything until like about ten seconds before we walked out on stage.

For what it's worth, my sense is that such criticism would be a minority opinion in the Dylan fan world. The only thing I see that's negative is people wish that there had been more.

Well, that's nice to hear. After the show was over, we weren't so sure. It was hard to watch and even listen to it, because it's pretty raw. It's not a polished show by any means.

The only part that sounds really bad is not because of any of you. It's his endless harmonica search on "Jokerman."

Yeah, that was a tough spot. We just kind of freewheeled it and kept going and just waited to see what the hell was gonna happen. On live TV! Just don't stop. Same old thing you always learn when you're in a band: Something goes wrong, never stop. Just plow ahead.

What's going through your mind?

What's going through our mind is "What the fuck?" And if you see Bob's face, you could read his mind, and he's thinking the same thing. So we just looked at each other and kind of laughed. Like, here we go, now you're *really* flying by the seat of our pants. Hold on. If things were raw and bad before, we don't know where this is going. But it's live, so just go with it, and that's what we did.

One thing I'd never noticed until rewatching it last night is how on the previous song,

"License to Kill," there's no one-two-three-four count. Dylan just starts singing, and the band is not even playing yet. Then halfway through the first line you stagger in.

It's very hard to come into a song without a count. Advice to young musicians: Watch the singer at all times. Don't take your eye off him. Especially if you're playing in front of millions of people on TV. You don't want to screw up too bad.

We later found out he's kind of notorious for keeping things loose, but at the time we didn't know that. It's just get up there and play and hope you get through it.

It's funny that it was still so loose, because you guys have had way more rehearsal than a lot of bands would have. You've been woodshedding for months.

Yeah, but very informal. I mean, had we known what songs we were going to do it, we could have gotten it a lot tighter and more focused. Had he said, "Why don't you guys focus on these five songs and learn these really good?" But it was never like that.

We didn't know what we were going to play. If it sounds raw, that's why it's raw. I figured we'd play at least one from *Infidels*, but when we were walking out on stage, he just said, "Sonny Boy in E." It was like, oh, shit, here we go.

And that's the first song too, which is funny because he's ostensibly there to be pushing this record. Dave has just held up the cover of Infidels, *and then Bob does an old Sonny Boy Williamson song.*

I never thought about that. It's like, "Aren't you here to promote your record?" Weird.

There's a video out there from the show soundcheck. Most of the tunes are totally different. You do "My Guy," you do "Treat Her Right."

I know, what the hell? He was real loose at soundcheck. He was just having fun. Paul Shaffer tried to jam along with us at soundcheck. It didn't go well for Paul. Bob told Bill Graham, "Lose the clown on the keyboard."

Ouch.

You know, I felt bad. He did get axed from that gig, but I read about a year ago, there was some list of Paul Shaffer's favorite performances, and the Dylan one was his favorite.

Did you have any interaction with Dave while you were there?

No, he was surly from the get-go. I've been on a lot of TV shows. He's one of my least favorite guys to be around.

Oh wait, I did have one interaction with Dave. This was before I was on Letterman. I was waiting on him in a store and he yelled at me. So that was my initial meeting with Dave, as an unsatisfied customer.

Yelled at you about what?

I was working in an art store. Something wasn't framed right or something, and he started going off and being a jerk. Then when he got kind of semi-famous, he was on daytime TV, I was like, "Oh, that's that guy that reamed me at the store the other day." Before you know it, I'm on a show. I did think he was funny, but he was not the friendliest guy to bands. He was probably excited Bob was on there, but he didn't really give a shit about us. He looked at us like we were threatening to him or something, out of corner of his eye.

We did have interaction with the other guest. We hung out in the green room with Liberace which was a real treat.

What do you talk about with Liberace in the green room?

Not much, other than to tell him, "You're one of my mom's favorites." What am I gonna say to Liberace? I asked for an autograph and he was out of pictures, so he said, "You're definitely going to get one." Sure enough, it came in the mail a couple weeks later.

He was with his boyfriend at the time, the guy who was the infamous boyfriend in the Liberace movie. He wore a full length fur down to the ground.

It was a very surreal evening. Liberace did a cooking segment, and then we played with Dylan. Like a weird fucking dream.

So what happens right after? You finish "Jokerman" on a weird note with the harmonica, you walk off, how does the evening end?

It's kind of a blur at this point. I think we went out to a bar, just me and the band. Dylan split. He went to a Knicks game.

I'm not sure of the chronology here, but your one other bit of overlap is there's a Cruzados song called "Rising Sun" that Dylan plays harmonica on. Is that later?

Yeah, maybe six months or so.

At the time when we were with Dylan, we were called The Plugz. But the music was changing, so not much after Letterman we changed our name to The Cruzados. We got signed to some subsidiary of EMI Records and they were gonna put out a record we recorded in West Hollywood at Cherokee Studios. Which never came out, by the way; the subsidiary folded. But we asked Bob to come down and play on this song "Rising Sun." It was actually one of my songs early on called "Some Kind of Bad;" we'd rewritten it with all four members. It was one of our real raucous, fun songs that we liked to play.

So we asked him to come down if he wanted to blow some harmonica on it. He just dropped into Cherokee Studios one afternoon, you know. It wasn't a long session. He came in, he blew some harmonica, we said hello and thanked him.

Are you all playing together or do you have the track and he's overdubbing it?

He just overdubbed to the track. He did a bunch of takes. Just kind of let the tape roll, the way he does. It was kind of loosey-goosey.

It never came out, but things work out for a reason. Later, we re-recorded that whole record and some other songs for Arista. We didn't have Bob, but we had Paul Butterfield playing harmonica on that version.

I haven't seen Bob since.

Was there any disappointment when you do these three songs on TV and then don't get another call? All those months leading up to Letterman, than nothing after except that one harmonica guest spot.

Well, there was some disappointment, but not really, because we had a lot of really good offers coming in at the time, and we were really excited. We got signed to Arista Records by Clive Davis. David Byrne wanted to work with us. He brought us a cassette one day; he wanted us to do one of his songs. We didn't do it at the time, but Tito from our band would record that song for his movie *True Stories* later on.

So it wasn't like we didn't have anything else going on to fill the void of "damn, we didn't get to go to Europe." I thought about it for a second maybe, like it would be nice to go to Europe [for the summer 1984 tour that became *Real Live*], but I was so excited about putting out our debut album on Arista. It was kind of good the way it all worked out. Our buddy Gregg Sutton got the bass gig on the tour.

A few years ago someone [an artist named Daniel Romano] covered the entire Infidels *album in the style of the Plugz. Did you hear that?*

I did. I'm fascinated how someone has so much time on their hands. It was really weird, but I was very impressed by it. I thought it was us, but it sounded way better than us. It was as if we had practiced. *[laughs]*

Colin Allen drumming for Dylan in Offenbach, Germany, 1984.
Photo by Norbert Kohlhauer

Colin Allen

Before Bob, Colin Allen already had quite a career as a blues drummer, logging stints with John Mayall's Bluesbreakers, Focus, and a pre-Police Andy Summers. In addition to his own bands, he's written songs for Paul McCartney's Wings, Fleetwood Mac, and others. And, most relevant to his time with Bob, he had done a lot of work with guitarist Mick Taylor, both before and after Mick's stint in the Rolling Stones.

It was through Taylor that Allen got the call to be the drummer on Dylan's 1984 European tour, which was captured on the album *Real Live*. In 2018, Allen released his memoir *From Bournemouth to Beverly Hills: Tales of a Tub-Thumper*.

. . . .

How did you get involved in the band? Was Mick Taylor the connection?

It was exactly that. Generally in the music biz, it's who you know, not what you know, just as long as you are considered good enough to do the gig. Since playing together with John Mayall in '68-'69, Mick and I never really lost touch, and from time to time I found myself involved in various projects with him.

In '82, I was living in Los Angeles, which had led to my playing with Mick and Mayall again in the Bluesbreakers Reunion band. When the Dylan European tour band was being planned, there I was in LA and relatively fresh in Mick's memory, so he called to say Bob was checking out drummers and would I like to try out for the gig. I did and got the job, mostly, I think, 'cause I had Mick in my corner.

Were you a fan of Bob's prior? When he suggested something relatively obscure like "When You Gonna Wake Up," would have you have known it?

Fan would be a little strong, I was never a fan of much music that was reminiscent of the US folk scene — two exceptions being Joni Mitchell and Tim Hardin — but I of course knew of Bob. You can't escape his songs. He was always on the radio and in the newspaper for one reason or another. The tour was to promote the *Infidels* album and luckily my flatmate had a copy, so I listened to that and of course knew a lot of his more popular songs. Anything I didn't know could soon be learnt — his songs aren't really complicated. He gave each of the band members about four cassettes full of his songs to help us along.

My first day of playing with Bob, Tony Marsico was there playing bass. We didn't say a word to each other — guess he wanted his Plugz drum partner Charlie Quintana on drums. He'd also been trying out for the gig, as had my friend Ian Wallace, who had previously toured with Bob. The second day at Bob's house, [bassist] Gregg Sutton was there and we immediately hit it off. Like myself, he had familiarized himself with the *Infidels* album, so any songs we played from that album sounded somewhat like the recordings, which may have been the reason we both got told the gig was ours.

When exactly did you know the job was yours? What did Bob say?

I found out the gig was mine on the second day, when I first met Gregg. At one point, Mick disappeared into another room with Bob. When they reappeared, Mick walked over to me, bent down and said softly in my ear, "You've got the gig." That was about it. Gregg was told the same day.

Can you say more about how the audition process went? I'm trying to picture what it looked like, who was there, how long it took, etc.

To meet Bob initially meant driving north along the Pacific Coast Highway to his dusty ranch-like abode at Point Dume, about two and a half miles past Malibu. Mick greeted me as I got out of my car and took me into the house. I said hi and shook Bob's hand and proceeded to set up my drums with the rest of the gear in the kitchen area. Not much more was said to Bob. I greeted the bass player, but that was it. Mostly I exchanged comments with Mick, who I hadn't seen in quite a while.

I guess I spent about four hours in the great man's company, running through songs. I don't remember anyone else being there, although there could have been others in the house. I was ultimately asked to turn up the following day. I said okay and then left.

The rehearsals at Bob's home only continued for about three days, mostly to find a keyboard player. Both Benmont Tench and Nicky Hopkins came along to play but, for individual reasons, couldn't accept the gig. Finally Ian McLagan came along and was a perfect fit — another old friend in the band.

Once Ian was in, the next phase of rehearsing took place at the Beverly Hills Theatre. It was always the same procedure, Bob starting up songs by strumming and the rest of us joining in. Sometimes it might be a Stones song, just for a laugh. One time he started singing Boy George's "Karma Chameleon."

Basically, I'd say Bob was making a mental list of all the songs that found an acceptable feelgood level, organically, without any "You play this and I'll play that" approach — there was never any of that. Eventually, I guess, he thought he had a set list. Apart from a couple of things being dropped in the beginning of the tour, things stayed more or less the same, although there was always a chance of him wanting to play something off the top of his head. We played "Knockin' on Heaven's Door" a few times towards the end of the tour — never ran through that. "Señor" was another song that became a late arrival in the set. We also played "Lay Lady Lay" one time in Spain — just played it in front of thousands. Also, anything could happen during the encore section and often did.

How are you coming up with drum parts? In many cases the arrangements are quite different than the studio recordings.

Drum parts aren't something I ever gave much thought to unless it was an odd time thing. Mostly I listened to what was being played and joined in — if it feels good, then that's the drum part, apart from spicing it up a bit as you get used to the song. There were a handful of songs I counted in, but Bob started the rest by strumming his guitar. The band would then join in by playing their instruments' signature intro licks, if any.

Although I'd be tapping the tempo on the hi-hat, I always waited for the first line of the song, so my backbeat on the snare drum was in the right place in relation to the melody. Artists like Bob, who have spent a lot of time playing by themselves, can sometimes lapse and start singing without thinking where they are in the bar, which means the poor old drummer has to turn the beat around. I was determined that wouldn't happen on my watch, and it didn't.

Did Bob seem comfortable? He hadn't done a smaller-band tour quite like this in a few years.

Even in the beginning, when all kinds of stuff was happening, journalists saying how bad the shows were, etc., etc., none of us had anything but a totally positive attitude. Those scribblers had no idea that we were making adjustments on stage as we were performing, on the edge, in real time. After about a week things fell into place, as we knew they would. Impossible to know what Bob thought; it was "here we go, see you at the end."

What were things like backstage and on the road? Was everyone hanging out, or doing their own thing?

Backstage was fun. Lots of laughs, especially as the tour progressed. It was great having Santana on the tour; he and his band were great guys. Also nice to have our own tour plane, an old Vickers Viscount, so we were all together traveling as well, including promoter Bill Graham. Also Bob's sons Jesse and Jakob were along for the ride, plus Bob's cousin, Los Angeles "Dentist to the Stars" Stan Golden, who was acting as the big man's travel companion. The tour carried a table-tennis table, I believe, and, as I had played quite high-level club table tennis for the YMCA as a teenager, I often played with various people including [Bill Graham] and a young Jesse Dylan.

In her memoir, Joan Baez described being frustrated with this tour — for one, she apparently had been told she'd perform with Bob a bunch, and didn't — and leaving early. Did you have much interaction with her while she was there?

I had no interaction other than the odd greeting with Miss Baez. As to her being part of the tour, that's news to me. Her name was never mentioned, prior to her first appearance, I think in Germany. She maybe performed at about four shows. I can't remember her singing anything by herself. We sure as hell didn't rehearse anything with her. She just came on stage, did a kind of impromptu duo singing thing with Bob, performed a bit of free form dancing whilst solos were played and that was it. All a bit superfluous, really — but I would say that, 'cause I was never a fan.

Anything in particular you remember about either of the final two shows, Wembley Stadium or Slane Castle in Ireland?

Well, of course, Wembley was the big one. Eric Clapton, Mick Taylor and Carlos Santana on stage together, plus Van Morrison and Chrissie Hynde. [Backstage,] I believe Mark Knopfler was there. I spoke briefly with former Traffic drummer Jim Capaldi. Tennis party-boy Vitas Gerulaitis was hanging 'round also. Pete Townsend was sitting next to my brother-in-law in the Royal Box. He said he thought the band sounded like the Stones, which was not surprising, considering two former members were in the band. My dear old Mum backstage gave Mick Jagger a surprise kiss on the cheek. He recovered well.

Straight after the show, it was off to Luton airport for the flight to Dublin. At

Slane Castle, the final show, we were again joined by Van the Man and also Bono, who apparently was living in the castle at the time.

Wait, how did your mom kissing Mick Jagger come about?

I looked a lot like Mick. Backstage at the Wembley show and finding myself in close proximity to Mick, I decided to tell him I was annoyed not to have received payment for a session I had done for the Stones' label. At the time, many years earlier, Mick had been producing tracks for a proposed album by former Mamas and the Papas singer John Phillips. As I was speaking on the subject with Jagger, my mother suddenly appeared next to me and after exclaiming, "There's my son's look alike," grabbed Mick and planted a smacker on his cheek.

Did you think that the album Real Live *did the tour justice?*

Not really. A few tracks were okay. There were other songs [that didn't make the album] I always enjoyed playing. "Simple Twist of Fate," for example; I seem to remember us having a nice groove on that. "Every Grain of Sand" as well was usually good. In the encore section, we played "Leopard-Skin Pill-Box Hat" — that was a shuffle and could have been a nice addition. Only the last few gigs were recorded, maybe the best takes were the ones that got on. I guess Bob decided what should be on the album. Who knows — doesn't really matter now — it's almost 40 years ago and I didn't get paid a penny for the recording anyway. There was something in the gig contract that stipulated any live recordings would not mean any extra remuneration.

When the tour ended, was there ever talk of more? Or was it known that that was it?

No talk, no nothing. We had no idea what the future held. I heard within about a week of the end of the tour that Bob was in the studio, fooling about with another bunch of musicians. Anyway, it was fun traveling around Europe with such a great bunch of people. It's not everyone who gets to play with a living legend, is it?

From left, Steve Wickham, Dylan, Gregg Sutton, Bono, Leslie Dowdall, and Mick Taylor onstage at Slane Castle in Slane, Ireland, 1984.
Photo by Ken Regan/Camera 5

Leslie Dowdall

At Bob Dylan's final show of his 1984 *Real Live* tour, a mammoth gig at Ireland's majestic Slane Castle, a host of special guests joined him on stage. Van Morrison. Carlos Santana. Bono. And…Leslie Dowdall.

If you're saying "who?," you probably didn't live in Ireland in the '80s. Dowdall's band In Tua Nua made quite a splash locally, first signed by U2 to the band's own label Mother Records. They broke up before they could fulfill all that buzz outside their borders, but Dowdall went on to have a strong career under her own name.

Before that, though, when In Tua Nua had only released a single song, Dowdall found herself onstage singing a song with Bob Dylan himself. A song she, unfortunately, didn't know. She tells me the story of how she got there, and how Bono helped her through.

. . . .

Set the scene, especially for those of us outside of Ireland. What is Slane Castle?

It's a beautiful castle in Ireland. There's been huge gigs run there for many, many years. The Rolling Stones. David Bowie.

It was 1984, and we were at an Elton John concert in Dublin. We got a phone call in the middle of the show to say that we got the support for Bob Dylan in Slane Castle. We were jumping up and down. We couldn't believe it.

You were a pretty new band, right?

Yes, very early days. Somebody got wind of us, and we were asked to join the big lineup that day. Obviously, we were on first.

I know you were on U2's label early on. Were you were already signed there?

Yes, we were on Mother Records. We later toured with them on the European leg of the *Joshua Tree* tour. That doesn't do us any harm.

Were you and Bono fairly close already?

He'd support our band. I think in a photograph [from the Dylan show], Bono has his arm around me as I'm singing with him.

What do you remember about your own set at Slane? Was that the biggest stage you played at that point?

Yes. I remember the excitement of it and the massive crowd of 80,000 people. The crowd was phenomenal. It's scarier to play in front of 50 people than to play 80,000. It's just like a sea of faces.

I saw this old TV news clip talking about riots there, with so many people clamoring to get in.

There was a drowning on that day. I think a boy drowned in the river. Kids trying to get over to the gate.

Did the Dylan fans seem into your band?

Yeah. It was great, I suppose, because we were the only Irish band. We had a small following, and people are always proud of their Irish band.

After we played our set, Bob Dylan's tour manager came up to us and said that Bob Dylan would like to meet me and Steve Wickham, our fiddle player, in his dressing room. We were like, "Oh my God. We're meeting Bob Dylan?" We never thought we'd meet him. It's one thing to play the concerts, but you never actually get to meet anybody.

We were summoned to a dressing room. I remember just standing there, completely gobsmacked. "Oh, there's Bob Dylan standing in front of us." I remember being fascinated by just looking at him. He was covered in Pan Stik [foundation] and eyeliner.

He said, "I love your band. I think you're amazing. Could you come and join us for one of the songs in the encore?" I was thinking, great. "Blowin' in the Wind" or something that we'll know. He says, "I'd like you to join us on a song called 'Leopard-Skin Pill-Box Hat,'" which I'd never heard of, truthful to say.

I remember being on stage standing beside Bono. I said to him, "I don't know the words." He said, "Just sing *nah nah nah nah nah.*" I mean, there were so many people on the stage. It was all a flurry, what was going on.

It was a huge honor and a privilege. When you're young, you take it into your stride. It was only years later, people would say, "You sang onstage with Bob Dylan." I'm like, "Yes. Imagine. I did!"

The most extraordinary thing about it, I've never had any photographs from that day. My brother about six years ago was at a Bob Dylan photo exhibition in Dublin. The photographer's name was Tim O'Sullivan. My brother went up to him and said, "My sister sang with Bob Dylan. Do you have any photographs of that day?"

He came up with these amazing pictures, and he sent them to my brother, and he said, "You can have these if you don't publish them." My brother framed them for me and gave them to me on my birthday.

Dylan sits in with Paul James at Toronto's Nags Head North, 1986.
Courtesy of Paul James

Paul James

Paul James has sat in with Bob Dylan so many times he can't remember them all. He'd just show up to a Dylan show and, often as not, get called onstage.

Their relationship started, though, not with him sitting in with Dylan, but with Dylan sitting in with *him*. In 1986, Dylan was filming the movie *Hearts of Fire* around Paul's home base of Toronto. Paul gigged constantly then, shlepping all around Canada. And at one night's show at a bar in Toronto, he gained a very unexpected new guitar player. He told me about how it all started.

. . . .

I started using a wireless guitar in 1982. I was one of the first guys to be using that, because I had to learn how to be an entertainer in the early days. On a rainy Tuesday night in Chelmsford, there wouldn't be a lot of people there. You scratch your head and think, "How am I going to get those three drunks in the corner to pay attention?" With my wireless guitar, I could wander over to the bar, order a drink and play with one hand, then play slide guitar with a beer bottle.

So one night I'm doing my shtick at the Nags Head North. I spin over to the bar while playing and I order a drink. Then this guy steps up to me. His face is about a foot away from my face. It's Bob Dylan. I go, "I won't tell anybody you're here. I'd really like to meet you." He said, "Well, meet me at the bar after your set." Everyone just thinks I'm talking to some guy at the bar.

I went back to the stage and realized there's still half an hour to go on my set. "Oh, shit." In my brain, he's going to be recognized and he'll leave. But, as fate would have it, I go to the bar after this set and he's there. He's wearing a big beret and he's got a poncho on. We go backstage. I have my acoustic guitar. I played some Robert Johnson stuff. He went, "Oh, do that again." He was a big Robert Johnson fan. Now everybody knows who Robert Johnson is; in 1986, not as many people did.

Then he said, "I'd like to sit in with your band." I said, "Wow, that's fantastic. We know a lot of your songs." "I don't want to do any of my songs." "Oh?" "I'll just play backup guitar for you." I went, "Okay…" Like, *what*?

I said, "Well, we're going to go on now. Do you want to come up with us?" He says, "Why don't you do one or two songs, and then introduce me as a hitchhiker from Vancouver." So I did. I mean, people didn't know. No one was expecting anything. We were supposed to do a one-hour set, and I got so lost in the time, we played an hour over.

Did people recognize him at a certain point?

No one said anything, but I had the feeling that people did. It's one of those things where no one said anything, but then, later on, "Oh, I was at that show." "I was at that show." All these people were supposedly at that show.

Way more than would fit in the room.

Right. So then we all piled into my van. He was with a lady, and I had my band with me. I don't know if there were seatbelt laws then, but we were all crammed in there. We drove back to my place. We sat and drank and smoked and laughed all night. We were sitting on the floor with two acoustic guitars. He would initiate stuff, some sort of chord changes, and I would play along with them. They weren't really songs or anything; we didn't do any singing. We'd just do different chord changes. I love doing that, and we just laughed.

Bob was saying, "I can't understand how come you haven't made it big yet." He says, "You know what it is: There's nothing happening here." If you think of Canadians— Neil Young was a Canadian, but he couldn't make it here. He had to go to the States. Joni Mitchell, same thing. Canada is a dead-end street. It's better now. Back then in the '80s, you would go around and play and play and play and play until you played yourself out.

Anyway, we finished playing at about ten o'clock in the morning, and we were all tired by then. It was an amazing, incredible night. It just came out of the blue.

Bob said, "Where else are you playing?" I said, "I'm playing at the Diamond and I'm playing the El Mocambo in the next week or so. I'm doing three gigs with Bo Diddley as well." Bob showed up to one of the Bo Diddley gigs and he showed up to the El Mocambo with his daughter Anna. He didn't get up [onstage], he just came to see the show. It was pretty incredible. Bob Dylan at another Paul James show, and then he was at *another* one. I couldn't believe it. I had to touch myself to see if this was really happening.

It really helped me out because after the Nags Head North, there was a picture in the paper. "Bob Dylan sat in with Toronto's own Paul James" — it was this big deal. People were coming to shows to see if Bob was going to show up.

Everyone thought he'd come to the Diamond because that was the big club. He didn't come there. He showed up in all the places you wouldn't expect. One of the Bo Diddley gigs we were playing for the Ontario Police. They had their own place where the officers and their wives would go. Bob comes to that one.

When he came to the Bo Diddley show, we were chatting. He was going, "Dude, we could get a recording studio or something like that real quick." I was like, "Okay!" I figured he'd do it. I should've taken the bull by the horns. Like, "Oh, I know a place we can go right now." I just didn't have it together.

Like I said, he came to a couple of other shows while he was in town. And then he was gone. It was like, "The post office has been stolen, and the mailbox is locked."

How'd you reconnect with him four years later?

At another Dylan show, I'm getting on the guest list. But [a friend of mine] calls me and says, "Hey, Paul, would you do this benefit for these quadriplegic people?" I said, "When is it?" He tells me the date. I said, "Oh, Bob's going to be in town, and I'll probably get on the guest list and go and see the show, and maybe I'll see him or something." This was when he was playing the Hummingbird Centre or the O'Keefe Centre. All these places change names so often.

My friend says, "Here's the problem. I told them that maybe you do it, this benefit thing. They put posters up all over the place saying you're going to play there." I said, "You're kidding. Aw jeez, I'll do it."

I went and did it. It was an early gig. Then I got home and I listened to my messages. It said I'm on the guest list for the Bob show. I figured, "Okay, maybe it's still going on." So I whip downtown and park. I run up to the will call. "Is my name on the list there?" "No, sorry."

I start walking away. Somebody comes running out of the blue and says, "Are you Paul James? You're on the guest list. Come on in." I didn't have a backstage pass. It was just admission. I went in. Ronnie Hawkins was singing with them.

The show ends. I go up to the front of the stage to see if I can get in there. No. So I go around the back, and I see Ronnie Hawkins there. I wave at him and he says, "Oh, it's Paul James. Let him in" I go in, see Ronnie. Ronnie says, "You're looking to see Bob?" I said, "Yeah, I thought I might say hello." He said, "Elvis has left the building."

What happens when he finishes the show, he gets right onto the bus. He's on the road before people get out of their seats.

I go to leave. I'm walking to my van, and then this girl comes out of nowhere and says, "Are you Paul James?" "Yeah." "You want to see Bob?" "Yeah." "Follow me."

I followed her car down the highway. We get to a hotel a little ways out. The parking lot is like a football field. All the cars are parked up close to where the hotel is. Meanwhile, at the very back, there's this bus under the trees. She drives over there. There's Bob, and he's laughing. He says, "Did you bring a guitar with you?" I said, "I got one in my van." He said, "Play 'Hot Tamales' for me." It's a Robert Johnson song. I recorded it on my first album, and he had that. So I did.

We sat and we talked and played a little bit. That's when he was wearing the hoodies. He had these nice bicycles that he was biking around the city on, with his hoodie on.

Then a year later, the tables turn and you sit in with him, the first time of many.

The next time he's coming to town, it was at Canada's Wonderland.[71] Three or four days before the show, I get a call. They want me to open the show. They want me to play solo acoustic, do the Robert Johnson stuff and all that jazz.

Before the show, I'm sitting in my dressing room and a knock was on the door. I open it up and there's Bob. He's got a hoodie on and he's got a baseball cap. He comes in. "What kind of guitar you got?" I go, "I got a National Steel Body, I got this…" We just talked about nothing. Then he says, "Okay, have a good show." And he's gone.

The thing that's funny is I never know that I'm getting up [on stage], ever. For another show a few years later, I got on the guest list and I got a backstage pass. I went backstage. I saw Bob and he said, "Oh, you got in. Hey, how are you?"

You're basically having no interaction between all these? He vanishes and he's gone.

That's right. Everything was like a strobe effect.

So I'm backstage, and he's happy that I'm there. He said, "Okay, enjoy the show." Then he goes on. I figure, okay, well, I'm not going to see him anymore.

The view from backstage wasn't very good. You got the side angle, and the sound wasn't as nice as in the front. My girlfriend, who hadn't been given a backstage pass, was in the front. But there was all this beer backstage. So I filled up two

71 An amusement park that contains the Kingswood Theatre venue.

beers and I went out front with my girlfriend. We'd watch the show, and then I'd go backstage and get two more beers. I'd be going back and forth five or six times.

Once when I'm coming out with two more beers, this guy says, "You Paul James?" I go, "Uh-oh, I'm busted. I shouldn't be doing this." I said, "Yes?" He says, "Bob wants you on stage right now." I said, "What?" I ask, "Does he have a guitar up there?" "Yep." "He's got an amp?" "Yes, he got it all set up."

Then I hear [Bob say] over the speakers, "I got a friend here tonight. His name is Paul James, maybe you've seen him around."[72] He talks so funny.

Another few years on, you do a number of sit-ins that I gather also functioned as auditions to join his band?

In 2008, I'm going to one of his shows again. He's playing in Hamilton, not Toronto, at Copps Coliseum. These big guys come over to me and say, "You Paul James?" "Yeah." "Here's your tickets. At the encore, we're going to come and get you and bring you backstage." I said, "Okay, great." Sure enough, at the end of it, when the band leaves the stage before the encore, they show up, they take me down there, and they bring me backstage. It's almost like an X on the floor, "Stand right here and just wait there." "Okay." I waited.

Bob finished the encore. He came out, and sauntered over by himself. "Hey, how are you?" Then we started talking. He says, "Hey, was that you playing with Mink?" They had just put a DVD out of my performance with Mink DeVille at Montreux in 1982.[73]

Bob had seen the DVD?

He was a fan of Mink DeVille. I didn't realize that. He asked me, "How did you do that stuff with the two guitar solos going on at the same time?" I said, "Oh well, it was Willy's band, so he was soloing. If he'd go up, I'd go down. We could mesh together." It was this song called "Lipstick Traces" that I guess he was referring to.

It was interesting because, if you look at stuff that he's doing with Eric Clapton later on [at the 1999 Crossroads Festival, where Bob sat in], they got that same two-guitar solo thing going on. Eric could be playing a solo while Bob was playing a solo. I think it was on "Not Dark Yet."

72 Dylan said at this 1999 show: "I have an old friend here. Tried to get him in my band a long time ago. He had his own thing to do, but he's here backstage and we're gonna try to get him out and play. His name is Paul James, if you can see him around. I don't know, I just saw him out there a minute ago. Hey Paul, come on up here!"
73 Rock band in the CBGB punk scene in the '70s and '80s in New York, fronted by Willy DeVille. Freddy Koella in a later chapter also discusses playing with DeVille.

Anyway, for me it's like second nature to do that. So he says, "Do you think you could play guitar for me?" I went, "Well, yeah." He said, "You'd be playing the lead, not the rhythm. Because I have two guitar players." "Yeah, sure." He said, "Okay, well, let me think about that for now" or whatever. I was like, "Oh God."

I started listening to a lot of Bob's stuff. I go to a website with all the setlists of shows. I started looking there to see what songs he was playing. In the last 10 years now, his setlists don't vary that much, but back then, it was almost like a different show every night. On a tour, he'd do something like 100 songs. If you ever had to sit in, it'd be almost impossible to guess what songs you're going to do. And he does everything in different keys than he recorded them in, and he does different arrangements for all the songs.

Anyway, so then I got a call from his manager Jeff Rosen. He said, "Can you come down to California tomorrow?" They wanted me to come down right away and join the band for that tour. We were going to rehearse for two or three days and hit the road.

Now, I do all my own business. I had all these gigs that I was going to play, so I had signed these union contracts and stuff. If you don't show up, you can get sued. I said, "I'll have to get out of a whole bunch of stuff, but I think I can do it." I was so responsible, you know? I just couldn't get it together fast enough.

Then Jeff called me back, he says, "Okay, forget about it. Maybe what we'll do is we'll get you to jump in when we come through." Sure enough, Bob was coming to town. They weren't playing Toronto; they were playing London [Ontario] and Oshawa. The night before the first show, Jeff Rosen calls me and says, "Are you still going to those two shows?" I said yes. He says, "Bob wants you to bring your guitar." "Okay, what's he got on mind?" "He's going to pull his two guitar players off the stage, and you're going to do the first five songs both nights."

I said, "Do you know what songs he's going to do?" Because like I was saying, he was doing 100 songs, and I don't know every one of his songs. Plus the arrangements and the keys were different. To get out there and be the only guitar player, I was thinking, I just want to do as good a job as I possibly can. I'd like to listen to the song, know the arrangement a bit. Jeff says, "He'll tell you when you get there." It's like, aw shit.

There was a soundcheck. That's when I found out what songs we were going to do. We didn't run down any full song or anything. We did a verse or two max of each song in its new arrangement with its new key, and that's it. I think about a half hour. We went backstage, and I was going, "Oh God." Everything was in A flat, C sharp.

Bob's playing piano mostly at this point. He's using piano keys probably.

Yeah, there was no A, C, G, D.

We did "Stuck Inside of Mobile," and I had to start it. It was funny because he gave me three solos in the song. There really aren't any solos in that song originally.

I was looking at the setlists and you played practically totally different songs both nights. So it's not like by night two you know the routine.

That's exactly right. I think he did "The Levee's Gonna Break" both times. That was the only one he repeated.

I was so nervous. I don't get nervous when I go on stage, but I was hoping to remember all the changes and stuff. Because they weren't like three-chord songs. They were all like "Spirit on the Water." He was throwing solos at me for all of them, too.

Something like "Tangled up in Blue," it was a totally different arrangement. I guess he was just waiting for me to start and he went like *[plays riff]* on the harmonica. I do the song now and I do that same riff. I remembered it later, the exact thing that he did. I made up a harmonica solo at the beginning based on that riff he played.

Anyway, so then after the second show, [road manager] Jeff Kramer comes over and says, "You're going to play with Bob. You got the gig." Then they're gone. I'm sitting there going, "Oh my God, I'm going to play with Bob Dylan!"

Then I start thinking. In a way, I understood exactly the dilemma that Larry Campbell had in your interview. You don't have a life anymore. You're dedicating your life to playing guitar for Bob Dylan. You have to be on call at all times. I'd have to leave home. I had a new girlfriend and it was like, I may as well forget about having a relationship. To me, it was the gig that you hope and fear to get.

Then near the end of the tour[74], Charlie Sexton sits in. He had been in the band already before, and I think he wanted back in. I think he wanted back in badly.

For me to be in the band, being from Canada and the distance between everybody and all that, I think that just made it difficult. And I think that the fact that Charlie wanted in, and he already knew all stuff because he was there already, Bob went for it.

Anyway, it was interesting. Simple twist of fate. He's an older guy now, and he's busy. I know that doing these shows is a lot. But him getting me up so many times, it was always humorous and fun. I never knew. I never, ever knew.

---

74 It was technically a few months later, not that same tour.

Mike Campbell, Dylan, Stan Lynch, and Tom Petty in in Los Angeles, California on the 1986 *True Confessions* tour. *Photo by Chris Walter*

Stan Lynch

Following a trial collaboration at the first-ever Farm Aid in 1985, Dylan hired Tom Petty and the Heartbreakers to back him for much of 1986 and then, following a few summer dates with the Grateful Dead, 1987 too. He later wrote in *Chronicles Vol. 1*, "Tom was at the top of his game and I was at the bottom of mine."

But Heartbreakers drummer Stan Lynch disagrees with the second half of that statement, and I do too. Those '86 shows in particular are about as fun as it gets, a joyful mix of hits and deep cuts and old-time-rock-and-roll covers, all backed by as a white-hot band as well as the Queens of Rhythm backing singers.

Talking to Lynch, his enthusiasm for these tours with Dylan is infectious. Lynch was a member of The Heartbreakers from the band's formation in 1976 until an acrimonious split in 1994, but he calls the Dylan tours the peak of his many years with Petty and the band. As he puts it, "If there was ever a part of my life I could relive, that might be it. The rest of it, I'm cool. I'm glad I did it. That's one I would like to do again."

. . . .

What was your experience like backing Bob?

It was joy. The whole time, I was flying. My life was great, my body had never been stronger, no one ever told me what to do or what not to do.

There was never a playbook. My joke was, I'm going to count four and then Bob is going to just start playing and, in about a minute or so, we'll know what song it is. It was glorious. I found the whole thing close to jazz. The front man is John Coltrane. I felt like Philly Joe Jones[75] in those three hours. Everybody was just

---

75 Iconic jazz drummer who played with Coltrane as well as Miles Davis.

masters of improv.

Do you play?

Some guitar.

Do you know when you're having the best jam session of your life? One of those where you just go, "My God, I don't know where we're going, but this is really cool." It was like getting to jam, but the skeleton of the jam was "Like a Rolling Stone"! As long as you stick to the intentionality of that song, and you stick to the passion of the lyric, there was nothing you could do wrong from the drummer's seat. I just listened to Bob and did what he did. It was like serve and volley, punch and counterpunch. It was aggressive and exciting when it needed to be; it was beautiful when it needed to be.

The only time I knew I'd stepped out of line— there's a great scene in *Hard to Handle*[76] when I think I'm supposed to kick in, so I play this big drum fill announcing the band. And Bob just simply puts his hand up behind his back, without stopping the harmonica, and just shows me his palm. Which says to me, "Not now, kiddo. Back off. Save your rattlesnake bite for a later moment."

We'd probably done it a million times the other way, but I loved that you couldn't close your eyes and do anything by rote, ever. I found that to be so exhilarating. I never slept better in my life, because you were on your toes physically, emotionally. It was almost sensory overload to play with Bob.

Did you feel prepared for that, from your work either with The Heartbreakers or elsewhere?

Chaos is my middle name. I was born for anarchy and it's like, that's Bob! He's just a natural at it.

We're playing a big gig. I think three songs into it, Bob turns to me he says, "Hey, Stan, what do you want to play tonight?" I'm thinking, "Uh, loaded question?" But I took it right at face value and I went, "Well, how about 'Lay Lady Lay'?" Because we'd never done it. I wanted to do that cool beat that's on the record, that beautiful mandolin swing. It just feels like mandolins are bashing into the wall. I really wanted to try that rhythm live.

That's how fearless you are. It didn't even occur to me that that might not be a good idea, to pick a song we'd never played before. He says, "What key?" You never ask a drummer what key! I see Mike [Campbell] in the corner going, "A! A! A!" I go, "How about A?" Everybody has a big sigh of relief. Then Bob walks up to the microphone and proceeds to play a song I can't even recognize. Like, if

---

76 An official concert film taped at one of the early Dylan/Petty shows in Australia, 1986.

this is "Lay Lady Lay," I have no fucking idea, but it was fun as shit. It was the Ramones doing "Lay Lady Lay."

The band was a little horrified maybe, but I was only horrified for about a second. I realized, "We're really going with this!" We went with four minutes of "Lay Lady Lay" as a punk song, replete with the Queens of Rhythm all trying to find their way in. It was fantastic, but it was absolute anarchy.

Obviously by that point, you've got quite a comfort level together, but let's rewind back to Farm Aid 1985. First time in the room together rehearsing, what does that look like?

Interesting story, I think it was the first rehearsal. We were supposed to start at two and Bob showed up at five maybe. I already had tickets to see Frank Sinatra and Sammy Davis at the Greek. I'm a big fan. I remember saying around six o'clock, "I got to go." I just figured, fuck it.

Bob walked right up to me. He said, "Where are you going?" Like, what the fuck's wrong with you? I said, "I got to go see Frank and Sammy."

The whole band backed away from me as if I had radioactive dust coming out of my ass. Bob took a big beat, and, God as my witness, he said, "Frank Sinatra? Sammy Davis? I love those guys!" So I took Bob as my date to go see Frank and Sammy.

What was your date like?

I was scared shitless. Like, he's in my car. Do I turn on the radio? What if Bob Dylan comes on? I think we just sat in silence.

We went to the Greek. Bob had the hooded sweatshirt on. Nobody really knows he's there. I did somewhere between buddy and security, and we watched the show.

I think Sammy came out first, and it was fun as hell. I was probably stoned and just digging the show. Sammy ended and everybody stood up. Bob went to leave. He thought the show was over. I grabbed him by the back of the sweatshirt and went, "No, Frank's next!" "Oh, right."

I remember during intermission thinking to myself, "Gosh, I guess we should talk. That's what guys do." And so we talked. He's just a guy. I figured, "Well, guys like to talk about motorcycles and girls." So we did.

Then Frank came out. I'm watching Frank, and I'm watching Bob watching Frank. I'm just going, "Wow, this is a Fellini moment." We make it through the whole show, and somebody backstage figures out it's Bob. Somebody comes out and goes, "Frank says come by the dressing room after the show and say hello." I'm thinking, "Fuck, yes, this is going to be great!" I had a long-term love affair with the Rat Pack my whole life. It's been a thing for me.

So we go by the dressing room. I go, "Bob, over here. Let's go in and say hi to Frank." He goes, "Nah. Let's go."

So close.

It was so perfectly Bob. Like, "Nah, fuck it. I'm outta here."

Every time he was in the room, there was this energy. Talk about a guy who can read the room all wrong, that's me, but what I read was Bob was ready to have fun, play some music, don't stress, no posturing. Can we just make a joyful noise unto the Lord? Every time he turned around, he would rock with me. If I was catching a groove, Bob did all the things that you want your frontman to do. Hips are swaying, shoulders are moving, he's looking at you and he's pointing. I loved every inch of it.

Did that come from day one, the band and him gelling like that?

Yeah. I felt energy from him and freedom from him like I couldn't even imagine. The only fear I had was, I didn't want to disappoint Bob Dylan. I don't want to play something that he just thinks is offensive. But I figured he'd tell me. He was just that kind of guy. He'd walk up to you and go, "That's a pile of dog shit." Fortunately, I never heard it. Matter of fact, I actually got some really nice attaboys from him, that, really, I didn't get that often.

Like what?

I remember one day he walked up right to the drum riser. I thought, "Oh, shit, I'm about to get it now. This is the moment I'm fired." I think all he said was, "Man, you're playing great right now. I love this." Part of me was wondering, "Is this a joke?" Maybe that's his way of saying you suck so hard I can't believe it. I figured I might get the call the next day from Elliot [Roberts, Dylan's manager then] and he'd say, "Hey, Bob thinks you suck." I never got that call.

I loved what he did to the chemistry to the band. It just changed the dynamic. You add a sixth member on anything— oh, and that other guy is Bob? Like, "Well, this is dynamite in the baby carriage right here. Carry it carefully." We were all very reverent. I saw it immediately in the other guys too. It was like, "Oh, shit, we're in the presence of somebody who can really do this!" We thought we were seasoned vets, and we realized, "This had been pre-cooked way before us. He's been good a long, long, long time."

What do you remember about that first actual show, the Farm Aid one months before the tour?

I don't remember much except I think we did "Maggie's Farm." It was funny as shit, because none of us really knew what was going to happen.

I think Willie Nelson came out for that too.

I was probably shitting my pants. I was going, "Wow, this is a *Wayne's World* moment for me. I'm playing with Bob Dylan *and* Willie Nelson *and* Tom Petty and The Heartbreakers! Pinch me. This is the kind of shit I dream about, and it's happening." I was pretty much in that mode for my entire rock career. I never could believe it. I was just going, "Holy shit!"

I hope you can convey in this interview the big grin on my face when I think of Bob Dylan. I was experiencing zero pain — physically, emotionally, spiritually. I was only experiencing joy. I'm getting to play amazing songs with amazing musicians in amazing places all over the freaking world. It wasn't like, "Oh, yeah, you're playing Spank, Idaho." You're going to go to New Zealand, you're going to go to Australia, you'll be playing in East Berlin and all over Italy. It's like, "Oh, fuck!" He's universal. Bob speaks the universal language of brilliance.

You mentioned Australia. One of the things you did there was record the first Heartbreakers/ Dylan song, "Band of the Hand." Do you remember anything about that?

It was quick. I think we learned it in the studio. You can hear me trying way too hard, because I'm still in live mode. I'm like, "I'm not making a record, I'm making a live document of our aggressive fabulousness." I probably came in, beat the shit out of my drums for a couple of hours, and they said, "Get outta here." *[laughs]*

You've got the Queens of Rhythm singing backup too. Dylan had been doing stuff like that in the gospel years, but was that new for you and The Heartbreakers?

I'd never experienced anything of that caliber. They were fabulous. They also played rhythm, tambourines and shakers. They were bringing the church to this shit.

What a show for me, because I got the best seat in the house. I'm looking to my left and there's those wonderful women just physically involved with the music. I look to my right and it's Benmont [Tench] and Mike Campbell, and I looked to the front and it's Bob Dylan and Tom Petty. It's like, shit, everywhere I look, it's great.

What does it look like when you're not on stage? Are people hanging out together during the off-hours or keeping to themselves?

There were nights in the bar you'd see everybody. You never knew who would be there. The people that Bob attracted, and the people that were coming to me with stories about, "Oh, I was Bob's masseuse. You have to tell Bob that Joe said—." I'm getting like five of those an hour.

There was one show we did where it finally hit me. I wasn't the sharpest tool in the shed with music back then. I was very self-absorbed, as many young musicians are. Then when we were in Italy one night, I remember I really heard Bob Dylan. I *heard* him.

Usually when he did his solo stuff, I was like, "Well, if I'm not involved, I'll leave." But I was sitting there at the drums still. I sat behind the kit and I smoked a cigarette and I watched this man. It's one guy, one guitar, and he's singing "Blowin' in the Wind." I melted. I started to actually weep because it hit me in that one moment finally. Like, this guy wrote all this stuff and he's doing it tonight. It's pouring out of him like sweat. It feels effortless, but it's killing me. Every line ripped me to shreds. He did a song, I wish I could remember it. It was about a young man who volunteers to go to war, and he comes home with the medals.

"John Brown."

Yeah. Just thinking about it now can choke me up. That was the moment I was never the same on the tour again. I was never the same. I remember walking up to Bob at the end of that show while we were all still sweaty. I put my hands on his shoulders and said something like, "You really fucked me up tonight." He looked at me with that billion-dollar look and he said, in that voice, "Stan…are you all right?" Like he didn't understand what I was saying to him. What *should* have come out of my mouth was nothing, but, of course, being me, I had to say something. What came out of his was like, "No, no, not you!"

It was strange. I don't know if the relationship— I'm not saying we *had* a relationship, but I looked forward to seeing Bob. I loved talking to him. Everything you say to him, whatever came back was not what you expected. I remember once saying something like, "Wow, I love that outfit." He said, "Yeah, what do you like about it?"

Bob was fantastic at keeping you on your left foot all the time. I did not find that uncomfortable, I found it growth-inspiring, exotic, enticing. Challenging, in a good way. Like, "Bring it."

Did you have any favorite songs to play, either ones you did every night or something you did once or twice?

"Positively 4th Street" used to blow my mind. "Like a Rolling Stone" blew my mind. "Knockin' on Heaven's Door" blew my mind. I'd have to look at the song list because probably every freaking song I go, "What??" For me it was hard not to just be excited to be there every second. How amazing to know that I'm going to play three hours of songs that are etched in my soul. At one point Roger McGuinn comes up and sings "Mr. Tambourine Man" in front of hundreds of thousands of people in East Berlin. The place looks like a sea that's going to erupt. Even at the time, "This is going to be an apex moment. This is a zenith." I felt it. "From here on out, it's going to be a letdown."

You did some shows with the Grateful Dead, big stadium shows in the US. Do you remember anything about touring with those guys?

I was not a fan, so I didn't care. The guy you're talking to now knows what a stupid thing that is to say. The man you're talking to now, 30-plus years later, knows what an idiot that kid was.

You didn't know me then, but I was more of a hedonist. I was like, "I'm in a rock and roll band and all that implies. Take no prisoners. I want it all." That was me. I was not really a session guy or a guy that wanted to be taken lightly or not noticed. I had a big mouth and I played a lot of drum fills and probably made way too much noise coming out of my mouth and my drums. Fortunately, everyone was tolerant.

To me, what's so special about these tours listening to recordings, it's like the most pure fun you can hear at a Dylan show. Even the great Dylan shows from other eras, "fun" isn't necessarily the key word.

I played those gigs as ferocious as I was capable of. Most drummers will tell you, "Never go to 10." If you go to 10, you blow your wad. But I did. I went all the way. Benmont went with me too. Everybody did. Everybody was fully willing to engage. When it was time to throttle up, it was all the way.

You mentioned McGuinn. I was looking through the setlists, you had so many people sitting in. Stevie Nicks, Mark Knopfler, John Lee Hooker, Ron Wood, Harrison. Any good stories about anyone else?

Where was John Lee Hooker? Was that in San Francisco, with Al Kooper there too?

Yeah.

It's a story. It's not a good story. Maybe I'll hold onto that one. That was a bad night for Tom and I. Tom and I had a very, very bad night. We argued terribly. John Lee

Hooker and Al Kooper came out and saved us from being assholes. That's about as nice as I can put it.

The presence of outsiders got you back on your best behavior?

Actually, it was probably a turning point for Tom and I. We never recovered from it, but the evening was saved by the presence of greatness. I love Al Kooper. He's essential. He's just essential in so many careers, including mine. He's a lodestone and he doesn't even know it.

It's funny you mention him, because Benmont told me that he knew the Al Kooper parts on stuff like "Like a Rolling Stone" and was playing off of those. Did you have an equivalent? Were you thinking about the "Positively 4th Street" drum part or Sam Lay or—?

No. That's what's so pathetic! That shows you the absolute arrogance and profound stupidity. It wasn't until after the tour that I started hearing what the records really were like. I don't think there's one thing I ever did with Bob Dylan that was ever from the record, except maybe…let me think… No, I fucked up everything. *[laughs]*

I had no clue what anybody did. Never studied a record in my life. I'm not sure if idiot is the word. Ill-informed. The fact that that guy was tolerated is extraordinary.

Obviously, you knew the hits at least. Did you know the deeper cuts?

No. I owned a few Bob Dylan records. I loved them, but I never studied them. All I knew was, I loved the way he sounds. When everybody would tell me like, "Bob Dylan can't sing," I'm going, "No, he sounds cool as shit." I loved the way he looked, I loved what he wore, I loved his record covers.

He was a cult figure to me that you could never know, so I didn't really bother trying. I didn't really think about his life, or the depth of it. I was young and dumb, man. A rock and roll fan. I loved what I loved, and Bob was part of it. I loved Steppenwolf, too. I was more like, "I wonder what kind of chicks Bob gets. I wonder what he drives."

I've got a couple specific shows from your two-year run to ask you about. One was the opening of your final tour in Israel. It was a big deal at the time, him playing there. What do you remember about that?

I remember the security. They literally carried scimitars on their belt. I said, "Why do you carry that instead of a gun?" He said, "A gun's great from a distance, but up close a gun is worthless. With this, if you get close to me, you're mine." I went like, "These guys are serious. They'll just rip my entrails out."

I remember going to a seder; I think maybe the Prime Minister put it on. I remember Bob being there. I remember talking to girls on the beach and thinking they're going to be knocked out. "I'm here with Bob Dylan! What do you guys do?" "We're in the military. All four of us are aces with confirmed kills. We're going to be working tonight." I'm like, oh, right, okay. There's reality.

I remember being on my balcony in the Hotel David in Tel Aviv. I smelled smoke, so I called down. By the time I hung the phone up, two armed military show up with nine-millimeter sidearms. This is serious shit. They push me aside, literally, and walk to the end of my balcony. They walk out and they smell and they look. They turn around and they go, "It's nothing, just a garbage fire. Thank you for calling."

They take that call seriously.

Fuck yeah. Here's what else I remember. We went to a disco in Israel. You know, going out partying. Come home late. The hotel lobby's dark. You can't see a thing. I'm with the guys and they're complaining. "What the fuck, man. Who turned the lights off?" I walk in and my eyes adjust. There's six fucking military men with Uzis in all four corners in the lobby, just looking at us.

On stage, I was pretty emotionally blitzed. That was the most somber moment of my musical life.

That's the beginning of the '87 tour. Then the end of the tour, the grand finale at Wembley, a whole bunch of special guests. Anything you remember about those shows?

I got to meet Ringo. That's a great drummer moment. Oh God, I shit my pants trying to come up with something funny to say and blew that too. I tried to thank him for everything. What came out of my mouth was something like, "I want to thank you for my haircut and my car and my—" I don't know. I was completely sideways. He just gave me a big hug and went, "I know. I know." Because every drummer just craps their pants when they meet fucking Ringo. What would I be without that first Ed Sullivan show? A plumber?

I would gladly wear a *True Confessions* tour T-shirt today. I've tried to meet Bob. I've gone to several shows and never been invited to come say hello. All I could say would be, "I love you. Thank you. I hope you have any good memories of anything I contributed to your life at all. If you even remember it." It was so memorable for me. It's as memorable as your first girlfriend.

You have that Sinatra story. Do you remember any other outings along the way with Dylan?

I remember going out to Sydney Harbor with Bob. Somebody had a sailboat. We went out and we anchored off a little island. I remember thinking, I'm going to go in and take a swim. I jumped over the side. The next thing I knew, Bob jumps over the side, and we both took off swimming. We swam for the island, and we made it. There was a rope on a tree. I said something like, "You want to climb the rope?" "I will if you will." So I climbed the rope, and Bob climbed the rope. The people from the boat said, "Do you want us to come and get you?" I said, "Bob, you want to swim back?" "I will if you will." So we swam back to the boat.

To me, that's my takeaway. Everybody thinks they know Bob Dylan. I think I know my version. It was very simple. "I will if you will" kind of says it all to me. That's the experience I had with him on stage. I said that to him musically, every chance I could. "We going to do this?" "I will if you will."

One thing I wanted to hit on not related to this tour is the 30th anniversary concert a few years later, in 1992. You're onstage playing with Jim Keltner. How did that happen?

That's just good fortune. Somebody might have said, "Is it okay if Stan plays?" and Jimmy's like, "Yeah, sure." That's another one of those, with what I know now, could I have taken real advantage of that? I just sat down and blew thunder out my ass. I didn't listen enough.

Jimmy Lee Keltner, that's the mother church of rock and roll drumming right there. There's not a cooler guy. There's not a groovier guy. There's not a more soulful guy. If he would adopt me, I would move in. There's nothing about Jim Keltner that you don't want to emulate.

I didn't play but maybe one song. I did shake the tambourine on "Mr. Tambourine Man." I do recall that. I remember thinking, "I *am* Mr. Tambourine Man." *[laughs]* It's not much. I remember thinking, "The world doesn't need another drummer right now." I did get a cool attaché case that says "Bob Dylan 30th Anniversary." That still sits in my storage locker.

Remember, I haven't been in The Heartbreakers since 1994, so just to even say, "Yes, I played in Tom Petty and The Heartbreakers, and we went out with Bob Dylan," that's great! So much has happened since then for me, musically and cosmically. I've had two more careers since then. But that one, it's pretty cool.

Not a lot of people can say that.

It was fun to get the stories. Once I got in a dressing room with Ronnie Wood and

Garth Hudson. I remember Ronnie walking in and going, "Stan, want to smoke?" He had two packs of Marlboros. I go, "I don't smoke." He flung one at me and hit me on the head. "Take it up, then."

These guys never let me down. They never fucking let me down. A guy like Ronnie Wood, I've idolized him since Jeff Beck records. Shit. It's like you go, "Wow. I wonder if they'll let me in."

The same with Roger McGuinn. We toured together; I made a record with him. I can't tell you how many times I stared at every Byrds album cover and listened to the records with headphones on. Then the fact that he's standing right in front of me, and he'll let me in— I always felt like the redheaded stepchild with a lot to prove. If they'll let me in the club, I'll try to prove that I'm worthy to be there musically, and more importantly be a good hang. I won't be a drag.

For me, the road was never a place to dread. You hear the other guys, and they go, "Oh, fuck, how many weeks are we going to be gone?" I'm going, "Shit, pack my suitcase for the next 10 years, I don't care!"

Rock and roll is a litmus test. It's a mirror. If you smile at it, it smiles back. If you shit at it, it shits back. If you're angry at it, then it's angry at you. That's how I felt about audiences. You're in front of 15,000 people, and, if you're an asshole, you probably deserve to be booed. That's what I never understood. Even in the old days, it would be like, "Why are you bringing a bad attitude to people who just shelled out a lot of money and showed up?" Just never made any sense to me. If you're in a bad mood, you should probably get your ass in a good mood. "Hey, man, everybody knows the road sucks." Fine, but does it really, or do you suck?

Were The Heartbreakers changed by the tour? After '87 ends and Bob is now removed from the equation, are you all performing differently on your own tours and recordings?

I thought the band was going to continue to be that great and sound like that for the rest of my life. It didn't. When the tour wrapped, I probably figured everybody felt the same way as me, that this is so fucking good it's going to be like this always. And boy, was I wrong. That's probably where it started. Everything shifted for me right around then, I think.

You were on different tracks coming out of it?

Completely. There is a joke about blind men discovering an elephant. They all are touching it, and they're all describing it, but they're describing something completely different. One guy's got the trunk, and he's going, "It's probably a snake." One guy's holding the ear, one guy's holding the tail, one guy's touching the foot. It's five people describing an elephant.

That's how I would describe the end of that tour. I walked away thinking it was the coolest thing I've ever seen in my life. The other people walked away probably going like, "Thank God that's over." I would love one day to be interviewed en masse and go around the room. Because then you'd get the truth. It takes everybody there to give you the truth. I don't know the truth. I just know what I think I saw.

I loved everybody in the band. They were my brothers. [Bassist] Howie Epstein and I couldn't keep a straight face 90% of the time, because we were so enamored that we were actually making it happen. You couldn't pose. You couldn't go strike a shape and think anybody was going to believe that shit. You couldn't play at rock star when you're playing with Bob Dylan. You just fucking get out there and knock the music down.

That's what I thought everybody in the band was doing. Benmont Tench, get the fuck out of here. That guy, you put a hand behind his back, it still is going to be magic. He'd make shit out of smoke. Mike Campbell, if you look at his hands, you can't even tell what chord he's playing because he knows so many. I got no fucking idea what he's doing, but Jesus, he's that good. He owns 21 frets. He owns them. Like they're his bitch. And then he's listening to Benmont, and he's sending *him* off into another direction, and the two of them are making music out of G, A, and D that you've never heard before in your life.

If I ever needed to be musically entertained, I just put my right ear over [to them]. If I ever wanted to be biologically entertained, I'd look at Tom and the Queens of Rhythm and Howie. This is some foundational shit right here. It's like not cerebral. This is from the waist down. Rock and roll has to entertain you from the neck up and the waist down, you know what I mean? The right side of the stage is entertaining me so heavily, and the left side's got my balls in a sling, and I'm just going, "This is rocking me." And then, oh yeah, by the way, it's Bob Dylan! Like there's a crown on top of the whole fucking thing. So did I enjoy myself? I reckon I did.

Do you think any of that has to do with the fact that it wasn't a Heartbreakers tour? Was there less pressure, not doing your own songs the entire night?

Nobody wants to think of themselves as being in a backup band. Even when you're in The Heartbreakers with Tom, we never wanted to think of ourselves that way. You never had the freedom of just being a backup band. You could be responsible for the crash of a gig.

With Bob Dylan, and Tom Petty and The Heartbreakers as the backup band, you *couldn't* crash the gig. I mean, Bob Dylan doesn't need you there anyway. He proved it every night by going out and playing four or five songs on his own that were like, "Oh my God!" So the pressure was never really on the band. You're right, I think there was a little air out of the balloon. I didn't own those charts. The thing with Petty and The Heartbreakers, I own those. If you're playing "Refugee," it's got to sound like fucking "Refugee." If it's "Listen to Her Heart," I've got to sing that shit. With Bob, I didn't own any of those charts. I didn't even fucking *know* 'em, I'm so stupid and belligerent. As long as I'm just bringing some heat, there really was no pressure.

To a man or woman on that stage, they were all extraordinary. It was a very fortunate convergence that all came together. You couldn't plan for that. It had all the things that great theater has, but all there for a reason. Tom sang together with Bob on one mic. They never rehearsed that, ever. When Tom would do, "How does it feel?" he'd be on one mic screaming with him. If those guys had bad breath, they knew it. They were smelling each other's tobacco. We all were. It was so intimate and so real.

I remember starting a song once with some stupid beat. Bob started playing something reggae, and I decided, well tonight I'm going with— I got about four bars into it. It's the only time he ever did it to me, he looked at me and gave me the international "No."

What do you mean?

He took the cigarette and butted it out on the floor, and did the thing under his neck, where he went like, "No."

Like, cut it out?

Yeah. Like, that's not going to fly. Don't make me commit to that for four minutes, you idiot. I was a little insulted for about a half a second, and I just went "*Riiiight.* That's a terrible check to try to write for the next four minutes." Because once a drummer puts his foot down, this is where it's going. And sometimes I was off. Sometimes I was probably off by a fucking country mile. Usually the band would always just honor it. They would go like, "Okay, Lynch has spoken. Let's go."

I read somewhere that Bob didn't think he was that good during that time. That broke my fucking heart. It literally reduced me to like emotional rubble, because I thought the motherfucker brought the shit. I'd never seen anything like it. Not that he'd ever want to talk about it, but if I had a chance, I'd be like, "God, I read somewhere that you thought you weren't bringing it? Man, you have no idea how inspiring you were for me. You never let me down."

Above: Promo shot from around the time Xanthe Littlemore opened
for Dylan.
Left: Littlemore's All Access Pass
Courtesy of Xanthe Littlemore

Xanthe Littlemore

Xanthe Littlemore is a singer-songwriter and guitarist based in Melbourne. Over the course of a four-decade career, she has won the Australian Songwriters Association's "Song of the Year," among a host of other awards. She's recorded and toured under her own name and as a member of an array of Australian bands like the Rock Follies, Maiden Oz, and Rebel Union. She's collaborated with local legends like Tommy Emmanuel and Paul Kelly.

But, before all that, she opened for Bob Dylan and Tom Petty. For a single show, and on very short notice. A not-entirely chance meeting led to the invitation from Dylan himself. She's never told the story before now.

. . . .

In 1986, I was 22, living in Sydney. At 14, I had become a professional musician, singer, songwriter, guitarist, totally inspired by Dylan and other '60s/'70s music. I was doing lots of gigs around Australia, the States and Europe. I learned to write songs from playing Bob's songs every day.

My brothers are all musicians too. Musicians, you've got the days free, you do what you want. My younger brother Justin and I were sitting around on Valentine's Day, 1986. We went, "What should we do today?" "Let's go and see if we can meet Dylan." Just, why not?

We went over to the Sebel Townhouse, which is where all the big stars stay. My goal was to just shake Bob's hand. That's all I wanted to do, I just thought I would be so happy if I could do that.

We got all slicked up with our best clothes on. We said to the guy behind the hotel desk, "We're here to see Bob." "Who are you?" "We're journalists and we're here to interview him." The clerk said, "We'll get his manager down."

Seems like he's got a lot of managers, but one of them came down. Again, he's like, "Who are you?" We tried to bluff saying, "We're journalists and we have a scheduled interview with Bob." He asked, "When was this organized?" We caved in and said, "Actually... we're musicians, and we just want to meet Bob." He said, "Well, you write him a letter. I'll take it up to him and he can decide if he wants to meet you or not. He's just waking up." It was 2:00 PM or something. That's breakfast.

I have to say it was a good letter, because I quoted a lot of his lyrics. Like, "we don't want to waste your precious time" and things like that from his songs. The manager ran it upstairs and came back and said, "Yeah, Bob'll meet you."

It took a long time. Maybe a couple of hours. My poor brother had to go to a gig, so he didn't get to meet Bob.

I was starting to think, "Well, if he's this hard to meet, I don't want to meet him anyway." I had just stood up to walk out and he comes down the stairs surrounded by seven-foot-tall bodyguards, about four of them. He walked straight over to me. I was like, "What am I going to say?" Thankfully, he made conversation. He said, "Hey, where'd you get those boots? I need some boots like that."

They were fireman's boots I suppose you would say, up to the knee. Just really cool Italian leather boots. We were chatting, just everyday stuff. He said that he'd been sitting up all night with Lauren Bacall drinking and talking. She was staying there too.

Bob said, "Did you see the shows?" I said, "No, I didn't. I was doing gigs myself." Then he gave me free tickets to his shows and said, "Look, I've got to go, we're flying to Adelaide." We walked outside and there's a big stretch limo. I said, "Why don't I come to Adelaide with you?" He says, "I don't think my wife would like that."

No one knew he was married to Carolyn Dennis at the time. He'd actually been married about two weeks prior. I thought it was a joking throwaway line.

I thought, "Oh well, I gave it a shot." I started walking off down the road, and he goes, "Why don't you come to the airport with us?" I'm like, "Okay, I will." Just turned on my heel, got into the limo. All the bodyguards. I remember them standing back, watching this unfold. They moved aside to let me sit next to Bob.

We were driving out to the airport, talking about songwriting mostly, because that's one of my favorite things. I was saying how good it feels when the song comes through and Bob was agreeing about the joy of songwriting. Then he said, "Tell me the first line of one of your songs."

I was surprised, thinking, how are you going to impress Bob Dylan? Don't even try. Don't try to be too poetic or arty or whatever. Just keep it simple and straight. The song I'd written the day before, it was called "Lost and Found," and the first line was, "We've got the chance to make things happen." I thought, that'll do.

Then I said, "Now you tell me the first line of one of yours." *[laughs]* He didn't expect that. He leans over — he talks in a whispery sort of voice — and he says, "There must be some way out of here." That's when I got a bit starstruck. I'm like, oh yeah, this is the guy. The guy who wrote that line.

Then Bob says, "You *got* something." I'm like, hang on, I'm sitting in a limo and my lifelong hero has just said I got something? I'm not going to ruin this moment by saying anything at all. I just looked out the window, soaking up that happiest moment.

Then he goes, "But are you any good?" I said, "Would I be here talking to you if I wasn't good?" I think it was this confidence that made him say, "We'll get you on the show." With his American accent, I didn't know what he was saying. I was just like, yeah, whatever, floating on his compliment. Then he goes, "No, we'll get you on the show." Finally, I realized what he was saying. I said, "What show? When?" He said, "Tomorrow. My show." I'm like, okay… That was the trippy thing, that he didn't hear my music at all. He just took a shot. That amazed me; he had that much confidence. I could have sounded really bad!

I said, "Well, okay, what do I do?" He said, "When you go back home, ring this guy and he'll organize it for you."

At one point during the airport drive, I remember the driver passing back an autograph book and asking Bob to sign it. Bob does this childlike scrawl. It looked like a three-year-old's writing. I said to him, "You're not left-handed, are you?" And he goes, "No, but if I write with my right hand, they'll analyze my handwriting and find out all about me." I said, "But they're going to find out all about the left side of you." "Oh yeah… I didn't think of that." I thought, wow. It's sad, how he has to guard his privacy. Which is the reason I didn't tell this story for 30 years.

When I got back home, I rang Marty Feldman, the manager I was told to ring. That was funny in itself, because here's this stranger ringing up him and saying, "Bob says to buy me a plane ticket." Who is this nutcase? He didn't believe me. I said, "Well, ring Bob up and ask him. It's all true." He did, and he rang back five minutes later and bought me the plane ticket.

Then the next morning we flew to Adelaide, a couple of hours' flight from Sydney. We went to this big outdoor stadium with 20,000 people there. I went backstage, just to get a drink or something. I was starting to get nervous. I wasn't worried about the crowd; I've never had stage fright. I was nervous about Bob. He would see if I was any good or not. I wanted him to like my music.

Bob wasn't backstage, but the entire Australian record industry was. The guys there just owned the whole show, the record companies, the agencies, the tours, everything, and they didn't want me in the club. So when I got there, they were like, "What are you doing here?" Almost like, how dare you be here without us booking you? I just said, "Oh, Bob wants me here." That was nice. Just to have that.

Then Dylan's stage manager said, "Come up to the side of the stage and get ready." I was so nervous, I handed the bodyguard the water that I had, so then I didn't have water to drink. I planned to play my songs that were the most Dylanesque because people were there to hear Dylan. The ones that sounded inspired by him.

The sound of 20,000 people clapping, it's just so loud. It's like a tidal wave. I made them laugh a couple of times, and the sound of 20,000 people laughing, whoa.

The stage was really high. I looked down, and Bob's standing with his arms crossed looking up at me. Later the bodyguard said that he doesn't often come to see the support act. He usually comes just before he's going on. But he came down to check if I was any good.

Did that add to your nerves when you saw him standing there?

Yeah, a lot. Like I said, I wasn't scared of the crowd, but seeing him standing 20 feet away watching, real serious. It's like, ohhhh…

As soon as I got off stage, one of the security people said, "Bob wants to see you backstage now." I went backstage, and he's on his own in a dressing room, pacing up and down, like he was nervous. "What did you think? How did I do?" He goes, "You are good." I went *[sighs with relief]*.

I said, "I was so nervous, though. When you were my age, did you get nervous?" He goes, "Aw yeah, all those *people*." The way he said it made me feel he still gets nervous.

I said, "Bob, after the gig can I hang out with you a bit more?" Because we hadn't had that long to talk yet. He goes, "Yes, this is my room number, listed under Frank Murphy." That was his pseudonym.

Then that was it. I knew not to hang around while he was getting ready to go on. Since I had an Access All Areas card, I just went and stood on the side of the stage watching him and Tom Petty and the whole band and everything.

After the show, Bob rings and says, "Oh, I'm tired." So we won't hang out. I was happy anyway. I wrote him a little letter, just because I wanted to say how happy I was for what he'd done, getting me on the show and everything, and how kind it was. Then I went to sleep.

I woke up to the phone ringing in the Adelaide Hilton hotel. "Hey, this is Bob.

I've got half an hour before we got to go; come up and we'll talk."

I go up to the room. He's lying on the bed with his hat over his eyes and his arms folded. He goes, "Get some paper and a pen." I brought it over to him and he goes, "No, not me. You. Write down 'Rock and Roll' and underline it." I did and then he listed all these artists that he thought I should listen to. Elvis Presley, Howlin' Wolf, Muddy Waters. Then he said, "Write 'Folk.' Underline it." And he gave me a list: Carter Family, all the artists that influenced his style.

I think that was his way of saying, this is the area you need to improve to get more your own style. At 22, he already had an amazing style, way beyond his years, but I still sounded a bit immature, I suppose. I felt he was trying to just give me some help.

He gave me the names of all these different records to buy and artists to listen to. It was a big list. We chatted a bit more about a few other things, and then he said, "Well, I got to go now." I said, "I'm so happy to meet you. I'll come to the shows back in Sydney." Because I had the All-Access badge.

Then I just said, "Oh, just one more thing, Bob?" He's like, "What?" I said, "How do I get back to Sydney?"

He goes, "Didn't anyone organize that for you?" I said, "No…" He said, "Pick up the phone and call Marty. Tell him to come down here and bring money." Marty brings wadges of American dollars. He was like, how much do you need? He's handing me $100 bills. I think he gave me about seven of them and I'm like, that's plenty, thank you.

What happens next?

It's a bit of an anticlimax after the gig.

How could it be anything but?

Yeah. I will say that I was so happy that day. Like, all I ever wanted to do is meet him and shake his hand, if I was lucky. Everything else was just such a total bonus. It was one of those days where you're so happy and you think, "I'm going to wake up. This is going to be a dream," and it's not a dream. It's real.

I don't know what people will think reading this, but they will probably assume that I'm a cute young 22-year-old and he's Bob Dylan and that I probably would've slept with him. It's important for me, as it was important then, that I was only ever seen as a musician. It was never anything more or less than that. I never wanted it to seem like it was just a way to get me in bed sort of thing, because it wasn't. It was totally like musician to musician. That was the energy of it. It was all just respect.

No funny stuff was ever suggested or mentioned, and I really appreciated that. That's why I didn't ask him for photos or autographs, because I just didn't want to make myself like a groupie or a tourist. In retrospect, I do wish I had a photo.

A week later, Dylan and Petty's band came back to Sydney. I'm at the shows and didn't see much more of Bob, just small meetings, but not for very long. Like one time, I was there and he was getting ready to go on. He goes, "Xanthe, why aren't you at home practicing?" I'd be offended if it was anyone else, but not him.

Another time, there was a TV special being filmed. I couldn't tell you which night, because it all blurs together, but I said, "Oh, can I be in the TV special?" They said, "We don't need anything." I said, "I'll open the limo door," so I did that in the TV special.

The backstage scene that night, the whole vibe of it was really amazing because it was then that I realized the respect that Bob's got. He wasn't there yet but everyone else was, including the King and Queen of Japan. The whole vibe was, we're all waiting for Bob. The party hadn't started yet. It's a hard thing to describe, but the attitude was, "I'm only talking to you because Bob's not here." Including the King and Queen of Japan. I just thought, "What would it be like to be him?" He once said he never gets close to real life. Everyone changes when he shows up. That everyone else has got something that they don't value, our anonymity. I just really sensed that. To see the King and Queen of Japan bowing to him like he's some amazing guru or something—

Everywhere Dylan goes, people bring him gifts. There was this big, long table with lots of gifts. One of his employees was told to go along and pick out the good gifts. Bob went and looked as well. I remember him picking up this painting of him that was a copy of the *Desire* cover. I remember Dylan looking at it like he didn't like it. He said, "Do you want this?" I'm like, "Yeah!" I've still got that in the other room.

Then another night, I was backstage going somewhere in the elevator and Tom Petty and his band got into the elevator. We started talking about songwriting and music. What someone says behind your back is what they really think about you, so I asked them, "What did Bob say about my set?" I forget who it was, I think it was the guitarist, he said, "She's got balls."

I didn't like that compliment. I thought, "Okay, well, it *is* a positive thing, not a negative thing." As a female, you'd prefer him to say something different, but that's what he thought of me.

Not act as if being compared to a man is the highest compliment.

Yeah. I know what he meant by that. "She's really courageous. Got up there and did it" and all of that.

Another amusing thing that happened when I was talking to them in the elevator, I said to Petty's band, "I feel useless, like I'm just hanging around doing nothing now." Then the whole band said, "So do I." That was a funny moment. I was like, "Oh, it's not just me."

When you said earlier that it was going to be an anticlimax, did it feel weird, like you start off with this amazing thing opening this show, and then now you're attending shows but you're not playing them?

It felt like a comedown. I'll tell you, it felt even worse the following week when they all left for Japan, and I was back playing shit gigs in Sydney. Last week I played to 20,000 people with Dylan and now I'm back here? You're supposed to get discovered, this is how it happens in the movies, and then from then on you're a big star. That's how it was in my head, and it's like, wait, what? Aren't you supposed to go up and up and up?

You did *get discovered, but then the person who discovered you moved on. Now you're back at the same shows you were playing before.*

Yes. Very depressing.

I'll tell you what else was depressing. I was practicing and playing and doing everything I could to be successful in music because I truly believed it would lead to happiness. When I met Dylan, he was very obviously not happy. He looked really sad, like he'd suffered a lot. He was only 44, but when you're 22, that's super old. I thought he'd be the happiest guy on the planet because he gets to be rich, famous, respected, write the best songs in the history of the world. He gets to be Bob Dylan! When he didn't look happy, I'm like, "Well, my whole motive for doing music was just ruined."

I did go on to get a great manager and do much better gigs, headlining concerts of my own, and got a name in Australia, but not straight after the Dylan gig. That took me right up and then smashed me back to the ground.

Before Bob left, I said to him, "I want to stay in touch. Can I write to you?" He said, "Yes, here's an address you can write to."

I was really self-conscious writing to Dylan. I knew he would never write back because someone might analyze his handwriting. *[laughs]* I wish I could read my letters now. It was probably talking about songs and music and, "Thank you for getting me that gig. You didn't have to do it, but you did, and it means so much to me."

Bobby Valentino onstage with Tom Petty at a different (non-Dylan) show.
Courtesy of Bobby Valentino

Bobby Valentino

When I was working on a newsletter post about Dylan's second year of touring with Tom Petty and The Heartbreakers in 1987, a footnote on one show caught my eye. It appeared in the setlist for Wembley Arena attached to the eighth song, "Lenny Bruce." It read, simply, "8 – Bobby C. Valento (violin)."

I'd never heard of him, and, Scarlet Rivera aside, a violin player sitting in with Dylan is pretty unusual. A quick glance confirmed he'd never appeared with Bob before or since (also, that his last name is actually *Valentino*). So I called Bobby Valentino up to find out how he ended up playing violin on a single song one night in 1987. We talked about Dylan and also about Petty, with whom he had a much longer relationship.

. . . .

I gather you'd never heard the recording of your appearance until I sent it to you a week or two ago. What were your first thoughts?

I was aware it existed, but I've never heard it. I could have done better, but it wasn't too bad. Had I known the song, it would have been nicer!

Yeah, "Lenny Bruce" is a fairly obscure choice for a sit-in.

I'd never heard it before. I wouldn't say I'm a Bob Dylan completist. I mostly know the singles and a few famous albums, and that's about it. The singles, I would have had no trouble with at all. Once you hear it on the radio a couple of times, it's in there.

I played with Tom Petty on and off ever since I'd done the *Damn the Torpedoes* tour. The Fabulous Poodles, we were a support act on that tour, and we got on really well. I ended up doing odd guest bits with Tom in Europe quite a lot. He said, "Oh, come along and do the Wembley shows." I was playing with Tom Petty each night. I think "Louisiana Rain" was one night and "Stories We Could Tell."

One of the nights [after Tom's set], I was sitting quietly in the VIP section next to the stage watching the Heartbreakers deal with the strangeness that is Bob Dylan. Suddenly, a guitar tech turned up and said, "Bob wants you. Get down on stage now." I got down there and plugged the violin in. Tom Petty was shouting the chords at me as we went through it.

Did you have any inclination why or how? Had Bob seen you with Tom earlier that night?

I have no idea. Maybe Tom said, "Oh, get him up because he can wing anything." I'm pretty good at winging things. I'm quite quick about figuring out how it all goes. Often, I just don't play for the first verse. "Oh, that's how it goes. All right." It was quite lovely. All of a sudden, play along with a song, totally making it up as I went along, in front of 9,000 people, which I'm quite happy to do.

I remember one of the nice bits was Bob didn't like lights coming straight at him. I don't blame him; it can be really painful on the eyes to have these bright lights pointing at you. He wasn't lit from the front, which made being on stage very pleasant. You could see out to the audience.

Did you interact with Bob either before or after that one song?

Not very much. He seemed pretty shy to me. I think I said, "Oh, that was fun." We chatted a bit in a bar afterwards at the Mayfair Hotel. I can't remember what we said. It was pretty bland.

Then, on the last night, I recall George Harrison was there, Jeff Lynne, Ringo, and whoever he was with at the time. Afterwards, they all piled into Bob Dylan's dressing room for a bit of a party. I went to Tom Petty's dressing room because I wasn't really in the same league as these people. Tom came to get me. He said, "Hey, come on to Bob's dressing room." I think the main reason was because we all used to smoke in those days, and I had some very good black hash with me. About the only other thing that Bob said to me was, "Roll up a joint, Bobby."

If you were in that dressing room with Tom, Harrison, Jeff Lynne, Bob Dylan, that's basically a proto-Traveling Wilburys.

In fact, George Harrison gave me a plectrum with "Traveling Wilburys" written on it. Nobody had heard of the Wilburys at the time. I think they were possibly doing odd bits of it in George Harrison's studio during the days.

You mentioned your band opened for Petty's Damn the Torpedoes *tour. How did you get on that initial tour?*

I'd absolutely loved Tom Petty's first and second album. They were quite big in the UK before they were big in America. The Poodles, we had a manager called Brian Lane. He knew whoever was managing Petty at the time and got us the job of the support act.

They were a bit nervous with us because we were thought of as an English punk band. They'd had some problems touring with punk bands in Britain. Then they found out we were quite funny. We grabbed a lot of promotional photos from Tom Petty's tour manager, drew mustaches and beards and stuff on them, and sent them back to them. They thought it was hilarious and did the same to us. We started getting on really well. You wouldn't know who'd be in whose bus in the morning. We'd get out of the hotel, they'd pour into our bus, and we'd pour into their bus.

People don't sit in with Bob Dylan that often. He's not someone who is constantly inviting people in.

If I'd had a run-through or something, I could have done a lot better job. I'm not bad at winging things. There's an awful lot of session stuff that I've done that is, literally, they recorded the run-through and just used that. I've usually had somebody shouting chords at me.

Like in this case, you said Tom Petty was just shouting the "Lenny Bruce" chords at you mid-song.

On stage, he was just shouting at me. He's like, "C, F, A minor." I can't remember what key it was in. I think it was in C.

Did you ever go back and listen to the original song "Lenny Bruce"?

No. I should check it out, but I never have.

Richard Fernandez (in hat) leads Tom Petty, Dylan, and the touring company through the Wellington,
New Zealand airport, 1986.
Courtesy of the Alexander Turnbull Library

Richard Fernandez

In a career spanning five decades and counting, Richard Fernandez has served as tour manager for too many iconic artists to name. When he won the Parnelli Lifetime Achievement Award, the concert industry's highest honor, in 2016, Graham Nash said, "When musicians are out on 'the proud highway,' we need all the help we can get. The secret is a good tour manager. For decades, Richard has been that lifesaver." Ric Ocasek said, "There was chaos, but he was always calm and cool… Of all the crews I ever worked with, he's really the only one I remember!" And who should show up at the actual ceremony to present him with the award but Tom Petty, who Richard worked with from 1978 all the way until Petty's death in 2017.

It was through Petty that Fernandez entered Bob Dylan's orbit. He worked as tour manager when Tom Petty and the Heartbreakers backed Dylan in '86 and '87 and then, while Petty took a break from the road, continued with Dylan alone for the early years of the Never Ending Tour that kicked off in 1988.

I called him as he was preparing to hit the road once more with Steely Dan, for a freewheelin' conversation about his years with Dylan in the late '80s and early '90s, Tom Petty, and what life looks like for a tour manager in general.

. . . .

Was your first time working with Bob the first time he worked with Tom, at Farm Aid in '85?

Yes. Bob came to [his and Petty's shared manager] Elliot Roberts and said he was going to do Farm Aid and he wondered if The Heartbreakers could work with him.

We were rehearsing up at Universal Studios. Bob would come to rehearsal and he'd only talk to Tom and the band, which was cool. Nobody talked to him or anything, but the rehearsals went down well. Bob would just come in and do his thing and then he'd leave. That's about it. But when we got to Farm Aid, and they actually performed it in front of people, it was pretty amazing. They played unbelievably together. I thought it was just going to be a one-time shot. Nobody knew what was going to happen after that.

Were the Heartbreakers and Tom jazzed about it after the show, do you remember?

Yeah. That's the one thing about the Heartbreakers that I didn't know when I first joined up with them, but learned. They were so respectful to the people that came before them. I took Tom and Mike [Campbell] and Ben [Tench] to see Muddy Waters at a club in Phoenix one time. During his encore, his road manager came up to me and said, "Hey, do they want to come back and meet Muddy?" We went back, and they're in his dressing room. The door opens, and here's Muddy. He's coming off the stage. He's got a towel around his neck and he's all sweaty. He looks up and the first thing he goes, "*Tom Petty.* How are you?" Tom was like a little kid going, "Oh my God, he knows my fucking name!"

That's one thing I really dug about them cats. They respected everybody that came before them. That's the way they were about Bob.

What is that first joint tour like, in Australia in '86?

I remember it going down very well over there. I remember promoters coming up to me and going, "Wow, this is the best band he's been with! He's actually doing the songs!"

"He's actually doing the songs"?

I mean, doing them in a way they recognized them.

The band, the Heartbreakers, they played *together.* Sometimes when [Bob] was singing, if he had his electric guitar, he'd be hitting the wrong chords and stuff like that. It never bothered the Heartbreakers, because they just stayed right there. "We got our rhythm section. We know where we're at." Tom would go, "Here we are. Here we are." And Bob would go, "Oh. Yeah."

On that first tour, once we realized we were going to go do a tour in New Zealand and Australia, Bob would still just come to rehearsal, talk to maybe the band and nobody else, and leave. That was about it. Then we did a couple of shows.

We'd already had a few shows under our belt, we went to Sydney, and it was one of the backup singers, Queen Esther Marrow's, birthday. I talked to one of the girls and said, "Listen, I'm going to set up a thing on the day off for the band and some of the crew guys. We'll set up at a restaurant, have a party for her. I'll get a cake." She said,

"Oh, that'd be great. Let's not tell her." I said, "Okay fine, don't tell her." I tell [Bob's road manager Jeff] Kramer. He goes, "Oh, that's a great idea." I get this restaurant, I set this party up, I sort transportation for the band and the crew to get over there and back.

I haven't even talked to Bob once yet, since before Farm Aid. I haven't spoken one word to him.

I'm sitting there in my room and it's about 11:30, something like that. We're not leaving until six. The phone rings. I pick it up, and he goes, "Hey Richard, it's Bob." The first thing in my mind, I got a lot of new guys in the crew. I pick up my itinerary, I'm looking through going, "Bob fucking who?" He goes, "I was wondering what time the transportation is leaving for Queen Esther's party." I'm looking down, going, "Yeah, I think about six o'clock…" Suddenly I realize, "Oh, fuck, it's *Bob*."

We'd already been through two full rehearsals and the Farm Aid thing, and that's the first time I actually spoke to him.

What would a typical show day look like on the road for you?

Well, it starts the night before. I printed out these sheets and stuck them underneath everybody's door. It says, today, you do this, this, this and this, soundcheck, whatever is happening. After the gig, this is what we're doing. Even though they have a book that says that, this gives them specific times if any changes have to happen. Tom liked it because he said in the mornings, he sees it, it's underneath his door, and he can look right over and go, "Okay, yes, that's what I got going on." He leaves it there.

Then in the mornings, it's checking up, it's calling the venue. Let's say they load in at nine or ten o'clock. I'll call the venue about eleven and see how it's going. If there's any problems that have come up, if there's any problems that they foresee, whether they be technical, they can't get something in or out, or a logistical problem where there's some equipment that's [still] on its way. Just anything that might arise.

I want to know what's going on in the building, so when I talk to the artists when we get to the building, there are no surprises. Then once I've talked to building people, I start getting in touch with the people in my staff and say, "Okay, this is what we're doing today." Then check up on transportation, make sure it is going to be there when we go into the venue for the soundcheck.

I've been working with Steely Dan for many years now. Donald Fagen is a guy that does soundchecks every day, and I really respect him for it. I worked for Tom for 38 years. After the first 10 years, Tom never did a soundcheck. The only time we ever did a soundcheck was when we did the Super Bowl. He would just walk in the building, plug in the guitar. He paid everybody really good money, and he expected it to work.

That's one thing Tom cared about. He goes, "The lights are the lights, whatever, but don't ever try and save money on the sound."

Was that what happened with the Dylan and Heartbreaker shows? The soundcheck was done by band or crew guys?

If we were doing multiple shows, Tom would go in there and do a soundcheck with the band out of respect for Bob. Even if Bob didn't show up. He just wanted Bob to know, "We're here for you. If you want to come down, you've got a full band ready to go. If you want to work up something, or if you got a new tune you want to do." We were on Bob's clock. Tom understood that, and he wanted to make that apparent.

Would Bob show up much?

Oh yeah, he would show up. I got a funny story about Bob at a later show. When I was working with the G.E. [Smith] band,[77] for the whole tour, Bob wore a gray sweatshirt, sunglasses, and a baseball hat. He came into every building that way. Sometimes he played on stage that way.

It was Halloween. G.E. comes to me and says, "Hey, I want to get the whole band and crew gray sweatshirts. I'm going to have them wear baseball hats and shades when he walks in the building." The band, the crew, everybody that was associated with us, the guy at the soundboard, the monitor guy. Gray sweatshirt, baseball hat, and shades.

We did the soundcheck, and Bob came. He just looked. He didn't say nothing. Played the whole soundcheck — 20, 30 minutes. Put the guitar down. I'm leading him and his security guy to the dressing room. I opened the door, and he stops. He goes, "Hey, tell those guys I want my clothes back when this is over."

Hilarious.

The other good thing that happened on the G.E. tour is, we were doing Radio City Music Hall for four or five nights [in 1988]. We had just played Philadelphia, and Bob was unhappy with the performance of the band. He called my room the night

---

77 G.E. Smith was Dylan's guitarist for the first few years of the Never Ending Tour, beginning in 1988.

At Madison Square Garden, if you go over curfew, they charge you like $5,000 a minute. Dylan comes out for the encore. They only play a minute or two then, boom, it's done. Bob walks up to the mic and goes, "I'd like to play more, but it costs too much."

. . . .

we got into New York. It was unusual for him to call that late for anything. He goes, "I really didn't have a good time. It just wasn't clicking." I said, "Okay, let me talk to G.E. We'll make sure they're down there for soundcheck early."

Soundcheck usually doesn't start 'til 4:30 or 5 because we had a 8:00 show. They were down there at three going through everything. About four o'clock, Bob and his wardrobe lady and his security guy walk in the building.

I'm in the production office, and the production manager comes in and goes, "Bob just walked in. Oh, man, he is on it." I go, "What do you mean?" He goes, "He's yelling at everybody he sees."

Then his wardrobe lady comes in. I said, "How's Bob?" She goes, "Oh, he's in a fucking surly mood. He's been screaming at me all morning. As soon as [security guard] Callaghan got there, he started yelling at Callaghan. He walked in, he yelled at Al [Santos, production manager] on the way up." I said, "Oh shit."

I call Callaghan, I says, "Callaghan, bring him down to rehearsals." Dylan goes out there. He's not saying much, but he's not yelling at the band. He just goes right back to his dressing room.

I go back to the production office, and I'm just sitting there. Suzi, his wardrobe lady, comes down. She says, "Bob wants to see you." I'm like, "Oh, fuck. Jesus Christ."

There's one thing Tom Petty said when I got a lifetime achievement award a while back. He goes, "You know, the road manager is the toughest job on the whole thing, because if anything goes wrong, it's your fault."

So I go, "Okay, just put your best game face on and do what you can do. Tell him you tried as hard as you can, and I'm sorry, dude."

He's gone to these long dressing rooms with mirrors all over the side, for a chorus line or something, but he's the only person in there. As I opened the door, he's got his back to me. There's a mirror there. He's plucking away on a guitar. He sensed there was somebody there, and he looks in the mirror. He sees me. He turns around and looks at me and goes, "How about those fucking Dodgers?" *[laughs]*

The night before was a big night, the first night of the 1988 World Series where the Dodgers played the A's. Kirk [Gibson] goes in at the bottom of the ninth with two outs, they're down by one run, and hits a magic home run. I'm a big Dodgers fan. I'm sitting in my room by myself watching the game, and when that happens, I just went nuts. I went yelling around my room, just hysterical.

So at Radio City, the door closes, he senses there's somebody there, and "How about those fucking Dodgers?" I say, "I couldn't fucking believe it!" He goes, "Yeah, what the fuck was that?"

Did he know you were a big fan?

We had been to baseball games together. We'd been to some minor league games where I didn't have to sneak him in. We also had been to Yankee Stadium.

The Yankees were really nice to us. We'd get three seats in a row, one of them on the end. We'd go to the Yankees office before the game and wait there. Then before the game started, I would go down and sit on the inside seat of the three, the one that was closest to the crowd. As soon as the bottom half of the first inning ended, Bob and Callaghan would walk down. Bob had his Bob Dylan uniform on, with the hood, the shades, the baseball hat, Levis, and just a ratty gray sweatshirt with no writing on it. Everybody was watching the game because it's the first inning and stuff. They would walk down and just sit right next to me. Bob would sit next to me, and Callaghan would sit on the aisle.

We'd watch the whole game like that and talk baseball. He would notice stuff and go, "How come he did that?" I go, "Because that's a decoy. He wanted them to think…" He goes, "Oh, yeah yeah yeah."

You were like his baseball whisperer. You knew all the ins and outs.

Yeah, but he was pretty hip to the game. The other thing that we did on the G.E. tour is five or six of us would go to batting cages on days off. Bob started coming. So he'd get in there and start hitting the ball. I go, "Dude, you have a batting stance like Rickey Henderson, holding it straight back." He goes, "I like him!"

It sounds like you didn't talk much early on. How did your relationship develop to the point where you're talking baseball at Yankees games?

Only because I never tried to initiate any conversation, other than if it was something business-wise — "we can't go on for five minutes because there's a guitar thing" or something like that. He understood that part of it, that's why I was there. To make sure everybody is in the place where they're supposed to be with the right things. One time he called me a wrangler.

Being a tour manager, it's a fine dance because you're the guy that communicates with the management, the artist, and the crew. You're the guy that walks that whole line. You got to go to the manager and say, "We can't do this. We're changing this and this and this." Then you have things with the artist: "Rehearsals are doing this. Is this going to be okay for you?" And then the crew guys: "Oh, we need to get a guitar tech. Why don't you call what's-his-name in New York, see if he's available?" There's a lot of hats and a lot of people that I talked to.

It's just a fine line that I have to walk, especially with Bob. At first, there was not a lot of communication. Then, all of a sudden, he realized that if he wanted something, if he let me know, it would get done.

Those early tours even with the Heartbreakers, they had so much respect for that cat, and continue to. I remember Tom telling me a story one time. I've always liked the song "Something Big," but I never told Tom, "You should play that song." I didn't want to be one of those cats. Then one day at rehearsal, he came and said, "Hey, let's do 'Something Big.'"

I was stoked. I was talking to Tom, I said, "Hey, you've decided to do 'Something Big'." He goes, "Yeah, I was in the studio at home and I was deciding, what songs am I going to play for this tour? I'm pulling up different stuff. All of a sudden, the buzzer rings, and I go to the gate." "Yeah?" "It's Bob." They lived close to each other, down the road in Malibu. Bob came in, and said, "What are you doing?" Tom goes, "I'm trying to pick out some songs that I might do during the tour." Bob's looking at what he had and goes, "How come you don't play 'Something Big'? That's one of the best songs that you've ever wrote."

He pulled it up and he started playing it.

How did it happen that you transitioned to doing Dylan shows without the Heartbreakers?

The Heartbreakers were not working. I never missed a Heartbreakers tour. They were working opposite each other for a while. There was one year where I did a Bob tour, I did Neil Young, I did Bob again, and I did Tom. That was a crazy one.

Then in '91, I realized we were going to have a major [Petty] campaign in '92. I told Bob, "You know what? I don't think I can be here next year. Tom's got a big thing going on. I'm going to be busy all year with that."

I wasn't sure what to expect, to be honest with you, but he was very gracious.

He goes, "I understand. That's where you came from. You belong there with Tom."

Were you there before the Never Ending Tour, when Bob was doing stuff with the Grateful Dead?

Yes. Bob played with them, I think, two or three different times.[78] I remember especially the time in Akron at the Rubber Bowl. That was the first time they played together. I remember me and Callaghan taking Bob over to their dressing room after his set, so they could work out what they were going to do on stage. It was like the Heartbreakers, nothing but respectful of Bob. "What do you want to do? Okay, we'll do it like that, then." You could tell that they were digging it. They wanted to be up there with him.

It's the same vibe I got the first time walking into a building when Crosby, Stills, and Nash opened up for Tom Petty and the Heartbreakers. Me and Tom were walking into the building before they went on. We're walking by their dressing room, and David, Stephen, and Graham were getting ready vocally. They were tuning up. Tom goes, "Stop." He just listens for a second. He goes, "That is so cool."

There's only one cat that I can remember who was on the same plane as Bob when they would meet and talk. That's George Harrison. He respected Bob, but wasn't in awe of him.

There were the shows Dylan & the Dead played the next year without Tom Petty and the Heartbreakers. Were you a part of the Dylan touring organization for those?

Yes. I was there.

They made a live album. Jerry Garcia later said Bob picked all their worst performances.

He thought a lot different than everybody else. His whole perspective on things was different from most people's perspective.

I remember, him and Kramer, his manager, were having a discussion. We were in Europe. Kramer wanted him to go on a bus somewhere. Bob didn't want that. He wanted to be in a car. I was walking by the office, and Bob called me. He goes, "Richard, come in here. Tell Kramer it's more comfortable for me to ride in a car than it is in a bus." So I'm like, "You know, Bob likes to ride in a car more than he likes to ride in a bus." Then Bob goes, "*See?*"

---

78 In 1986, one of the Dylan/Petty tours was alongside the Grateful Dead. Then in 1987, Dylan hired the Dead as his actual backing band for a short summer run without the Heartbreakers. That became the live album *Dylan & The Dead*.

I never would question Bob, whatever he wanted to do. He's got his reasons. I don't know what they are, but he's got his reasons.

What do you typically do during a show? Are you able to actually watch any of it, or are you running around backstage doing stuff?

That's the one time when I got 40 eyes watching the people that I've been watching. All these 40 eyes, the crew and the light guys and everybody, they're right there. They're making this thing happen. I'll go back to the production office, but I never missed Tom Petty [doing] "Wildflowers." I never missed that song.

If there was a problem, I was there. There was a time at the Outside Lands festival in San Francisco, where Tom was playing, and the PA was intermittently cutting in and out. The monitors were great, though, so Tom has no idea. He's having a fucking great time.

Sounds great to him, but bad to everyone else.

Yeah. I'm standing behind his amp looking at him. He's like, "What's going on?" I had to pull them off the stage. He goes, "Why? I can hear." I say, "The PA is cutting off in and out." I knew he was pissed off.

Steve Winwood was standing at the side of the stage. Before I walked up, I said, "Steve, stay right here. Don't go anywhere." Because I knew Tom would be really pissed off if he came off stage in the middle of a performance. He goes off, and I lead him right to where Steve is. Steve goes, "Hey, hi, Tom!" "Oh hey, hi, Steve. How're you doing?" Steve goes, "Yeah, that's okay. They'll get it fixed." Then Tom goes, "Yeah, I know." I was thinking, "Thank you, Steve."

Cheered him up. Smart, very clever.

The other person around who was good like that, and I've had around to help me out is Jackson Browne, who was a close friend of Tom's. I've had to pull Tom off when Jackson was around, and as soon as he sees Jackson, he just cheers up.

Do you ever have to interrupt Bob on stage, pull him off for some emergency or other?

No, but I'll tell you something funny. At Madison Square Garden, if you go over curfew, they charge you like $5,000 a minute or some ridiculous amount. Me and Bob had talked about this beforehand. I said, "After 11:30 PM they're going to start charging you." He goes, "Okay, fine." He comes out for the encore. I said, "You got five minutes, dude, and then we're going into big time." He goes, "Okay. G.E., we're doing this but we're doing it really fast. We're only going to play like two minutes."

They only played like a minute or two into the song and then, boom, it's done. Bob walks up to the mic and goes. "I'd like to play more, but it costs too much."

Ha!

He's the same guy that, we were playing at the Greek Theatre in Hollywood, he's having a great time, they're kicking ass. He turns around to G.E. and he goes, "'My Way', the way Frank Sinatra did it!" G.E.'s like, "Oh, okay…" *[laughs]* This is onstage! But they did it, and that's part of the genius.[79]

Were there any other days or shows or events that jump out at you?

What always sticks out to me is the time that we played in East Berlin. We were on tour in Europe and [promoter] Barry Dickins called me up and said, "Hey, you've got a show here and you've got two days off and then you've got a show here. In between, we can do a show at East Berlin." I called up our production manager. I said, "Hey, can we do a festival in East Berlin?" He goes, "Yes, if we only pull out backline, and as long as they got some kind of lights, but if it's in the day, it really won't matter, what are they going to use for PA…" blah blah blah.

This is before the Wall went down. This has been put on by the Communist Party, a free concert in the park. We get to the gig and there's 100,000 people. We're just like, what the fuck? It was heads for miles.

I'm thinking, if the Communist Party put this on, they're trying to appease people. Why would they bring Bob Dylan here? He's singing all of his songs and these kids are just so into it. I went to the side of the stage, and am talking to this kid from Yugoslavia, all excited. "As soon as we heard about it, we started driving to get here."

These are people that thought, "I *never* thought I'd ever see Bob Dylan." Just that alone to me was like, whoa, this is deep. This is way deep. They're all singing their anthems back to him, and we are in a communist country.

I remember when the Wall went down. We were on the road, and I remember seeing Bob at the gig and he goes, "See what happened today?" I go, "I bet you one of the reasons is because of you, dude." He goes, "No, no, no." He would never take credit for anything.

Were you involved in the Grammy Awards when he played "Masters of War" in '91?[80]

79 Richard's probably thinking of a different Sinatra song, "I'm in the Mood for Love," which
   Dylan played for the first time at the Greek in '88. He has not performed "My Way"…yet.
80 A fairly infamous night where Dylan gave a bewildering acceptance speech and played an

That's when he got the Lifetime Achievement thing or something. I remember Bob being up in his dressing room with Jack Nicholson and Yoko, then him coming down.

I think he gets nervous accepting these kinds of things. He doesn't know how to really do it. I think it's something that makes him uncomfortable, to be the recipient of somebody putting you on a pedestal.

Both those guys, both Tom and Bob, I noticed they would get nervous at certain times. Tom would get nervous every time he walked on stage.

Really? Even after performing for years?

After years. When we walked into the Super Bowl, it really freaked him out. Because at halftime, what happens is, the teams come in the tunnel, and we're walking out of the tunnel to go out to the stage. You're walking out of this tunnel, all of a sudden you've got 80,000 people yelling.

I'm walking on with the band. Tom is behind me. He's got his hand on my shoulder. We've got Secret Service guys. That's who they use for security, the Secret Service guys, because they don't fuck around. They talk nice and everything, but they know what the fuck is going on. I've got the Secret Service guy here, Tom's behind me, and Tom's hand's on my shoulder. All of a sudden we get out to where there's people, and Tom puts both hands and he's like this on my shoulder *[tightens grip]*.

The Secret Service guy looks back, and he can see that. He says, "Stop." He turns around and he looks right at Tom. He goes, "Tom, you're in the safest place you can be right now. We do this all the time. Nobody's going to get near you." I can tell Tom was thinking, "This is what I needed somebody to tell me." If I told him, I'm five foot seven and 140 pounds and I don't carry a gun. I'm like his pal. With this guy, he knew that this guy was here for us. "We're doing this now. Come on. Let's go." "Okay. Fine."

Both Tom and Bob would get nervous at certain times. Tom more so than Bob, but Bob had his moments where he would get skittish or afraid. I remember some threatening calls to Kramer's office when we were at Radio City Music Hall. Kramer had hired some extra security, the same kind of Secret Service guys. George [Harrison] was in Bob's dressing room, and I went up to get Bob because it was time to go on. Him and George, we walk into the elevator. George notices the guy at the elevator. George goes, "Bob, what's up with the suits?" Bob goes, "Oh, Kramer had some threatening calls and decided to call in some extra people."

---

almost punk (and lyrically incomprehensible) version of "Masters of War."

George goes, "Good move. Good move."

Was that generally stressful? Bob has some overly intense fans, you might say. I imagine there's a certain amount of nerves or tension. How was that for you to deal with?

Bob stayed in his rooms a lot. He'd go out for walks with Callaghan, but that would be very, very late at night. I took a couple of strolls with them late at night. We'd have to walk about 50 feet behind him.

One of the things that intrigued Bob was buskers. He would stand across the street and watch people. I think, in his mind, he goes, "I wish I could do that." He couldn't.

Those people probably never knew that Bob Dylan had been standing there.

Callaghan came to my room one time and said that him and Bob were out for a walk, and Bob had seen this busker and told Callaghan that he wanted him to open up the show. Callaghan went and got his number, and the guy goes, "Are you kidding me?" He goes, "No. Somebody's going to call you."

Callaghan gives me his number and says, "Hey, call this guy. Bob wants him to open up this show." I called the guy up. He didn't believe me. I said, "Why don't you come to the Sebel Townhouse here in Sydney? We're going to fly you with the band to—" I think it was Melbourne. I said, "We'll get you a hotel room. We'll fly you back the next day." He just couldn't believe it. He came to the townhouse and he goes, "This is really going to happen?" I go, "Yes, it's really going to happen, dude."[81]

That's amazing.

I think in the back of his mind, [Bob] really digs that at some level. He was the most interesting cat I've ever worked with, let me tell you. Being a big jazz fan, I've seen a lot of video of Miles, and the way he handles rehearsals reminds me of Bob in the way they get things done. It's not really the normal way, but it's a little cryptic, how they get people or musicians to do what they want to do without really saying, "Play a G" or something like that. I found those similarities and it cracks me up.

Bob was, if not the most, at least the top two most interesting people I've ever worked with. I respect the hell out of him, let me tell you, to this day.

---

81 Dylan may have made a habit of doing this on this tour; Xanthe Littlemore told me her story of being invited to open a show in another chapter. It's also possible this is what Fernandez is referring to and just misremembering some details.

One time I was in town in LA, getting ready for something with Tom. Bob was doing a charity at the Beverly Wilshire Hotel. It wasn't long after I'd left, maybe like three or four or five years after. Their production manager went, "Hey, come on down to rehearsal." Because I knew everybody. It's the same crew and everybody; I had hired a bunch of those guys.

I got there early and I'm standing at the mixing board with a mixer guy. Bob and the band walked on stage. Bob's looking around and goes, "Is that Richard out there? Get up here where you belong!" I felt really honored.

[A while before this], I was on my way back from a Tom Petty tour. I used to have to go through Honolulu before they booked nonstops from LA into Lihue [Hawaii]. I was in Honolulu waiting for my connection to go back home. I see Sam, Bob's son, sit down. He goes, "Richard, what are you doing?" I say, "I'm going home. What are you doing?" He said, "Oh, I'm going to Lihue. I'm on my honeymoon." I went, "Congratulations. If you need anything, let me know. I'm there."

The next day [Sam] calls me. He goes, "I'd really like to go surfing." I said, "My next-door neighbor has like 30 or 40 boards of all different sizes. Pick out what you want. I'll take it down there." I got a local beach about two miles down the road for me. We throw the boards in the back of the truck. Me and Sam go down there. We go out, we go surfing.

When I got up on stage, Bob shakes my hand. He shakes your hand like a gangster shakes your hand. They just put it out there and they don't grip back. Then, all of a sudden, I start to pull back and he holds it. He goes, "I really want to thank you for taking care of Sam. He had a great time." I said, "Anything for your boy, dude."

It's funny, we have this relationship that's not a friendly relationship like, "Hey, Bob, what are you doing? What's going on tomorrow? What have you been eating?" But if we see each other, it's like, "Hey, how's it going?" "Good. I'm glad." "How's your family." "Are your kids good?" "Great."

I remember him calling me the day after Tom passed, just to check in. He just wanted to call and say, "How are you doing?" He goes, "I know, it's tough, but we got to hang in there." I don't talk hardly any to him, but knowing that he called up and cared about a mutual friend that we both really loved…

Marshall Crenshaw promo shot from a few years before he auditioned to be Dylan's bass player.
Courtesy of Marshall Crenshaw

Marshall Crenshaw

Marshall Crenshaw's songs have been recorded by Bette Midler, Ronnie Spector, and The Gin Blossoms. He played Buddy Holly in the 1987 Ritchie Valens biopic *La Bamba*. He's been nominated for both a Grammy and a Golden Globe. But you know what's *not* on his list of accomplishments? Playing bass in Bob Dylan's band.

He tried, though. In 1988, Crenshaw was invited to join what would become the first backing band of the Never Ending Tour. He rehearsed with Bob and the other musicians for three days. Then he was fired, before he played a single concert. He hasn't told this story until now.

. . . .

Tell me how you got involved in that in the late '80s.

What happened was, I was sitting in my kitchen in Nashville on a Saturday afternoon. At that point, I'd been in Nashville for maybe five months. Some friends and business associates were whispering in my ear the idea of moving there. A lot of music business types from LA and other places were moving to Nashville during this period.

I decided I didn't want to live there. It got a little rough between me and my wife during that time, so she split about a month before I could leave. I'm sitting in my kitchen on this Saturday afternoon, like literally staring out into space, in a really bleak frame of mind. The phone rang, up on the kitchen wall. It was G.E. Smith. At that time, I hadn't really spoken to him in maybe four years or so. The call was really out of left field.

How did you know him from four years prior?

I first met him when I was on tour with Daryl Hall and John Oates. I went all over North America with them as an opening act on an arena tour. The guys in the band were really nice people, and we just bonded with them.

Anyhow, he called me up out of the blue. Again, I'm in a shit mood and shit frame of mind. I don't know whether to kill myself or go bowling. We're talking for a second. He knew that I played bass on some of my own records, and he complimented me on that, then he said, "Would you be interested in going on a tour as a bass player with Bob Dylan?" And I just said, "Yeah, sure, fine." You know, like that. That's all I had the energy to say.

Then he gave me the backstory. What he told me was that one night Bob Dylan was sitting at home watching *Saturday Night Live*. The show goes to a commercial break, and he sees *[SNL* bandmembers] G.E. and T-Bone Wolk and Chris Parker up there playing into the commercial. He just picked up the phone to his manager and said, "Get me those guys."

T-Bone Wolk, the bass player, I guess that he first said yes, but then changed his mind. So G.E. was looking for somebody to fill in. He just thought it would be cool, a different approach I guess, to bring me into it.

The thing is, G.E. and other people I know, they know Bob Dylan's body of work like jot for jot. Like G.E. went to school on every album as they came out in turn. And I'd never done that really. I loved Bob Dylan, but at the time that I talked to G.E. on the phone, I'm going to say that maybe I knew 20 of his songs.

But I wanted to try and make it work. I was flattered that G.E. asked me. So I called a friend of mine at Columbia Records, asked her to help me out and send me all of Bob Dylan's albums. She did. They came in these big boxes. I think I had three weeks to try and cram Bob Dylan's whole catalog into my brain.

Had you ever done anything like this? Instead of fronting your own band, you go out as the bass player for someone else?

No, I never had. If I'm playing bass on one of my own things, I can make it work, but I don't really have the comfort level on the instrument that a bass player would have. I don't have a sound on the instrument just normally. And again, it's like this massive body of work. The scale of it and the scope of it is just overwhelming.

Then I hear from G.E. again. Again, this is sketchy information, but he said, "The plan right now is for the band to rehearse for three days, then we're going to go do the first gig and Bob will just meet us on stage. It's going to be like a Chuck Berry gig." I said, "Wow, that sounds crazy."

Another few days go by, and I hear from G.E. again. "Okay, change of plans. The band is going to rehearse at this place in New York for five days, then Bob's going to come on the sixth day."

Of course, it's one of those famous Bob Dylan curveballs that we've all read about: He shows up on either the first day or the second day. I'm nervous, to say the least. I have a bad feeling about the whole thing.

We played for a couple of days, but I'm sure that Bob could see the flop sweat and smell the fear on me. Anyhow, I did the best I could.

What do those days look like musically? Are you running down Dylan's songs, or are you just kind of jamming?

I think we did play songs of his. I have to say that I'm standing next to his amplifier, and a lot of times I just really couldn't fathom what was coming out of the amp. Like maybe G.E. would take a solo and then Bob would start to mimic the solo, and I'm supposed to be the one that's holding the whole thing together. It's not working at all.

Anyhow, after three days or so I was given the news that I was going to be replaced. I felt bad because I really was hopeful about the whole thing, but part of me was relieved.

I left, but I went back the next day. When I walked into the rehearsal space, people seemed shocked to see me. I just wanted to say to Bob that I understood his decision, that it made sense, and that I was really happy that I got to meet him. I wanted to be classy and pay my respect. He was very cool about it. On a personal level, he was cool the whole time, really, although it was no secret in the room that there was a problem, and *I* was the problem.

By the way, Chris Parker, I could be mistaken, but I don't remember him saying a single word the whole time I was there. I never really got to know him, but it was cool that I played with him.

Yeah, I think he talked to me about his nervousness.

We're probably all nervous. G.E. was nervous too, I'm sure, but he's got that real seasoned session musician brain, so he was keeping his cool.

Anyway, they brought in Kenny Aaronson to replace me, who's definitely a real bass player. Then when they decided to get someone to replace *him*, they got Tony Garnier, who I've been friends with since about 1980. I feel like that was a really positive turning point for Bob, because ever since Tony came on board, he's had quality bands consistently. Tony's just one of those people that makes other people relaxed in his presence. I certainly wasn't doing any of that when I was there, I can tell you for sure. Sometimes I joke with Tony and say, "Hey, man, you took my gig!"

Drummer Christopher Parker wailing away in Santa Barbara, California on September 5, 1989 with an early Never Ending Tour band (left to right: G.E. Smith, Parker, Dylan, Tony Garnier).
Photo by Joseph Peduto

Christopher Parker

Christopher Parker was the first drummer of Bob Dylan's Never Ending Tour. For three years starting in 1988, he split his time between the road and his day job in the *Saturday Night Live* house band, alongside Dylan guitarist G.E. Smith. Parker was seated a few feet behind Dylan for all the formative moments of the Never Ending Tour, playing more than 250 shows before he left at the end of 1990.

We discussed how he got involved in the earliest days of the Never Ending Tour, his relationship with Dylan, obsessive fans, songs they rehearsed but never played, and a whole lot more.

. . . .

Can you walk me through how you joined the band? I know you were on SNL *with G.E. Smith in the years leading up to it. Was that the connection?*

Yeah. G.E. was the band leader, as you know, and said, "Would you be interested in doing this?" At that time, the bass player on *Saturday Night Live* was T-Bone Wolk, so the three of us went to Montana Rehearsal Studio, which no longer exists, and started playing with Bob. We probably played 100 tunes or something over a couple of days, a lot of great stuff. Not all Bob's material; other people's material, too. It was really fun, and he seemed to dig it.

How did you know G.E.?

I met him at *SNL* when they called me to be in the house band. That was '86, I guess. Steve Ferrone was the drummer, and he was leaving to go on the road with Duran Duran. I had done the show over the years as a drummer for guest artists, Quincy Jones, Leo Sayer, Boz Scaggs, Linda Ronstadt and Aaron Neville, Elvis Costello, Paul Simon, and stuff with Joe Cocker and Belushi, but that's just playing in the guest spot. I had never been in the band before.

So you get the call, you go to the rehearsal space. At this point, are you a fan, or do you just know a few hits that everyone knows?

To be honest, I wasn't a fan, but there was an interesting intertwining of lives. In 1970, I auditioned for this band in Woodstock. I answered an ad in *Rolling Stone*, "Drummer Wanted." The band was called Holy Moses.

I got the gig and started working up there. I met a girl who eventually became my wife. Her mother was a huge Dylan fan and ended up buying Bob's house on Byrdcliffe. The first time I took this girl home, we went to Byrdcliffe, Bob's house. He wasn't there, but his vibe was certainly there.

People in Woodstock were always talking about Bob. "Well, I saw him… He might be around… He was supposed to come here… He's supposed to…" Everybody was always mentioning him in some context. At that time, I don't think he was currently living there.

But getting to know this woman who later became my wife, we explored the property and explored the rooms and it was amazing. At that time, I started to listen to the records. I really liked *Nashville Skyline* and *John Wesley Harding*. I wasn't really aware of the poetry at all. I still wasn't a *fan*.

After rehearsing with him and meeting the guy, listening to him sing and to the poetry, I became an instant fan.

What does that first meeting look like? You show up at the studio, what happens next?

We're introduced. Not much is said. We start playing.

G.E. and T-Bone knew a lot of the songs, and I didn't. They were quoting things; they seem to know whatever he wanted to play. I just fell in, like Colin Allen talks about in your interview with him. Bob starts playing something and you fall in. There was never any, "Here's the count off and here's the tempo and this is the kind of feel I want." He didn't tell me, "That's good" or "Don't do that," but looked at me like, "You wouldn't be here if I didn't dig what you were doing, so just keep doing that."

I had the gall at one point to say, "What do you want me to play on this?" Bob said, "I'm just a fucking poet."

It was all very, like Jim Keltner said[82], like jazz. Feel it and get a groove and don't play the same thing twice. When we played the song that we had played yesterday, it was completely different. We did probably three or four different versions of "Heart of Mine." A guy who does the archives in Tulsa, he sent me tapes of some

---

82 In my interview with him, printed earlier in the book.

of those rehearsals and you can hear all these different versions of "Heart of Mine." That was fun to listen to.

Wow, that sounds amazing.

Quality is not great, but that was the genesis of the band. T-Bone, who was an amazing musician, not only played bass but played acoustic guitar and played accordion and sang. He and G.E. were singing backup at some times. Sometimes T-Bone would put down the bass and play accordion, so it was Bob on acoustic, T-Bone on accordion, and me playing brushes or something.

We got a lot of really intimate feels going on, not only his tunes but stuff like "Barbara Allen," a song that they sang in the Alistair Sims version of *A Christmas Carol*. Bob loved that song. We played that a lot on the road, actually.

There were explorations by everybody. Should I play guitar? Should I play brushes? Should I play accordion? G.E. often played acoustic or just Telecaster. Bob sometimes played acoustic with a harmonica around his neck, traditional Bob-style, or he played the Stratocaster. The band could be really, really electric or it could be very intimate and folky. Even jazzy. Tunes would float like a Bill Evans Trio record.

One time he said, "I'm trying to write a song here." I don't know what song it was, but he's writing it on a paper towel on the windowsill. Deep in thought. I wonder what song that was.

During all these rehearsals, do you have the gig, or is it a long audition?

It's still very much an audition. I think we did four or five days one week, and then another three or four days the next week. It was based on the *Saturday Night Live* schedule. He was very accommodating, because the show was pretty busy with pre-records and guest artists and everything leading up to the Saturday night.

Then one day [Dylan manager] Elliot Roberts showed up. He pulled me aside and said, "He's got something coming up. Would you be interested?" That's when I knew I had a gig, because they were talking about dates, starting at some amphitheater in California. I said yes. That was the beginning.

T-Bone didn't want to do it, because he was committed to Hall & Oates, but they found Kenny Aaronson, who I'd never played with before.

Obviously in retrospect this is the beginning of Dylan pretty much touring forever. Is it presented as the start of something big or just like, "We're doing a couple months on the road"?

This was presented as a one-off thing. "Could you do a little summer tour?" It was definitely not presented as a never-ending tour. Six weeks or a month would go by, and they would say, "We got another bunch of dates. Can you do it?" I kept saying, "Yes."

Do you have to turn in your notice at SNL *at a certain point?*

No, no, because G.E. was in the band and he wanted to keep doing this.

So you'd do both?

Luckily for us, we never had to give notice. Bob and Elliot Roberts worked around our schedule. They didn't book gigs on a Saturday night. They didn't book gigs on a Thursday if we were doing pre-records. G.E. and I racked up thousands of miles flying back and forth.

That sounds like an exhausting schedule.

It was exhausting, but really fun to go from the confines of NBC Studio 8H to wherever it was, New Mexico or Canada. We played all over the place. I found posters yesterday from Turkey and Italy.

That was very fortunate, right up until G.E. decided he didn't want to do it anymore. Then there was this long audition process trying to find another guitar player, which was really painful. By that time Kenny Aaronson had left, so we had Tony Garnier. I was teaching him the tunes in the back of the bus after the gigs. He was really thrown into the fire and did great, as he's been doing for 30 years since.

Was there a change in the sound or the vibe when Kenny left and Tony joined?

Yes, the vibe changed *and* the sound changed. Tony came in playing acoustic bass — he played electric too, but it was a different approach. He's a different musician, a great musician, but it definitely disrupted the thing that we had had, which was this flexibility to go in a rock direction or a folky direction or a jazzy direction or reggae. Any direction he wanted to go, we would fall in.

We didn't play the same thing twice. Play something different every night, or play something that is current to that night. That happened a lot, especially on familiar tunes, like "Rainy Day Women" or "Times They Are a-Changin'." That had a 12/8 kind of feel, but when it got too comfortable in 12/8, he would change it to 4/4. Bob would put it in strict eighth notes instead of shuffling.

How is he communicating those changes? As a drummer, something like time signature really affects what you're doing.

He *didn't* communicate it. I would watch. He was standing directly in front of

Always people wanting to see him, talk to him, show their painting, give a manuscript they'd written about how this one song saved their life. Legal pads filled with handwritten stuff, photographs and sculptures, car bumpers from a '49 Mercury. Skulls, steer horns, you never knew what was going to be in his dressing room.

me, and I would watch his body language most of all. That was the only clue. He never gave me four fingers or six fingers or said "shuffle" or "straight eighths" or any of that stuff. That was never spoken. It was solely my interpretation of his body language. And a lot of times he didn't like the lights, so it was hard to see him.

Not only that, there were some shows where he's playing in a hoodie with his hood up, which probably made it that much harder to see what he was doing.

Oh yes. There was a very funny moment one Halloween. We were playing in Chicago. He had been in a hoodie for a while, hoodie with a prayer shawl and Ray-Bans and blue jeans. So somebody on the crew gave everybody a hooded sweatshirt, blue jeans, a prayer shawl, and sunglasses.

Bob never came to soundcheck, but he would sometimes after dinner come and check out the stage. So that night when he did, everybody dressed in a hoodie, a prayer shawl, blue jeans and sunglasses. When he came on stage, he saw everybody in his exact outfit. There was dead silence for what seemed like 10 minutes, but it was probably 30 seconds or something. Then he smiled a little bit. He got the joke. He didn't say anything, but he got the joke.[83]

There was another backstage event, we were playing this place called Memphis Mud Island, which is an island in the middle of the Mississippi. You take a tram to get out there and everything. There's one room where you can tune up and stuff before you hit the stage. This time of the year, [it's] probably 110 degrees, and giant mosquitoes everywhere, so everybody was trying to take cover in this room.

For some reason, a member of the Eagles was in the neighborhood and wanted to come and hang. We're sitting in the room, just the band and Bob, silent. Nobody

83 Richard Fernandez tells a different version of this story in Chapter 32.

is saying anything. We're just trying to mentally prepare for the evening. Then this Eagles guy comes in. Silence again. He finally said to Bob, "So Bob, how's your dick?"

There was dead silence. Then after about 10 seconds, Bob had to smile.

Those were rare moments to see him smile and get a kick out of something that happened. Because he's Bob. He's seen everything, played everywhere, knows everybody, nothing fazes him really, but it was great to see a moment like that when he actually smiled.

Speaking of guests, Neil Young joined the band for three entire shows at the start of your run. How did that happen?

We were playing in California and he lived nearby. He would drive up in his Cadillac convertible and pull his Silvertone Amp out of the trunk and his guitar and set it up next to me, left of the drums, and play all night. He was fucking amazing.

Jerry Garcia sat in. Ringo sat in. We played double drums in France. I had enough spare parts on the road to put another kit together. Two sets of drums set up alongside each other. [Ringo and I] talked a lot before shows, hearing directly from him about the early days with the lads. Some great conversations, talking about drums and technique and equipment and stuff like that.

Van Morrison sat in in Athens. It was in a soccer stadium and the crowd was throwing M-80s onstage. You know, like a quarter stick of dynamite. They're exploding at Bob's feet and Van Morrison's feet. I'm back on a riser, seeing these flashes and stuff. Didn't faze 'em. They just kept playing.

There was a woman who had a passport that said Sara Dylan. Had her name changed, I guess. She probably came to hundreds of gigs and always had a roll of nickels. She would throw nickels on the stage. If you hung around after the show— we never did, but my drum tech and different crew guys would pick up these nickels. It's always $5 or $10 worth of nickels.

That is very bizarre.

Yes. Totally, totally, totally bizarre. She would show up in Helsinki or she would show up on this island in Norway. How the fuck did she get here?

There was always an entourage, a group of people who wanted to see him, wanted to talk to him, wanted to show him their painting, wanted to show him something they had made for him, wanted to give him a manuscript they had written when they were in Vietnam with Agent Orange exploding above them and how this one song saved their life. Legal pads filled with handwritten stuff, photographs and sculptures, car bumpers from a '49 Mercury. Sometimes you'd get a peek into his dressing room and look at this pile of stuff in manila envelopes. Skulls, steer horns, you never knew what was going to be in his dressing room.

Nobody was throwing the stuff away. It all got cataloged. Especially in LA or New York, people just besieged him.

Are you ever having to deal with that personally?

Yes, by association. I had a house in Kent, Connecticut at the time. When I started working with Bob, it didn't take long. Even after the very first tour, people would pull up the driveway and say, "Can you tell me a little bit about what it's like to work with Bob?" People in pickup trucks with shotgun racks and people on bicycles would just show up at the house and knock at the door. Really not a good time. How do you deal with this? Nobody was— I was going to say nobody was crazy, but they're *all* kind of crazy. They were Bob-obsessed.

Some people would show up more than once. "Here's a painting I did. Can you get this to Bob?" or "Here's a letter I wrote. Can you make sure Bob gets this?" I was the conduit to Bob. I said, "I really can't." I'm not going to take this and then give it to Bob. "This is from somebody in Connecticut who's obsessed with you." I drew the line there.

I tried to be polite and dissuade them from coming again, because I'm there with my family. It was weird. There were some weird moments.

Musically, how did the show and the band evolve over the three years? We already talked about Kenny going and Tony coming, but otherwise, in terms of the sound and in terms of how you all interacted with each other?

We got more comfortable. Over the course of the three years, a lot of things got changed. We played different tunes or tackled different things.

When stuff is getting added late in the tour, covers of obscure songs, when are they getting rehearsed? Do you work a lot at soundchecks or are they things you rehearse before the tour?

Some of the things we had played before the tour. "Oh, yes, I remember playing this," or G.E. and Kenny or Tony would say, "How do you want to do it?" "He likes G, you want to do it in G?" "Let's put it down half a step just in case." Sort of go through it. I would listen. I wasn't at the drums; this would be backstage or on the bus. I was listening. "Okay, I could do something like this. Maybe this will work." I'd play it for the first time at night with Bob singing.

His phrasing is the other clue to what I'm going to play, besides the body language. His phrasing is as unique as Frank Sinatra. Back phrasing, waiting for the change to go by before he sings the lyric that goes with that change, or singing the lyric that goes with that change way in front of that change, so that the end of the line is when you hear the change that goes in that spot of the song — to be able to do that is just brilliant. There's no other singers besides Frank Sinatra or maybe Ella Fitzgerald or Ray Charles. I guess Willie Nelson too. Somebody who's got such command of the song that they can stretch lines, or shrink lines, or truncate lines, scrunch words together or stretch words out however they want the phrases to reflect their mood at the moment, literally at that second. I evolved to really enjoy that as I'm playing with him more and more and more.

Was there any disappointment that at the time he wasn't using his road band for studio stuff? He didn't use G.E. or you or anyone for Oh Mercy *or* Under the Red Sky.

Yeah, because we would hear these tunes and be ready to play them. Then we'd see the record come out and think "I could have played on that. Jeez!" Sometimes it was a bummer because the feel we had live was hipper than what they had on the record.

Now that they're releasing all these bootlegs, maybe at some point they'll release stuff from '88 to '92. There were some amazing performances, Bob himself playing acoustic guitar and harmonica. Like Jim Keltner says, it would make you weep.

Speaking of acoustic, it looks like the earlier acoustic sets were just him and G.E., and then on later ones you and Tony were playing too.

I remember one night they were doing "Knockin' on Heaven's Door" and I was on the side of the stage. I just said, "You know what, this could really use drums." My mics were on and I snuck up to the drums and did this gigantic fill going into the chorus. Bob turned around and smiled.

I didn't do it the next night or subsequent concerts where they played "Knockin'." He didn't like that. If anything sounded predictable to him or he could tell we were phoning it in, he would change it.

I loved when guitarists would sit in and try to see what chords Bob was playing. He would turn the neck of the guitar towards the back of the stage. They had to use their ears and their instinct and whatever else to fit in. You can't use the Cliff Notes with Bob Dylan.

After G.E. announces he's leaving, there's a whole succession of other guitarists on stage, a new one every night or two. Kind of a series of auditions, in front of live audiences. Some of them probably are *trying to look at his hands, I'm guessing. That seems like a weird experience for a band member.*

It was very tough, and it was very painful. Heartbreaking, really.

How so?

There was some very, very awkward moments at the guitar auditions. There were a bunch of guys who would have been great if given a chance, but they made various faux pas, for lack of a better word, by asking Bob for an autograph or by asking if they could get something special. I don't know what they were asking for, but I know for whatever reason, certainly not a musical reason, they didn't get the gig. The guitarist he was most comfortable with was the guitar tech, César Diaz, who would tune Bob's guitars and give them to him. He was always at the side of the stage.84

And César, God bless him, was not a guitar player. I mean, he could play the guitar, but he wasn't a band member. This was really heartbreaking. He became the de facto guitar player. He was so nervous and not used to being in the spotlight. Not used to performing, period. That made it really hard to make the band gel.

That was kind of the last straw for me. Plus, I was having my second child and I missed a lot of my first child's early life. It was tearing me apart. I had waited 19 years with this woman who I met, whose mother had bought Byrdcliffe, we'd waited 19 years to have children because we wanted to do it right. We weren't going to make a mistake that we'd seen other people make; we wanted the relationship to be solid.

My first son was born in '88 and I was on the road for the following 18 months. Then my second son was born, and this guitar chair scenario was going down. I asked Bob to let me go and do what I need to do with my family.

It was a great ride, and so much great music. That's what's heartbreaking about not being on any of the records, there's no official document of that period. Some interpretations of the tunes were as good as the classic records or better.

Listening to some of the bootleg recordings, you talk about the versatility and that's definitely there, but one thing that jumps out is just how hard you guys rocked. It's almost close to punk at times.

Yeah. I remember some great takes on certain tunes. We were playing at West Point Academy and he played "Masters of War" and that was killing. That was like The Clash doing Bob Dylan.

It seemed like West Point was pretty controversial at the time. Do you remember that

---

84 Guitar tech César Diaz stepped into the lead-guitarist shoes in 1990 and 1991 after G.E. Smith left the band.

media brouhaha, about Bob Dylan playing at a military academy?

It was a tension-filled night. We're getting off the bus. We'd been on the road for, I don't know, three or four months. To interface with the cadets and the structure of this place and the militaristic vibe was very anxiety-provoking. Nobody knew what the show was going to be like. Are the cadets going to boo us? Are they going to throw stuff at us? We didn't know what was going to happen.

Clearly, there was a bunch of cadets who dug him and dug his music and wanted to be there. The place was sold out. That was an amazing show.

How about Toad's Place, 1990? Probably the craziest setlist of Dylan's entire career. "Dancing in the Dark," all these weird covers, his own songs he never played. What was the story with that show? Sort of a rehearsal with an audience?

A rehearsal with an audience, yes. It's not really a theater, so everybody's on the same level. Drums are on the floor. Guitars are on the floor. Bass is on the floor. There's no proscenium. I don't think we had played anything up to that moment that was with that much audience contact. There's usually a stage and security and fences and whatever else to keep the audience and Bob separated, but this was really the dissolution of the fourth wall. The people were right there. There's somebody watching me play drums three feet away. You could feel the energy. People were into it, screaming tunes. "Play 'Baby Blue'! Play 'Highway 61'!"

Had you known going in that it would be like this?

No, I thought it was going to be empty and we were just going to rehearse.

You didn't know there was going to be an audience?

No. I thought the first few people who trickled in, "Oh, they must be friends of the management or owners of the place or something. But people kept trickling in. Pretty soon, it was a full-blown audience.

Of all the Springsteen songs to cover, "Dancing in the Dark" a bizarre choice and it works...not super well. How would an off-the-wall thing like that happen?

He'd just yell it out. Or he would start singing something and G.E.'d say, "Oh, okay, well, jump in there." I'd try to fall in without ever having played it before.

Couple of things he did at rehearsal that I wish we had played live. We did "God Only Knows," the Beach Boys song, which is really a tough tune. It's got an odd number of beats and an orchestral figure in the interlude. We did — what's it called? — "Father of Time" or something?

"Father of Night"?

"Father of Night," yes. We did Willie Nelson songs and Hank Williams songs, some of which were great. Woody Guthrie songs.

I've talked to various band members. It seems to fluctuate pretty wildly whether Bob is hanging out, whether he's even talking to the band off stage. What was the vibe there during your years?

The vibe with him was great, unless we were in LA or New York, where, as I mentioned before, people were just besieging him with requests. When we played Radio City, the dressing room was full of stars, George Harrison, Allen Ginsberg, Peter Gabriel, Joan Baez. All these folks are coming by and they're besieging him. What are you going to do? In LA, an insane amount of people. Jack Nicholson, Harry Dean Stanton, Brian Wilson, Joni Mitchell. There were 100 people waiting in line to see or give something to him. I can't imagine dealing with that kind of attention and that kind of neediness being presented to you in some tangible form as an object of this neediness.

[But] if we were out in Oklahoma or New Mexico or Colorado or something, he was a normal guy. He had a fighter named "Mouse" Strauss, an ex-boxer who had been hit so many times he really wasn't all there. He would come and train Bob. They would box together. We would ask later that day, "Hey how was your session with Mouse?" Bob would say, "Oh, I knocked him down" or "He gave me a tumble." We were just normal. We didn't have endless conversations, but we certainly conversed. After I had my first son, when I went back on the road with him that was the first thing he said to me. "Hey Chris, how's that baby?"

You said he didn't give you much in the way of instruction in advance. Would you ever get feedback after the fact? "I want it slower tomorrow" or "I liked this thing you did."

Never.

Does that make it difficult to know if what you're doing is working?

Not any more difficult than playing jazz with somebody. You get a feeling; you get a vibe. If he turned around and smiled, I knew, "Well, I didn't fuck that up." If he wasn't happy, I didn't know, but maybe the song was different the next night. I learned from that one moment at a rehearsal, when I said, "What do you want me to play on this?" "I'm just a fucking poet."

Karl Denson sitting in on sax at the Beacon Theatre in New York City, New York, 1990.
Photo by Duncan Hume

Karl Denson

Karl Denson plays for tens of thousands of people every night in his current gig as saxman for the Rolling Stones, where he replaced the late Bobby Keys. But for a couple nights in 1990, he played a much smaller room: New York's intimate Beacon Theatre. He was there to accompany Dylan's opening act Lenny Kravitz, then a new artist promoting his debut album. Pretty soon he found himself playing with the headliner too.

. . . .

How did you come to be up there? Were you in Lenny's band then, opening the whole tour?

I was in Lenny's band, yes. The saxophone sound was kind of in at the time. We were opening just the Beacon shows. A week at the Beacon.

Before one of them, G.E. Smith, the guitar player with Bob, came and said, "Hey, Bob wants to know if you'd like to play a couple of tunes?" I was like, "Hell yeah!" We ended up playing "Gotta Serve Somebody," which I really loved at the time, and "All Along the Watchtower," one of my favorites also. It was pretty amazing.

How did he come to think of inviting you, or even know you were there? Had he been watching Lenny's set?

You know what? I think it partly came from Lenny's set, but I also think it might have been because we ran into each other a couple of days in a row when I was coming early to practice.

Coming early to the Beacon?

I come in early in practice, and Bob would be slinking around quietly with his lady at the time. He's so freaking quiet, it's funny. You never notice him, and then he'd pop up somewhere and I'd be like, "Oh, there's Bob Dylan." I think maybe he just noticed me practicing. My conscientiousness paid off.

At what point do you actually meet Dylan himself? You said G.E.'s the one who made the ask.

This is the best part. I'm a gangster, but I'm not a made man. I never actually talk to the boss.

So Bob invited me, and I got up on stage. I was all excited. I played the songs, and then they invited me back the next night. I came back and I played again. Then the third night, Lenny and a couple of the other guys from Lenny's band came and played. At the end of our little stint there, Bob walks over and whispers in Lenny's ear. I thought, "Lenny's only been here one night. I've been here *three*, and he didn't say boo to me." That was when I realized, "Dude, you're just a regular mobster. You're not a made man." So I'm still working on being made.

Are they telling you the songs in advance? Are you running them down with the band at all before you get up there?

No. I knew the songs. They're standards. You should be able to keep up with those kind of songs.

When I spoke to another sax player, Dickie Landry, he was telling me how nervous he was. The first few songs, he barely played. Whereas you sound extremely assertive from the moment Bob gives you the nod. And you were pretty young then. Had you had experience in those sorts of high-pressure situations to have that confidence?

Let's call it bravado. That was just pure bravado. What I was doing with Lenny was playing wild and assertive. I'm happy that you said that because I have no idea what we sound like back then, and so it'll be interesting to hear it.

I've always been a sound guy, as far as "my sound," so I think that's part of it. I can play very loud. Back in those days, that might have even been before I got my second saxophone and changed my setup, but I was definitely playing a loud setup. It was made for playing over amplifiers.

That makes sense to me because this era is Bob in his most garage-rock phase. He's got two guitars, and they're distorted and loud as hell, and his drummer is just wailing away. You need some power. This isn't a subtle acoustic thing you're playing along with.

I had been playing with Lenny, who was playing this— we called it the roach motel. It was this little fender amp that he had. It wasn't even as big as a twin. It was like a little box, and that thing was so freaking loud and gnarly. We would have the sound all dialed in on stage, and then Lenny would walk up and plug that thing in and just destroy everybody. So I was used to very high volumes.

Bob must have liked what you're doing because he gave you a lot of solos. It's not just like you get, I don't know, eight bars and then get out of here. You're going for a while.

The next day or the day after, I thanked G.E. again for inviting me. He goes, "No, man. I didn't invite you. Bob invited you." It was really funny. Just once again the fact that he didn't speak to me, but he must've enjoyed my playing, so I'm glad about that.

I guess all of it was surprising on some level, but did anything particularly surprise you or stick out from what you might've expected playing with Bob Dylan to be on paper?

I didn't expect to get to play my two favorite tunes at the time. That was the most unexpected part of it. "Gotta Serve Somebody" was on a later record, and then "All Along the Watchtower," just from listening to Jimi Hendrix as a kid and then hearing Bob Dylan do it, I was already sold. Those choice of songs was exactly what I wanted to play.

This is a fairly apples and oranges question, I realize, but I'll ask it anyway. How does playing with Bob Dylan compare to playing with the Rolling Stones?

It's exactly the same in a certain way because you're playing with somebody that's got that kind of a catalog. That's the thing that blows my mind with the Rolling Stones all the time. It is always surreal that I get to be a part of that unbelievable catalog. Bob Dylan's the same way. So many great songs and such a great songwriter that being a part of that for even a moment is surreal.

Dylan and the band in Santa Barbara, California, 1988. Keith Dircks was running sound on the stage monitors you can see in front of Dylan, guitarist G.E. Smith (left), drummer Christopher Parker (rear) and bassist Kenny Aaronson (right).
Photo by Joseph Peduto

Keith Dircks

While most of the people in this book are musicians, we've already heard from a few people who work behind-the-scenes to make Dylan tours happen. Now we hear from one of the men who made up Dylan's sound crew: Keith Dircks, who did the sound the band heard onstage during the first few years of the Never Ending Tour.

You should know going in: His job did not require much close interaction with the man himself. There are a couple choice Dylan anecdotes sprinkled in, but, to me, his stories are most interesting as a window into what daily life was like if you're a crew guy on the road with Dylan. If you've ever gone to a show and wondered what the people scurrying around onstage before the band comes on are doing, or what the people standing behind those giant boards are actually up to, Dircks helps break it down.

. . . .

I worked 22 feet away from him. In the first year, he said maybe 40 words to me. Truly.

When I first met him, we were in the [rehearsal] studio, Montana Studios in New York. The band had showed up first, like the day before. When Bob came in, I asked him, "What's your philosophy on monitors?" His reply was, "All around..." So that's what I had to work with.

At first, he was all, "Turn that down. I don't want that, I don't want that." Then we went and did the first show in some shed. Management called me to [Bob's] suite the next morning. I was getting fired, because Bob hated the monitors. And Dave [Robb, the other main sound guy] interjected and said, "Well, what don't you like?" And Bob goes, "Well, they weren't loud enough." And Dave goes, "Really? You want *loud*?"

At the second show, [Dylan's manager] Elliot Roberts was next to me. Because now I'm on thin ice. After the third song, he goes, "Turn that shit down!" Nothing was ever said again about how I did monitors.

You know, Bob's just a guy of few words. One thing stood out, out of the 40 words he spoke at me in the first year. We were up in Montana Studios, and it was just him and I in the room. I'm at the back of the room doing something. He walked back, and he goes, "When it's all said and done, it comes down to two things." And then there was a long pregnant pause. You know, the Bob pause. Then he said, "Kids and food," took a bite out of a jalapeño, turned around, and walked away.

The next year, in '89, my first daughter was born. And 25 years later, God damn, he was right on. It's all about kids and food. He had totally nailed it. I couldn't appreciate it at the time. I kind of went, well okay, that's a Bob-ism. But then, 25 years later: oh, I guess he had something to say.

In the States, the crew all had mountain bikes, and we took them on tour with us. And whenever you had an hour to get away, you just go for a ride. When we went to Europe, the crew didn't take any of their bikes, but Bob and his entourage got bikes in Europe to peddle around. Every time that they did, they left the bikes unlocked, and they would get stolen. So in the next country, they'd have to buy another set of bikes.

There were not a lot of groupies. Other rock tours, you go to the bus, there's groupies hanging outside. So I go to go on the bus one day and there was a girl standing out there. I go, "Can I help you?" She goes, "Can I ask a question?" "Sure." "Do you guys need any more poets on tour?" I said, "Well, geez, you missed the boat by one day. We hired our last poet yesterday."

I never know if Bob knew who I was, but I worked 22 feet away from him every night for two years. In '89, my wife was pregnant with our first one. Every night I'd call her and go, "Is today the day?" We were in Poughkeepsie, and I get back to the hotel and there's a message that I had to get home. So I leave the tour for 10 or 11 days. The guy that replaced me was Dave Taylor, who was out on tour with us anyway. My nickname on the tour was Mel. And when I came back, I said, "So how did it go?" And Dave goes, "I don't think he missed you." "Why is that?" And Dave goes, "He walked past me and said, 'Hey Mel, how's it going?'"

Bob would talk to G.E., and then G.E. and I would talk. The next morning, G.E. would go, "About last night, he wants you to fatten up the guitar a little bit." We kind of figured out what was best for Bob, how Bob could play with the rest of the band. If I had two monitors in front of him they were totally separate from each other. One just had his guitar, and then the other one had his voice. And then the side fills had the majority of the band.

My favorite part of the show is the four or five acoustic songs where it was just [Bob] and G.E. Most of the time G.E. was on like a 12-string, and Bob on his guitar, a Takamine. For me as a sound guy, I appreciate the quality of sound more than, you know, the individual sounds themselves. And just the quality of what those guys were playing, and the air in between the notes, you could pick everything up.

I eventually left the touring business because I had totally missed everything with my kids. The next-door neighbor taught them how to ride a bicycle, that kind of stuff. It was the price you pay for living on a tour bus. Everybody you talk to goes, "That must have been so great! You've been around the world!" And it's like, you see the bus door as you're closing it and then you see the stage door as you go in. You know if you've been there before if catering or the showers look familiar. Other than that, it's the same day.

Richard Thompson performing with Dylan at the Guitar Legends festival in Seville, Spain in 1991.

Richard Thompson

Richard Thompson has been singing Dylan songs since the earliest days of his band Fairport Convention. Their 1969 album *Unhalfbricking* alone includes three Dylan deep cuts: "Percy's Song," "Million Dollar Bash," and "If You Gotta Go, Go Now" (that one translated into French, no less).

Thompson didn't actually meet Dylan for another few decades, though. In 1991, Dylan played a five-day festival in Spain called Guitar Legends. The bill also included B.B. King, Keith Richards, Les Paul, Dylan's old Band-mate Robbie Robertson, and many more. To accompany him during his short set, though, Dylan didn't call on any of them. He asked Richard Thompson.

Thompson told me about that experience and about, another two decades later, learning that Dylan had covered his song "1952 Vincent Black Lightning" in a concert. Thompson had in fact been the opening act at that very concert, but was already on the road to the next town by the time Dylan sang his song.

. . . .

Was that 1991 Guitar Legends thing your first interaction of any sort with him?

That was the first time that I'd met Bob, and the first time that I played with him as well. I was in the middle of a European tour with Bonnie Raitt, and the Guitar Legends thing came up, so I decided to come off the Bonnie Raitt tour and run down to Spain.

I did my soundcheck for my little bit, my three songs, then Bob's road manager said, "Can you play something with Bob?" I said, "That's a great honor." We went up and rehearsed, I think, the three songs that we did: "Along the Borderline," "Boots of Spanish Leather," and "Answer Me, My Love," the Nat King Cole song. We went through everything once and that was it.

We performed those as a duo. Then we did "All Along the Watchtower" with a very accomplished and luminary house band as well. I think it was Simon Phillips on drums, Bruce Hornsby on keyboard. That was fun.

Who picked the songs? "Watchtower" is a fairly obvious song for a thing called Guitar Legends, but the three you two did alone are definitely not obvious. Two of them he didn't even write.

No, not obvious. Perhaps he chose "Boots of Spanish Leather" because he was in Spain. Perhaps he chose "Along the Borderline" because it has a slightly Mexican–Spanish inflection to it. The Nat King Cole song, maybe it's just a song he was enjoying at the time. I can only speculate.

A lot of people tell me Dylan is a hard guy to accompany because he's not going to do it the same every time. What did you feel that your role was in those acoustic songs?

I felt that my role was to fill in the gaps and play bits of lead here and there. To do a bit of the Bruce Langhorne thing that Bruce used to do on Dylan's records.[85]

What do you remember from the actual performance?

A lot of feedback. I mean, literal feedback from the monitors. The monitors were way too loud and feeding back quite badly from time to time. I'm trying to get in tune somewhere between the dressing room and the stage, but I think both our guitars had gone out of tune, so I spent the first number trying to tune up to Bob, really.

There's a moment in the video, in between the first two songs, where it looks like you're frantically trying to tune and Dylan's not waiting. He's just barreling ahead.

Yeah. It was a little out of tune, to say the least. That was a little distracting.

Later you come back with everyone for one of those big all-star finale type things. You sing a verse or two of "I Can't Turn You Loose" with Roger McGuinn. Bob's just playing guitar. Generally, what's your feeling on those all-star jams, where some festival gets every single person on stage at once?

People like to see it, but I don't think musicians like it. They like to feel included in the big finale, so it's good in that way, but it's usually chaotic in another sense. It's not always the most musical experience.

---

85 Langhorne played on a number of Dylan records in the '60s. Most relevant to Thompson's comparison perhaps, "Mr. Tambourine Man" is also a simple two-guitar number, with Langhorne's leads accenting Dylan's strumming.

The second day [the day of Thompson's set, after Dylan had left] we did a Jimmy Reed song. That one was more memorable because you had Les Paul up there and Robbie Robertson. From a guitar nerd point of view, that was a bit more interesting.

I wonder if there was scuttlebutt that Robbie was going to play with Dylan. You can imagine that rumor circulating.

Could be. It was a strange event. I've never been able to watch the video of the performance.

Never been able to watch as in just haven't, or as in don't want to?

I'm not always a fan of seeing my performances on stage.

The one band song you did that Bob actually sang was "Watchtower." In your book[86] you wrote about how you and Fairport were trying to focus on English, Irish, Scottish music and purge yourself of American influences. So I wondered if you were a big Hendrix guy, or if he was the sort of performer you were trying to discard then.

I saw Jimi when he'd just got to town. He did a little show in the London suburbs quite near to my house. It must have been early days of the Jimi Hendrix Experience. It was really, really impressive. People talk about the guitar playing, which was obviously great, but also, he's a really good songwriter, a really good arranger and a really good singer. It's this all-around thing that was really impressive. A full musical package.

There's a kind of authenticity to Jimi, as well. British blues guitar players are brought up basically on the records. They didn't come from Chicago. They were good imitators. I thought Hendrix was head and shoulders above anybody else at that point on the London music scene.

That was '66, '67. By '69, Fairport were weaning ourselves off of American-influenced music and trying to do much more UK sounds and UK style. In '67, we got hold of the Basement Tapes and we covered quite a few of those songs. We got hold of Joni Mitchell's demos before she made an album, because we really were a band that loved lyrics.

At that time, the best singer-songwriters were coming out of America. There weren't so many in Britain. Bert Jansch, maybe Ewan MacColl, but mostly Bob Dylan was the standout writer who changed the culture. That was a real focus for us with the lyrics. I felt in that way, in London at that time, we were about the only

86 *Beeswing: Losing My Way and Finding My Voice 1967–1975.*

band doing that.

When you say get ahold of the Basement Tapes, this is obviously before the official album in '75. Did you buy it in a bootleg shop? Did Bob's publisher bring it to you?

We went to his publisher and said, "Have you got any unpublished Dylan songs?" They said, "Oh yeah, come over." They gave us, I think, 12 sides on acetates from the Basement Tapes. "Open the Door, Homer," "This Wheel's on Fire." "Mighty Quinn." About a year later, Manfred Mann got ahold of that, and Julie Driscoll got ahold of "This Wheel." It was songs that ended up getting quite covered by quite a lot of people.

Why did you end up doing "Million Dollar Bash" out of that 12-song batch?

I think because we thought it was a fun kind of throwaway. We could have guests singing on different verses. I don't think we were thinking, "This is a single" or "This is a permanent part of the repertoire" because it never was. It was just something that we threw at the wall, pretty much.

You covered a couple other unreleased Dylan songs that are not Basement Tapes, "Percy's Song" and "If You Gotta Go, Go Now." Were those from the publisher as well?

"Percy's Song" I think we found in a songbook of Bob Dylan's songs. It might have been the first one that ever got published in the UK. I can't remember whatever else is in there, but mostly stuff that appeared on the first two or three Bob Dylan albums. "Percy's Song" was in there for some reason, which was amazing, really. We thought, "Nobody knows this song." Joan Baez sings a verse of it in *Don't Look Back*, but that's it. That's the only place it surfaced at that time.

"If You've Gotta Go, Go Now," I can't remember where that came from. Another song that we did was "I'll Keep It With Mine," which we found on a Judy Collins B-side. We felt the way that Judy Collins did it didn't do the song justice. We felt it was better slowed down and given much more emotion, so the Fairport version was a lot slower. I think we did a good job on it.

Jumping forward a few decades, let's talk the "Americanarama" tour in 2013. What did you think when you were invited on that?

I suppose I thought, "This is exciting. It's a tour. We can get paid. That's good; we like to get paid. Dylan's on the bill, Wilco's on the bill, My Morning Jacket's on the bill. How bad can it be?"

The only downside for us was we were basically opening the show, usually

I didn't really believe Bob Dylan covered one of my songs... why would he? When it sank in, I thought, "Well, that's fantastic. I've covered 75 of his; he's covered one of mine." I think that's the right ratio.

. . . .

something like 5:30 PM, when there were about 500 people in the arena. People slowly trickled in during our set. So our sets were a bit throwaway in that sense. But we had some fun. We did a lot of jamming with Wilco, who like that sort of thing.

Towards the end of the tour, I met Bob. He invited me to his bus, and that was very nice. He was very gracious and friendly. He said he was appreciative of the stuff Fairport had done with his songs. That was lovely.

Was this before or after he covered your song "1952 Vincent Black Lightning" onstage?

It could have been the same day, possibly. Can't remember.

You said afterward you had no clue that he was going to cover the song. You were not even still in the building when it happened.

That's true. We had to get to the next date, wherever that was, and in order to do it we had to leave pretty much after our set and then drive 600 miles or something. It was a necessity, so I missed it.

Do you remember how you first heard about it and what your reaction was?

I think I read it on Facebook. Someone commented about it. I thought, "Well, I don't really believe that. Why would Bob cover one of mine?" When it sank in, I thought, "Well, that's fantastic. I've covered 75 of his; he's covered one of mine." I think that that's the right ratio.

What did you think when you finally heard a recording of it?

It wasn't apparent that there *was* a recording for a long time. But, as we know, these things surface sooner or later.

I thought it was great. I would not expect to have a verbatim version from Dylan.

I like the fact that he plays around with things and he doesn't do stuff the same way twice. That's a wonderful thing when you get to 80 or whatever he was then. It shows that you are still experimenting musically, and you're still alive musically. You're not going through the motions. I liked it and I treasure it.

You just joked that you covered 75 of his songs, which is probably a slight exaggeration, but on setlist.fm I counted and there were 29 Dylan songs — and I'm sure that's missing some. What about his catalog works well for you to play?

I think he really understands tradition. He understands the American music tradition and he understands the European music tradition, where American music largely came from. Some of his earlier songs are based on traditional ballads. "Masters of War," for example. "It's All Over Now, Baby Blue" seems to me like a rewriting of a song about Mary, Queen of Scots.

I think in that sense it is easy to access for me, and for Fairport Convention back in the day. It wasn't a leap. As we were discarding American influences, probably Dylan was one of the last influences that we actually discarded because it was so close. A song like "Percy's Song," melodically it's very close to the British tradition. I could say that about quite a few Dylan songs. He understands the history and I think that's something that Fairport always loved as well. And I still do.

Winston Watson drumming with Dylan
in Dresden, Germany, 1994.
Photo by Manfred Neugebauer

Winston Watson

Winston Watson sat behind Dylan's drum kit for a large part of the '90s. He joined on extremely short notice in September 1992, filling in a second drum stool for a friend midway through a tour, before equally abruptly finding himself not only sticking around, but becoming Dylan's sole drummer for four years.

Along the way, he played high-profile shows like Woodstock '94 and *MTV Unplugged* and behind all-star guests from Sheryl Crow to Van Morrison (not a person Watson remembers fondly). He even found himself playing a bit part on *Time Out of Mind*, a year after he left the band.

. . . .

How'd you join the band?

I was in a little three-piece band in Los Angeles and working at a movie set company, doing a lot of side hustles because I had a two-year-old daughter. My best friend at the time, Charlie Quintana, was playing with Dylan. Charlie had played with him at the Letterman thing with The Plugz. I would meet him three or four years later, and we became neighbors and best friends.

Charlie had invited me to the Pantages Theater in LA. They had a long run there, seven nights in '92. I didn't know anything about Dylan. I had heard the songs everybody heard, and made fun of his voice just like anybody else. It just was not my thing at all. I was into Soundgarden and Alice in Chains.

At that Pantages show, I remember nobody really being happy and everybody drinking. It just seemed like no one was having a good time. I remember saying to myself, "Man, you couldn't pay me to play in that band!"

I was living in Studio City at the time, and Charlie would keep in contact. One day a few months later, he called me and said, "Hey, what are you doing next week?" He asked me to fly out to Kansas City to play with them. I thought he was pulling my leg. I was like, "What does that mean? Like you and I? Because I know it's you and Ian Wallace [both on drums] right now."[87] He says, "No, it's going to be *you* and Ian." "I don't even know the guy, man. What the fuck am I going to do?" "You'll be fine. There's not much left in the tour, and I got to go play with Izzy Stradlin." I said okay.

I flew out to Kansas City. I had to pay for my own cab with the last bit of money that I had and made my way to the hotel. I went to the room, ordered room service, had a bath. I was just laying there in the tub going, "What the fuck am I doing here?" I was terrified. I had no idea what's going on.

One of the first people I saw was [tour manager] Victor Maymudes, who was preoccupied with something, not really interested in talking to me. So I went out to the buses. [Driver] Tommy Masters says to Victor, "This is the kid that's coming out to play drums." Victor turned around and had the biggest smile on his face, and he's like, "Yes, we've been expecting you." At some point, the rest of the band gets on the bus. I'm trying to ask anybody I can get my hands on, "What's going on? How does this work?"

Before the show, are you given any instruction musically? "Learn these songs, do this—?"

No. At one point, they had a backline kit that I could check out, and I sat on it for a minute. I thought, "Isn't there another drummer here?" I didn't meet him until later. I thought, "I don't know what I'm going to do. I'll just try not to get in the way."

We get to the venue, and there's like 80,000 people there. It was like looking at the Grand Canyon, but of people. Albert King went on before us. When he finishes, we're admonished to go on. I stepped up behind the kit. It felt basically like strapping on a rocket pack and going forward. There's no going back. Tony [Garnier, bassist and bandleader] just said, "Watch me, and watch him. It'll unveil itself to you."

Luckily, I had been there at Pantages checking out what they were doing. It was a lot of shuffles and stuff that I thought I could do, but I couldn't make heads or tails of the songs arrangement-wise. It didn't sound like anything that I'd ever heard before. I just knew that people seemed to know the songs when he started singing them, whether he sang them the way that they remembered or not. When the words finally come out, you got the hoots and hollers.

---

87 The late Ian Wallace is one of those artists to enter Dylan's orbit several times many years apart; he played drums on the entire 1978 tour, then, a decade later, returned to Dylan's band in the early '90s.

When you step on stage in Kansas City, have you even spoken to Bob?

No. Hadn't met the man. Hadn't said a word to him in my life.

That's nuts.

It was just the strangest of all gigs. It seemed to be over before it started. I thought, "Wow, okay, that didn't hurt so much. It wasn't as terrifying as I thought." I had Ian there to be my guide basically. I just tried to duplicate what he did and stay out of the way. Any time he wanted to do a flourish, I tried to keep it down.

What was funny was, Bob knew that someone was coming out, but he didn't know *I* was coming out. You know what I mean? When he stepped up to the mic to sing, he hadn't turned around and looked at the band yet. At one point, he was singing, and then he slowly turned around to his left and looked back at me — and *kept* looking at me. There I was, hair bigger than Angela Davis and my California Hurley gear on. [He would look] in between verses and choruses for like two hours or however long we played. That was a little unnerving.

What are you thinking when you're getting those looks?

I don't know. [Rob] Stoner said something once about him shooting looks and I said, "Boy, do I know that." I just remember thinking, "Is this what it's going to be like the whole show, or is it just me?" Like I said, he was expecting someone, but I don't think he was expecting *me*. I had just barely turned 30 years old.

We finished the set, and he went off stage right. I thought, "Okay, I'm going home." The only thing I could think about was how the hell I was getting out of there and where my personal stuff was. Because I didn't bring any clothes. I just had an actual pilot's flight suit and some long underwear and shorts and an apple cap, like I was in Pearl Jam, which was the thing at the time.

Bob came up to me and said he liked the way I played and that he'd see me tomorrow. I was like, "What does that mean? Like, am I playing with him forever, or is he dropping me off at the airport tomorrow?"

I finally got a chance to call my wife, and she says, "Okay, so when are you coming home?" I said, "I don't know." I kept saying that for two weeks or however long the tour was.

Every night was something different. How can I describe it? All this gravity started to set in because people were writing about it. I wasn't used to any of that. Not at least on that level. I'd been in *Circus* and *Kerrang!* and all the rock magazines, but to be in *USA Today*? That took some getting used to. As you go back and research his history, there's no part of that that includes you. You have to step forward as if it's a minefield, and there are no footprints to guide you through.

I think all he ever wanted from me was to be myself. I immersed myself in older stuff, rootsier stuff, like Levon Helm or [Jim] Keltner, who I met before but never appreciated until I started really digging in and listening to those cuts. When I got rid of all the crap I had on stage and just pared it down to a four-piece kit, things were a lot better and more fun and not as tense.

Why did the smaller kit help you in that band?

It didn't look so ridiculous, like a big Phil Collins kit. Ian had a pretty big kit, and I thought I had to compete with that, but I didn't. I was better on a Bonham-sized kit anyway. But I like two floor toms; Levon had one. The more I watched that kind of stuff and remembered what it was like to play in my mom's band, instead of being in a loud rock band, it was basically what turned the corner for me.

I'd grown up listening to country music from '55 to '76. When things started getting more pop, it's when I got off the bandwagon. Funny thing about my discography is there ain't much hip-hop in there, but there's a lot of American stuff, like starting from past the Civil War up until now. That history with country music saved my butt in Bob's band.

I'm a rock player, period. I grew up playing rock and roll. That's what I am, and it's where I move best, but I like to play a lot of other stuff too. When people call me to do singer-songwriter stuff, I try to summon guys like Keltner and Levon and Richie Hayward from Little Feat. Those guys have a certain thing that's quintessentially American. There's an unspoken swing. The more I learned about those cats, the more I learned about swing and not being so loud. Because I'm pretty loud. I play with the MC5 now. We're pretty loud, and a lot of that's my fault.

I've listened to the recordings, and you've got some songs to rock out on too. It wasn't all country stuff. You're doing "Watchtower" every night, going pretty hard.

Yeah, because he wanted to rock. Neil was out with Pearl Jam. Rock was the thing at that time. According to some of those cats that I talked to in management, it brought in a lot of the kids. The fact that we were rocking and rolling, that we could do Woodstock '94 and *Unplugged* and all that stuff, that was speaking to a generation that hadn't even heard him, really.

Whatever contribution I made to that, I hope is cool. A lot of cats that I play with now who are younger, *MTV Unplugged* is when they first heard of me. It's like, "Wow, you're the dude with the hair on the drums?"

It's like Miles Davis. I don't think he gave a shit what you were going through the night before or tomorrow, he wanted whatever it was you had that night.

Now everybody's got my hairdo 20 years after the fact. I was one of the only people who walked around with, not a tight afro like [MC5 singer] Rob Tyner, but it's like the big curly 'fro, you know what I mean?

Yeah, that thing was big. Didn't it make you hot drumming?

No, it was like a giant heatsink. It actually drew stuff away, like how dogs have an upper and inner coat. But there were some nights we would play in places where it was heavy, like Louisiana or Alabama where there's a lot of humidity. It would not leave you alone. Tying it in a ponytail, getting by the air conditioner, even a bucket of cold water wasn't enough. I'm from Arizona, I know what fucking heat is like, but the humidity they have in the South is just sick. It'd be like having a bear suit on while you play.

I used to complain about getting a ridiculous amount of camera time. I would always be behind him in still shots. I had to jeopardize my privacy. It's bad enough that he has to have security. I don't need that kind of stuff.

And with the big hair, you're a recognizable figure. The other guys, some of them look a little generic.

Yes, and people think you're a certain way and they project stuff onto you. Then you don't fulfill that projection, and they're either hurt or sometimes worse.

What do you mean? What did people project onto you?

Like I'm Animal in the *Muppet Show* all the time. I'm not. I'm the polar opposite. I would like to go back to the hotel and watch TV or whatever. I haven't raised hell in a long time. Even when I did, it was in sensible shoes.

When people want to hang out, they want to drag you out to do nightlife stuff. Go to bars, introduce you to girls. You're nothing like they expect. Sometimes they understand, sometimes they're just offended.

I didn't know how to deal with that on such a large scale, because we toured a lot. I couldn't make people understand that the interaction I'm having with them that night, it's a one-time deal for them, but I have to repeat it over and over and over and over again. Even though I don't feel like it, or I'm heartbroken, or homesick, or have food poisoning, or whatever. But it's not in me to be rude or aloof. Because I'm no different than anybody that comes to see us. I just got really lucky.

It was different than going out and contracting to play with someone like Sheryl Crow. You knew more about that stuff because it was contemporary, but gosh, his stuff reached so far back. I didn't get a break to try to digest all his stuff for the first year or so. Even then, it didn't make any difference because none of his songs were like that anymore.

If you go back and listen to the records, that might not help you play the songs now.

How do you play darts when someone keeps moving the board?

It's like Miles Davis. I don't think he gave a shit what you were going through the night before or tomorrow, he wanted whatever the fuck it was you had *that night*. I understand that, more now so than ever, mainly because of Bob and someone like Howe Gelb from Giant Sand. I had initially played with Howe in the '80s, which kind of prepared me for the unpredictability of Dylan in the '90s. The two of them, they were parallel. They're very prolific, they're very idiosyncratic, and they're really special. They're the kind of people that come around every once in a while and you take note.

A lot of the purists thought I had no business being up there, and I can understand why. I go through the same thing with MC5 people. It's like, "You people realize I was five when that band first started, right? You realize I was three months old when Dylan's first record came out, so what the fuck am I supposed to know?" I didn't go looking for anything. I was asked by Dylan's people, and I was asked by [the MC5's] Wayne Kramer himself to join, and I said yes. There are people who talk about it, and there are people who do. I'd rather hang out with people who do.

You said the only person whose opinion mattered was Bob's. How do you tell his opinion? He's not someone who is going to give you detailed notes at the end of every show. Other band members say he's a little inscrutable.

My wife kind of keyed in on something at the time. We called it the Charlie Chaplin thing. He would do this movement, like he's really feeling it. When that happened, I knew that "the Bob and Winnie Show," as some of the fans were calling it, was happening.

He has this cool and innate sense of rhythm. If he likes something at 116 BPM, he'll always play it within a beat. If he says something's too quick, I'm not arguing. He says something's too slow, I'm not arguing.

So getting back to the early days, after that first two-week tour, do you know that you're going to come back?

No. He and I sat down at a restaurant near Lafayette [the last tour stop] and had a conversation and smoked some cigarettes. I told him I had a blast. Because as terrifying it was, that knife's edge of stage terror— I don't need to fall out of an airplane or climb Everest to feel that. There's just nothing like it.

So then what happens after that next fall run? When the tour resumes in 1993, you're now the only drummer. Ian's gone.

Yeah. We went over to Ireland to rehearse at U2's place at the Factory. That's when all hell broke loose, basically.

Tell me.

[laughs, sighs, long pause]

If you want to…

Ian's gear was there, but he wasn't. I didn't know why. I remember getting into a panic.

You don't know going into these rehearsals that it's not gonna be two-drummer, like the last time?

No, I didn't. His stuff was still in the hallway, and I thought he was there. I thought, okay, I'm going to have to deal with him and fight for territory.

Bob had mentioned earlier that he wanted me to not be deterred. That I was here for a reason. Because I was intimidated at first. Then when I got used to it, he basically said that I wasn't going anywhere.

So I got to Ireland thinking that I was going to stand my ground, and, if Bob wanted it to feel a certain way, I was going to do what I was asked. I walk in and all the backline's set up, but it's only one drum kit. Mine. That's when I put two and two together. I remember going, "Okay, now it's up to me."

You get into a situation working with a bunch of cats and they have a way of doing things, and you don't want to upset the herd. You want to fall in, and that didn't happen. Instead of me coming around to what they were doing, Bob played bass for a little bit with me playing drums. I remember thinking, "Jeez, he doesn't play bass. What's Tony going to do?"

He's singing while playing bass?

No, just playing music for the most part, trying to get with my foot and my swing.

When you're doing these rehearsals, do they have a loose jam session feel, or is Bob dictating certain songs or ideas?

It started with a feel. We'd either build on that or it would go immediately into the trash. We'd have to retool, have dinner, and start something else. Drink and smoke a lot of cigarettes and get back to it.

I never thought I had to fill anyone's shoes. No one ever said, "Play like this or play like that." That is a relief, but it's also terrifying because it's all up to you to be intuitive. That's more intimidating than putting staff paper in front of me. I can fake my way through a chart, but you can't fake your way through a vibe. People are like, "How can you memorize all this stuff?" I said, "Easy. You don't play it like everybody remembers it. Just play it however he wants it today."

I will tell you, whatever came out in those early years, that was *hammered* out. Like all day. Fully catered, yes, I've had worse jobs, but it was a mindfuck that I wasn't prepared for. After the first night, I think we had two or three days, like all-day rehearsals, just to get ready for that first show in Dublin.

That show was really important. Anybody who was famous and Irish and alive at the time was in that building. U2 was there because we're in their place all week, plus Carole King and Chrissie Hynde and Kris Kristofferson and Elvis Costello.

I can honestly say, on the last night we packed up rehearsal, he wasn't convinced we could do anything. He wasn't happy until we started the first show at this venue across the street, the Point Depot. We lit the joint up and burned it down. Because there was nothing to lose. I played like a man being chased by wolves. They say, "one gig is worth ten rehearsals." Abso-fucking-lutely. It was ragged but glorious. There was nothing perfect about it. It wasn't like a Steely Dan song. It was rock and roll.

We then had that long run at the Hammersmith and worked out a lot of stuff there. John [Jackson] wasn't G.E. Smith and I'm not Levon, but we weren't really aiming for that softer sound, as far as the rock part goes. Because he had that vignette in the middle where he would do the three acoustic songs. Like "Little Moses" or "Boots of Spanish Leather" or "It's Alright, Ma." So they'd do that, then I'd climb back on my kit and start making my little racket with "God Knows" or "Wicked Messenger." The encores were fun too. It was usually "Rainy Day Women" or sometimes "Alabama Getaway" after we'd played with the Dead. That was always a riot to play.

He did a lot of stuff that I liked. We did a lot of stuff off of *Oh Mercy* and *Blood on the Tracks* and *Blonde on Blonde*. I didn't really know any of it, but my girlfriend after high school loved Bob Dylan. She would always put *Desire* on, and I would always want to throw it across the room. *[laughs]* She would put it on so much, and sing along to it out of key all the time, that eventually I started putting it on myself. It became a background to our romance. I think I even told Bob that story. I said, "If it wasn't for *[Desire* drummer] Howie Wyeth, I probably never would've listened to your music as much as I did." Howie was tearing it up on that record.

You mentioned the quieter acoustic sections, what would you be doing during those when you weren't playing?

When Bob plays acoustic guitar, I think it's the most beautiful thing someone could hear. Aside from Ry Cooder, I don't think I've ever met anybody do it better and sing at the same time. There was one time we were rehearsing part of the acoustic set. It was the first time I'd actually listened very closely to how they were doing "Hattie Carroll." I was really moved by it, so much so that I didn't want to get back on my drums and play the rock part of the show. I wanted to hear more of that.

I told him that one night. I said, "I could sit there and listen to you play all night and not ever get on my drums." He says, "Do you think a room full of people would sit there and do that?" I said, "Don't give me that, man. Come on." I could talk to him like that, which was pretty cool. I was still a fan. I know you're not supposed to show that, but I couldn't help it.

He's at best an *interesting* electric guitar player, but I love that too. It's impressionist for sure. He would say this nonsense about it being math— I think he plays what he wants to play. He's a brilliant piano player, but as far as guitar playing goes, even after all this time, there's still a naivete about it. He knows what's involved, but there's still a bit of innocence there. You're not doing it for commerce reasons, you're doing it for purely artistic sake and not caring. He's not Eric Clapton, which is great. Neither am I. The part of me that plays guitar embraces that part of him so much. Even though it may not sound pretty in some places, it still speaks to me. Now, whether we come out on the other side together, that's something different.

He's a riot. I don't think he gets credit for it, but as serious as "Masters of War" is, he's a really funny guy. He and my daughter always got along because the both of them, they're just ridiculous together. I know grown women that would kill their own relatives just to be in a room with the guy. When my kid shows up, she's like, "Oh, hi Bob."

She would come along for some of the tours or some of the dates?

Yeah. He would always run off with her somewhere, and they'd have their little talks. She was two to six when I was with Bob, and then she was nine when I was with Alice Cooper. She's been on a lot of stages and backstages a lot. To her, it's just another day at Dad's workplace.

I'll tell you this one funny story about them in the Warfield Theatre in 1995. We were getting ready to do the show. I'm getting my clothes on. I see my wife in the green room, and I don't see my daughter. I said, "Deb, where's Marcella?" She looks at me, the color drains from her face. She's like, "Isn't she with you?" I go into a panic. At one point, one of our guys sees me and I said, "I'm looking for my kid. Have you seen her?" They're like, "No, man, we'll help you look."

Everybody helped. At one point, I'd looked everywhere except Bob's dressing room. I go up and knock on the door real quick. His assistant opens it or whatever and there she is.

We were already five minutes late going onstage, and the two of them were holding the show up. I said, "Babe, come on. Bob's got to go to work now." She says, "Oh, okay." He says, "I want to talk a little more about that later, okay?" She's like, "Okay, Bob." And she grabs her drink and comes out and meets my wife.

At that point, I go to stand with the band and wait for him. They bring the house lights down. Bob stops me with his arm. He says, "We got to do something about that girl."

I said, "Oh man, I'm sorry, she just loves you. I didn't want her to disturb your show." He goes. "No, that girl in art class. She's real mean. We got to do something about her."

We'd gotten Marcella these cowboy boots and there was this mean little girl in her art class who splashed paint on them. Bob asked her, "How'd you get that paint on your cowboy boots?" So while I'm looking for my daughter, she's telling Bob that story, and they're holding the show up. He stops me and says, "Hey, we got to do something about that girl."

You played some notable shows with Dylan. What do you remember about Woodstock '94?

We stayed at a hotel in Albany near the airport. I met Nine Inch Nails, Cypress

Hill and some other bands all raging at the airport bar. The Nine Inch guys thought I was in Cypress Hill, and the Cypress Hill guys thought I was with Nine Inch.

We go to the site the next day. It's raining and it takes forever to get there. At one point, I asked Bob if he wants a cigarette. The two of us were smoking stage right, and I remember a million cameras clicking. I remember thinking, "Wow, I wonder who just showed up." I looked past his shoulder, and they were all pointed at us. That was pretty shocking.

The stage was huge. I wasn't near anybody. I hate those gigs. I grew up playing in bars. Even if you're in an arena, I like my boys close. I know arenas make money or whatever, but I would rather do a multiple-night stand in a nice theater. It was too big. Did anybody hear anything? I don't know.

Pete Townshend would say [about the original Woodstock], "Oh, I hated it. It changed my life, but I hated it." I know exactly what you're talking about, Pete. Not my favorite gig, but to have everybody you know from home call and tell you that they just saw you on TV, that was pretty cool.

Not long after, you taped MTV Unplugged *with Dylan.*

There's the show they released, and then there's a whole other show that had no hits, nothing anybody would really recognize. I think it was two nights. After we taped the first one, all the executives were complaining that there were no hits. No "Once upon a time you dressed so fine," no "Everybody must get—" There was none of that. They were bent about that. At one point, Bob said okay. The finished product is what happened.

They got plenty of hits after they badgered him. I'm surprised he capitulated.

It was a good idea in the end, I guess, but I thought the cool part about it is that we *weren't* going to do that stuff. That was me being eager to see what he was capable of outside of that stuff. I don't think the general public gave a shit what he was doing, aside from the hits they could tell their kids about or they did their dissertation on or whatever.

Sadly, people don't really want to remember you as you are, they want to remember you as you were. They have that embalmed memory of you.

It seems like Bob has been fighting against that since the mid-'60s.

Since day one. Wayne Kramer [of MC5] would tell you the same thing too. I mentioned that term I use, "memory embalmers." He thought that was fantastic.

The next year you guys toured with the Grateful Dead.

I remember being one of the only people, according to Jerry's crew, that talked to him during that period. [Longtime Dead roadie] Ram Rod told me that. I thought he was putting me on.

I was notorious for breaking sticks. During the first Dead show, I was chopping lumber like a beaver. Bob thought it was funny, because stuff was landing all over the place. The next day, we were soundchecking, and Ram Rod says, "Some of us in the crew want to have a word with you when you get a chance." I thought, "Oh fuck, what did I do now?"

We finished our soundcheck. I said, "Man, if it's about the sticks, if I broke anything, see our accountant, I'll pay you a check or whatever." Because a couple of times I saw that the broken sticks flew toward their backline. I thought I had knocked something out or ruined one of Jerry's precious little stage tokens or whatever.

They look at each other and they start laughing. They said, "No, fuck all that. We want to know what you talked to him about." I said, "Who?" "Jerry." Ram Rod says, "I've been with the guy longer than you've been alive. I haven't said a word to him in 13 years."

I thought that was the funniest thing. We didn't really talk about anything! I remember him saying that I looked so young. I'd just gotten into my 30s and I still looked like I was 18.

At one point, we were playing with them at RFK Stadium, and I had exhaustion. I actually fell out and had to be given oxygen. When I came to, my friend was there with me. Right next to him, I saw the beard and the glasses. He's looking at the medic, serious as a heart attack. "Take good care of my man here. We need him tomorrow."

I said [imitates wheezing]: "Don't worry, Jerry…I'll be fine…" I thought that was pretty cool, that he actually cared.

I believe the last time Garcia sat in with Dylan was at one of those RFK shows. What do you remember about that?

That Bob wouldn't let him play!

What do you mean?

I wanted to hear what I'd been waiting to hear. It kinda never came.

You want to hear Jerry be Jerry, go into outer space.

Yeah! He doesn't need to be doing Johnny Winter and Floyd Radford. As we were playing, I just remember thinking, "I hear *your* part, Bob. You going to let Jerry get in there?" But it was obviously the thing they do as brothers, do you know what I mean? It's like Bob was going, "Oh, *yeah?* Well, check *this* out."

What do you remember about playing "Restless Farewell" for Frank Sinatra at his televised birthday concert?

We rehearsed a couple other songs. "This Was My Love," I think. But I think Frank liked "Restless Farewell" a lot. I could hear him saying "When's that Dylan kid going on?" When you watch it, you can see the genuine affection that both of them have for each other.

Anyone you could imagine was there, like Don Rickles, all the Rat Pack, anybody that was like a Soprano or whatever, they're all there. Our table was really fun. I sat next to Bob. There was Frank and Barbara Marx, his wife. Clayton Cameron, who plays with Tony Bennett, was sitting on the other side of me. So the two of us were sitting next to Bob, and on the other side of him was Danny Aiello and Rickles. Then the table next to us, there was Patrick Swayze and Roseanne Barr and Johnny Depp and Kate Moss. It was like we were in one of those Hirschfeld drawings, caricatures of people decorating a room in a Hollywood event like you'd see in a *New Yorker* magazine.

Did you see just the way that they showed the crowd, watching us as we did the song? It was reverent. Everyone was moved by it. At one point when they cut to the audience, no one is saying a word, no one's talking. These are people that I've been seeing my whole life in one medium or another, and there they are looking at us. You can see the solemnity as they do the wide pan stuff. It meant that musically, we had done our job, which I always felt we did in that band to the best of our ability. Even though some nights we didn't get it right, I think no one would ever say that we didn't try or that I didn't give 110%.

Did you have a favorite run from all those years in the band?

I would say '94, '95. We were really moving those years. By the time we got there, the innocence was off. It was all business. We had something.

But just when you think you start to believe that, that's when he pulls the plug. I knew it was coming, because we had this thing that we used to do every night and he wasn't doing that for a while. I felt like I was alone sometimes. I still enjoyed it but there was less of that interaction. I wasn't doing anything different. Maybe that was the problem.

Your exit must have happened fast because I think it's only like six or seven months between that '95 run you love and you leaving in summer of '96, after a couple shows around the Olympics in Atlanta.

Yeah. During the Olympics and all that stuff in '96, he wasn't happy. His manager was talking to the band about it. I said, "Man, I'm on the verge of a divorce, we haven't played with each other in I-can't-remember, I could go any time. Don't feel like you have to not say anything to me. I could get on a fucking plane right now and never look back." I'd been there a good long time; I could understand.

So what happened was, I got a call from management. I said, "Okay, who'd you get?" They're like, "What?" I said, "Obviously, you're calling me either because you want me to come back out, or you got somebody else. Who did you get?"

They said it was David Kemper. I said, "He's a great player. I think it's what Bob's aiming for now. We've been loud long enough." That's how I exited that play. I knew better not to stay in Mississippi a day too long.

On the DVD you recorded years ago[88], you also mention a time Van Morrison told Bob he should fire you. Was that around the same time?

That was part of it. It was at dinner. Van was visibly impaired and just blathering on about whatever. At one point I was mentioned and hung out to dry. I got up and unceremoniously put my napkin in my chair and walked out.

I almost didn't play that next day. I didn't care what anybody thought, and I didn't need anybody helping to put mines in front of me or trip me up. Especially not someone like that. I didn't need anybody to tell me I suck. I only want to hear that from Bob, and he didn't tell me that.

You're credited on "Dirt Road Blues," but Time Out of Mind came out well after you left the band. What's the story there?

It was sort of a scratch idea I had done earlier. They had two guys in there, Keltner and Brian Blade, try to replicate what I did, and they couldn't do it. They couldn't duplicate the feeling, I guess, that was on mine. I called it a porch stomp. It's like you'd sit on a porch and hit spoons and stomp your foot. It was Keltner that said, "Well, why don't you just loop that? That's Winnie on there. Just loop that, and that's the song."

It's interesting that a little bit of drum that you played maybe several years earlier he'd remember, or that someone would dig out the file.

---

88 *Bob Dylan Never Ending Tour Diaries: Drummer Winston Watson's Incredible Journey* (2009).

As I remember the story, either Lanois or Keltner himself said that they were working on that idea and Bob or somebody played the original thing, which was a cassette, from what I understand.

Mark Howard's book[89] explains it. I think I have it here, hold on a second. Okay, here we go:

[Reading aloud:] "The song 'Dirt Road Blues' was created from a cassette tape Dylan had from a sound check. He asked me if we could use it, and so I made a loop of the best eight bars and the band played on top of it. Because it was a soundcheck recording, Daniel didn't like it — he said the steel part sounded like the *Bugs Bunny / Road Runner Hour.* That's why Winston Watson played drums on the album."

So there you go. An offhand thing. I had no business playing on the record. At least that's my fragile ego saying that to me.

Well, that's one more studio recording than G.E and so many of the Never Ending Tour band members got up to that point.

Right. I'll take it.

Was there any sense in your era that his songwriting days might be behind him? He'd taken a fairly long break by the time you left, just doing the folk covers albums.

Not at all. Does the well ever dry up completely? I don't think someone with a fertile mind like his would ever do that.

Will he stop? Maybe at some point, but I think he needs to do it like anybody else, and he'll be the first person to tell you that. It's just something he does.

Watching him work was a lot to take in at an apprentice age, when all the journeymen around you are questioning why you're even in the fucking room in the first place. One quote that I liked, which I agree with and disagree with in part, was that "it's interesting, but it's never fun." I disagree. To me, it was interesting, and many times it was fun. Not all the time. It was serious business all the time, but you could have fun with it.

There were times, like I said, that were raucous enough to where we could grin at each other, all of us, where we did burn the barn down like the roadhouse band that we were. There was nothing really refined about any of it. We could have been that way, but not with *me* in the band.

---

89 *Listen Up!: Recording Music with Bob Dylan, Neil Young, U2, R.E.M., The Tragically Hip, Red Hot Chili Peppers, Tom Waits* (2019).

Dickey Betts bends Dylan's ear at the Rock and Roll Hall of Fame concert in Cleveland, Ohio, 1995.
Photo by Sidney Smith / AllmanBrothersBookBySidneySmith.com

Dickey Betts

Though his last name wasn't Allman, Dickey Betts helped found the Allman Brothers — he was the one who suggested Duane recruit his younger brother Gregg to sing — and wrote some of their most famous songs, including "Blue Sky" and "Ramblin' Man." The former, Bob Dylan shouted out in "Murder Most Foul" ("Play Oscar Peterson, play Stan Getz / Play, 'Blue Sky,' play Dickey Betts"); the latter, he performed onstage with Betts himself.

That "Ramblin' Man" performance took place in Tampa, near Dickey's home, in 1995. It's not the only time Betts and Dylan shared a stage. For a decade or so, whenever Dylan played a show in central Florida, Dickey was likely as not to pop onstage to jam. We talked about those sit-ins, as well as hanging with Dylan and The Band on their 1974 tour, recording a song for a Jimmie Rodgers tribute album Dylan produced, and his reaction to Dylan's "Murder Most Foul" nod. Oh, and about the guy he beat up in front of Dylan at Bill Clinton's inauguration. Dickey's wife Donna occasionally popped in to fill in some details.

. . . .

Let's start at the beginning. When did yours and Dylan's paths first cross?

In the 1970s. I went out and joined Bob on one of their tours for a couple of days. I knew Bill Graham, so I called Bill ahead of time to see if he'd like it if I came out. So I met Robbie Robertson and Bob on that little two-day sabbatical. I was trying to refine my songwriting a little bit. Me and he and Robbie hung out a little bit, just the three of us. It was really interesting meeting Bob, but I didn't really get to know him then.

What were you doing when you were hanging out with him and Robbie?

Just screwing around. It was like an after-show in a hotel suite. He and Bill were playing chess. In between games, me and Robbie Robertson went to the bathroom to do a little line.

You can delete that if you want to. Or print it. Whatever. If you know the situation, you know the situation.

Anyway, that was about the extent of that. Ever since then, I go to see Bob when he plays [the Van Wezel Theater] in my little hometown here. I went to see him there two or three times. He always had me backstage.

When you were on the road with the '74 comeback tour, you said you wanted to refine your songwriting. What were you hoping to achieve?

I just was trying to learn something, which I did. I don't know what it was, but I learned something. Just listening, being around people like Bob. I used to hang around with Billy Joe Shaver all the time. In fact, he and I ran around together during his whole life. He's one of the great songwriting artists like Bob, but he writes blue-collar old cowboy, dusty-boots type of songs.

Donna: I think Dylan mentions him in a song. "I'm reading James Joyce and listening to Billy Joe Shaver."

That's right. Dickey, you and Billy Joe share that, being mentioned in a Dylan song.

Yeah. Anyway, that's why I was out there getting to know Bob. It was kinda selfish on my part, but that's the way you learn, you get around people. I'd written songs before, but I was just trying to improve myself. And it helped. I wrote some pretty good stuff.

I know you sat in a number of times in the '90s, but did you have much interaction between that Bill Graham–Robbie Robertson tour and then?

No. I just barely got to know Bob. I didn't hang around while he was writing songs or nothing like Billy Joe. Bob lives way out in California and I live on the other side of the United States. I lived in Nashville for a while and that's where I really got to know Billy Joe. But Bob has always been on my radar.

A funny story happened when Bob was playing here at the theater we have here in Sarasota [in 1992]. The Van Wezel. Donna, my wife, she'd never met Bob. So Donna and I were going up into Bob's bus. I knocked and said, "Hey, it's Dickey." He said, "Come in." Donna went in, thinking I was right behind her. Then a bunch of fans got me, so I was hanging around signing autographs and shit, and I got delayed. So she goes and sits down thinking that I was right behind her.

Bob, I don't know if he thought they sent him a girlfriend or what. *[laughs]* She was so awkward, and he felt awkward. "So…nice to meet you…"

They went on like that, and she would kid Bob. She would say things like, "You do really well with those words. You ought to think about really making a career out of that." That'd just tickle the hell out of him. He's not used to people making fun and joking around with him, because everybody's so in awe of him.

Another time, Bob wanted do "Ramblin' Man." I said, "You don't know the words to that, do you?" He said, "I know all the words to 'Ramblin' Man.' I shoulda wrote that song myself." I said, "Okay, let's check. If you don't know, just make shit up, and you'll do well." So we sang "Ramblin' Man." He sang every word exactly the way I wrote it.

Wow, he knew it.

I mean, he knew it! And he sang it better than it's ever been sung before. *[Dickey busts into Dylan impression:]* "I'm on my *way* down to New Or-*leans* this *morning*." He was talking and singing at the same time. It was great.

You've got a pretty good Dylan impression.

[Dickey's really belting now] "I'm on my WAY down to New OrLEANS this MORNING. I'm LEAV-ing out of NASH-ville"… He'd just go, and the words meant so much the way he sang it.

Do you remember sitting in with him at Jazz Fest in New Orleans?

I sat with him a bunch of times. He used to do "Rainy Day Women" all the time when I'd seen him, except that time he wanted to sing "Ramblin' Man."

I remember in Tampa he had that Western swing band. They had Nudie suits and standup bass. Oh, man, it was totally different from what he had been doing. The crowd, of course, they loved him. I sat there with him that night and he did that "Rainy Day Women." Bob was playing lead guitar, and then I would play lead. We'd go back and forth. I asked Jeff [Kramer, Bob's manager], I said, "Bob is so reclusive and everything, but I'm the only guy that I've seen that he invites to just come backstage. Why is that?" He said, "Man, he would give anything to be able to play guitar like you did. You're his favorite guitar player."

I don't mean that now as just self-aggrandizing or nothing. It sounded like I was, but I don't mean that. It just was a surprise. Bob, he does try to play lead guitar. It's simple, but he does a good job of it.

What do you guys typically talk about when you're hanging out backstage shooting the shit?

Songs and boxing stuff. I don't say much at all; I just hang around and listen. I don't talk much anyway. Doing this interview is the most I've talked in a week.

Donna: You talked about him playing for the Pope.

Dickey: Oh, yeah! He said, "Yes, that was just like another gig to me, playing for the Pope. I think he took a tip from Dalai Lama and decided to befriend some rock stars."

Donna told you the story about the presidential inauguration, I guess.

[Donna earlier, before Dickey got to the phone: "We went to the '92 Clinton inauguration. There were 13 different balls going on, and the Allman Brothers played one. Dickey's old friends Don Johnson, the actor, and Melanie Griffith, his wife at the time, were hosting it. It was called the Blue Jeans Ball. They had a big jam. Some of the things that evening became a little infamous."]

I'd love to hear your version of it.

It was quite a ruckus. There was this guy smarting off to everybody in the green room the whole time. He had been telling us all that he was a senator. He was pretty mean.

I went out to play. The band couldn't play a three-chord blues. We kept losing the chord change and screwing all up. So I just walked off the stage. Let them do it.

When I came back, I guess they had a TV in there. This guy told me I'd better go to the woodshed if I'm going to try to play with the big boys.

I said, "You know, I'm about fed up with your bullshit. I've been listening to you all night and I'm tired of hearing it." He said, "I'll just take you outside and kick your ass." I said, "No, you ain't fucking taking me nowhere. You'll never make it to the door."

He started to get up off the couch with his fist balled up. So I just knocked him out. He landed right in Bob's lap. Bob said, "Well I'm glad somebody knocked that sonofabitch out!"

I split my hand wide open on one of this guy's teeth. There was blood going everywhere. Don Johnson rushed me to the hospital. When I went back to the hotel, I was scared, really. God, I thought, I done knocked the fucking senator out. What's going to happen now?

Stephen Stills called my room. He said, "Man, I just want to apologize for that sonofabitch I brought to the show." I said, "*You* brought? He was telling everybody he was a senator." He said, "Bullshit! He's my goddamn gofer. He goes and gets me some drugs when I need it." I said, "Well, I sure am relieved to know that."

She would kid Bob, like, "You do really well with those words. You ought to think about making a career out of that." That'd just tickle the hell out of him. He's not used to people joking around with him, because everybody's so in awe.

Bob, I don't know if he still does, but he used to practice boxing. He'd go to the boxing gym all the time. Now, every time I see him, he throws a right hand at me in slow motion. He says, "Hey Dick, how's that right cross doing?" He's talking about, I guess, President Clinton's inauguration.

In 1997, Bob put together a multi-artist Jimmie Rodgers tribute album, which you appeared on. How did that come together?

Now that I'm so old, I don't remember a lot of them word for word, but I used to know so many Jimmie Rodgers songs. I'm very academic when it comes to music. I study a lot of stuff. I sang all kinds of Jimmie Rodgers songs. I guess Bob heard about that, or maybe I sang one in front of him, I don't know. Anyway, he asked my manager if I wanted to be a guest on that record. I said, "Hell yeah!"

He got a bunch of people that knew who Jimmie Rodgers was and sang some songs. You could do a Jimmie Rodgers song any way you wanted to do it, except you couldn't change the words to it. I did "Waiting for a Train," which is not the easiest one to sing.

You got a good yodel going there.

Oh, I tried. A lot of people didn't try the yodel and that was Jimmie's whole thing, that blue yodel. I didn't cowboy yodel or nothing; it was like a blue yodel. It's more like a moan kind of thing.

I said, I want some old horn players. I don't want no new guys around town here. I told the producer, I said, "Find me some old guys that played back in the '40s. I want somebody that really knows how to play." He found two guys that played for Benny Goodman — Jerry Jerome and a trumpet player. Jerry was so beautiful. He was about 80 years old, and I said, "Did you know Charlie Christian when you played with Benny Goodman?" He said, "Yeah, he was a good boy, but he did too much of that dope stuff."

I've got one more question. What did you think when you heard "Murder Most Foul" a couple of years ago with the line "Play 'Blue Sky,' play Dickey Betts"?

Oh, that was such an honor. All my friends were coming to me saying, "Man, did you hear Bob Dylan's mentioned you in a song?" I said, "No shit."

I heard the song. I was so embarrassed, I would say, "Well, he just used me because it rhymes with Getz." *[laughs]* People would tell me, "Oh, bullshit," but anyway, I was very embarrassed because it was such a flattering thing for Bob Dylan to mention you in a song.

The next time you see him, are you going to mention "Murder Most Foul"?

Yeah, probably so. When Bob plays in our hometown here again, I'm going to go see him. I had some good times with Bob, some good experiences. When you sit and play music with people, you never forget it.

Michael "Soy Bomb" Portnoy

Dylan fans know performance artist Michael Portnoy best under another name: Soy Bomb.

With those two mysterious words scrawled in black marker across his bare chest, Portnoy stage-crashed Dylan's 1998 Grammy Awards performance, bursting out from the rows of extras behind Dylan to undulate wildly while Bob and the band played "Love Sick" until he was forcibly dragged off.

Portnoy is the one person in this book Dylan did not intend to collaborate with. All these years later, Dylan (or his team, at least) still doesn't seem thrilled about it. All the versions of that Grammys performance on Dylan's official channels edit Soy Bomb out. But, whether they like it or not, Soy Bomb became the most memorable part of the performance and can't be erased from history.

It should be no surprise, perhaps, that the most unusual performer in this book gave me the most unusual interview. He answers some of my questions straight. He uses others to add new layers to the legend of Soy Bomb. And he leaves it up to us to determine which is which.

. . . .

How did you come to be one of the extras on that stage in the first place?

I was hired by a casting director who I'd worked with before on an Elton John video. We were instructed to "give Bob a good vibe."

What was your background as an artist up to that point? Had you done similar things before in other settings?

Around that time, I was performing experimental stand-up comedy, making solo theater shows, and working as a dancer for a New York-based company.

Talk me through your decision to crash the performance, and what preparation work was needed.

Once I got the job and heard it would be on live TV, I knew I had to do some kind of absurd intervention. Something with dance and an inscrutable message scrawled on my chest. To get my body in shape, I went on a high protein diet of goat breasts and moved no other muscles but my deltoids for an entire week.

What were you setting out to achieve with your appearance?

I had a few simple objectives: to dismantle capitalism, to replace 4/4 with 11/4 as the dominant time signature (my dance was in 11/4), to abolish song verses in favor of a chorus-only reality, and to defame the soy industry to pave the path for oats. Luckily, all of these were achieved instantly the moment I tore off my shirt.

At the time, your statement about the meaning of "Soy Bomb" was: "Soy represents dense nutritional life. Bomb is, obviously, an explosive destructive force. So, 'soy bomb' is what I think art should be: dense, transformational, explosive life!" Many years later, anything to add as to why you chose that phrase?

There are seven letters in soy bomb. The only seven letter words are: albumen, keekers, and tumping — words which will become crucial in this decade.

How did you feel standing among the extras during the first half of the song waiting for your moment? And what was your moment? Was there some sort of cue you were waiting for?

I just thought "good vibe, good vibe, blend in," but all the while I was terrified my shirt, which I'd unbuttoned and taped closed to make it easier to remove, was going to come undone prematurely. I hadn't set any cue; I was just waiting for what felt like the right moment.

What inspired your dance style? If you were just generically bopping around or something, it would have been much less memorable.

I was very into Butoh at the time, a Japanese dance form which is contortive, trance-like, at times grotesque, and in which the body transforms along with different internal states of being. So I guess it's Butoh meets flailing buffoon. In 11/4.

What were you thinking while you were up there?

I was trying not to think at all.

I had a few simple objectives: dismantle capitalism, replace 4/4 with 11/4 as the dominant time signature, abolish song verses in favor of a chorus-only reality, and defame the soy industry to pave the path for oats. Luckily, all were achieved instantly the moment I tore off my shirt.

. . . .

Why do you think they let you stay on as long as they did? Were you surprised?

I was very surprised it went on so long! I thought it would last all of about three seconds. We only had one rehearsal earlier that day, so I heard later that the guys in the control booth genuinely didn't know if it was part of the act or not. That's why they didn't send anyone out sooner to stop me.

If Bob and the band had just stopped performing entirely, what would you have done?

To be honest, that was the most frightening thought to me, that Bob would just stop the band and turn to me and calmly ask, "Hey man, what's this all about?" I was much more prepared to be beaten to the ground than to have to answer that question.

What happened after you got dragged offstage?

I had my eyes closed for most of the dance, and at one point I felt some hands on my waist. So I tensed up all my muscles and there's a very funny photo of a guy trying to lift me up as if I were in rigor mortis. The security guys were very kind, actually, and just escorted me through the back door of Radio City Music Hall out to the street. It was February, though, and I was just standing there, freezing, still topless, and without my coat or wallet. Soon some reporters came out to interview me, and then eventually some cops came over, gave me a white sheet to cover myself, and let me in to the subway so I could get home.

In my research, I came across an old website called "Soy Bomb Nation," which hasn't been updated since '98. Was that you?

I remember that! They were trying to turn it into a whole movement. But I had nothing to do with them. There were a bunch of Soy Bomb-related things that popped up at the time. My favorite was some guy in the Midwest who knitted a Soy Bomb sweater vest with the letters appearing exactly the same way they were written on my chest!

Ever hear from anyone in Bob's camp about it? (They should have thanked you for making the performance so cool and memorable, but somehow, I doubt they did.)

No, I never heard from any of them.

I gather you weren't much of a Dylan fan when you did it — Bob just happened to be the one artist who had extras on stage that night. Did you ever dig into his music later?

To give everyone who's reading this even more reason to hate me: sorry, no, I never got into him. I do understand his cultural and historical significance and that his lyrics are genius, but I never could get past his voice.

Did the Soy Bomb performance influence your later work?

Yes, there has been considerable flailing about in most of my work since. At least in the development stage. Seriously though, I think I'm always looking for ways to insert something totally unpredictable and joyously stupid in whatever I do, whether that's film, visual art or performance.

I know you've got other claims to fame in the art world, but in the music-history sphere, how do you feel about being "the Soy Bomb guy" all these years later?

Oh, it's wonderful, so much easier to say than "Guy who led an abstract game show on a spherical lavender stage inside a massive mound of mud in an important quinquennial exhibition in some city in Germany you've never heard of."

Have you ever gone back to watch the video in recent years? If so, what did you think?

Well, I didn't have time or money to build it then, but I really regret I didn't go with my first plan which was to make a hidden mechanical suit with six-foot-long protractible metal spikes that would have poked out in every direction, like a porcupine. They would have had to use a magnetic crane to remove me from the stage.

Dylan plays cards with his band on the tour bus. Larry Campbell is seated next to him.
Photo by Ken Regan/Camera 5

Larry Campbell

In 2013, Bob Dylan fan site *Expecting Rain* ran a poll to pick the best guitarist among the dozens who have backed Bob on the Never Ending Tour. The winner? Larry Campbell. In 2016, they ran another poll. The winner? Larry Campbell. And then a *third* poll in 2018. Who won that time? Charlie Sexton…in a tie with his erstwhile bandmate Larry Campbell.

Larry Campbell played with Dylan from 1997 through 2004, and it's a testament to Campbell's career that that's probably not even the thing he's best known for at this point. That would be his decade-long relationship with Levon Helm, producing his records and playing in his band alongside Campbell's wife Teresa Williams. Since Levon's passing, Larry and Teresa have continued backing up friends like Jackson Browne and Hot Tuna while recording their own albums as a couple.

In 2021, a documentary called *It Was the Music* traced the path of their careers apart and together. Around the time of its release, we got on the phone for an extended conversation about his eight years in the band. It's a subject he hasn't talked too much about in the past, but he was willing to open up and share an inside look at what his world was like playing next to Bob all those years.

. . . .

One thing the documentary makes clear is how deep in the roots music world you were before getting connected with Dylan. How did you transition from that career to playing with Dylan?

As concise as I can make this… There had been so much great music going on through the '60s that really spoke to me, from the Beatles on *The Ed Sullivan Show* all the way up through the FM radio, psychedelic music, Bob Dylan, Rolling Stones, all this fertile stuff in the world of rock and roll and popular music. I was really entranced by this music. All this overlapping with the folk boom. I couldn't get enough of this stuff. I was insatiable.

By the early '70s, I started to get a little bit disillusioned about what was going on in rock radio. I was really leaning towards the rootsier end of music. I decided New York City is not the place for me right now. I packed up and moved out to California with some blind ambition. Long story short, ended up touring with a band, settling in Jackson, Mississippi for a couple of years, where I really absorbed the culture of this music that spoke to me the most.

I ended up coming back to New York in the late '70s, just in time for this *Urban Cowboy* boom where country music was fashionable. It turned out to be a really lucrative situation for me, because I was finding work in the studios and playing at clubs every week. The Lone Star Cafe, City Limits — all these places where this type of country music, the roots music that people were attracted to, was performed.

One of the guys I had met in California — and we became very close in New York — was [longtime Dylan bassist] Tony Garnier. When I met him in California, he was the bass player with Asleep at the Wheel. He moved to New York about the same time I moved back. We would play a lot of gigs together and studio work and all that. I was playing in the clubs and touring with people like Doug Sahm, Rosanne Cash, kd lang, Cyndi Lauper. There's a long list.

So it's the end of 1996 and I've decided I'm not going to tour anymore. I had just finished this tour with kd. I just wanted to be a New York studio musician and get more into producing records. A few months later, I get a call from Jeff Kramer, Bob's manager, saying Bob was interested in hearing me play and could I come down and hang and do some playing together? Bob's awareness of me came through Tony.

I initially turned it down. I had made this decision; I wasn't going to tour anymore. Then I woke up the next day and remembered what my impetus for being in music was in the first place. It was the Beatles, the Rolling Stones, and Bob Dylan. I thought, "Wait a minute, I'm going to turn this down, this opportunity to work with this guy?" I called Kramer back. We worked it out. I came down, we played for about three days, and then the next thing I'm on tour for eight years with Bob.

You went from not touring anymore to touring with someone who tours about as much as any human being alive.

Exactly. *[laughs]* That was a conflict for the whole eight years I was doing it. In fact, ultimately, that's why I left. I wanted to produce records. These opportunities were coming up, but I couldn't take advantage of most of 'em. I would try to schedule a day to do it and then we get called to go out on tour.

Playing with Bob is great. You're playing great music with this guy who's a total American original. Probably our best. But I still had this need to express myself. You could only do that to a limited degree when you're in this band with Bob. There are parameters around your own personal expression. It's completely understandable; it has to be that way because it's his music. So that need was surfacing. If I was ever going to do this, I had to get on it.

There's a moment in one of the episodes of It Was the Music *where Teresa's showing a photo of you guys on your 10th anniversary in Hawaii. She says, "Well, we were there because he was there with Bob." It got me thinking, your personal life too. If you're on the road eight, nine months a year every year — like, what personal life?*

Exactly right. That's just the reality of it. That's the price you have to pay to do something like that. I was drawn to do it for as long as I could.

Getting back to the beginning of your time with Bob, Tony introduces you, you show up. Is there an audition process? How do you go from there to your first show?

Well, they weren't quite calling it an audition. Although, ostensibly, that's what it was. I showed up at the studio, and I met Bob, and we started playing. It was about three days of playing together. Mostly what we were playing was old rock and roll and country tunes. We'd do a few of his tunes, but it was mostly just running through like Hank Williams and Buddy Holly songs. It was a lot of fun. I guess Bob was absorbing what I was putting out. After that third day, Kramer called and said, "Okay, so we're going on tour next week. You coming?" I said, "Well, yeah, I guess I am."

That first tour was Nova Scotia. We flew there, and the boat with all the gear in it got stuck in the ice, crossing whatever strait that is. We're in Nova Scotia and all these dates are being delayed because the gear is not there. So that was a little nerve-wracking because I was ready to get into it, but everything worked out.

That first tour was great. We had rehearsed — not really *rehearsed*, we just played a bunch of music together — and then next thing I know, I'm on stage playing all these Bob Dylan songs, most of which I have never played before, and some I've never even *heard* before. You just jump in and do what you can do.

How are you learning those? Was someone giving you a tape like, "Here's what he played last tour. Go learn them."

No. I had a box full of cassettes of all his records. Once we got to Nova Scotia, I would just try to listen to his stuff as much as I could. In soundcheck before the first gig, we'd run through a few tunes that we would do that night, and that's the way the rest of the tour went. Most of the rehearsals for the shows were at soundchecks. Some tunes we would do, some tunes we wouldn't, and then there'd be songs that we didn't run through at soundcheck that we would just start doing. It was interesting!

Did you feel intimidated being the new guy and stepping into the shoes of a bunch of iconic guitarists who have played with Bob before you?

I don't know if intimidated is the word. I was definitely on my toes, as I would be with any musical situation. Once you're up there doing it, if you've done it for long enough, you just fall into, "Okay, that's my gig. I got to do the best job I can do. I got to just listen to everything that's going on and react to it." I'm sure if I thought about it, and I probably did at some point, it was a pretty heady place to be. This is a guy that I've always respected as one of our greatest artists, and here I am six feet from him playing the stuff that made me respect him. I didn't want to mess it up, that's for sure. But you sorta fall into a professional mode. With any gig you're doing, you just put that hat on, and it keeps you from freaking out.

Speaking of freaking out maybe, sounds like things are going great, then all of a sudden, one month in, Bob's rushed to the hospital, the next tour gets canceled. Do you remember when you heard, and what your reaction was?

We had played somewhere in the Midwest, and there was a dust storm. The dust was really thick. I was walking around the street, and I ran into Bob on his motorcycle. He was driving around in this dust storm. Apparently, the dust that was kicked up came off the river and had dried goose droppings in it. That's what he inhaled. I did too. I got a little sick also, but he ended up with histoplasmosis from that, which is a real serious thing.

I found out about it as we were preparing for the next tour, which was canceled. When I heard how serious it was, I mean, I just was hoping he would get better. I heard he was in a lot of pain, and certainly my sympathies were with him. I was concerned that nobody could give me a definitive answer about the potential for some sort of lasting or permanent damage from this. I was prepared for the possibility that that might have been my first and last experience with Bob.

Tracy Chapman called me because she heard that our tour had been canceled. I did a few dates with her during that time, waiting to hear about Bob. Fortunately,

The TV director with his headphones on comes walking up to me as I'm playing. He says, "He's got-a go meet-a the Pope! He's got-a go meet-a the Pope!" He's looking at me like I'm supposed to do something about this. Typical Italian fashion, man.

it all worked out, and he came back as good as new.

Do you remember the feeling or emotion at that first show back?

Oh, it was great. He was in good spirits, and we were all pumped too. I think he began talking about wanting to do the next record at the beginning of that tour and that he was planning for a new record. I was excited at the prospect of doing an album with him.

At that second tour, I started to feel more comfortable. Bob was starting to venture into rootsier music, cover bluegrass and old folk songs and all that, which I thought was great because a lot of that stuff was really right in my wheelhouse. I think with that particular band it seemed like we were trying to color everything with a rootsy feel — which was highly satisfactory to me, I could tell you that.

How would those old folk or bluegrass tunes come to the band? Would Bob during a soundcheck suggest, "Here's an old Stanley Brothers song, let's work it up"?

That's pretty much it. Or he would give us a cassette with like three or four songs on there. We'd go back to the hotel, listen, and then come to the soundcheck next day and start working them out. Or he'd just pick a tune at a soundcheck and we'd see if anything came from it. We'd either continue and get somewhere with it or just drop it because he wasn't feeling it or something. It was a lot of fun playing these old Carter Family tunes and these Ralph Stanley tunes and folk songs that he had played in his early days.

I wanted to ask you about arranging songs. Even his own songs could sound pretty different. Near the end of your tenure, I was learning guitar myself and I found this site that tabbed out a cool fingerpicking thing you created for "Girl of the North Country" — which, by the way, took me like two years to learn. For something like that, are you coming up with a part and suggesting it to the band? Is he giving instructions: "I want the guitar to sound like X, figure something out"?

It's all that. He would maybe suggest a riff for certain songs. He'd play like a three-note riff, which I would grab, or Bucky [Baxter], or Charlie when he eventually joined the band, and then embellish on it — or not. With certain songs he would say, "Let's play this riff every time after every verse." We would play that riff note for note.

In case of something like "North Country," he would just strum his guitar and then I would play along once I knew where the verses were going and in a style that I felt would enhance what he was doing. Then [drummers] David Kemper or George Receli, they'd start with a groove. Bob may ask them to change it, or try something different, or keep this but change that. Everybody was throwing in with their own ideas, but we would also honor what he was able to explain. Very often he didn't even know what he was trying to get out of it. He just wanted it to land in a place that felt good to him. We'd kick each one of these songs around until it felt right.

Any particular favorite songs you enjoyed playing on stage?

Man, to put one above another, boy, that's tough. I mentioned in our documentary series doing "Mr. Tambourine Man." Playing that, playing "Blowin' in the Wind," playing the iconic Dylan tunes when he was into it and giving it up. These tunes that meant so much to me when I was just learning about who I was. Those moments were really special.

The bluesier tunes were a lot of fun to play with him. "Crash on the Levee" and "Maggie's Farm" and "Serve Somebody," that stuff was fun to play.

What about the blues stuff jumped out at you?

Bob is not an old Black guy, but he's got this authenticity in that genre that I don't know where it comes from. The blues comes out of suffering. It comes out of what African Americans experienced in the United States. You feel like can only be really authentic if it's being expressed by someone who it had been handed down to through these generations of the Black American experience.

When Bob would sing one of his or anybody's blues tunes, he still found a way. Although it's not the Black American experience coming out of him, there's still something about his ability to do this. I felt the same way with [David] Bromberg, too. Bromberg, this big Jewish guy from Brooklyn, can deliver a blues tune with his own personal authenticity that gives him license to do it, and it was the same with Bob. How to define or explain that, I'm not sure. It's just a visceral thing you would get. A couple of the deep blues things we did on *Love & Theft*, when we would play those live, on a night when he's really giving it up, you just get this deep feeling.

What was a typical day on the road with Bob like?

Get into the hotel at 3:00 in the morning or whatever it is because we drive at night. Wake up, hopefully after a few good hours of sleep. Get some food. Maybe, if you're capable, go to the gym before you do. Go to soundcheck. The band would warm up for about a half-hour. Bob would show up, and then it would be another two hours of running through stuff. Maybe two hours on one tune, maybe a few tunes, maybe some songs that we would never play again. Soundcheck was always interesting that way. Then we break, go to dinner. The caterers traveled with us. The food on this tour was unbelievable. It was the best thing about it. It was a catering company out of Knoxville. Oh, boy, that was something to look forward to.

I don't usually hear people raving about road food backstage.

I know, but everybody on this tour, all the crew, and the band, they did this right. We'd eat, and then chill for a half hour, and then do the show. That was the routine. Then, after the last song, off the stage on the bus right away. No hanging. On the bus and down to the next town. If you're lucky, it's a two-hour ride and you get to a hotel at a reasonable time, but very often it would be five to eight hours. The road ain't for the faint of heart, man. It's pretty grueling.

After a show, was there any post-game recap or something where the band or Bob or anyone saying, "This worked, this didn't work, let's try this tomorrow"?

When we would get off the stage, there was a little curtained area behind the stage that was set up every night. We'd all get off the stage and go there. Bob would comment on whatever he wanted to comment about. "Yeah, that was great." "No, that didn't work." "We've got to change this." That was pretty regular. Some comment one way or another. Then we would either address it at the soundcheck the next day or not.

Was that enough for you to go on? From the other musicians I've spoken to, some people find it frustrating. People feel like it's hard to read his mind.

I mean, Bob can be mercurial, for sure. You would think that you were giving him what he expressed that he wanted, and then the next day it could be the furthest thing from what he wanted that day. That would happen, but you just go with it. I think that could be frustrating, but we can all be that way to some degree when you're trying to be a creative artist. That's not uncommon. I think with our band, with Teresa and I, I might have been guilty of that myself a few times. It's just part of the game, you know?

You had some memorable shows with Dylan, but I'm guessing maybe none more memorable than playing for The Pope.

There's 400,000 people out there. The Pope's been up there all day long with all these international acts performing, acrobats and magicians. Then we get up to play a few songs. We're facing the audience and off on stage left is the Pope's throne. He's sitting there, and he's got his chin in his hand. He must have been exhausted.

We play a couple of tunes. I'm at stage right and Bob is doing— I forgot what song, maybe it was "Knockin' on Heaven's Door." The TV director with his headphones on comes walking up to me as I'm playing. He says, "He's got-a go meet-a the Pope! He's got-a go meet-a the Pope!" He's looking at me like I'm supposed to do something about this. Typical Italian fashion, man. He's shaking his head; he's looking at his watch. "He's got-a go meet-a the Pope!" And I'm trying to play this song.

The song ends, and I walk over to Bob. I go, "Hey, Bob, this guy is telling me you got to go and meet the Pope." Bob looks around like, "What?" Then the TV director looks at him with hand signal and he points to the Pope. So Bob hands his guitar to somebody and goes over and shakes the Pope's hand. The Pope gives him a rosary or something. He comes back, we play one more tune, and then that's over. That was an experience I never expected to have. It was just surreal.

The next year Dylan did some dates with two other icons, Van Morrison and Joni Mitchell.

That was a great tour. I felt like the competitive thing was sort of there, but in a good way. Bob wanted to up the show every night, and it wasn't coming from a place of frustration, which could happen with Bob. It was coming more from a place of, "We're all in this together. Let's get out there and do something cool." And we did. The gravity of the artistry of these three people was a good launching pad for us to get out there and do the best we could every night.

What did you mean when you said the competitiveness sometimes came from a place of frustration? Was that something that was happening elsewhere?

Yeah. Sometimes you'd get this feeling if there was a particularly good show from the opening act that Bob would get competitive and seemingly insecure. Seemingly. I don't know that for sure, but that's my amateur psychiatry analyzation of it. We're all insecure, and this would seem to come out in him sometimes.

How would that affect you and the band? Something you noticed on stage or you're getting really drilled during soundcheck the next day?

Both. You see him uncomfortable on stage and there's nothing you can do about it. Just play the best you can play and move on. But I don't want to seem like Bob is the only cat that does that, because everybody does that. That's a normal thing when you're trying to be the best artist you can be, that kind of insecurity and frustration and not feeling like you're delivering what you want to deliver for whatever reason.

Another big newsmaking performance you were part of was Dylan's return to Newport Folk Festival in 2002, for the first time since he'd "gone electric" there in '65.

The most notable thing to me was, we get on stage and here comes Bob with a wig and a fake beard and mustache on and a hat. He hadn't said anything to anybody about this. There was no warning. We're absorbing that on stage at the same time as everybody in the audience is absorbing that. I was amused by it. What the purpose of that was, I didn't know at the time and I still don't know, but okay. I'm not going to try and analyze that.

I remember it being a cool performance. I also remember realizing the importance of this, the monumental significance of this. Bob Dylan, whose 1965 performance at Newport was an iconic moment — now I'm able to participate in this thing with him for the next and possibly only other time he's ever going to do it.

Was there a particular period that you look back on especially fondly?

There was a tour we did where we were doing some Warren Zevon tunes and we were doing some Rolling Stones tunes. When everything just started to click in a lot of ways. Everything just felt like a smooth machine that tour. I don't know how to explain it or why, but the material we were doing, Bob's seeming contentment with everything — it just felt like we were all clicking.

When you left the band at the end of 2004, did you know it was your final show? Had you already given notice?

No, I didn't. That tour was when I started mulling it over. That last tour, there were these projects that I wanted to do and I wasn't able to do them. I think one of these things was playing on a recording with McCartney, and I just couldn't do it. That in itself wouldn't have been the catalyst, but these things were adding up.

That's a tough one, though. One of your heroes.

Exactly. Also, I wanted to be with Teresa. When I got off that last tour with Bob, Teresa was in the middle of this run of a play about the Carter Family. We got together around Christmas, and then she was going back out on this Carter Family thing. I came back home, and I was looking at the potential tour schedule for the next year with Bob, and things just started adding up.

It was in that time off that I decided, I got to do something. I called Kramer. The next tour was going to be with Merle Haggard. I wanted to do that, but I just told him, "I can't do this anymore. I'll give you as much notice as you need." I explained the whole thing and he got it. He thought maybe I should come out and do the Merle Haggard tour, but after he discussed it with Bob they just said, "Okay, go ahead, we'll get somebody else for this next run."

It was scary. That's a big ship to jump off of. I just knew I had to do it and something cool would happen. Then, two weeks later I get a call from Levon. He said, "Hey, I heard you left Bob, come on up here and let's start making music."

John Fields

On October 20, 1999, Bob Dylan played one of the most surprising gigs of his career: The television sitcom *Dharma & Greg*.

Though on a certain level there's probably no good answer to the obvious question — *why?* — Dylan did have a connection on the show. One of the show's writers, Eddie Gorodetsky, was friendly with Dylan (he would go on to produce *Theme Time Radio Hour*). The show made the ask, Bob's manager asked for tapes of a couple episodes, and a month later he agreed to cameo.

Dylan's appearance comes right at the end of the episode. It has practically nothing to do with the episode's central plot: Dharma (played by Jenna Elfman) joins a teenage boy's rock band until one of their moms kicks her out. The main plot wraps up with three minutes left to go. Then, out of nowhere, Dharma tells Greg, "Oh, by the way, I've got another audition." Suddenly she's in a studio drumming with Bob Dylan and a band.

I wanted to learn more about what that day was like, so I spoke with one of the band members, John Fields. He plays organ in the scene, having never met Dylan before.

. . . .

This was, if I remember correctly, July of '99. Although I lived in Minneapolis, I was producing a record for a band called Evan and Jaron at The Village studio that summer. This was early in my career; no one had heard of me in LA. The band fought for me to be involved. Columbia kept saying, "We need a figurehead, someone who can help with cred on the record." They met with a couple of people, and they liked T Bone Burnett.

What was great about having T Bone involved was his Rolodex was thick. He'd say, "Hey, why don't you get Jim Keltner over to play drums for a couple of days?"

"Bring in Marc Ribot and have him play on whatever songs." I had never really worked that way before. I was so budget-conscious coming from the Minneapolis indie music scene. You don't really bring in session players just to fool around and see what happens. It was a real luxury for me as a producer.

Anyway, that had been going on for a month or so. T Bone would come in at the end of the night and I'd play him what we were working on. One day he comes in and he says to me, "Hey, I've got a pick-up gig and I wonder if you want to play organ?" I said, "Sure, no problem." I'm thinking that it was one of his buddies down in Santa Monica. I had no idea who, and he didn't tell me. He just said, "It's Friday and I'll tell you more when we know more." I didn't even think about it much.

T Bone finally said, "Oh, the gig is over at the Fox lot. It's with Bob Dylan. I put together a little group to jam on this show *Dharma & Greg*. We don't know what it's really going to be, but just show up at five o'clock." I was thinking it was something a lot smaller time, not a televised gig with no rehearsal. I'd never been on a national TV show before.

It's not that I have a history with Bob; it's just that *everyone* does if you're from Minneapolis. I'm a Jewish kid, and my mother was from St. Paul. She went to camp with Bob at Herzl.[90] His mother and my grandmother were best friends in the '80s at this assisted living apartment complex in St. Paul. I'm sure I met his mom back then. It was just a little bit of extra electricity when I met him. The last thing I'm going to say is, "Do you remember my mom from camp?"

When we got there, there was a bunch of gear set up. It was Tony Gilkyson from X, Joe Henry played acoustic, I played organ, T Bone played bass, Bob played guitar. I think it was T Bone's guitar he was playing. And then Jenna Elfman, who wasn't really a drummer. She'd been taking drum lessons for the last several months. She had one beat she knew; you can hear her playing it on every song. She wasn't versatile, but she had this one beat, so we worked with that.

I didn't know what we were going to play. There was no vocal mic, so it wasn't like he was going to sing. We just jammed. He'd say something like, "Let's play a Memphis blues." You would just watch his hands. Luckily, I also play guitar and could decode what he's playing. I'm a huge Al Kooper fan and there's this interview with him where he talked about the "Like a Rolling Stone" organ session and how he didn't know the song. Al would let the chord hit first so that he wouldn't make a mistake and then follow in on bar two. Now I'm playing organ in the same situation.

90 Louie Kemp told me about this camp way back in Chapter 10.

I actually think he was having a fun time. Jenna is super charming and funny and makes you feel relaxed. She's not some big superstar or something. Obviously, Bob's a superstar, but I don't think he looked at himself like that. At some point, there were red Solo cups and drinks. I remember having a vodka cranberry. I don't know why I remember that, but I do.

It took an hour or two, then they invited us to stay for the actual show taping, which goes down real quick because it's live. Evan Lowenstein from the band came with me and we stayed for a little bit of the show and then left. That was it. Never saw Bob again.

It was definitely one of the weirder pick-up gigs I've ever played. I still get residual checks for being an actor on a major syndicated sitcom, 20 years later. It's like four cents.

Ray Benson sits in with Dylan and his band (Larry Campbell to the left of Dylan, Ray and Tony Garnier to the right) in Denver, Colorado, April 2000.
Photo by Larry Hulst

Ray Benson

Ray Benson has been leading Asleep at the Wheel since he co-founded the Western swing stalwarts way back in 1970. Fifty-plus years on, they're still going strong. In 2000, Bob Dylan commented onstage that they were "the best group I've ever heard, probably... the most genuine group."

Benson didn't know about that quote until I told him, but he was in the building when Bob said it. Asleep at the Wheel opened Dylan's Spring 2000 tour, and Benson himself sat in with Dylan a number of times on that run. We talked about that, as well as Benson's experience playing with two longtime Dylan sidemen, Tony Garnier and an 11-year-old Charlie Sexton, decades before Bob hired them.

. . . .

Before we even get to Bob Dylan, how did you first meet Tony Garnier?

He was a student at UC Berkeley. He was playing with some folks and heard that we were looking for a bass player. He dropped out and joined the band.

How long had Asleep at the Wheel been active at that point?

This was end of '73. I guess we had one record out, but we had been playing around the Bay Area, so he knew who we were. Tony was there from end of '73 until '78 or '79.

And now he's been with Bob for decades.

Tony Garnier has been an addition to Bob that has been immeasurably positive. Just look at his track record, been with Bob for 30-some-odd years. I call him the Bob Whisperer. Bob listens to him in terms of musical things. It's one of the reasons I think that Bob is out there doing new things every day. Because it ain't easy. What Tony does is not easy at all.

Was Tony your connection into Dylan world?

Yeah. The first time I got to meet Bob was when Tony was in the band. Steve Earle was opening their shows [in summer 1989]. We were recording in Harrisburg PA, and they were playing a gig. I went over to see Tony and Steve Earle. Bob was very nice. We just shook hands. That was the first meeting.

What if anything do you remember about the first time you played on stage with him? Which I believe was at Austin Music Hall in 1996. Charlie Sexton was there too, sitting in before he had actually joined Bob's band. So a historic night in retrospect.

You have to watch Bob. That's the whole game with Bob, just to see where he's at and try to complement what he's doing. Because that's what's going on. It's not what was played a year ago or ten years ago. It's what he's doing at that moment. You got to pay attention.

I remember at the Austin thing, Bob asked me about Charlie. I said, "Charlie would love to go [play with you] man. He's fantastic." I called Charlie up and said, "Hey, Bob was asking about you. You could probably get a call sometime." Sure enough, a while later he called up and hired Charlie.

Had you known Charlie for years around Austin?

We go way back. I've known Charlie since he was 11 years old.

How did you meet him at 11?

He was hanging out in Antone's. There's a video somewhere of him when he was either 13 or 14 jamming with me at the Continental Club. Somebody filmed it.

I read somewhere a story about you telling Bob that in the song "Stuck Inside of Mobile," he flubbed the line. Does this ring a bell?

That was at Willie Nelson's 60th birthday, I think at the Austin City Limits studio. We're sitting there talking about making records and about how it has changed over the years in terms of the technology. I can't remember why, but I said, "On 'Stuck Inside of Mobile with the Memphis Blues Again,' there's your line, 'He built a fire on Main Street and shot it full of holes.' You flubbed the words. You say shot before: 'You shot— *built* a fire on Main Street…' When we first heard that, we would play that over and over again and just say how cool that was."

Bob goes, "Yeah, they wouldn't let us do that now, would they?" In other words, the engine or the producer would say, "No, Bob, you got to do that again. You flubbed the word up."

You have to watch Bob. That's the whole game with Bob, just to see where he's at and try to complement what he's doing. Because that's what's going on. It's not what was played a year ago or ten years ago. It's what he's doing at that moment.

Talking about Willie Nelson, a song that he did, "I'd Have to Be Crazy," Steve Fromholz wrote the song, and he's singing the words off mic to Willie, because Willie didn't know the words. It comes out as this beautiful echo before Willie's singing. He went back in, and the engineer said, "Oh, you need to do this again, Steve leaked in your mic," and Willie said, "I like that."

My whole thing about recording is letting it happen, don't beat it to death, make it spontaneous. Because the technology enables us to fix *everything* now, a lot of things come out a little too clean and processed.

Let's jump into the tour in 2000. I saw in an old interview, you called this tour a highlight in the band's career. What made it so?

Well…Dylan! The same reason why you're asking me about it. I first heard Bob Dylan when I was a kid. His influence on every musician that ever hears him is immeasurable. To me, it was just something that I had hoped would happen from the time I picked up a guitar.

How did it happen? I know these things are often just booking agents talking to each other.

I really don't know. From what I understand, Bob decides. It was a rough tour for us, because we were in the middle of a George Strait tour also, opening these stadiums. I think we're about the only band that could go from a Strait country tour to a Bob Dylan tour and pull it off.

How do the audiences compare on a Dylan tour versus a Strait tour?

I always felt that we had a great reception from both. They're there to see Bob, and of course they were there to see George. It's the hardest thing to do, but every night we'd pull it off. They would clap at the end of the set. That's all you can hope for.

During the off-stage hours on that tour, how much overlap or interaction is there between the Asleep gang and Bob's people?

They were all pals. It was, at the time, [David] Kemper on drums, and, of course, Larry Campbell, one of the greatest musicians that I know.

I read somewhere about Larry teaching you a guitar tuning that you used for your own song, "I Ain't Lookin' for No Trouble."

Yeah, D-A-D-G-A-D. Larry said, try this one out, it's pretty cool. He's a master. I have the greatest respect for him. I guess at the end of his tenure there, they weren't getting along, but in my mind Larry played brilliantly.

So you're hanging with the band on the road. Is Bob hanging out? A lot of people I talked to say he keeps to himself.

I was lucky. Bob liked to talk to me. We would trade music sometimes.

What do you mean, trade music?

He'd say, "Have you ever heard so and so?" I go, "No." "Here's some stuff." Or I would give him some music to listen to. He never stops learning. Bob is a creature of proximity. Whatever he's around, he is influenced by. I remember he gave me some Sam Peckinpah movies that he liked. I gave him some Cliff Bruner.

One of my favorite things was Bob telling me a joke. One time, we were playing in Rochester, Minnesota. He said to me, "I played here once." I went, "Really?" He said, "Yeah, 1958. I was playing piano for Bobby Vee."

Literally the same room?

Yeah, same hall! It was this municipal auditorium, big old brick building.

Later the same night we got off stage. Me and Jason are sitting there. Bob walks up and goes, "What does a train hear with?" I said, " I don't know Bob. What?" He said, "Engine-ears."

That's so corny, I love it.

That was my favorite Bob Dylan moment, to be honest with you.

You mentioned Jason Roberts, your fiddle player. I know you guys both sat in with Dylan a few times. How does that come about? A lot of times people open for him, but never get on stage.

Tony asked Bob. He said, "Hey, you want Ray to sit in?" He said, sure. Like I said, Bob changes over the years. At that point, he was much more open. I've seen him in recent years. He's changed, as we all do.

Changed in terms of what?

Like having people sit in. He's not doing that anymore, last time I saw him a few months ago in Austin. At this point, the music that they're playing is more complex musically than it was in years past.

I don't think he's had anyone sit in for a few years at this point.

No, because they rework everything. That's part of what he's doing in this part of his life. He's reworking stuff on a daily basis.

Were you able to say hi? I don't know what the COVID protocols are these days.

He wasn't visiting before the show. I went backstage and just hung out with the band, then watched the show. Went backstage after, but he had already left, so I just went home. His manager called after and said, "Hey, Bob asked about you!" I just said, "Tell him I said howdy."

In terms of the sitting in you did do back then, was there any rehearsal at soundcheck or whatnot?

You just wing it. That's what it is. You got to see, what's Bob doing, whether it's on piano or guitar. He's a moving target.

At one of those shows, there's that quote that Dylan said on stage about how Asleep's the most genuine group. Did you catch it at the time?

This is the first time I ever heard of it. I didn't know he said that. That's pretty nice.

Here it is then: "Ray Benson is up here tonight with us. Asleep at the Wheel's been on a lot of shows with us and they're the best group I've ever heard, probably. They're the most genuine group."

Honestly, I had no idea. He's heard a lot of groups and I appreciate it. Let's put it that way.

    I knew that we got along, and that was about it. I just try to respect his privacy, and any chance I get, I love to see him, but he does—

    That's very nice. I had no idea.

He's had plenty of people open for him. Doesn't give a lot of quotes like that about most of them.

I couldn't ask for anything more. You believe me, that's…that's wonderful. Made my day.

Freddy Koella with Dylan (and drummer George Receli)
at New Orleans Jazz & Heritage Festival, 2003.
Photo by Duncan Hume

Freddy Koella

Freddy Koella only played guitar with Dylan for one year, from 2003 to 2004, but a passionate group of fans swear he's Bob's greatest guitarist of the Never Ending Tour. One fan compiled a selection of Koella's best performances with Dylan; the compilation ran to nine discs long!

How did someone who wasn't with Bob for very long and never even played on a Dylan record earn such a cult following? "Weird" is a word that comes up a lot when fans discuss Freddy — as both a compliment and a criticism — and perhaps explains why he sticks out in people's minds two decades after his short stint. His lines and solos drew on classical music and free jazz and were often a far cry from the blues template other guitarists stuck close to. As one fan put it on an internet forum, "I always thought that Koella's kind of weird style was what Bob would sound like if he was really good at guitar."

When I caught up with Koella, who now lives back in his native France and speaks with a fairly thick French accent, I started by asking him if he knew about the Freddy-frenzy.

. . . .

Are you aware that you have a cult following all these years later among fans? One person put together nine full CDs, called Freddy Or Not, *of great moments of you playing with Dylan.*

I have no clue about that, you know. Because I just played with him and that's all. As I do with all the singers I'm working with. I'm not interested in what's beside that.

Where were you before you got connected with the Dylan world? You'd been playing with Willy DeVille, right?

I was still playing with him. Dylan and Willy knew each other a little bit[91], so my name was not completely unknown to them. I mean, Bob's camp knew who I was even if they didn't know my name. That was the connection, I guess.

How does that lead into you joining Bob's band?

This guitar maker, James Trussart. He's a French guy who makes metal guitars in LA. He's a very old friend of mine, 40 years, I would say. Tony Garnier went to his workshop when I was there. We were all three talking together. Tony said to James, "We're rehearsing tonight, but I don't know about this player." He didn't seem very enthusiastic. James said to him, "You should try Freddy!" Half joking. I didn't say anything; I was surprised. Tony was, "Oh, yeah, I don't know…"

The day after, they called me. Where I was living in LA, it was five minutes from the studio. I just went. We played, we had a good time and that was it.

Were you familiar with the Dylan repertoire? Were you a fan?

I knew the average stuff. I had *Blonde on Blonde* a while back. I liked him, but I wasn't like a fanatic. Absolutely not. When I went rehearsing, I didn't learn the songs. I just went and we played.

Are you getting any instruction?

No. He just throws a song. "One, two, three, four," and you play. Because the material he's playing is familiar to me. I've been playing this type of music forever.

What about it was familiar?

Blues and folk music. The chord changes, the harmonies, the grooves. I've been playing that since an early age.

Are you running through actual songs, or are you just jamming riffs and chord changes?

Dylan songs, of course. You see, the drummer and the bass player are from New Orleans originally, and I spent 10 years in New Orleans. So their playing was very familiar to me. I connected very fast, I would say.

What division of labor did you establish with Larry Campbell, the other guitarist? How do you pick your spots in the band?

---

91 In a 2015 interview with Bill Flanagan, when asked who he thought should be in the Rock and Roll Hall of Fame, Dylan responded, "Willy DeVille for one, he stood out, his voice and presentation ought to have gotten him in there by now."

We decided at the rehearsal what each would do. Because every time we went on tour, we had two or three days rehearsal. I was relying mostly on Larry, because he'd been there for years. I was adapting to what he was doing.

What happens at the end of that first rehearsal? How do you eventually find out you got the gig?

We end the rehearsal and Bob was smiling. He said, "We're going to Australia tomorrow. Are you coming?" The next day!

But my wife was super pregnant. I said, "No, I can't. I cannot leave my wife by herself. I'm sorry."

Bob was not happy. He wanted his way. I said, "Okay, but what can I say? Too bad." The manager came to my rescue. He said, "Bob, come on, he has a family. Just have him the next tour." So they went, but they called me for the next tour.

In between those tours, do you think you're not in the band?

I thought I'd lost it. Definitely.

What do you remember about your first show?

It was in Dallas. It was the Gulf War, with W. Bush. France said it's a mistake to go in Iraq, so Americans were anti-French at the time. They boycotted the French fries and all that. I said to the band, "Oh, man, Dallas? They're going to shoot me, I'm French!"

I always enjoyed playing with him, but remembering all these songs was very difficult for me. That was the hard side of it. Musically, it was great all the time.

I'm not surprised remembering songs was difficult. You played 100 different songs in a year. Were there any times he starts into a song onstage and you're trying to figure out what it even is?

Oh yeah, definitely. I had a book where I had all the charts, in case before the show I didn't know one song at all, I'd just peek into the book. But Dylan at some point told me, "Freddy, you know what? Just don't learn the songs." Which was fine with me.

This was the beginning of Bob playing piano rather than guitar. You're standing right next to him onstage by the end. How did that affect your playing?

His body expression and his face, it's like conducting. So you go along with that. In fact, you watch him all the time. I sensed when he liked my playing by his face expression. And when he liked it a little less, I could build something more efficient for him.

I think one of the reasons people remember you so fondly is that you played a lot of solos, and they tend to be very distinctive. You'd never do it the same way twice.

I don't like to repeat myself. I find it boring. I have an impressionistic attitude towards music. In fact, I think Bob has the same aesthetic. I think that's why it worked so well with him, because I like the same music he does. We know the same music and we kind of have the same approach. Of course, I have blues schooling, but I did lots of classical music also. So my solos are a blend of different stuff. And, *voila*, that's what it is.

Had you done any tours like that when you're on the road for so many months a year before?

That long? No.

Did you like it? Some people like that lifestyle and some people can't stand it.

It was fine with me, but except that my wife didn't like it at all. So that was not good.

The only band change during your time was by the end you're playing with two drummers, when Dylan added Richie Hayward from Little Feat to go with George Receli.

Since I was listening to Lowell George a lot when I was a kid, it was great I met [Hayward]. We talked about Lowell George on the bus.

There were also a few shows where Bob's guitar tech Tommy Morrongiello sat in. What was the story there?

I don't know. Bob can be— you cannot read his mind. I don't know why Tommy played, to be honest. To please him? To say to us you're not good enough? I don't know. No joke.

How much offstage interaction did you have with Dylan himself?

Not much, which was fine with me. The musical discussion was good enough for me, to be honest. He's private; it's okay.

You mentioned the ups and downs. Were there any particular shows that stand out to you all these years later that you remember fondly?

I had a book with all the charts, in case I didn't know a song, I'd just peek in the book. But Dylan at some point told me, "Freddy, you know what? Just don't learn the songs." Which was fine with me.

. . . .

I remember we did a tour in England in small venues, like Hammersmith and some classics. Those shows were really cool. Bob was really excited because it was a small venue, so much better. I think I started to get more comfortable with everyone and the music.

When you were there, he would sometimes introduce you as "Fuzzy" Koella. Where'd that come from?

Because I'm a hairy bear. When you change after the show, because you're sweating, you can see the body sometimes. He saw me.

So that wasn't a nickname you already had?

No, he invented it. It's a good one.

I was thinking it was maybe because of your fuzzy guitar tone or something.

No, no. It was that.

Did you know the last show was going to be your last?

Not at all. I fell sick on the time off. Really sick. I had kidney failure from a sinus infection, a very rare disease. I went to the hospital, and I was really in bad shape. They didn't know what I had at first. I thought I would die.

I called the manager and I told him. This is when I'm at the hospital in really bad shape. I missed the tour after, and I was still sick for the next one, and the third one I was *still* sick. So they said, we're gonna keep the guy who replaced you. I lost the gig because of that, which I will say was very depressing at the time.

I'm sure. How long were you in the hospital?

Two weeks at the hospital, then the recovery was very, very, very long. I was out of business almost a year. It took me a while to get on my feet.

Did you ever have any contact afterwards?

In 2012, I believe, I did one or two songs in Santa Barbara, which was close to where I lived. Watching them on stage at the time, I was scratching my head and I was wondering, "Would you like to go back?" I wasn't sure, to be honest. I think that night, Bob wasn't really in a very good mood, and I sensed that the musicians were quite tense. I didn't like it.

What was funny is that I started to play, and a pick was underneath the strings on the neck. [Charlie] Sexton was looking at me and making signs. I didn't know what he wanted to tell me. Finally, I found out. The pick was stuck in the strings.

Then they called me maybe two or three years ago. I talked to the manager. I said, "You know, I'm living in France now. I don't know if that would be possible." He said, "Yeah, I don't know. It might be complicated," and that was it.

They were calling you to see if you might want to rejoin the band?

Yeah. He said, "You know, your name fell on the table again, so I just was seeing what you were doing."

The problem was he wants people nearby, or who can get to him on short notice?

Exactly, and I didn't want to go back to America.

The guy I'm working with now, Francis Cabrel, he's a Bob Dylan fanatic. I can see in his music his influence. Of course, it's in French, so it's completely different, but musically, you can sense the influence. I wish that one day — and I know that it's like one chance in ten — at a concert I could call the manager and try to let him meet Bob. That would be amazing for him, because now he's 68. He's not getting younger.

All these years later, how do you view your one year in the band?

Quite magical, I would say. The artistry of Bob, he's so beyond all the other artists I've worked with. Playing with a guy that talented, it's like a gift. I really looked at it as a gift of life. Now I think about it fondly. But I don't think about it often.

Jeff Bridges

Jeff Bridges is — well, he's Jeff Bridges! The world may better know the actor as The Dude from *The Big Lebowski*, but for our purposes, his claim to fame is as Dylan's co-star on 2003 movie *Masked & Anonymous*. In that film, he played muckraking journalist Tom Friend, out to get a story about Dylan's musician character Jack Fate.

Bridges answered a few questions about acting with Bob — and playing music with him, too. During downtime on set, the two would jam on their guitars in Bridges' trailer. We also, naturally, touched on *The Big Lebowski*, since one of that movie's many achievements is raising "The Man in Me" from a deep album cut to one of Dylan's best-known songs.

. . . .

Were you surprised when The Big Lebowski *had such an impact on "The Man in Me"? It was a semi-obscure cut beforehand; now it could plausibly appear on a Dylan greatest-hits album.*

Yeah, man. I mean, it's a wonderful song. I got a band that I put together largely because of T Bone [Burnett] and *Crazy Heart*, The Abiders. We do "The Man in Me" when we play Lebowski Fest or anywhere else we're playing.

You've covered "Ring Them Bells" with The Abiders too.

Oh yeah, "Ring Them Bells," I love that song. I'm trying to think of all the lyrics right now, give me a hint about what I love about it so much. *[sings]* "Ring them bells, you sinners…" It's a wakeup call.

If you could play a role in making another Dylan deep cut more well known, which song would you pick?

Gosh. That's a good question. I'd have to look at a list of the songs. Well, this is a very popular song, but I love "Highway 61 Revisited." John Mellencamp did a version at a tribute to Bob that was just phenomenal.

Bob Dylan, he has to be my favorite writer, favorite musician and creator of music. I love all his different seasons that he's had in his life. I love his stuff he's done with the American Songbook; those albums were so great. I feel so blessed to just be alive with the guy and to have acted with him— God! In *Masked & Anonymous,* to hang with him on that level, to play with him basically, was wonderful.

One of the great things about Masked & Anonymous *is that the scenes are occasionally broken up by the musical performances by Bob Dylan and the band.*

What a band!

Were you around when they were taping those?

Oh, yeah. Charlie Sexton, who's one of his guitar players in the band, is also a terrific actor. I've seen him in some other things. Why do I remember the drummer playing like a cardboard box or something? It all sounded so great, wonderful.

I'm surprised that that movie hasn't taken off and wasn't a bigger hit, man. I mean, that's an intense movie!

You mentioned in another interview guitar-picking with Bob in your trailer. How did you end up playing "You Belong to Me"? Any other songs you two jammed to?

I'll occasionally go down the Bob Dylan Google hole and just let my mind go into that realm. Just prior to that movie, I came across that version of "You Belong to Me" from the movie with Woody Harrelson *[Natural Born Killers].* It's just him playing the guitar. He's such a wonderful guitar player, people don't know that about him. I remember walking by his trailer, and he'd be sitting out smoking a cigar and picking on the guitar, man. Just his approach and his freedom of chords was just beautiful.

His version of "You Belong to Me" from that movie was just wonderful, and so I learned it too. I'm in my trailer one day and I get a knock on my door. There's Bob with his guitar, man. He says, "You want to jam?" I say, "Shit, come on in!" So I played that song, and then I also played him a John Goodwin song, who's my old, old friend whose music I play.

My hands were shaking, you know, being next to— I don't want to say hero and idol, that's not quite it, but my guy who I admire so much who I get to play with. Not only with good music, but acting. Bob was such an incredible actor. I was very impressed with him.

Larry Charles, the director, said, "Why don't you and Bob get warmed up and do some acting exercises? You know about that stuff." I said, okay. Well, so we just jammed for about an hour or two, just playing pretend within the movie. I can't remember specifically what it was, but I remember we just jammed, and he was so open and willing to jam, man. It was so much fun. To do that in the acting realm and in the music realm with someone that you admire so much was just a real turn-on.

Have you seen Dylan in concert?

Yeah, I've seen Dylan in concert! Maybe three or four times. I saw one where he was with Paul Simon, and they would switch who would open for who. The night that I saw him, I think at the Hollywood Bowl, Paul Simon was opening for Bob. Paul opens with "American Tune." He's got like two drummers and violins and horns, this huge orchestra, and he proceeds to just kick ass after that incredible song. He just does an incredible concert. Now I say, "How is Bob going to follow that?"

Bob comes out and he's got like a four-piece: a drummer, a guitar, bass, him, maybe he's got another guitar guy there. What does he open with? "Hello darkness, my old friend…" You know, the Simon tune. You didn't know if his tongue was in his cheek or if it was a real sincere homage.[92] Actually, I think it was [sincere] because he's done "The Boxer" too. Then he proceeded to just kick ass in the most incredible Dylan way that was so stripped down. Like Elvis. I was watching that movie [2022's *Elvis*] and some documentaries. He had that big full sound but when he had it stripped down, it was so cool. Bob stripped it down to its essentials.

---

92 This "Sound of Silence" performance Bridges is referring to was actually a duet with Simon himself.

Dickie Landry playing Einstein on the Beach with Philip Glass, 1971.
Courtesy of Dickie Landry

Dickie Landry

Before April 26, 2003, saxophonist Dickie Landry had never played with Dylan before. He's never played with him since either. But one night in New Orleans, Landry sat in with Dylan. And not just for a song or two, but for the entire show.

Though new to Dylan, Landry was already well established in the avant-garde music world. He'd played for years with Philip Glass and Laurie Anderson, collaborated across the globe with Robert Rauschenberg, hung out with Ornette Coleman and Moondog, and even guested on the Talking Heads album *Speaking in Tongues*. So this Dylan sit-in is a small blip in a long career, but, as the veteran Louisiana musician explained to me, an interesting one.

. . . .

I have a friend in New Orleans who owns a restaurant. Name is Kerry Boutté, the restaurant Mulate's. He had been friends with Dylan for a while and also the bass player from New Orleans [Tony Garnier]. He invited me and a couple other friends to dinner at the restaurant, and Bob was going to be there.

But, if you know Bob, he doesn't like to meet new people. So the minute Bob walks in, he saw about six of us that he didn't know and was about to walk out the door. Tony Garnier said, "No Bob, you gotta meet Dickie Landry. He's played with Laurie Anderson, Philip Glass." Bob said, "Well, where is he?" I said, "I'm right here, Bob."

He said, "You must have interesting stories. How did you meet Philip Glass?" So I went through the whole story of my meeting Philip. At one point, Philip and I were both plumbers. He said, "Philip Glass was a *plumber*?" I said, "Yeah, while you were making your money, we were scrambling!"

He's got his manager, Tony Garnier, the drummer [George Receli], me, a date, and somebody else at the table. I started talking about music I'd heard recently. I asked Tony Garnier if he had ever heard Hank Williams III play. He said no. [I told him] the first half of his concert was pure country, and the second part was pure hardcore punk. And I love to play punk. So [during Hank's show] I ran to my apartment which is about two blocks away from the club and got my horn and jumped on the bandstand and started playing. And there were shouts like, keep going! So I did like an hour and a half set with him.

Bob's saying, how did you follow him? I said, even in punk music there is a structure. The structure goes around once, and in the middle of that you improvise. The band members move, somebody's giving a cue when they're going somewhere. And he said, "Well, my music is very structured. If you could do that, you could play my music." I said, "What do you mean?" He says, "What are you doing tomorrow night? Why don't you bring your horn and play?"

My immediate reaction was, I don't know any of your fucking music!

In the meantime, there was an audible gasp at the table from all these managers and people. I mean, it was literally out loud, audible. Like, he just asked somebody to sit in? He never does that! Who is this man? Anyway, we kept talking about bands and musicians. At one point, I turned to Tony Garnier, I said, "Tony, is he serious?" He said, "I don't know, sometimes he changes his mind. Call me in the morning."

So [the next day] I called Tony Garnier at one, two o'clock in the afternoon. I said, Tony, what's up? He says Bob's been up since eleven o'clock this morning asking if I was going to show up at the concert.

I show up at the venue and Tony gives me the list. Sixteen, seventeen songs, the keys, watch Bob for the solos and stuff. I'm looking over everything and I don't know the songs. I never played any of them in my life. I'm a great Dylan fan; I never played his music. Philip Glass does not play Bob Dylan songs. Most bands I played with never did either.

Bob walks in. He said, "Are you ready to go on?" I said, "Hell yeah." He said, "Well, take us on stage." So I'm the first one who gets onstage. As I walk onstage, he's got me dead center of the stage, and the band is behind me. I can't see anybody! All I can see is Bob, about ten feet away to my right on piano.

We started playing. The first song, I hobbled through it. Second song, I hobbled through it. Third song, I got it.

The rest of the concert followed. He's changing songs every song. The first two songs were in the setlist. The rest were not. So I'm in completely blind territory. Not a clue what song was coming up. My balls were sweating onstage.

At one point, the light goes down and Tony says, "We got a folk song coming up. I don't think a saxophone would sound good." In my mind, this is the way they get me off the stage. So I go off the stage, I'm standing by the guitars, and the guitar tech runs up to me and says, "What the fuck are you doing offstage, man? You're killing it!" I said, "Well, Tony—" He said, "Fuck Tony. As soon as the light goes down, you're going back onstage."

They play two songs, and I go back onstage. The first word out of Bob's mouth was, "Where did you go, Dickie?" I said, "Well, Tony Garnier—" He said, "This is *my* band. Don't leave the stage again."

After the concert, he and I spent about a half hour together. I had a date with this girl. He asked her, "So what did you think of the concert?" She said, "Oh Bob, it was great." "Well, what about the saxophone player?" "He was fantastic!"

I said, "Bob, I want to thank you for letting me perform with you tonight." He looked at me with his steely blue eyes, and he goes, *[Dylan voice]* "Any tiiiime."

Duke Robillard in Charleston, South Carolina during his abbreviated 2013 stint in Dylan's band.
Photo by David Oppenheimer

Duke Robillard

Duke Robillard is one of those musicians who has come in and out of Bob Dylan's professional orbit a number of times. He differs from the others in two respects.

The first is that, when Dylan asked him to play with him, Robillard said no. Many times. He has been a prominent blues guitar player since the late '60s, recording dozens of albums under his own name and in a wide array of bands alongside artists like Robert Gordon and J. Geils. He was too busy with his own career, he says, to drop everything to join Dylan's Never Ending Tour. He only eventually relented when the ask became to record a studio project, *Time Out of Mind*, rather than an ongoing road gig.

The second key difference is that when he finally said yes to hitting the road with Dylan, many years after *Time Out of Mind*, things did *not* go well. Or rather, they did… until they suddenly, abruptly, dramatically didn't.

I'll let him explain.

. . . .

Before you had a professional relationship, were you a fan of Dylan's music? Did you listen to him when you were younger?

Soon after he started, my friends turned me on to him. *Bringing It All Back Home* got me because it was bluesy and electric and a lot of fun. I got hooked on his music then.

That was your sweet spot, bluesy and electric?

Well, I'm a blues player, so yeah, I got more interested when it became electric.

At what point did you first get connected professionally?

I had been requested to audition several times over the years, starting in— I can't remember if it was the early '90s or the late '80s. Probably the early '90s. The first time it was requested that I audition for him, I really wasn't interested. I was my own bandleader and I had been for many, many years then. It's just not something I was interested in doing. But for some reason, it kept coming up every few years. I would be called by his management or his musical director and asked if I would be interested in coming down and auditioning for the band. I kept saying no.

Finally, probably about the third time they called me, they had just started the *Time Out of Mind* album. They were in the studio for one day, and Bob just decided that he really wanted me there. That was a different story, of course. I was really interested in *recording* with him.

The next day, I flew down to Miami. They were already started. I got in the studio, strapped on a guitar, and recorded immediately. It was crazy. They were in the middle of working up "Dirt Road Blues," but the version that I came in on, [producer] Daniel Lanois didn't use. I thought it was a great version. He used a demo they had recorded back in Oxnard, California, that Lanois played guitar on.[93] But immediately, Dylan got very excited after one take of it, and I knew it was going to be a fun session.

It was an odd situation. Daniel Lanois wasn't in agreement with having me there, but Dylan insisted. [Lanois] kept telling me to sit out songs, that he was going to play guitar. So he'd go in and play a little bit, but then before they actually started rolling, they'd have a meeting and Bob would tell Lanois that he wanted *me* in there. That kept happening the entire session. Nearly every song, I was thrown out of the studio and then Lanois would play, then *he* was thrown out, and I'd get called back. It was a funny way to make a record.

Funny, and sounds probably stressful too.

It was. I knew, first of all, Lanois didn't want me there. He didn't like blues guitar players; he actually told me as much. He didn't want to hear one blues lick or one lick he ever heard before. So I already knew he didn't want me there, but it was very obvious that Bob Dylan wanted me there. It did make it a little odd, but I just figured, "Well, the boss wants me here so I'll just do as I'm told, go back and forth."

In retrospect, that album is thought of as Bob's big comeback. Could you tell even in the

---

93 This is the demo with Winston Watson's drum loop that earned him a credit on *Time Out of Mind* even though he had already left the band.

moment that the songs were that good?

Oh, yeah. I thought the songs were incredible. As they're going down, we had the headphones on, listening to him change the lyrics from take to take. I just thought it was a completely fascinating experience. I loved it.

I think of Bob as mostly doing stuff live with his band in the studio. Was that the case for these?

Absolutely, 100%. I think he might have fixed a line or something. Something he didn't like, he'd maybe fix it while we were all sitting there. It was only maybe once or twice at the most. The rest of it was all just completely live.

Is that how you like to record, or do you prefer the modern piecemeal approach?

I prefer to record live, but I like the idea of being isolated in case you don't like something that you did. Everybody else had a great take, but you didn't. I like the option to fix things, which we had there. It was a big studio so things were isolated enough that, if you needed to fix something, you could.

Were you ever doing that? Like what you're saying in terms of Bob revising lines, you're redoing a guitar part?

I think there was one song where Bob had an idea about how he wanted me to play a solo or something. I overdubbed on one song.

How long were you there for?

Nine days, about 8 or 10 hours a day.

Do you remember roughly how many songs you're getting through in that time?

Multiple songs per day. I would say minimum of three songs a day, maybe more. I'm sure we recorded quite a few more tunes than we used. I think a lot of them came out later on like one of those authorized Bootleg Series things that they did.[94]

We did a lot of work in there. It wasn't like, play a song and hang around a while. We were constantly working.

How does that lead, 16 years later, to you joining the live band? Is his manager still calling you up every couple of years to go on the road?

---

94 He's referring to *Tell Tale Signs*; later, after Robillard and I spoke, even more came out on the Bootleg Series *Fragments*.

I'm trying to think. In between doing *Time Out of Mind* and from when I joined the band, I don't remember whether or not I was asked to come in and audition again. I might have been.

When I did join the band, it was a particularly slow winter when they asked me. I didn't really have as much work as I wanted or needed to have. I finally said to Tony Garnier, the musical director, who I had known since he was in Asleep at the Wheel 40 years ago, "How many times can you say no to Bob Dylan?" So I joined.

He has a lot of songs at that point to learn. How do you get prepared for show number one? Are you crash-coursing his recent albums?

They gave me a rough idea of the material that they had been doing most recently. Of course, it really wasn't an indication as to whether or not that would be the same material we'd be doing once we got to rehearsal.

I did have a rehearsal with Tony and the longtime guitarist that was there, Stu Kimball. They came over to my house and just prepared me as to what to expect, what Bob liked and what he didn't like. I think we went over some of the most frequent tunes they were playing, that they figured we'd probably continue playing. Other than that one rehearsal, it was just basically doing a crash course with material from all periods of his career.

Speaking of Stu, with you as the two guitarists, what's the division of labor? Are you talking in advance: "You take solos on this. I'll play acoustic on that."

Bob, at that point, had had Stu switch over to acoustic guitar, and then me playing electric. That's what he was hearing as being how the sound of the band would be at that point. Stu was playing more electric guitar before that, when he was playing with Charlie Sexton. I think Bob was trying to get the volume level on stage down a bit, and also maybe represent more his style of playing with Stu playing acoustic guitar.

Because Bob is playing entirely piano at this point.

He wasn't playing guitar at all. He had some operation on one of his fingers on his left hand, and it prevented him from playing guitar at all at that point. He was frustrated about that. He did go back to playing some guitar after I left, I believe.

He's a famously unpredictable person to follow. Now on top of that, he's tucked behind a piano where I'm guessing you can't really see what his hands are doing. Does that make it complicated to figure out where he's going?

Really, there wasn't a problem if I knew the song. I could hear him. He's in my

For years, they'd asked me to come and play. I didn't want to give up my own personality and my music. When I did decide to join, I really thought I was going to be with him 'til he stopped playing. For me, it was a big thing to just stop, break up my own band, and do that. I wish it had continued to go right.

. . . .

monitor. Occasionally, we'd learn a tune quickly at a soundcheck and then play it that night. If I wasn't as familiar with that song, you had to listen closely. But that's what I'm used to doing anyway. The music that I play is very much based on playing with other people and things changing. Jazz material or blues material, you don't have a set-in-stone part. I was used to following. Keeping my ears wide open and following.

In an interview at the time, you said that playing these songs was making you a better guitarist. You thought they were adding a new style to your playing. What was that?

Anytime you play different material, you have to approach it differently. Especially me in this position. I had been my own leader for 30 or 40 years, so playing someone else's music, you have to change your approach. I was learning new material and different styles of songs than I had played before. It made me focused on new things, and it was a lot of fun.

I've talked to a few other people who played with him in the last 15, 20 years, and one thing that comes up is some people wish they got more feedback. That it's hard to figure out what he wants, they don't know if they're doing well or not. Is that something you experienced?

[laughs loudly] Yes, that is absolutely true. You look to the musical director for that, because people just don't go up to Bob and ask him. And he doesn't seem to offer those kinds of things. You're supposed to, I don't know, have mental telepathy or something to know what it is that he wants.

What really happened with me was very strange. We had done one tour, maybe a month or something, before we took a break. He was very happy with how it was coming along and how I was responding to his playing. He actually let me know that quite often.

So I was feeling, "this is nothing like what I've heard playing with Bob Dylan was like." I seemed to be doing stuff that he really liked. I was trying to really be tasteful, but also be responsive to what he was doing. I made sure to not overpower him in any way. It went really good until we took a break.

Then we started off what was called the "Americanarama" or something like that. We went out with— What is the name of that band that Jeff Tweedy…

Wilco. And My Morning Jacket.

Yes, that's right! Dawes was another band that was on. They were good and they were really nice guys.

When we started up that tour, right from the rehearsals Bob was looking for something different. He did request a few things that maybe wouldn't have been impossible for somebody else, but for me, it's slightly impossible to go from one end of the neck to the other really quickly back and forth. I tried to do it, but it was something that was just a little beyond where my hands were at my age. At that point I was 65 years old.

Was it a different genre or a different style of playing that was way removed from the blues?

They were the same songs that we were playing, but he was hearing a few different kind of parts. He was developing more of an idea of something new he wanted to try. Some of the things that we rehearsed didn't really gel. We ended up going back to the way we were playing before, because they just weren't working that well.

Right from the beginning of that trip, for some reason, he seemed to be frustrated or unhappy with me. I've been told that the lead guitar chair in his band is kind of like the hot seat if something's bothering him. If he wants to get out his frustrations, the lead guitar is usually where he takes it out.

Strange things started happening. He would take me upstage and yell at me. He'd ask me, can I play different than that? I said, "Sure, I can. What do you want me to play like? One of your former guys?" I can do that, because I'm a versatile musician. He didn't respond to that. He didn't say, well, play more like Bloomfield or like Robbie Robertson.

For some reason, I was bugging him. But the odd thing about it is that what I played that he loved the trip before, now it appeared like he hated it! *[laughs]* I had no idea. I'd ask Tony like, "What should I do?" Tony would give me a suggestion, then I'd try that, and he'd be even more pissed off at me. He'd swear at me over the mic.

On stage?

Oh yeah. He'd come up near me with a harp mic, and he'd start swearing. Obviously it was at me, because he's right up next to me. I'm going, "Okay, he hates what I'm doing. Well, I'm doing what he liked last month." So I'd try something different.

After about three days of that, I just told the manager, "Look, I'm going to leave. I can't be treated like this." Bob got very upset about that. He and I had a long talk. When we got to a hotel at 4:00 in the morning, we talked for about two hours outside the bus. He tried to calm me down and straighten it out. I told him, "Well, I can't tell you right now for sure, because I don't believe this is not going to keep happening."

So he wasn't giving you any helpful advice or something?

No, he didn't give me a suggestion. He was just saying he'd wanted me to stay. He really wanted me in the band and he didn't want me to leave. I said, "Look, it would really help me if I just went home for a week and really thought about this. I'm not going to go on like this. You're not going to be doing this to me on stage." I said, "I'll do whatever you tell me. If you just tell me what you want, I'll do that." He said, "Well, if you just play this last gig in Nashville, I'd really appreciate it. Not just leave me flat." I said sure. He had called in Charlie Sexton to come down to that gig in case something went wrong.

Then Bob came on the bus and he told me that he wanted me to play all my solos on the bottom three strings. Just make believe I only have three strings, which is a *very* odd request. But I said, "Sure, I'll do that for you. No problem." That's what he wants and that's what he gets. I was determined I was going to do a great job, and I did. The show went great, people loved it, and I played everything on the bottom strings.

But I still was packing my guitars up because, as I had said, "I'm going home, give me a week." He got very mad at me for actually continuing to leave. He really blew up at me. Between him and his road manager, they just wanted to know like, "Don't mess around with us. Let us know if you're not coming back." Bob said all kinds of horrible things to me. Finally, I said, "Okay, you're right, I'm not coming back. I told you I'm not going to take this shit."

This is right after that Nashville show where you're playing on the lower three strings?

Yeah, that was the night right directly after the show. I just went to my hotel and packed up and that was it. That was the last time I saw him.

And you know, I didn't want it to be that way. For years, they had asked me to come down and play. I wasn't going to do it because I didn't want to give up my own personality and my own music. When I *did* decide that I was going to join, I really thought I was going to be with him 'til he stopped playing. Because, for me, it was a big thing to just stop, break up my own band, and do that. I thought I was going to be there until the end.

When I got the impression that he was enjoying my playing and he was letting me know that on the first tour, I figured that it was going to continue that way and it would be a good experience. *[chuckles softly]* I wish it had continued to go right.

Before things went bad, did you have any favorite shows or songs to play from that first tour?

The one in particular that he just called out a couple of times, it's from, I think, *Bringing It All Back Home.* Maybe "Love Minus Zero/No Limit." I hadn't had a chance to practice it, but I knew the song enough that we could just play it off-the-cuff and I could follow him. I just felt like that was a tune I could really sink my teeth into.

Basically I enjoyed playing absolutely every song because they're all great songs, including the newer tunes. Those newer bluesy tunes that were from the last two or three albums, I really enjoyed them.

A lot of his newer stuff then, not that he's ever gotten far from the blues but on those last few albums, they were real bluesy. I would think that'd be something you would get into.

I had heard from someone who was at the session for *Tempest*, or maybe one of the other ones, that he had said that he felt like he needed me there.

When I recorded *Time Out of Mind*, he was really impressed that I was doing albums of old jazz tunes and filling them with vocals, which is something he got into a bit later. I had this feeling that he wanted me there because he was going to do some of that. Plus, he knew that I was a blues player, which is also something he loved.

Speaking of the jazz-standards stuff, did you ever listen to the stuff he did a few years later?

I listened to a little bit of it. I've had friends that have played me a few tracks, but I never listened to it really seriously, because that is just not the way I hear those songs. The band, they're a great band, but using steel guitar and stuff like that, it's not the way I hear that music. Bob interpreted them his own way, which— I've spent a lot of my life listening to that material by great singers of that stuff, so I can't really say I was ever fond of his concept of doing that.

You've played with a million people; how does playing with Dylan on stage, trying to follow him, compare with some of the other people you've played with?

Like I said, that first tour, he was easy on me. Perhaps because he was older, he pretty much stuck to the same material. We didn't vary it a lot. I know when he was younger, he would pull out songs that maybe only one guy in the band knew. He didn't do any of that when I was there. Thank God. I don't know how I would have felt about that if I literally didn't know the song and it was hard to follow. He didn't make it hard on me in that sense at all. I think possibly because his memory wasn't as sharp as it was, he would need to rehearse things too to feel good about them.

Maybe that's just not true. Maybe the reason we stuck with a very similar setlist is just that he was playing what he wanted to play. Who knows? But it was fun. Like I said, when it started off, I felt like I was learning more about how to back him nightly and I enjoyed it. It was satisfying; I got to play enough that I felt like I was expressing myself through these songs.

I just enjoyed the whole experience until it went south. When it went south, it was only about three or four days of that. I just decided, I'm just too old to take this. If I was 20, I think I would have just shivered in my boots and done anything he said, but I was 65 years old.

You mentioned things had been a little slower in your own gigs which is why you joined in the first place, and then, all of a sudden, the gig ends suddenly. Was that tough to recover from?

I ended up being able to start working right away, but it affected me psychologically for at least a year or two. I actually sold all of my Dylan CDs and albums. I got rid of everything that had anything to do with him. It really scarred me.

But after a while, I started to come back and say, well, I *knew* he was a difficult person to communicate with when I went in. He's got that reputation. I finally just let it all go and said, "Well, that's what happened. I'm glad I had a chance to do it and I'm glad I enjoyed *some* of it." It didn't turn out the way I thought it was going to turn out, but that's okay.

The Queens of Rhythm, Benmont Tench, and Dylan in Mansfield, Massachusetts, July 1986.
Photo by James Iwuc

Benmont Tench

In Chapter 29, I spoke with Tom Petty and the Heartbreakers drummer Stan Lynch. Now, in this final chapter, we hear from the band's keyboard player Benmont Tench.

Unlike Lynch, Tench has collaborated with Dylan several times beyond the two Heartbreakers tours in 1986 and '87. He recorded on *Shot of Love* and *Empire Burlesque* earlier in the '80s and then, decades later, reappeared in Bob-world: first on Dylan's 2003 soundtrack one-off "Cross the Green Mountain" and then on two tracks on 2020's *Rough and Rowdy Ways*. So he works perfectly as our grand finale, taking us from decades ago right up to the present.

. . . .

The bulk of what I want to talk about is the Heartbreakers tours, but you've intersected a few other times with Dylan. Were the Shot of Love *sessions the first time you guys connected?*

I went in to work on *Shot of Love* because Jimmy Iovine called me. He was kind of auditioning with Bob to see if they could work with each other. He brought me down because he didn't know anybody else on the session and he wanted my sound in there.

He and Bob didn't get along. So, unbeknownst to me, Jimmy left in the middle of the session.[95] He left me in the room with nobody I knew, including Bob. At the end of the day, Bob said, "Can you come back tomorrow?" I said, "I can't." There was a Heartbreakers meeting or something, I couldn't skip it. Not even for Bob.

But he called me a couple of months later [when he was still working on] *Shot of Love.* Maybe it's because I said I can't. Maybe it's because I said no.

That was my first experience working with him, and it was marvelous. The

---

95 *Shot of Love* guitarist Fred Tackett gives his view on this story in Chapter 24.

Heartbreakers worked with him four or five years later as a whole. But in the meantime, most of us, I think all of us except for Tom, had played on some things on *Empire Burlesque*. So he knew us a bit before [shared manager] Elliot Roberts suggested that we be a band for him on a tour.

I read a rumor that you also were involved in rehearsals for the 1984 tour a couple of years before that, but you couldn't do it. Is that right?

He did ask. Somebody called me and said, "Can you come down to this address and just sit in?" I said, "I can't tour, because I'm working with Tom." He said, "He just wants to see what it would sound like to have a keyboard player."

So I went down there, and it was Colin Allen from Mayall's Bluesbreakers on the drums. It was Gregg Sutton, I believe, playing bass. And they said, "This is Mick." This guy playing guitar. I said, "Cool."

We start jamming. Bob just wanted to jam and play some songs and stuff. Slowly, it dawns on me that "Mick" is *Mick Taylor*. He started playing, and I went, "Wait a minute, wait a minute. Wow!" But it was going to be impossible for me to play on the tour. I think he just wanted to see what it would sound like. They wound up getting Ian McLagan, which was a very brilliant call. Mac was one of my heroes.

Take me to Farm Aid in 1985, before the full Heartbreakers tour. You mentioned earlier Roberts was the connecting glue there. How did it happen that you and the Heartbreakers and Dylan get paired up?

There's a couple of ways I understand it. When we did *Shot of Love*, Debbie Gold was Bob's assistant. She was a character, but she was smart. She and I hit it off. Then Mike Campbell came in; that was [producer] Chuck Plotkin's idea. They did a version of "Heart of Mine" and put Mike on it, but they didn't wind up using that version on the record.

Debbie told me that she had said to Bob, "Well, if you like Ben and Mike, you should try playing with some of the other Heartbreakers." Maybe she said Howie [Epstein, bass] and maybe she said Stan, so then when *Empire Burlesque* came around, the four of us were on parts of that record. So he already knew us. I don't know if that's exactly how it went down. That's what Debbie told me.

Anyway, by Farm Aid, Elliot was representing us along with Tony Dimitriades. My understanding is that it's Elliot that finally connected all of the dots. Tom had probably met Bob at some point, but I don't think he had recorded with him. He wasn't on *Empire Burlesque* like the rest of us. So Elliot or whoever it was, said, "Why don't you do this one-off with Bob?"

It made me really happy, because I had enjoyed my studio experiences a lot. He became a legendary songwriter-performer because he's so damn good. I got to play this great music with the *creator* of this great music on *Shot of Love*. And the band, Jim Keltner, Tim Drummond, Fred Tackett, Steve Ripley, Danny Kortchmar, the Queens of Rhythm singing background, just ridiculous. You've talked to Keltner, right?

Yeah.

Okay, good. Keltner's one of my best friends. I saw him just yesterday. I moved into a new house two years ago. It turned out that, if I walk down the hill for five minutes, I'm at Jim's house. During this whole pandemic, our pod has been Jim and his wife Cynthia and the nanny. Pretty good pod.

Jim seems kind of like you in that there are these people that Dylan brings back again and again. There are gaps of sometimes decades, then, once again, they're back on the stage or in the studio.

I think he and Jim have a tighter relationship than he and I do. But then, Jim's a marvel. A lot of the most special people know that Jim is really special. Bob Dylan, oh yeah. That's a cat. It's kind of our job to learn what we learned from Bob and tell other people, "Hey, how about this?"

I thought Farm Aid was transcendent. We did maybe five songs. You can find bad copies of it on YouTube and stuff. I thought it was thrilling. Not because Bob's name was Bob Dylan, but because it was great rock and roll. So a little while after, they said, "Do you guys want to do a tour?" Of course, we said yes — or Tom said yes, because he knew the rest of us would. That's how we got started on a two-year journey playing with Bob.

When you were doing Farm Aid, was it thought of as a one-off? That this was going to be it.

Probably. When we did that, maybe that convinced Bob that we would be a good fit. Maybe Bob really enjoyed it. Maybe he felt we were really good. Maybe we worked cheap. *[laughs]* I don't really know.

We wound up backing him up for a few tours. He made us a much better band because he taught us— we already had a really good swing. We paid a lot of attention to Howlin' Wolf records, to Little Richard, to the country records that really swung because they had the great rhythm sections. But Bob is a man who helped create the true rock and roll swing. He inherited it somehow through the spirit, through the wind, through something in his bloodline, through just being the cat. He inherited the Charley Patton, Robert Johnson, Tom Johnson, Memphis Minnie, Howlin' Wolf, Elvis Presley, Buddy Holly, Earl Palmer, Little Richard swing. He knew it. He *was* it. To play with his rhythm guitar was just like, "Right, this is what we've been trying to do the whole time." We were there, but we didn't know there was another place to go. He brought us to that other place. That knowledge never left me, because I was hungry for it. I didn't know where the oasis was in the desert, and there it was, water to drink. Cool, clear water, what I needed for my soul.

The Heartbreakers were always able to play off the cuff. If Tom said, let's play "I Fought the Law," we were like, we don't need to practice that. We've heard it on the radio a million times. Let's go out and play it. I think Bob probably enjoyed that about us. It wasn't very hard to teach us a song — and sometimes he *didn't* teach us a song. He just started playing it. It didn't matter if there were 20 or 60 or 70 thousand people watching. Not often, but every now and then, he just would start playing. That's the best kind of playing, in a way, if you know the song inherently but you've never played it. I'd never covered "Desolation Row" in a band. I'd never played it in my life. I'd just listened to it a million times. At a festival, he just started playing the chords. Within four bars, I was like, "Good Lord, we're playing 'Desolation Row.'" We were off to the races, and it was beautiful.

He said in Philadelphia one night, "Can we play 'I Dreamed I Saw St. Augustine'?" I'm sure we didn't rehearse it; we may have done it in the dressing room at most. That song is one of the songs that brought me in deep to his music. When *John Wesley Harding* came out, I heard somebody playing it out of a dorm window, and I just went straight to the record store and got lost in it. So we got to play "I Dreamed I Saw St. Augustine."

Later on, he did that with "Lonesome Death of Hattie Carroll" and he did it with "Tomorrow Is a Long Time." He and I were walking next to each other when the band got onstage. For small talk, I said, "What do you want to do for a slow song?" He said, "Do you know 'Tomorrow Is a Long Time'?" I said, "Yeah." He said, "Let's do that, just you and me and maybe Mike." When the time came, he started playing "Tomorrow Is a Long Time" with just me and Mike. It was Gothenburg, Sweden, and it was 20,000 people. We had never played it with him before, or with each other. It was transcendent.

What was Tom's role in that band? Were they co-bandleaders? Was Bob the leader and Tom just another member of the backing band? How did the dynamic between them work?

The band got on stage. He said, "Do you know 'Tomorrow Is a Long Time'?" I said, "Yeah." He said, "Let's do that, just you and me and maybe Mike." Gothenburg, Sweden, 20,000 people. We had never played it with him before, or with each other. It was transcendent.

Well, to me, the Heartbreakers have never felt like any kind of backing band. With Tom, we worked as a band, and he was our guitar player and the lead singer. [After his early band Mudcrutch broke up,] he had been making a solo record with session people like Keltner and Al Kooper and Jim Gordon. Legends. And he chose to ditch that record and go back to the band from Gainesville, which was us.

My take on his role was he was still the bandleader for the Heartbreakers, but he was also kind of a liaison. Bob's going to say, "I want to play this song," "I want to use this ending," "That's wrong, the chords are this." We would defer to him, but we wouldn't go "Gee that's great" if we didn't think it was. And *he* wouldn't say, "Gee that's great" to us if he didn't think it was. He would be as harsh as he wanted to be, and between the whole bunch of us, we got it done.

Not to compare or discuss quality or anything, but The Band was Levon and the Hawks. They were a *band* and Bob started playing with them. It's the same thing. He gets a readymade band, essentially blood brothers. We'd all done the *Empire Burlesque* thing but to be really like, we've got the whole band, including Tom, everybody at once, and play those songs. Man, it was just gorgeous. The Heartbreakers had great songs all along, because we had Tom, but you'd fit Bob in there and you'd go another level.

Tom's role there was rhythm guitar player and harmonies. I think he was really happy. He was really happy to be the guy who's playing rhythm guitar, so he really doesn't have to wrangle everything. Tom isn't counting us in or anything. He isn't giving us any cues. We're all just watching Bob like a hawk, like we always watched Tom, and just locking in with him. It was glorious, just glorious.

What do you remember from the early days of the tour down in Australia and New Zealand?

I think the first show was a festival in New Zealand. We went down there for a week or so early to do some rehearsing, acclimate to the time. So we were in Wellington for a pretty long time. We played New Zealand, and, if I remember right, it was not good. For us onstage, at least. I remember several things were kind of like a train wreck. It's like, I didn't know it was in this key... Then we'd start in that new key and Bob would realize that he didn't *want* to be in that key, so he'd change back to the original key. It was pretty shaky. I don't know what the audience thought.

After one or two gigs in New Zealand, we flew to Australia. When we went to Australia, we were really good. We were really, really good. From then on, on that tour of New Zealand, Australia, and a little bit of Japan, I think it was really good for the most part. It was really a rock and roll show, so there were moments that were dodgy, but, good Lord man, who wants perfection? It's a lot more fun to be flying without a net. If you drop the ball and go, "Whoa, how am I going to get myself out of this?," then you get out of it and land on your feet, it might make things even better.

When it was rough, it was rough in a way that wasn't like, this isn't any good. It was rough in a way that rock and roll *should* be. Not out of tune, not mistakes, but alive and breathing and changing and living.

One thing that's striking watching the videos and listening to the recordings is that it really seems like everyone, including Dylan, is just having a blast.

We were all having a really good time. I was definitely ecstatic. You see the tour movie that was made by Gillian Armstrong *[Hard to Handle]*, and you're going to see that I'm practically jumping out of my skin. I'm like dancing behind the organ, jumping up and down because I'm so bloody thrilled.

By the end of [our run together], I don't think Bob was very happy. I don't think it was our fault, but I just think he was not very happy. In *Chronicles*, you can read his take on all of that.[96] But the beginning was wonderful, and all the way through there were parts that were just terrific. There were always gigs or parts of gigs that were transcendent. Always.

In Australia, we check into the hotel the first night, and who checks in at the same time? Lauren Bacall. So we all go down later to the bar, coffee shop, whatever it was. She's down there. Bob had had us learn some standards. He was just like,

---

96 "I'd been on an eighteen month tour with Tom Petty and The Heartbreakers. It would be my last. I had no connection to any kind of inspiration. Whatever was there to begin with had all vanished and shrunk. Tom was at the top of his game and I was at the bottom of mine."

let's learn "Lucky Old Sun," let's learn this, let's learn that. He had us learn an old standard called "All My Tomorrows." He and I sat down at the piano and played it for Lauren Bacall.

What a beautiful moment. Lauren Bacall and Bob Dylan. Just beautiful. That's something I remember really clearly from that tour. Things like that happening.

I unfortunately was at the height, or the near-height, of my use of cocaine, so I was in an altered state of mind. But I think I played well. I *know* the band played well, and I don't think I was the only person taking cocaine on that tour. I never saw Bob do anything except take a shot of whiskey and smoke a cigarette. I was definitely transgressive, which wasn't very responsible of me. I don't think it affected the gigs.

It's a beautiful performance, the one from the film from Sydney. There's much, much more. I think that Bob re-edited [Armstrong's] cut, so I've always been curious as to what her cut was and whether Bob will ever put that out in any form again.

He wasn't deconstructing the songs at that point. We played songs a lot like the record. These were songs we'd heard our whole lives, and we liked the way it was. He'd say, this song, and we'd start playing it, or he'd start playing and we'd fall in. We knew the opening licks to "Just Like a Woman" and all these things, so it just came naturally to us.

Later on, he found his way into changing melodies, or entirely changing chord structures. The bit that's in the film *Masked and Anonymous*, where they're thinking of getting Jack Fate, Bob's character, to play this telethon and one of the chairmen of the board says, "Jack Fate, nobody can even tell which song he's singing." I guarantee Bob wrote that line. But that was later.

We were playing it the way that we felt it and the way that we'd always heard it. We weren't being a cover band. That was anything but being a cover band. That wasn't karaoke. Like I said, it was living, it was beautiful.

One moment you can see in the film is you playing Al Kooper's organ part in "Rolling Stone." I wonder if there was an excitement of playing an iconic part like that. You have plenty of iconic songs with Petty, but you helped create them; maybe it's different with a song that pre-dated you.

It is different. It's a song that I've heard since I was I think 12 or 13. Our first tour was opening for Al Kooper. Al had long been a hero of mine. I knew Al, and so it was doubly sweet to play his organ part. So yeah, I think you can see me jumping around with glee on that clip.

Did you enjoy playing the oldies? The early '50s rock 'n roll songs Dylan put in the show? The shows open with "Justine," and there's you on the organ doing this fun riff.

I think I'm on piano. I think Bob's on the organ. He had a DX7 with a sound program. We'd come out and they'd drag the keyboard in front of the stage that Bob would play and we'd do "Justine." I didn't know "Justine." Songs like that and "Red Cadillac and a Black Mustache," I didn't know those songs. I don't know that they were all on the radio in Gainesville. If they were, I was three, four at the height of early rock 'n roll. I didn't know those songs. What better way to learn them than from Bob?

Do you have any memories about the time touring with the Dead in '86? I think you just did a few shows, Dylan with The Heartbreakers, and the Dead.

We split the bill; I think sometimes we'd open and sometimes they'd open. We would play stadiums. It wasn't like you'd step out of the dressing room and a couple of steps you're on the side of the stage, so it wasn't that easy to go out and listen. Those shows were too big for me. They were too big for me to get a grip on or get a focus on. It was kind of weird.

I'm a big fan of the Grateful Dead, and so I was really kind of in awe. I spoke to Bob Weir because we had a friend in common, but I don't think I spoke to anybody else.

You mentioned Chronicles. *One of the things Dylan writes in there is that you specifically were asking him to do more obscure songs and he would come up with some lame excuse not to do them.*[97] *Did that ring a bell?*

Well, I'm always annoying. I would say the same thing to Tom: "There's this great song on the second record, Tommy, it's fantastic, let's do it." Usually he wouldn't, because he wanted people to hear what he felt they came to hear. With Bob, I was probably being annoying. From what he said in *Chronicles*, in retrospect he thought I was right. That doesn't mean he doesn't think that I was being annoying.

He did play obscure stuff because he was playing stuff off of *Saved*, and a little bit of stuff off of *Shot of Love*. That was pretty obscure. In his solo set, he'd go back and maybe play "To Ramona." He'd definitely play the great acoustic songs like "Masters" or, good Lord, "Gates of Eden." He did these breathtaking renditions of "Girl from the North Country."

As far as going deep into the catalog, I don't know that on the Australian tour he

---

97 "Benmont Tench, one of the musicians in Petty's band, would always be asking me, almost pleadingly, about including different numbers in the show. 'Chimes of Freedom' — can we try that? Or what about 'My Back Pages'? Or 'Spanish Harlem Incident'? And I'd always be making some lame excuse."

did, but on the last tour, the European tour, was when he said, let's do "Tomorrow Is a Long Time," let's do "Hattie Carroll." That kind of thing.

Yeah, that last tour, the '87 tour, I think he wrote he was a little more open to your suggestions.

Yeah. You know, I didn't try to get close to him, because I don't think that I was qualified for the experience that was going on around me, to really take it in and appreciate it. I didn't shy away from him, but I didn't just go up very often and go, "Hey Bob, how're you doing? Did you sleep well?" I basically knew him as the guy who was leading the whole thing, whose songs we were playing.

He's always been terrific to me. I haven't had run-ins with any side of Bob that wasn't pretty much kind, unless he's frustrated trying to get a certain sound and I'm not figuring it out. In the studio, he generally will kick me off of the piano and play piano himself and tell me to go back to the organ. Well, nobody plays piano like him! I certainly can't.

It's his primary instrument in some ways, especially live. It has been for 20 years.

He started out as a piano player.

That's right.

In the studio one time, we'd been learning "I'll Remember You" off of *Empire Burlesque.* He was showing it to me on the piano, and I couldn't get the voices and the feel of exactly what he was doing. That's never been my strong suit. I just finally said, "Bob, why don't *you* play piano on this?" For a minute he said, "No, you can get it," then he realized he should play piano. He should always play piano if he wrote it on piano, because he's a very cool piano player.

One other Chronicles *question. I'm sure you remember the section about this show in Locarno in 1987 where he steps up to the mic and the words aren't coming out, then he finds another way of singing. He paints it as this pivotal moment, pointing him out of a rut. Is this something that was apparent at the time?*

First I heard about it was when he wrote about it. Locarno, to me, was not a happy experience. It was outdoors, it was drizzling. There had been some kind of kerfuffle or fight amongst the band. I mean, not physical fight, but some kind of unpleasantness among the band before we went on. I broke out in hives on my hands. It was a miserable show for me. The circumstances, the rain, the fact that my hands were constantly itching and I'm trying to play the piano, the fact that there was whatever small thing there was backstage with the band. I had no idea. I had no idea.

I knew that he had not seemed happy since the rehearsals for the European leg. He was like, "We're going to learn 'Frankie Lee & Judas Priest.'" I'm like, "That's great!" But the way we learned it was he sat and played rhythm guitar, did not sing. He played the pattern, which is the same throughout the song, for way longer than the song would have lasted.

It struck me that he wasn't happy. It struck me that it wasn't going to be a good tour. I actually asked our manager, "Can you get me out?" He said, "Don't be ridiculous, Ben. It starts in a couple of days." I was also extraordinarily messed up on drugs and alcohol at that point, so that colored it.

That tour, it started off kind of great. Like I said, *I* was a disaster, but we played Tel Aviv, we played Jerusalem, we played in Switzerland. We went through Italy, where I had never been and the Heartbreakers had never played, and there were some great shows. Really terrific shows, but it wasn't the best of times.

In retrospect, I think about it like this. I think about Sweden and him saying, "Let's just play 'Tomorrow Is a Long Time.'" "'Lonesome Death of Hattie Carroll,' just you me and Mike." The fact Roger McGuinn was on the tour; McGuinn would open playing a solo set, then we would come on and join McGuinn for a couple of songs. McGuinn was so terrific, he was such a wonderful guy to travel with. We started our career opening for McGuinn. We opened for Kooper, and we opened for McGuinn. Those are the first two people we opened for, and they're both heroes. Now McGuinn's on the tour, and McGuinn has history with Bob, and our extreme love for McGuinn and the Byrds, and so I can't look back and go, "What a horrible tour."

He did say in *Chronicles*, he couldn't find it, and that at the end of the tour in Locarno he cracks the code. Which is wonderful. I've seen comments from people who saw some of those shows and thought that we were terrible, and comments from some people who thought that it was marvelous. Kind of like you hear from anybody who goes to see Bob these days. I think he's playing great.

You have the splashy finale of the whole thing in Wembley. Four nights with George Harrison and Ron Wood and various people. Is there talk of more after that? Is it known that this is the grand finale?

I didn't think that it was a grand finale at the time. I wasn't told, "We're never doing this again." I always had to live day to day on any kind of thing. It's like, "Are the Heartbreakers going to tour again, or are they going to break up?" "Is Bob going to call us to tour again? Gee, I hope so, but I hope that it's happier."

Wembley is where— I'm not trying to make this about me, but this is my perspective. I was barely taking drugs or drinking on that tour. I was taking my sleep medication only at night, although I'd take twice as much, and I think I had some cocaine three times over the course of the seven weeks. And then I crashed into drug abuse the last three shows. I started drinking again after not drinking for seven weeks, and I drank a lot, so I kind of had a nervous breakdown in London. When a hurricane came and uprooted a giant tree next to the hotel we were at, when the Wilburys were kind of forming and all this stuff was going on, I was having a nervous breakdown.

It was still a good gig. I mean, I was not having a nervous breakdown on stage. Harrison came, and Jeff Lynne. George had been talking about something, I thought he said he wanted to have a band called the Trembling Wheelbarrows. But he had said Traveling Wilburys. It was some idea that he had in his head, I don't think he had cast it yet. There's a photograph because I think it was Tom's birthday. Tom, Jeff, George, McGuinn, Campbell, and me. Crazy, right?

Yes, four out of five Wilburys, already there together. Just missing Roy Orbison.

So I enjoyed those shows. Just offstage, I was a wreck. I came home and hit bottom and cleaned up.

I would like to have continued to work with him. Elliot Roberts called me up and asked me to do a tour with him after he was done with the Dead and the Heartbreakers. I was like 90 days sober, and I didn't trust myself to get on a tour bus and be alone in a hotel room, so I didn't do it.

This would have been the early Never Ending Tour, '88, '89?

Yeah. Playing with him on those tours.

So you skip that one. Then, in the early 2000s, you're back in the mix on his song "Cross the Green Mountain."

Yes, I was on that session. 2002–2004 or something. I have not heard it in so long. Where did you find it? Was it on the soundtrack?

Yeah, it was on the soundtrack of Gods and Generals.

That was one of the ones where it was very notable that he showed us on piano. I started playing on the piano. I think I may have said, "Why don't *you* play piano?" It took a long time to get it, but we got it. I need to listen to that again, because I remember thinking it was a beautiful song at the time. He knows a lot about [the Civil War]. He knows a lot about a lot.

The other thing touring with him was, the rehearsals for the '87 *Temple in Flames* tour, when he played over and over again the chords for "Frankie Lee and Judas Priest," he also would be playing something beautiful just in the corner. I'd say, "What's that?" It was like a Child Ballad or something from the 18th century or 19th century.

I got the Harry Smith *Anthology of American Music* or whatever it was called. But the songs that he was playing, they weren't on that. Everybody of his genre in his generation in that scene— had that record and learned the songs from that record, but he didn't do them like that. He went somewhere else. There are songs that are on the two records he made, *World Gone Wrong* and *Good as I Been to You,* that are on that anthology, I think, but they aren't like the way that Bob does them. He took them somewhere else. He really took them somewhere else.

It sort of kills me that they didn't release a proper live record of especially that '86 tour. He released one of the '84 tour and then he released one with the Dead in '87 that pretty much no one likes.

I don't know, maybe it's just too familiar in the arrangements. Maybe that's why he never put it out. Maybe he's like, "I don't want to sound like a nostalgia act. I don't want to sound like I'm covering my own song." We weren't slavish, but if I'm playing "Rolling Stone," I'll be playing that organ riff! I don't know why that's never come out, but maybe one day it will.

Bob Dylan, he's a guy with an extraordinary gift for storytelling, for songwriting, for not standing still artistically. Not repeating the same sound, not repeating the same style. Bob, if you pay attention to the last record, it's the real thing. It's the top-notch real thing. "Goodbye Jimmy Reed" — Jimmy Reed indeed! Not to mention "Murder Most Foul" or "Key West" or "Crossing the Rubicon."

Did you play on "Jimmy Reed"? I couldn't tell if there was an organ on that.

I didn't play on "Jimmy Reed." I played on "Key West (Philosopher Pirate)" and "Murder Most Foul." I played organ on both of those. I was trying for this ambient thing. I didn't have my gear, so I asked Chris [Shaw] the engineer to try to fake it. On there, it's ambient. You think it's the reverb, but it's actually the Hammond.

Those are two long songs too.

Yeah, they're two beautiful songs. It was wonderful to see Bob. It was wonderful to see the guys in the band. I knew everybody.

[When I first arrived,] I sat outside the control room and had a bite because they were working and they didn't want anyone who wasn't working in there. When I went in, they played me back a few things, I don't remember, it may have been "Crossing the Rubicon." I think he said, "Play Benmont that other song. Don't play him the whole thing, it's really long." It was "Murder Most Foul." It was gorgeous, really gorgeous, and they did play me the whole thing.

I played on "Key West" that day, and that was it. Then a few weeks or a month later, I got another call to come back down. I had heard a knockout version of "Murder Most Foul," and then, after I heard it, they put Fiona Apple on piano. He wanted Alan Pasqua to play some additional piano and me to play some organ.

So I got to go down and do that song, not in an overdub of keyboards, but with Bob and me and Blake [Mills] and Alan. Somehow we played to the previous take, because there's no time on that song. It was some kind of alchemy. We just played and watched Bob like a hawk for when to move.

Did you mean the previous recording was playing as you performed? Or was it just you, Alan, Blake, and Bob?

No. We didn't do like a bare take of just the three of us and Bob. It was alchemy, because it was playing along with something. Blake couldn't have made all that sound on the harmonium. But when it's there on the final thing, it's everybody in Bob's band *and* Fiona *and* us. It was gorgeous. What a lovely thing to work with him again, and be so relaxed and just get a chance to go, "Okay, I'm going to try to do my best on a song for Bob" again, after all that time.

I had a hell of a time. Learned a lot, had a hell of a time. Bob's played with a lot of people. I expect he had the same meaning for all of them that he had for us. It was a joy. Every time you're around him, something's going to happen.

You can read about Bob's life, and you can pay attention to what he says, and you can learn from it, but when you play music with somebody of that caliber, you learn something entirely different. It can only be passed on by that person. And those of us who have the opportunity to play with that person can pass on what we took away, but we only each take away a certain part of our experience with someone like that. Long may he live, because he's something else.

Acknowledgements

I haven't see Saint Annie, but I'd like say "thanks a lot" to plenty of other people.

First and foremost, to everyone who supported the Indiegogo campaign for this book. I feel like "This wouldn't have happened without you" is the sort of meaningless tripe a quarterback says to the fans after throwing the game-winning touchdown. Yes, it probably would have. But on a practical, financial level, this book *literally* wouldn't have happened without you. So thanks. A lot.

I'd also like to thank all the interviewees who participated. Many of them offered not only the recollections you just read, but additional help behind the scenes, sending photos, connecting me with other people to interview, etc. Thanks too to all the photographers who allowed their work to be used in this book. Shooting photos of Dylan has never been an easy task, so kudos to everyone who manages to get these killer shots under often trying circumstances.

Too many of my readers have helped me along the way to name them all, but I'd especially like to shout out fanzine historian James Adams and photo guru Dag Braathen, both of whom provided essential materials time and time again that enriched practically every interview I did. I hesitate to add any names for fear of the three people I'll forget for every one I remember, but a brief list of others who've assisted in the newsletter or book along the way: Karl Erik Andersen, Mark Bentley, Mitch Blank, Joe Carey, Craig Danuloff, Parker Fishel, Jake Fredel, Michael Gray, Tim Heidecker, Graley Herren, Harry Hew, Andrew Hickey, Matthew Ingate, Larry Jenkins, Les Kokay, Harold Lepidus, Daniel Mackay, Rob Mitchum, Tom Mohler, Franz Nicolay, Eyolf Østrem, Caryn Rose, Mark Satlof, Adam Selzer, Michael Simmons, Matt Simonsen, Michael Glover Smith, Bob Stacy, Emma Swift, Ben Taylor, Brian Walsh, Tyler Wilcox, Ian Woodward, Jon Wurster, and I'm sure many more whose names will jump out at me the moment after I sent this to the printer.

No one worked harder to make this book happen than editors Tim Edgeworth and Patrick Robbins and designer Noel Mayeske. That it's not full of endless typos or accidentally printed upside down is due entirely to them. And that I didn't lose my mind (at least, not completely) while working on this project is due entirely to Lesley and Ella.

Oh yeah, one more: Thanks to Bob Dylan, for giving us all so much to talk about.

Index

About The Author

Ray Padgett writes the Substack newsletter *Flagging Down the Double E's*, about Bob Dylan in concert. He is the founder of the cover-songs blog *Cover Me* and author of two previous books, *Cover Me: The Stories Behind the Greatest Cover Songs of All Time* (2017) and, in the 33 1/3 series, *I'm Your Fan: The Songs of Leonard Cohen* (2020). His writing has appeared in *The New Yorker*, *SPIN*, *Vice*, and *MOJO*. He lives in Burlington, Vermont with his wife, daughter, and two dogs.

Photo by Lesley Stephen